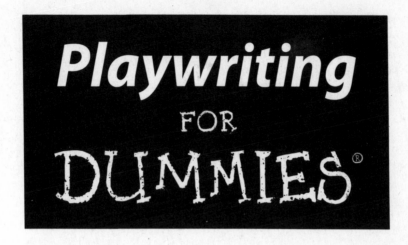

Playwriting FOR DUMMIES®

by Angelo Parra

WILEY

Wiley Publishing, Inc.

Playwriting For Dummies®

Published by
Wiley Publishing, Inc.
111 River St.
Hoboken, NJ 07030-5774
www.wiley.com

For general information on our other products and services, please contact our Customer Care Department within the U.S. at 877-762-2974, outside the U.S. at 317-572-3993, or fax 317-572-4002.

For technical support, please visit www.wiley.com/techsupport.

Wiley also publishes its books in a variety of electronic formats and by print-on-demand. Some content that appears in standard print versions of this book may not be available in other formats. For more information about Wiley products, visit us at www.wiley.com.

Library of Congress Control Number: 2011930315

ISBN 978-1-118-01722-7 (pbk); ISBN 978-1-118-12095-8 (ebk); ISBN 978-1-118-12096-5 (ebk); ISBN 978-1-118-12097-2 (ebk)

Manufactured in the United States of America

10 9 8 7 6 5 4 3 2 1

WILEY

About the Author

Angelo Parra, an award-winning playwright and playwriting instructor, has had productions of his plays Off-Broadway in New York City and in Los Angeles, Chicago, and Washington, D.C. He's also had productions at many prestigious regional venues, including Hartford Stage, Florida Stage, Cape (Cod) Playhouse, George Street Playhouse, Theatre Memphis, Passage Theatre, Penguin Rep Theatre, and Florida Rep, and at the Edinburgh International Theatre Festival.

Angelo is the author of *The Devil's Music: The Life and Blues of Bessie Smith,* the critically acclaimed play with music named among the "Top Ten Off-Broadway Experiences of 2001" by *The New York Daily News.* Another of his plays, *Journey of the Heart* (which dramatizes the seesaw struggle of a hospital committee to decide who gets a heart for transplant), won the Jewel Box Theatre Award, Mixed Blood Versus America Award, and David James Ellis Memorial Award. His screenplay adaptation of *Journey of the Heart* was a finalist in the Sundance Institute Feature Film Program. Two other plays, *Casino* and *The Slope,* were the recipients of a Fund for U.S. Artists at International Festivals and Exhibitions grant (a partnership of the National Endowment for the Arts, the U.S. Information Agency, the Rockefeller Foundation, and the Pew Charitable Trusts), awarded to sponsor the plays at the 1993 Edinburgh International Theatre Festival.

Angelo's honors include two New York Foundation for the Arts Fellowships in Scriptwriting, the 1998 Chicano/Latino Literary Award (University of California), and a prize for his play, *Song of the Coquí,* in the 1998 "The American Dream" competition sponsored by Repertorio Español. In 2000, he was named a Tennessee Williams Scholar at the renowned Sewanee Writers Conference. He is a member of the Dramatists Guild and a member emeritus of the BMI/Lehman Engel Musical Theatre Workshop. He was awarded a National Endowment for the Humanities Landmarks of American History and Culture grant in 2008 and, in 2011, a New York State Council on the Arts/Arts Council of Rockland grant to underwrite a new play in conjunction with the Kurt Weill Foundation for Music.

Angelo studied playwriting at Roundabout Theatre Conservatory's Professional Playwright's Unit, New Dramatists Playwrights Forum, the playwrights workshop at Playwrights Horizons, and the Playwrights Lab at T. Schreiber Studio, among others. He holds a B.A. in journalism from Fordham University and a master of fine arts degree in playwriting, earned under the late Jack Gelber at Brooklyn College.

Angelo Parra is the founder and director of the Hudson Valley Professional Playwrights Lab, teaches playwriting and performing arts at SUNY Rockland Community College, and is president of the board of Penguin Rep Theatre.

Dedication

To the four most important figures in my life:

My parents, Edith and Angelo, who always believed in me, no matter how harebrained my ambitions seemed to be.

My best friend, Sandy — also my proofreader, cheerleader, and wife (not necessarily in that order) — for her love, support, and patience.

And Charlie, who makes me laugh.

Author's Acknowledgments

This book would not have happened without the theatre career I've had, which, in turn, would not have been possible without significant help and encouragement and support along the way. My most heartfelt *thank you:*

To Joe Brancato and Andrew Horn for their confidence in me and my work and for allowing their gem of a showplace, Penguin Rep Theatre, to be my artistic home.

To the generous and perpetually optimistic Terry Schreiber and his T. Schreiber Studio and its Playwrights Unit, where my first plays were staged; to the Roundabout Theatre Company Conservatory, where my early plays were developed; to Peter Sylvester and his late, lamented Synchronicity Theatre Group for their friendship and presentations of my plays; and to Mark Judelson and Patrick Cacciola at the Arts Council of Rockland for their continuing support and encouragement.

To Nancy Golladay and the members of her Librettists Workshop at the BMI Lehman-Engel Musical Theatre Workshop for their expertise and friendship.

To my friends and fellow theatre-lovers Kim Hendrickson and Joe Grosso for advocating for me and encouraging me to take on the writing of this book. To the generosity of Sandoz (now Novartis) Pharmaceuticals.

To Patty Maloney-Titland who graciously allows me to teach playwriting in her Performing Arts Department at SUNY Rockland Community College.

And especially to my friends and playwriting colleagues who endured my self-doubts and whining over tight deadlines, and, more importantly, who functioned as an informal editorial board, providing me with input and feed-back. These theatre troopers include: Neil Berg, Miche Braden, Bill Bruehl, Steve Burch, Holly Caster, Tom Dudzick, Mike Folie, Jeff Fuerst, Earl Graham (of The Graham Agency), Erik Johnke, Jane Landers, Richard Manichello, Don Monaco, Jim G. Ramsay, Jennie Redling, Elaine Schloss, Paul Schwartz, Ralph Sevush (of The Dramatists Guild), Ric Siler, Judy Stadt, Staci Sweden, and Deborah Vines.

Publisher's Acknowledgments

We're proud of this book; please send us your comments at http://dummies.custhelp.com. For other comments, please contact our Customer Care Department within the U.S. at 877-762-2974, outside the U.S. at 317-572-3993, or fax 317-572-4002.

Some of the people who helped bring this book to market include the following:

Acquisitions, Editorial, and Media Development

Project Editor: Elizabeth Rea

Acquisitions Editor: Michael Lewis

Copy Editor: Caitlin Copple

Assistant Editor: David Lutton

Editorial Program Coordinator: Joe Niesen

Technical Editor: Todd Ristau

Editorial Manager: Michelle Hacker

Editorial Assistant: Alexa Koschier

Cover Photos: iStockphoto.com/James Steidl

Cartoons: Rich Tennant
  (www.the5thwave.com)

Composition Services

Project Coordinator: Patrick Redmond

Layout and Graphics: Claudia Bell, Corrie Socolovitch, Kim Tabor

Proofreader: Nancy L. Reinhardt

Indexer: Ty Koontz

Publishing and Editorial for Consumer Dummies

  Diane Graves Steele, Vice President and Publisher, Consumer Dummies

  Kristin Ferguson-Wagstaffe, Product Development Director, Consumer Dummies

  Ensley Eikenburg, Associate Publisher, Travel

  Kelly Regan, Editorial Director, Travel

Publishing for Technology Dummies

  Andy Cummings, Vice President and Publisher, Dummies Technology/General User

Composition Services

  Debbie Stailey, Director of Composition Services

Contents at a Glance

Table of Contents

Introduction

I'm guessing you're an individual who likes to have fun. Why? Because playwriting is fun (most of the time) and you've got this book in your hands; ergo you're the kind of person who enjoys a good time. Well, you've come to the right place. Pull up a chair, sit back, put your feet up, and stay a while as I give you a relaxed and user-friendly look the art and craft of playwriting.

Everybody comes to playwriting in their own way. My discovery of the art form was roundabout. Throughout my school days, I was terrified of standing in front of the class and speaking. Even reading aloud from a book caused me to stammer and tremble. This stage fright, I guess you'd call it, tagged along with me into my career as a writer for a big corporation. Making presentations or even voicing a point of view in a meeting would cause my throat to tighten and my hands to shake. If you had told me then that I would one day routinely and comfortably stand at the front of a college classroom with dozens of playwriting and theatre students eagerly awaiting my words of wisdom, I would have gone to court to have you committed.

Eventually, I decided to face my fears. I enrolled in an improvisation class, and, to my astonishment, I found that I loved hamming it up in front of the other students. The theatricality of the experience tapped into something in me. I enrolled as a student playwright in a theatrical studio where I discovered the exhilaration of writing lines late at night and having my words acted out by student actors at the studio the next evening. Writing had always been part of my life, but I had stumbled into my niche — playwriting.

Playwriting opened up a whole new world of artistic satisfaction, personal fulfillment, new and fascinating friends and colleagues, and just plain fun. I welcome you to join me.

About This Book

Writing plays for theatre is an exciting and enjoyable experience. I wouldn't trade away a day of it. But admittedly, at times it can be challenging and frustrating. *Playwriting For Dummies* is designed to maximize the "exciting and enjoyable" part of the experience and to smoothly and easily navigate you through those "challenging and frustrating" moments.

This book is about the art and craft of playwriting, but it's not intended to be a heavy-duty textbook or philosophical study of the field. *Playwriting For Dummies* is a practical, convenient, and nondemanding reference for people who are new to playwriting as well as people who are experienced in the art form but would like to explore further specific aspects of playwriting.

Don't feel like you have to read this book in order from cover to cover. Think of this book as a supermarket and each chapter as a particular aisle in that supermarket. As the reader — or shopper in this metaphor — you're free to wander every aisle to check out what you need and can use. Or, you can head immediately for the freezer aisle if all you want is a half gallon of chocolate ice cream.

Whether you're a casual browser or highly focused and goal-oriented, you'll find informative and useful information in this book.

Conventions Used in This Book

This book isn't heavy on special or unusual conventions, but here are a few you should be aware of:

- ✓ I *italicize* any words you may not be familiar with and follow them with definitions. I also use italic for titles of films, books, and plays I use as examples, and occasionally I use it to emphasize an important point.

- ✓ I use **bold** to draw your attention to key words and phrases in bulleted lists and to the actionable steps in numbered lists.

- ✓ In a few chapters, I use some lines from some of my own plays to illustrate how certain components of a play actually appear in a script. I do my best to replicate the standard style and formatting of a script in the text.

- ✓ All websites and e-mail addresses appear in `monofont`. When this book was printed, some web addresses may have needed to break across two lines of text. If that happened, rest assured that I haven't put in any extra characters (such as hyphens) to indicate the break.

What You're Not to Read

Anytime you see a Technical Stuff icon, you can skip that paragraph if you want to without missing key information. You can also skip the shaded gray boxes known as sidebars if you're short on time or if you conclude that that material isn't relevant to you. Sidebars contain interesting insights that can deepen your understanding of a topic, but you'll do fine without them, so take 'em or leave 'em; it's your dime.

Foolish Assumptions

In writing this book, I made certain assumptions about you, my reader, and your interest in playwriting. These assumptions are reflected in my efforts to give you what you need to quickly and skillfully get into the exciting world of playwriting. Here's how I imagine you:

✔ You've seen or read a play and enjoyed it.

✔ You want to understand what plays are and how they work.

✔ You want to experiment with writing in a genre — plays — that may be new and unfamiliar to you.

✔ You understand that before you break the rules, you should know and understand them.

✔ You've written a play and you want to improve it, or you're eager to write your first play.

In terms of your existing exposure to plays and playwriting, when I cite scenes from classic plays as models of the playwriting topics being discussed, I don't assume that you have seen or read the play, and you don't need to do so to understand the examples. Each time I bring up a famous play, the analysis of the scene and its relevance to the topic stand on their own. No prior experience with any given play is necessary to get the point.

That being said, if you have the time and interest in familiarizing yourself with the plays most often considered in this book, here are titles of most of them:

Hamlet, by William Shakespeare

A Doll House, by Henrik Ibsen

A Raisin in the Sun, by Lorraine Hansberry

A Streetcar Named Desire, by Tennessee Williams

West Side Story, by Arthur Laurents, Leonard Bernstein, Stephen Sondheim, and Jerome Robbins

The Miracle Worker, by William Gibson

Death of a Salesman, by Arthur Miller

Arsenic and Old Lace, by Joseph Kesselring

Bell, Book and Candle, by John van Druten

Inherit the Wind, by Jerome Lawrence and Robert E. Lee

If you haven't had to opportunity to see or read a lot of plays, the list above can serve as a suggested-but-not-required reading list. These plays are likely available at most public libraries, bookstores, and online. (A word about *Hamlet:* If you choose to read the play and you're not familiar with Shakespeare, it may be tough going. You may want to look for a copy of the play that features the text side-by-side with an explanation of Shakespeare's vocabulary and poetic turns of phrase. It'll make your first experience with Shakespeare a more enjoyable one.)

How This Book Is Organized

Playwriting is an art and a craft and, like it or not, a business. To be a success in this field, you need inspiration, particular skills, and the willingness to promote your work. This book is organized to help you deal with these and other aspects of playwriting. You can start at the beginning, or you can jump to the part or chapter of the book that has the information you're looking for. The road ahead is open and awaiting you. Follow the route that serves your needs best. And by the way, don't forget to have fun as you go.

Part I: Catching the Playwriting Bug

Warning: Playwriting and theatre are habit-forming. After you're bitten by the bug, you'll be itching to see, read, and write plays. But that's a good thing. In this part, you're introduced to the art and craft of playwriting. You explore what makes a play a play. You also delve into the sources of inspiration for plays and find out how you can use plays and playwriting to share your views and experiences with the world. You also get a glimpse of what the playwriting life is like.

Part II: Creating a Blueprint for Your Play

Having a focused vision of your play enables you to work more efficiently in the composition of your play. This part looks at some of the basic decisions and skills involved in writing a play. You zoom in on who and what your play is about. You explore all the factors involved in creating characters that are as detailed and complex as any real person you know, and you find out how to make them drive the story with action and effective dialogue. Furthermore, I guide you through some of the practical considerations involved in writing and staging a story that's enacted by real people in real time and staged by a small army of theatre craftspeople.

Part III: The Nuts and Bolts of Putting Your Story Together

Plays are composed of acts, and acts are composed of scenes. Each scene represents a crucial moment in the story you're telling, and how you tell the story involves a number of decisions, not the least of which is where your play starts. This part explores your play's point of attack and the obstacles your main character needs to face on his or her journey. It examines the concept of the climax, the point to which all events of the play are headed. And it also discusses the concept of a play's resolution — how the dust settles. Finally, in this part I also take a look at musicals and how a libretto (the story and dialogue of a musical) resembles and differs from a play.

Part IV: The Show Must Go On

Writing your play is only part of the playwriting experience. Another crucial component of playwriting success is getting your play produced and performed before an audience. This part walks you through all the steps involved in production: getting your play read and considered, working with your many theatre collaborators, and participating in rehearsals and using that experience to the advantage of your play's development.

Part V: The Part of Tens

In this, the final part of the book, you are exposed to three important lists of ten items that can help every playwright. You look at ten things every playwright should know about writing plays, ten hallmarks of great plays, and ten playwrights to know and emulate. Every artist stands on the shoulders of those who've come before, so you may as well take lessons from accomplishments of your illustrious predecessors.

Icons Used in This Book

To draw your attention to important and particularly noteworthy bits of information or advice, I use the following eye-catching icons in this book:

This icon points to time- or frustration-saving ideas.

For basic rules and information that you should take from the discussion and store away in your mental file cabinet, look for this icon.

This icon marks information that you don't necessarily need to know but may find interesting.

This icon alerts you to a pitfall or potential problem that you'll want to avoid. It signals a word (well, more than one word) to the wise.

Where to Go from Here

Pressing on with my supermarket metaphor, the store is now open for shopping! You can begin at aisle 1 or you can proceed to any aisle that features what you came to the supermarket for. In other words, you can go anywhere you like in *Playwriting For Dummies* and come away with interesting and useful advice and information.

The table of contents may spark some ideas and draw your attention, or you can head to the index if you're looking for information on a particular topic. You can jump to Chapter 3 to get a real feel for what a play is and its place in the world of theatre. If you have an idea for a play and want to start fleshing it out, head to Part II to create your blueprint and then to Part III to start writing. And Part IV can help you getter a better idea of how to get your play produced and performed.

Wherever you choose to start, good luck and happy playwriting!

Part I
Catching the Playwriting Bug

FOR WALTER, THE COMPONENTS FOR WRITING A GOOD PLAY WERE ALWAYS PLOT, CHARACTER, SETTING, AND MARTINI.

©RICHTENNANT

In this part . . .

You're here because you're writing a play, or you have an idea for one, or you're just plain curious about this art form. Not surprising. Men and women have been writing plays for more than 2,500 years. The idea and act of composing a story and then seeing it enacted by performers for a live audience are seductive and thrilling. Theatre is truly as real as storytelling gets. This first part of the book introduces you to the art and craft of playwriting, explores the sources of play ideas, and provides a glimpse into the life of a playwright.

Chapter 1

Introducing the Art and Craft of Playwriting

In This Chapter

▶ Looking at what playwriting is all about

▶ Getting your bearings as a playwright and getting to work

▶ Bringing your play to the stage

Playwriting is fun. Writing words that become the basis for what actors do and say in the presence of an audience is a heady experience. And fortunately, the enjoyment and satisfaction of writing plays is not reserved for some small, elite cluster of linguistic masterminds.

Anyone can write plays. It doesn't require formal training. But like any other pursuit in life, the more you know about a subject, the quicker you'll catch on and the better you'll be at it. This book is here to help. It provides you, in a straightforward and uncomplicated manner, with the practical knowledge and tools you need to get down to the joy of writing plays, sooner rather than later.

This chapter lets you get your toes wet in the world of playwriting so you can see how you like the water. It also offers you an overview of how this book will help you write and appreciate plays.

Understanding the Nature of the Beast

A playwright has a foot in each of two worlds: the world of art and the world of craft. For playwrights, the dividing line between art and craft is clear. The playwright as an *artist* conceives of an idea, a story, a statement to be made by the play. And the playwright as *craftsman* brings together the materials and construction skills to build the platform — the play — from which the idea, story, and statement can effectively reach out to audiences.

In a less metaphorical and more practical vein, a playwright writes plays for theatre. As obvious as that fact is, it's important to understand that plays and theatre, though inextricably interconnected, are distinct and therefore deserve individual consideration.

- **The play:** A *play* is a story written in the form of a script containing dialogue (what the characters say) and stage directions (what the characters do physically). A play is intended to be performed by actors in the presence of an audience.

- **Theatre:** *Theatre* is a branch of the performing arts that involves the presentation of a play by performers before a live audience. (Of course, *theatre* can also refer to the physical structure that the play is performed in.) Unlike the production of a film, theatre doesn't require expensive electronic gear, such as cameras, lights, microphones, sound equipment, and so on. In its most basic form, theatre doesn't require a director, and it doesn't even need the presence of a playwright after the script has been completed. You don't need to be an Einstein to grasp theatre's fundamental formula:

  Script + Performer + Audience = Theatre

Glimpsing the Life of a Playwright

The life of a playwright is, in many respects, much like the life of any other artist — it has its ups and downs. Working as a playwright, you'll have moments of artistic pleasure and satisfaction, and you'll also have periods of frustration and disappointment. The work requires persistent hard work, and it rewards you with a sense of fulfillment from a completed project. You'll find that personal sacrifices have to be made, but you'll get supreme gratification from knowing that your work has made the world richer.

Working as a playwright is exciting and challenging and fascinating. After you've taken the plunge, there's no going back. I've heard playwrights at low points grumbling about giving it up and leading a normal life, but I've never seen one do it. When theatre gets in your blood, you'll likely find that you don't want to be doing anything else.

The following tips for becoming a successful playwright apply to your day-to-day existence as well as your overall lifestyle. You'll find some of these practices invigorating and others more mundane, but they're all important.

- **Be an attentive observer of people and student of human nature.** If you want to create and stage believable characters in a play, you need to watch, listen to, and learn from everyone you come across, and you should be able to make use of what you take in.

✔ **See and read lots of plays.** You can learn a good deal from the successes and failures of others, and you need to know and understand trends and what producers and audiences are looking for.

✔ **Participate fully in life.** By interacting with others and staying active — from tweeting to traveling — you keep the mental shelves well stocked with fresh experiences to draw on.

✔ **Have a quiet and interruption-free place to work.** It can be a bedroom converted to an office or cubicle at your library, whatever works for you.

✔ **Have the self-discipline to sit yourself down to write, preferably at the same time each day.** Some habits are beneficial, and this is one of them. You become a better and productive writer by actually writing.

✔ **Make a living.** The vast majority of artists in any artistic medium need to have a day job. Man (or woman) does not live by art alone (most of us don't, anyway).

The following sections pull together all these practices — and then some — to give you an idea of what playwriting is all about and the process you work through to create a play that's ready for the stage. Chapter 2 also provides more detail on how to develop as a playwright.

Understanding stage plays

Plays are magic. For a couple of hours, a collection of strangers assembles and sits in the dark to witness other strangers enacting a story. The first group of strangers — the audience — is, without conscious effort or consent, drawn psychologically and emotionally into the story. The audience begins to care what becomes of characters who are played by the actors onstage. As if by hypnotism, audience members lose track of time and forget themselves and their personal concerns for the duration of the play.

Plays have a language that's common to playwrights, actors, directors, and other theatre people. This language includes terminology like *protagonist* (the main character), *antagonist* (the primary obstacle facing the protagonist), *conflict* (opposing objectives), *spine* (story line), *inciting incident* (the event that gets the plot going), *backstory* (events that occurred before the play begins), *exposition* (the gradual revealing of the backstory through dialogue), *climax* (the final confrontation between the protagonist and antagonist), and more. Use of this specialized vocabulary promotes clarity among theatre people as a play is developed and, ultimately, staged.

Compelling plays — plays that keep theatregoers glued to their seats — feature the following important characteristics:

- ✔ **Characters that the audience can understand and empathize with.**

- ✔ **Stories that keep audiences guessing; they never become predictable.** You never want an audience to get ahead of the story.

- ✔ **Specific details about the characters and the story rather than generalities and stereotypes.**

- ✔ **An essential simplicity and clarity at the core.** No matter how complex the characters and story may be, the play should build to the answer of one simple and unambiguous question: Will the protagonist succeed in achieving her objectives or not?

Coming up with and refining ideas

Inspiration is unpredictable. You'll never be able to tell exactly when you'll come upon the play idea you want to spend months and even years exploring. Ideas for a play can come from so many sources that listing and discussing the many possibilities would take a book in itself. However, the following list suggests a number of likely sources for good ideas:

- ✔ **Your life:** Good or bad occurrences in your life usually provide fertile material. A writer's life is her unique and most valuable resource.

- ✔ **Events you've witnessed:** Something you've seen, even if it didn't involve you personally, can inspire a good story for the stage.

- ✔ **Stories you've been told:** Family memories or other stories and events that have been told to you can spark a play idea.

- ✔ **Media reports:** Events, enraging or encouraging, that have been reported in newspapers, magazine, television, radio, and on the Internet can provide the germ of an idea that can grow into a play.

- ✔ **Your dreams:** Some of the most intriguing, if sometimes bizarre, ideas for plays can come out of your unconscious mind while dreaming.

- ✔ **Your imagination:** Sometimes ideas just pop into your head seemingly with no provocation at all. Write them down.

Carry a notebook or an electronic device that allows you to key in information. You never know when that great idea will creep up on you, and you don't want to trust it to your memory.

To read more about finding and developing ideas for plays, turn to Chapter 4.

Creating complete characters

Plays are about what their characters do and say. The key to creating complete, lifelike, and believable characters is specifics. The more detailed and fully fleshed out your characters are, the more readily audiences will empathize and sympathize with them.

A mantra you can embrace that will facilitate the creation of successful characters is this: Know your characters as well as you know your best friend. All the information you know about your best friend allows you to predict with great accuracy what he or she will do in a given situation. And that's where you want to be with your characters, even if most of the characters' details and specifics are never mentioned in your play.

Invest some time before you start writing your play in writing mini-biographies of your characters. Chapter 7 gives you plenty of ideas about what sort of info to include in these bios. When you're working with an intimate knowledge of your characters, it'll feel like your play is almost writing itself.

Factoring in the logistics of staging plays

One of the hardest things for the generations that grew up with movies and television as their primary source of storytelling entertainment is to internalize the essential differences between screenplays/teleplays and plays for the stage. They are as different as, well, apples and oranges.

Screenplays and teleplays have the technical ability (and usually the budget) to take audiences anywhere anytime. A story told through TV or film can be in New York one moment, in Hawaii the next, and at the top of Mt. Everest the scene after. Film and TV crews can travel to these locations to film and skillfully edit these very different locations into a seamless story line. In addition, today, much of what you see on a screen is created or supported by images produced with computers.

Stageplays, on the other hand, are limited to what can be done on a stage with real people in real time. Plays, of necessity, focus on the interaction of the characters and on their emotional lives. Theatre springs from characters trying to achieve their goals in opposition to the goals of other characters. That's what plays do well. What plays don't do well are car chases, explosions, alien abductions, gunfights, and other large, physically demanding activities; they can be simulated on stage, but they are more realistically done on film or TV.

Getting started on your play

As you get started on your play, you want to have your ducks in a row. Consider all the following recommendations:

✔ **Be sure your characters are detailed and specific and driven by clear objectives.** You want to be clear on which character is your protagonist and which is your antagonist and what each of them is after.

✔ **Be sure your cast is as lean as it can be.** It's an unfortunate reality in professional theatre today that the smaller the cast, the more attractive the play to producers. So you want to be sure that you axe those superfluous characters that appear for a line or two, never to be seen again. Playwriting today requires not only artistic imagination and vision but an inventiveness to do more with fewer actors.

✔ **Remember to use your environment in the play.** Where your play is set should not be arbitrary or ambiguous. A scene involving two brothers in conflict over an inheritance will play out very differently if it takes place in their home, in a restaurant, in a church, or in the room of their dying father. Where the dispute takes place can and should influence what they can say and how they can say it.

✔ **Be clear about your *inciting incident*.** This important term indicates the event that ignites the play and sets your protagonist on her journey. (Turn to Chapter 10 find out more about inciting incidents.)

✔ **Start your play as far into the story as possible.** Writing plays is about picking the crucial moments of your story and putting only those on stage. Early events and background information can be relegated to backstory and revealed through exposition. (Chapter 10 also discusses these components of the beginning of your play.)

✔ **Consider adding a ticking clock.** Suspense can be fueled by a limit on the time your protagonist has to complete her mission. (No, it doesn't have to be a literal ticking clock. And yes, you can read more about this subject — in Chapter 10.)

✔ **If you can at this point, have a vision of your climactic moment.** Knowing what the final confrontation between the protagonist and antagonist will look like helps guide you through writing the middle of the play.

Some writers outline their plays before beginning work. Some writers outline some of the time. Others prefer to plunge right in and see where the play takes them. You'll figure out in time what practice works best for you, but when you're beginning, my best advice is to outline. The time you invest in thinking through your play makes the writing easier and faster and helps you avoid the dreaded writer's block.

Developing your story line

The middle portion of a play is often the part that requires the bulk of the work. In the middle of the play, your protagonist encounters the obstacles to the completion of her mission.

One by one, the obstacles need to be overcome before the protagonist can move ahead. The obstacles should increase in difficulty, giving a sense of rising action. And to develop the audience's emotional involvement, you need to include setbacks, moments when both the audience and the character feel pessimistic about the prospects. The protagonist's journey toward the climactic moment should be anything but smooth sailing.

A tool for coming up with formidable obstacles for your protagonist is to ask yourself this question: What's the worst thing that could happen right now? And then make it happen. Chapter 11 further advises you on how to develop the middle section of your play with obstacles.

If you're writing the now standard two-act full-length play, you want to craft an ending to the first act that will have your audiences itching to come back to see how things turn out. It should involve a point of no return; the protagonist should be so far into her journey that there's no going back. If you create a cliffhanger (also sometimes referred to as a *hook*) at the end of the first act, the audience goes to intermission thinking, "How's she going to get herself out of that? I can't wait to get back to see what happens."

Building to the climax and resolution

The *climax* is the point near the end of your play when the protagonist and antagonist confront each other one last time. It's the apex of your protagonist's uphill climb. As a result of the climactic moment, only one of the two combatants can emerge on top.

In plays where the protagonist ultimately succeeds in her quest, the climactic moment — her victory — is often preceded by a low point, a negative condition from which it looks like the protagonist cannot recover. Then, like the mythical phoenix, the protagonist heroically arises from the ashes to achieve her objective.

In a play in which the protagonist is destined to fail to achieve her goal, the climactic moment often is preceded by a triumph or advance toward her objective. This temporary success sets the audience up to experience the irony and bittersweetness of the heroic defeat.

Plays have a cause-and-effect structure. One event, choice, decision, or action leads directly to another event, choice, decision, or action, and so on. This causality linking the events of your play should lead to the *earned conclusion,* an ending that's justified by the events that came before. It's a relevant and plausible conclusion that, in retrospect, seems inevitable to the story being played out. Chapter 12 guides you through the process of writing a good buildup to the climax and creating a powerful scene that determines the ending.

After the climax has occurred in your play, the characters generally have to deal with the consequences, the aftermath. Usually a brief moment or one last scene after the quest is over lets audience see how the dust settles. Audiences are given a peek at the new landscape. This closing is referred to as the play's *resolution.* The resolution is where you tie up loose ends if some of the threads in the play remain dangling. If your play has subplots, the resolution is your last opportunity to bring closure to the stories within your main story. Flip to Chapter 13 to find out more about resolutions.

It Ain't Over 'Til It's On Its Feet

Despite all your hard work, playwriting is not done when you finish a draft of your play you're happy with. Plays are meant to be produced — performed by actors for a live audience. Without performance, a play is like a custom-built car that's never taken out of the garage — it may look good, but it hardly serves any good purpose. So until a play is "on its feet," the playwriting process is not completed. (There's a quaint form of literature called *closet drama,* which is plays that aren't meant to be performed but instead be read as one reads a book. Fine and dandy, but where's the fun in that?)

The whole point of writing a play is to tell a story to an audience through the medium of theatre, via actors in live stage performance. So until your play gets there, until it's on its feet in rehearsal and performance, the goal is not yet fully attained. You want to see your words dramatically spoken by actors. You want to see your story enacted from start to finish. And you crave the applause that's earned by a job well done — not only by you but by a host of talented and enthusiastic collaborators.

Getting ready to collaborate

Novels, short stories, and poems are forms of writing in which nothing necessarily stands between the creator and the audience. A poet can recite his work for anyone who'll listen. A prose writer can make her work available to readers online, if not through a publisher. However, unlike those forms of writing, playwriting does not stand on its own.

The play is where theatre begins. When you type the words "The End," the play's journey is only partially completed. For the play to come to full fruition, it needs to be performed by actors. And the performance is enhanced immensely by the work of a director and a score of people working on the set, lights, sound, costumes, props, and so on. In other words, without the participation of a team of theatre professionals, your play doesn't happen.

The collaborative nature of playwriting requires the playwright to be open to the input and imagination of the other players. The director's vision impacts your play. The creativity of all the designers (sets, lights, sound, and costumes) is evident in the finished production. You can't have it all your way, and you shouldn't want to. Just as a child is not only the product of parental authority but also of teachers, classmates, and media influences, so too is the production of a play the result of many hands. And as a playwright, you'll want to adopt a team-spirit mindset to playwriting. (If you want to know more about that aspect of playwriting, Chapters 3 and 16 help you come to grips with the collaborative process.)

Promoting your play and understanding the business of theatre

When your play is ready to leave the nest, you need to prepare yourself for the realities of promoting your play with the intention of seeing it performed, which means getting the play produced.

Like it or not, a reality in theatre is that nothing gets done without money. And sad to say, it's not always the best plays that get produced; sometimes a production decision is about the prospect, from a producer's point of view, of selling lots of tickets. To get financing for your play, you must attract the attention of a producer or producing organization.

Before doing anything else, your first step is to copyright your play. It's simple and relatively inexpensive and gives you the peace of mind that comes with having proof of ownership. After that, your path to production will likely include some, if not all, of these phases:

- ✔ Critique and feedback from people who know plays and theatre
- ✔ Script-in-hand readings of your play by actors before a public or specially invited audience to get a real-world sense of how well the play works
- ✔ Submission of the play to contests and competitions in the hopes of getting exposure for the play and building your résumé

Looking at "theatre" up close

Theatre can be a puzzling word: Is it an art form or a physical location? Is it spelled *-re* or *-er*?

In addition to indicating the art form, the word "theatre" designates the playhouse — the building, auditorium, or other space in which plays and other performing arts take place. The word comes from the Greek *theatron,* meaning *viewing/seeing place.* And that's exactly what a theatre is — a place to see a performance.

To complicate matters, *theatre* can also be spelled *theater.* Some people make the distinction that theat*re* is the art form and theat*er* is the building. Other people say that *-re* is the British spelling and *-er* is American. What is correct? Well, it boils down to a "you say tom-*a*-to and I say tom-*ah*-to" situation: The answer depends on whom you ask. To keep things simple, I use only the *-re* form — *theatre* — in this book.

> ✔ Networking by showing up at plays and other theatre functions — seminars, workshops, conferences, and so on, where theatre-savvy people are likely to congregate — to introduce yourself and make your interests known

> ✔ Query letters inviting producers and the artistic directors of theatre companies that produce a season of plays to read your play

Some playwrights fancy themselves *artistes* and see themselves as above the commonplace undertaking of promoting and marketing their plays. If you're one of those, I have three words for you: Get over it. The successful playwright — the successful artist of any sort — is one who understands that you need to be your own best advocate. No one can speak to the merits of your work better than you.

When you're ready to take on the challenge of getting your play produced, plenty of info in this book will help you on your way. Chapter 15 discusses the process of holding readings and revising your script, and Chapter 17 helps you nail down a producer so your vision can finally be brought to life on a stage.

Chapter 2

Living the Life of a Playwright

*Y*ou want to put words in other people's mouths. You're dying to hear those words dramatically expressed in the presence of an audience. You can't wait to revel in the ecstasy of the wild applause.

You've been bitten by the bug — the playwriting bug.

You've probably seen plays presented by the drama club of high schools or colleges or performed by community theatre companies. Possibly you've acted in such productions. Very likely you studied some classic plays while in school or you may have had the opportunity to experience the excitement of seeing new plays done professionally. And during one of those theatrical experiences — somewhere between the heartrending dialogue and the laugh-out-loud comedic lines — you thought, "I can do that. I can write lines like that." That's how the obsession begins. Welcome to the art and craft of playwriting!

This chapter previews what you're getting yourself into. In it, I outline what it means to be a playwright, explain what a playwright does, list the traits of working playwrights, and describe what the life of a playwright is like.

And by the way, yes, you *can* do that!

Discovering What Makes a Playwright

A playwright writes plays. When you begin to pen dialogue or key it into a computer, you are playwriting. You may not be an experienced playwright and you may not yet have had one of your works produced, but by setting down lines to be said and enacted by someone else, you've become part of a long and (mostly) venerated tradition and history: You've taken on the mantle of *dramatist.* So hold your head high!

The playwright is an artist *and* a craftsman. Like an architect, the artist component of the playwright formulates the idea of the play, determines the form that will best serve the idea, and creates the blueprint for an engaging story. The craftsman component of the playwright is like an engineer, responsible for using the blueprints to design the infrastructure — the frame, water lines, power lines, communication lines, and so on — that will enable the building to function and fulfill the architect's vision. Both an architect and an engineer are needed for most building projects. So, too, are the artist and craftsman roles needed for the creation of a play.

Playwrights come from all walks of life

No single formula creates a playwright. Playwrights come from all walks of life, every type of job, all education and economic levels, all ages, colors, and creeds, regardless of gender, sexual orientation, or disability. The playwriting bug is an equal opportunity stinger.

I started out as a small-town reporter-photographer, segued into corporate communications for a decade, and was involved in local politics before my love of a good story — and an improvisation class I took for the fun of it — led me into playwriting.

And though it's not unusual for playwrights to have related pursuits (like journalism or acting) in their backgrounds, no special résumé or particular experience is required to join the club. All you need is the love of storytelling and the willingness to roll up your sleeves and get to work.

The Great White Way is great, but you don't need to live there

If you're under the uneasy impression that to be a successful playwright you need to reside close to "The Great White Way," relax. Broadway is a great place to visit, but you don't have to live there.

Funny spelling: Is *wright* right?

The word *playwright* is a combination of the product — the play — and of its maker — the wright. The word *wright* isn't used much today. It can stand on its own, meaning a person who constructs or repairs, but most often the word is found piggybacking on what the wright constructs or repairs. For example, a *shipwright* is someone who constructs or repairs ships, and a *wainwright* is someone who constructs or repairs, yes, wains (meaning carts and wagons).

Most people who have not had occasion to refer to this profession in writing usually go for *playwrite* as the spelling. After all, if the activity is play*writing,* then shouldn't the person who writes plays be known as a play*write?* Or should it be play*writer,* since a person who writes movie scripts is called a *screenwriter?* Maybe in some parallel universe, but not here

for us. And you can blame it on that snobby old dramatist and poet, Ben Jonson. While you and I are thrilled to be called a play*wright,* Jonson devised the term as an insult.

Ben Jonson, a contemporary of William Shakespeare, is known for his satirical plays. Jonson, like the great Shakespeare and Christopher Marlowe, wrote his plays in blank verse (a form of nonrhyming poetry), and he had no patience for dramatists who couldn't quite measure up to his artistic standards. Jonson belittled "lesser" writers as play*wrights* — implying that they were merely common tradesmen constructing plays. On the other hand, he was (visualize Jonson with his nose in the air) a *poet!* Jonson's sneering term *playwright* stuck, but over time the word lost his intended negative connotation.

Yes, New York City is to theatre what Hollywood is to filmmaking. "The Big Apple" is the home of the legendary and electrically gleaming Broadway theatre district. And despite Broadway's competitiveness and long odds against big-time success, it attracts some of the best and brightest performers, directors, and playwrights theatre has to offer. To bend a line from the Frank Sinatra hit "New York, New York": If you can make it there, you can make it anywhere.

All that being said, though New York is the Mecca of theatre activity in the United States, theatre is alive and well in many other American cities and communities, thank you very much. Other theatre-centric heavy hitters include Chicago, Los Angeles, Philadelphia, Boston, and Washington, D.C. But many smaller cities also have vibrant theatre communities, and, because 90 percent of Americans live within 25 miles of some city, you likely have the opportunity to see — and involve yourself in — theatre.

For those of you who ascribe to Dorothy's insight, "There's no place like home," rest assured that you can make it as a playwright without uprooting yourself and leaving your way of life behind.

Learning from Other Playwrights

If your dream was to be next hot lead guitarist in a rock band, in addition to learning to play a guitar, you would listen to tons of rock CDs and make your way to as many rock concerts as you could manage in order to learn from the experience and skill of others. As the great mathematician and scientist Isaac Newton said, too modestly but truthfully, about his groundbreaking discoveries: "If I have seen further, it is only by standing on the shoulders of giants." In other words, intentionally or not, as a playwright you build on the work of those who have come before you.

To develop skills in playwriting, exploring the theatre works of playwrights who have gotten their plays produced is strategically and educationally smart. In other words, before you strike out on your own, you want to understand what has preceded you and learn from the successes and failures of others — be they giants or not.

This section covers simple ways you can quickly get yourself up to speed on playwriting by surveying the theatrical landscape. Check out what others are doing. You don't need to reinvent the wheel to be successful.

Observing the rules before you break them

In my experience as a playwriting teacher, I frequently come across students who can't wait to shake things up. These would-be revolutionaries are eager to express their individuality and put their unique stamp on the theatre and the world at large. And they couldn't care less about story structure and playwriting guidelines. Dude, aren't rulz made to be broken?

As far as I'm concerned, you can't have too much of that kind of enthusiasm and drive. I admire and welcome the passion and energy of new writers ready to scorch the earth with their fervently held ideas and ideals. But — and it's a big *but* — if your credo is that rules are made to be broken, a caveat must be attached to that philosophy: If you're going to break the rules, first know the rules you plan to break.

Knowing and understanding the rules of any art form, including playwriting, will provide you with a launching pad from which you can soar to any heights and in any direction your heart and skills will take you.

Seeing lots of plays (good and bad)

If you want to be an informed and savvy playwright — and you should —
immerse yourself in plays and theatre. See as many plays as you possibly can.
Even without trying, you'll learn a great deal about plays and theatre — what
works or doesn't, and what's practical or impossible. If a play earns less than
stellar reviews, don't necessarily avoid it. The reviewer's perspective on the
play may be very different from yours. And even if the play is a dud, you can
learn as much by analyzing a flop as you can by studying a hit.

Here are some venues for you to see lots of shows:

- **Schools:** Almost every high school and college does plays; some do very
  fine productions. Don't shy away from school productions. But focus on
  the play — the story, the characters, the dialogue — and not so much on
  the abilities of the student actors and directors.

- **Amateur theatre:** Many towns and small cities have what's referred
  to as *community theatre.* (My own suburban county, though relatively
  small, enjoys two community theatres.) A community theatre company
  is composed of volunteer actors, directors, stagecraft people (set,
  sound, lighting, and costume designers, among others). *Volunteer* is the
  key; no professional theatre people are involved. All participants are
  amateurs doing theatre for the fun and satisfaction of it.

  Community groups tend to focus on productions of popular plays. The
  wonderful comedies of playwright extraordinaire Neil Simon are a staple
  of community theatre.

- **Regional theatres:** Regional theatres, sometimes referred to as *resident
  theatres,* can be found all around the country. These are professional
  theatres that mount their own productions of new shows or revivals.
  Usually regional theatres have a season of three or more shows, each
  performed for a month or so, for an audience of about 200–400 people
  each show.

  I've been privileged to have one of my plays, *The Devil's Music: The
  Life and Blues of Bessie Smith,* presented at such fine regional theatres
  as the Hartford Stage (Connecticut), the Cape Playhouse (Cape Cod,
  Massachusetts), the Florida Stage (near Palm Beach), Florida Rep (in
  Fort Myers), and the George Street Playhouse (New Brunswick, New
  Jersey), among others.

- **Touring productions in performing arts centers:** Hundreds of performing arts centers are located in and outside of major municipalities
  around the country. These venues typically bring in the road-show
  productions of Broadway hits as well as concerts and dance programs.
  Touring shows — like *Phantom of the Opera,* for instance — bring
  Broadway-caliber productions to the hinterlands, sometimes with the
  Broadway cast members and sometimes with different performers.

✔ **Broadway and other big-city theatre:** You can catch major productions of new and important plays in New York City on Broadway, obviously, but also in such other major cities as Chicago, Los Angeles, Boston, Philadelphia, and Washington, D.C. The quality of the plays you can see in the big cities may or may not be superior to what you see elsewhere, but the production values (sets, props, costumes, lighting, sound, and so on) generally will be first rate. And occasionally you'll catch big-name film actors in starring roles.

Finding ways to attend theatre without going broke

Compared with movie tickets, theatre ticket prices are high. Typically, tickets can range from $20 to $30 or more in community theatre, from $40 to $80 or more on the regional level, and $75 to $150 or more in the big cities. Going to theatre ain't cheap. So how, then, can you see lots of plays without taking out a second mortgage? Below are several avenues to less expensive (and even free) tickets. In some cases, you may find yourself up in the "nosebleed seats," but you'll be able to see plays without breaking the bank.

Never be reluctant to ask about discounts or freebies. Because everyone, particularly theatre people, knows that tickets are not cheap, no one will be offended. The worst that will happen is you'll get "no" for an answer.

Subscribing to theatres

Buy subscriptions to theatres that present a season of shows. Subscribers generally get their pick of seats, are entitled to perks (like after-show discussions with the cast), and, best of all, pay as little as half price per ticket. For example, Penguin Repertory Theatre (with which I'm affiliated) in Stony Point, New York, offers subscribers a season of four productions for the price of three. If you need encouragement to get out and see theatre, buying a subscription is a good way to prompt yourself to go.

Going through discount organizations

A number of theatre and entertainment organizations, most of them online, offer discounted tickets. Many of them will send you e-mails alerting you to the latest ticket opportunities. Discounts can range from 10 percent to half price or more (or even offer free tickets), depending on the nature of the organization. Generally, attractive discounts are available when a show opens (to help build audiences and positive word of mouth) and when a show is nearing the end of its run (to fill seats as the production schedule winds down). Some discount organizations charge a small annual fee; some charge a service fee. Following are some organizations that offer discounts and information about discounts:

✔ America Performs: www.americaperforms.com

✔ Broadway Box: www.broadwaybox.com

✔ Theatre Development Fund (TDF): www.tdf.org

✔ Playbill Online: www.playbill.com

✔ Audience Extras: www.audienceextras.com

Snagging student or senior discounts

Some theatres, usually those outside the Great White Way (Broadway), offer discounts to senior citizens or to students with student identification (see "Student rush" below for another discount opportunity for students). This courtesy, if available, varies from theatre to theatre, so the only way to know is to check with the box office or go to the theatre's website.

Attending previews

When plays open, the first handful of performances may be designated as previews, followed days or weeks later by the official opening performance. The purpose of the preview period is to see the show "on its feet" and make any last-minute changes or refinements to fix problems that may emerge when the show is done for an audience. Sometimes, though not always, tickets for a show are cheaper during the preview period. Why? Theoretically, a preview performance can be stopped to fix a staging problem, but it's rare. I've never seen it happen. Interrupting a performance is not something theatre people like to do, so most fixes are made between performances.

Participating as an usher or volunteer

Ushering — assisting ticketholders in finding their seats — is the simplest way of seeing lots of plays for free. Most theatres favor volunteer ushers. Some theatres keep a running list of available ushers, so ask about it at your local theatres. Unfortunately, the big Broadway houses tend not to use volunteers; they have their own staffs. But you can still ask.

An alternative to ushering is to volunteer to help in the costume shop, set-building shop, in theatre management, or other areas. If the theatre uses volunteers, you may be paid in free tickets. Again, ask. Volunteering also gives you the opportunity to make yourself known the various theatre professionals you'll meet and to build relationships with them that may give you a leg up in the future.

Taking advantage of student rush

Because theatres recognize that students normally don't have a lot of money, and to help develop a new generation of theatregoers, theatres sometimes offer students significant discounts to shows. This practice is called *student rush*. Tickets can range from $10 to $30 with valid student ID cards.

Unfortunately, there's no standard rule about student rush tickets. Some theatres offer them just before the curtain rises; others want you at the theatre two hours before the show begins. Some sell you tickets outright; others put you into a lottery for the limited number of tickets made available for student rush. Some will sell you only one ticket; others will permit you to buy two or four. Most of the time you'll have to do some waiting in line. With all these variations, taking advantage of student rush privileges requires some research. Contact the box office or go to the theatre's website for the theatre's specific guidelines.

Note: Whatever the rules are, you'll want to be dressed neatly for theatre, and you should *not* be texting during the performance. Reserve the torn jeans and the glowing smartphone screens for your next rock concert.

Filling the standing room

If you're willing and able to stand in one place for two hours, consider buying standing room only (SRO) tickets. Not all theatres and all shows do this. And generally, SRO tickets are available only when all the seats for the performance are sold out. Check with the box office, preferably in person, because theatres that do sell SRO tickets don't necessarily publicize it. After all, they'd much rather you buy a seat for a future performance.

Reading lots of plays

Read plays like your life depends on it, because it does, if you want to make it in the playwriting trade.

Dust off your old literature book from school to see what gems it contains. You may find plays like *Oedipus Rex* by Sophocles, *Hamlet* by William Shakespeare, *A Doll House* by Henrik Ibsen, or *Death of a Salesman* by Arthur Miller in that cola-stained, dog-eared volume. Another free option is to check plays out from your school or local public library — either collections by a single playwright or anthologies of exceptional plays by numerous writers.

You can buy published plays on Amazon.com or through other booksellers. And you don't always need to pay top dollar purchasing books new. You can buy used editions of published play scripts from many websites. And, of course, you can shop at those brick-and-mortar bookstores (how retro!).

When you read published plays, you see that the format used in books is different from professional script format (an example of which is included in the appendix of this book). Plays are published this way (the character's name on the same line as his dialogue rather than being above it and centered, for instance) to save space and keep the number of pages down. This formatting isn't appropriate for working scripts, though, so don't emulate it when writing your plays.

Avoiding movie versions

Watching a movie version of a play may seem like a convenient alternative to reading a play or going to a live performance. Unfortunately, it's not a very good solution. When a play is adapted to a movie, changes are made. The process of expanding on and adding new elements for the film adaptation is referred to as *opening up the script*. Locations only referred to in a play are shown in the film. Past experiences mentioned in the dialogue of a play can be shown in flashbacks. Characters that don't exist in the play are created for the movie version. (See Chapter 3 for more on the differences between theatre and film.)

In the case of movie versions of plays made from the 1930s into the early 1960s, the interactions between the characters of a play were sometimes changed entirely to satisfy the watchful, stern, and moralistic eye of the movie censors of the Motion Picture Production Code, often called the Hays Code. The movie version of a play of that period may be significantly different from the play in important ways.

For example, in *A Streetcar Named Desire* (1947) by Tennessee Williams, the climactic moment of the story is when Blanche DuBois is overpowered and raped. When the censors got finished with the script of the movie version (1951), the rape scene was so toned down that most people who don't know the story miss that pivotal action entirely. The Hays Code censors also insisted on a different ending to the story, one in which Stanley, who brutalizes Blanche, does not resume life as usual but, instead, finds that his wife and child are leaving him. According to the Production Code, Stanley had to be punished for his offenses.

Unfortunately, very few movie versions of plays have not been altered to accommodate the nature of film and the expectations of moviegoers. Occasionally, though, rather than a movie adaptation, you may come across a VHS or DVD recording of a live stage performance of a play. These versions are very much worth viewing.

Taking classes and doing workshops

Many playwrights benefit from the stimulation, challenge, interaction, and feedback that come from being involved in a playwriting class or workshop. And though some writers profess to work better independently, regularly going to a playwriting class or workshop also enforces a certain discipline on you: You need to be ready with a given amount of writing for the class or workshop.

Playwriting *classes* can be found at many colleges, in adult and continuing education programs, affiliated with theatres, and in theatre studios. Classes generally cover the basics of playwriting. Students sometimes do various writing exercises along with working on new plays.

Playwriting *workshops* are less "educational" and are more hands-on. Participants in workshops generally tend to be fewer than in classes. Workshops focus on plays in progress, with participants bringing in scenes to be read and critiqued. Workshop participants usually are not absolute beginners but rather playwrights who have at least some experience writing plays.

Unfortunately, classes and workshops can be costly. In addition, there is potential for confusion and discouragement if the teacher or workshop leader isn't careful to keep the feedback specific, constructive, focused, and balanced (addressing the script's positives as well as potential problems). The leader of one workshop I attended was careless and callous in her criticism, discouraging everyone but the most stout-hearted. I've also participated in workshops that provided a safe and supportive environment. Look for the latter, and avoid the former like the plague.

One of my strategies for avoiding writer's block is to participate in two workshops at a time, working on a different play in each. That way, if I stall on one project, I can shift my focus to the other project until the logjam breaks. (See "Battling the specter of writer's block," later in this chapter, for more on dealing with writer's block.)

In a discussion I had years ago with accomplished playwright, screenwriter, and director John Patrick Shanley about playwriting workshops, he said "It's never good to be the smartest one in your group." In other words, it may be gratifying for your ego to be the top dog, the person the others look up to. But from whom do *you* learn? Shanley's point is that being in a workshop with playwrights more experienced than yourself is far better because you can benefit from their advanced knowledge, experience, and input.

Working Like a Playwright

As stimulating and satisfying as the process of creation and writing can be, it's still work. And work takes time, preparation, direction, focus, effort, and stick-to-itiveness. As in any other pursuit, you'll have days when you're barreling along full speed ahead, and at other times you'll feel stuck in the mud.

As you venture into this bold new world of playwriting, you can put yourself on a more solid footing if you understand how a playwright thinks and works. Although individual playwrights can be very different from each other in their perspectives and processes, they share a number of common traits and methods that are useful to consider.

Living the dual life of a playwright

Writers lead a dual life. On one hand, most playwrights live their lives like anyone else. Their public lives include family, friends, jobs, places to go, and events to experience. As the saying goes, they put their pants on one leg at a time, like everyone else.

But writers also have a concealed side that observes and studies people — what folks do, what they say, and *how* they do and say it. This persona seems to float over life, watching interactions and analyzing events as they unfold, making notes for future use.

Years ago, an upset friend called me to talk through a very distressing incident. On one level, I listened and commiserated as good friends do. But, on another level, I was observing our interaction, listening to what she said and how she said it . . . and making notes, literally. In one hand I held the phone receiver, and in the other hand was a pencil scribbling on a pad, writing down the story she was telling me. After the phone call, I was disgusted with myself. *What kind of friend would do that?* The answer was obvious and unavoidable . . . a playwright friend. It was a landmark moment for me as a playwright.

Years later I wrote a play based on the incident my friend had related to me. I was lucky; she didn't object. (But what if she had? More on that ethical predicament in Chapter 4.)

Making a living — the day job

As a playwright, you face the tension between the heavenly freedom to pursue playwriting without distractions and the very down-to-earth need to pay the rent, put food on the table, and pay for cable.

In eras gone by, talented and promising artists of all sorts could hope to find a *patron,* who would provide the fortunate artist with financial support. It brought the patron prestige, and it allowed the artist to put aside mundane cares and focus only on the art. Leonardo da Vinci, Michelangelo, Shakespeare, Mozart, and Beethoven all benefited in some degree from the patronage of royalty, the nobility, or the church. Much of the great art of the Renaissance was created under the umbrella of patronage.

Today's equivalent of those patrons are arts foundations, grants organizations, and government arts agencies. They function to offer artists financial assistance to encourage the creation of art in all forms. However, the amounts of monies doled out to individual artists, while much appreciated, tend to be small and steadily shrinking. So, "heigh-ho, heigh-ho, it's off to work we go."

According to some estimates, only 5 percent of people who identify themselves as artists can actually make a full-time living doing their art. Conversely, that means that 95 percent of artists need to work to support themselves. We work at everything from the stereotypical "day job" — waiting tables, telemarketing, or temping in offices — to the entire gamut of full-time, blue-collar and professional positions — doctor, lawyer, or Native American chief.

As a writer, you may be inclined to try to find a job that involves writing. Maybe working for a local newspaper or writing brochures for not-for-profit companies. Writing is what you do, and such jobs keep your writing chops warmed up, right? After all, writing is writing, isn't it? Well, another school of thought on this point suggests that a shrewd writer ought to work at a job that involves anything *but* writing — driving a cab, drawing blood for diagnostic purposes, screwing the caps on soda bottles. The concern is that if you engage in writing for your day job, you exhaust your writing energy and creativity. Some writers swear this to be true, but that's not been my experience. Many of my playwriting colleagues have day jobs that involve writing. Therefore, the answer to this question must be your own.

Are you a failure as a playwright if you need to work for a living? Fuhgeddaboudit. Remember, 19 out of 20 artists need to work for a living. You're simply part of the overwhelming majority of dedicated and hardworking artists who create for the love of it, and maybe make a buck or two here and there. You work and work at your art with the dream that somehow, some day, maybe. . . .

Getting out in the world

Your unique resource as an artist is your life, so cramming in as much living as possible is to your advantage. Here again the playwright's duality as participant and observer kicks in. Immerse yourself in the experiences of life . . . but take notes.

Some writers insist that a writer ought to experience everything possible. Good and bad. Sounds like a good idea, but clearly that counsel goes only so far. You don't want to engage in criminal activity in order to create a criminal character or write about unlawful doings. Common sense and a hefty measure of self-preservation need to prevail in your choices of experience. Writing from behind bars or from a hospital bed gets old fast.

On the other hand, a playwright does need to recharge the creative batteries and broaden his horizons. And one of the most exciting and wholesome ways to do this is to travel. In the writer's context, travel can mean anything from casually exploring your neighborhood to apprehensively peering over the rim of the Grand Canyon to climbing the 463 exhausting steps to the top of the *Duomo* in Florence, Italy. The point is to get out and experience new people, places, and things.

Adventures expand a writer's understanding of human nature and can spark ideas for interesting characters and anecdotes for plays. In China, I walked part of the Great Wall, a breathtaking experience. And in the window of a Chinese butcher shop, I spied a carcass hanging that was, eerily, shaped like a dog. From the sublime to the chilling. In Spain, my traveling companion and I drank in the romance of Madrid, and, while motoring south to Seville, we were abruptly stopped and humorlessly scrutinized by soldiers in military camouflage with machine guns in hand. Again, from the sublime to the chilling. For a playwright, it's all good.

Using the D-word (Discipline)

In most jobs, the discipline to show up and put in the time doing the work is enforced by a supervisor and, more importantly, by the need for a paycheck.

When it comes to writing, most creative writers have no one clocking their comings and goings and no immediate paycheck incentive to make them show up for work. So writers need to be their own taskmasters, prodding themselves to sit down and pick up the pen or peck at the keyboard. In short, creative writers, including playwrights, need to be disciplined. For artists who fancy the idea of awaiting creative inspiration before getting to work, discipline is a dirty word — the D-word.

Some of my colleagues and I experience a curious phenomenon concerning writing discipline. Sometimes a real act of willpower is necessary to sit down and get started writing. As my writing time approaches, everything else seems to take on an urgent importance. I absolutely need to return a call, I've got to go out to get that quart of orange juice, I must trim my fingernails, and so on, as if I'm looking for any ploy not to face a firing squad. What makes this so peculiar is that I love to write. And when I'm seated and working, I'm totally into it and quickly lose myself in the fun of writing a play. I have no idea why I struggle to get my fanny into my desk chair when I know that the enjoyable (most of the time) experience of writing awaits me.

A key to successful writing is the discipline to actually get yourself to do it. And do it regularly, as I explain in the next section.

Establishing your writing time and place

Playwright Neil Simon is quoted as having said: "Writing is an escape from a world that crowds me. I like being alone in a room. It's almost a form of meditation — an investigation of my own life." The choice of writing time and place is a highly personal. It's something every writer needs to think on, make a realistic decision about, and stick to.

Writing time

Most committed writers establish for themselves a fixed writing regimen. The wildly successful novelist Stephen King brings himself to his desk seven mornings a week and doesn't call it a day until he has achieved his quota of ten manuscript pages. Other writers work by time rather than by word or page count. For example, Neil Simon has established for himself an 8 a.m. to 1 p.m. work day. After 1 p.m., he's free to enjoy lunch dates, return phone calls, do research on his projects, visit a museum, or do whatever floats his boat on a given day.

"I can't schedule myself that rigidly," you protest. "I've got a job to go to, a family to interact with, and a dog to walk. I can't regularly block out time. No way." Yes way. If you have that fire in the belly to write, to speak to the world through a story, you'll make it happen.

Writing place

There is no one perfect writing place for all writers. The choice of a customary place to work depends on your preference, what space is available regularly, and how conducive the space is to concentration.

With the advent of laptop computers, virtually anywhere can be your office. You may retreat to the relative quiet of a public library to write. Or you may hijack the dining table to work on in the wee hours of the morning. You may even prefer *Writing in Restaurants,* the title of a collection of essays by the Pulitzer Prize–winning playwright, screenwriter, and director David Mamet.

I'm fortunate enough to have a spare bedroom in my home that I converted into an office. The room contains my desk, my computer setup (computer, monitor, printers, Internet connection), my own phone line, overstuffed bookcases, file cabinets, a supply closet, and a hassock used by the dog, Charlie, as a sentry tower from which he protects me from copyright violators. And last but not least, my office has a door I can close.

Whatever little corner of the world you're able to commandeer, it should have the following features:

- ✔ **Solitude:** When you're working, you should be left alone. That means no interruptions from family members, the FedEx guy, or itinerant preachers. Concentration is fragile, and if it's broken you can lose your edge. Just ask Tiger Woods, who expects absolute quiet as he focuses to tee off, or Serena Williams, who concentrates mightily as she tosses the tennis ball high for a serve. Raw ideas and embryonic dialogue can be fleeting, and a sudden intrusion may be all it takes for a thought or some ideal wording to evaporate from your mind. So close your door or find a place to be alone.

✔ **Quiet:** The degree of sound or noise you want around you when you write is a personal choice. I generally work in quiet. Some writers enjoy having music in the background. Others find *silence* distracting and want the ambient noise of the world to keep them connected with humanity and, therefore, with their work. No matter what degree of sound you permit in your workspace, you must be sure it doesn't derail you. If music helps you concentrate, terrific. Just be honest with yourself, and yank out those earbuds if you find yourself humming and tapping your foot rather than writing dialogue.

✔ **Gear:** To avoid the interruption of having to get up to fetch something, keep all the gear and writing equipment you need close to you. For instance, my dictionary is close enough that I can flip through the pages without getting out of my desk chair. One of my computer printers is even closer than the dictionary. My desk chair swivels so that I can extend my arms in any direction to grasp my telephone, my cup of coffee, the lamp switch, or a pad and writing implements if I need to make some notes for myself. My workspace may be as cramped as a Gemini space capsule, but I have all the necessities for my work close at hand.

Avoiding the downside of technology

Modern technology, such as computers and smartphones, makes many aspects of life and work a lot easier. When I quit my last full-time job in the mid-'80s to go out on my own as a freelance writer, I was able to do that only because of computer technology. It enabled me to write quickly, easily make changes and revisions, and electronically fire off copies of documents to whomever they were intended. And the independence to do freelance writing on my own schedule enabled me to have the time to take the plunge into theatre and playwriting.

But the downside to all this technology is that it can be distracting, almost as distracting as it is helpful. And as you know by now, distractions are the enemy of concentration and productive playwriting work time. When the cellphone rings, or even just vibrates, do you have the willpower to ignore it? As you sit and work at your computer, can you ignore the tone that alerts you to incoming e-mail? Are you ever sidetracked by the temptation to play Grand Theft Auto or to join a Texas Hold 'Em poker game that's only a couple of mouse clicks away?

Technology may enable you to more easily get your playwriting career going, but I recommend that you turn off your phones, both land line and cellphone, when you start work. And if possible, keep those time-consuming games off your work computer.

In short, whether it's a knock on your workspace door or the phone's electronic equivalent of "The Vienna Waltz," the potential for distractions needs to be limited, or eliminated entirely, if you're to make the most of your work time.

Battling the specter of writer's block

Writer's block is the writer's version of that universal dream in which you need to run away from something but your legs are too heavy to move. In throes of writer's block, a writer sits in front of a blank sheet of paper or computer screen unable to think of anything to write. It's a horrible sensation, particularly if you're on deadline with a project. Inspiration just won't come. The Muses are not speaking with you that day. Help!

At some time and to some degree, writer's block happens to all writers. But I can let you in on a few strategies to avoid or minimize the downtime.

- ✔ **Consult your outline.** If you've written a detailed outline of your play, you'll very likely not have too much trouble with writer's block. If you stall in a project, consulting your outline ought to redirect you. If not, skip to another scene in your play and get to work. Jumping around in writing your play may not be the most logical way to work, but it sure beats sitting idle, pulling your hair out.

- ✔ **End on a cliffhanger.** Some writers stop work for the day in the midst of a scene rather than at the end of it. This tactic can be helpful, because when you come back to the script, you can easily pick up where you left off instead of beginning a new scene and possibly finding yourself blocked for ideas. This cliffhanger approach allows you to get a running start in your next session.

- ✔ **Work on multiple projects.** This solution is my favorite. I like to be working on two different plays at once (and generally working each in a different workshop). When I find myself stalled or running out of juice on one project, rather than sitting in front of my computer drumming my fingers on the mouse, I switch over to the other project. This approach keeps me productive, and it takes the pressure off me in the play I've temporarily put aside. Taking a break on a project sometimes allows you to consciously and unconsciously ruminate on the stalled work, relaxing your mind and opening it up for the free flow of ideas. It works for me.

- ✔ **Write anything.** One of the usual prescriptions for writer's block is to make yourself write anything rather than sit idle. Write poetry. Write a letter. Write some prose. The theory is that, at worst, you're practicing your art in some form, and, at best, the act of writing itself may just jumpstart the mental engine that's driving your work on the play.

Some playwriting instructors advocate writing scenes that aren't actually intended go into your play. This exercise has no pressure: No one will ever read the scene, so you can just write whatever comes to mind. Try experimenting with an "off-stage" scene that probes the relationships between the characters or between your protagonist his father or mother. Parental relationships are powerful, and exploring them for your character may lead to an interesting discovery, which, in turn, may unblock you.

✔ **Exercise.** Engaging in physical activity seems to put the focus on your body and relieve the pressure on your mind. Sometimes you can sweat your way back into gear on a play.

When I'm stubbornly blocked, and I don't have the time to put aside the intractable project, I'll lace up my running shoes and go out for a jog. If the weather's bad, I'll hop on my stationary bike and pedal furiously. A workout with weights or meditation for relaxation or mowing the lawn can achieve the same beneficial effect of relaxing and freeing up your mind.

Exploring the Tools of the Trade

Almost every trade or pursuit in life has tools to help accomplish tasks more quickly and efficiently. Playwriting is no different. The tools available range from the exotic to the mundane and from expensive to free. They serve to keep your scripts comparatively free of spelling and grammatical errors, and at the very least, they help you to look like you know what you're doing.

Spelling correctly for credibility

Does spelling count? In a word, positutely. "My spelling is close enough to be understood," you protest. "Why should I obsess over spelling?" Because even small and seemingly trivial errors get noticed. Unfortunately, multiple errors in spelling and grammar create the impression that you don't know spelling and/or grammar, are too lazy to turn on the word processor's spell-checking feature, aren't careful or thorough, don't have the self-respect to put your best foot forward, or all of the above.

Why create a credibility hurdle for yourself when most word-processing software programs come with spell-checking and grammar-checking features? These tools aren't perfect, but they help produce a script that's far cleaner than a script that hasn't been spelling and grammar checked at all. The spell-checker in Microsoft Word immediately flagged with red underlining the slang word *positutely* used above, giving me the opportunity to fix it or leave it if the "error" was intentional.

The only time that poor grammar is appropriate is if a character happens to speak poor English. Then, of course, his grammar would be flawed and would appear so in the script dialogue.

Formatting your script properly

Using the correct format for play scripts is essential, if not initially then certainly by the time you're working on the first draft you show people. "Why should I bother about format?" you inquire again. "Isn't the content of my play vastly more important than how it looks?" In theory, yes, but in the real world, not necessarily.

A comparison to illuminate the issue: Would you go to job interview at, for example, a bank wearing jeans and a T-shirt? Probably not, because you want to look like you fit in, like you're part of the environment you hope to enter. Inappropriate dress can lead the interviewer to conclude that you don't understand the world of banking and you're not to be taken seriously.

Similarly, when you begin showing your play to people who are in a position to make it happen, you want them to think you know what you're doing. If your script doesn't look like the ones producers and directors are accustomed to seeing, they very well may conclude that you don't understand the industry and you're not to be taken seriously. Why shoot yourself in the foot?

Believe it or not, script readers — because they receive hundreds, maybe thousands, of scripts to read — look for reasons *not* to read scripts. If a glance at your first page seems to indicate you're an amateur or clueless in your presentation of your material, your script can hit the circular file before a word is read. Is that fair? Of course not. Does it happen? Too often. Take the time to put your wonderful story and dialogue in the accepted professional format and you'll have a better chance at serious consideration.

Relying on scriptwriting software . . . or not

The touted advantage of using scripting software is that it makes script writing easy and it saves time. You hit a certain key when ready to write dialogue, and the software centers the cursor on the page for the name of the character. After typing in the character's name, it automatically positions the cursor down on the next line where it patiently awaits the magnificent words your character will utter. When it's time to indicate what your characters are physically doing at a given moment, hit another key, and the cursor moves into position for stage directions. Pretty nifty, right?

To see for myself how far interest in nifty features goes, I conducted a quick e-mail survey of a dozen playwriting colleagues. Collectively, the group, including myself, has had plays produced throughout the United States, in Europe, and as far off as Australia. My totally unscientific poll revealed that among this dirty dozen

✔ Ten playwrights, including myself, primarily work in Microsoft Word. (One of the ten also uses WordPerfect.)

✔ Two playwrights work in Final Draft, the 800-pound gorilla of the scripting software field, the industry standard when it comes to screenplays. (Most scripting software works for screenplays, stage plays, TV scripts, and others types of script, all of which have very specific formats.)

✔ Three playwrights, to my surprise, write the first drafts of their plays longhand, using pen or pencil and ruled paper. This manual approach to writing seems to provide those writers with a physical, hands-on connection to their work and ideas. However, all three eventually key their plays into Microsoft Word. Seems like twice the work, but who asked me?

If you're comfortable monkeying around with Microsoft Word, you can set up macros or a template that can do many of the common tasks scripting software can do for you.

The last word on scriptwriting software is this: personal preference. Well, that's two words, but the point is that scripting software, like any other tool available to writers, is a matter of what works for you. The software ranges from expensive (Final Draft) down to free (some of my students swear by Celtx, a free, downloadable scriptwriting program). If you want to know more about your options, look online for reviews of scripting software.

Making Money the Playwright Way

Being a playwright is not about money; it's about being an artist. Yeah, right. I don't know of any playwright who doesn't hope to eventually find a royalty check in his mailbox. A royalty is the creator's piece of the action when a play is produced for paying audiences. For some playwrights, royalty checks help keep them going financially. For others, they mean a little money on the side. But whether the possibility of making some money with your playwriting is essential or just a pleasant plus, you should have some idea how it works.

Earning money from your play

In the movie business, a screenwriter, if lucky, *sells* his script to a producer or studio. After the script is sold, the screenwriter has little or no say in what happens to his work. The work is now owned by someone else. In playwriting, you earn money from your work without giving up your ownership of it. The two broad types of earnings are royalties and licensing fees.

Royalties

In theatre, you in essence lease your script to a producer or theatre in exchange for a royalty — a percentage — from every ticket sold. The script must be performed exactly as written; no changes can be made without your permission. And, best of all, you retain ownership of the play, and you (and your agent, if you have one) are free to try to interest other theatres in staging the play. Therefore, your compensation comes not from a one-time sale of your work, but from multiple productions of the play.

When a producer (or producing theatre) decides to produce your play, you (or your agent) and the producer negotiate a contract that specifies, among other things, the number of performances planned, the ticket prices to be charged, the number of seats in the theatre, the royalty percentage (which may include a minimum weekly royalty), and, usually, an advance payment. The *advance* is money paid to you upfront that will be deducted from the last royalty check from the production.

The playwright's royalty for a play production is commonly somewhere between 6 and 8 percent of box office sales. For example, say you've negotiated a 7 percent royalty. If your play is being produced in a small theatre (100 seats), with shows are running about 80 percent of capacity, seven nights a week, and ticket prices average $20, then the following calculations determines the royalty for that week:

80% of 100 seats = 80 seats

80 seats × $20 a ticket = $1,600 in box office receipts each night

$1,600 × 7 performances = $11,200 in box office receipts that week

$11,200 × 7% = $784 royalty payment

Obviously, the larger the theatre (assuming good ticket sales) and the higher the ticket prices, the more substantial your royalties. (In calculating royalties, some exclusions may affect the gross box office receipts. For example, if the theatre gives up a percentage of the ticket income to a ticket-selling service, that obviously decreases the box office ticket income.) If your play is represented by an agent, the royalty checks go to the agent, who takes his cut, usually 10 percent, and then turns over the balance to you.

Licensing

Another possible way you can make money is by licensing your play for publication. A number of publishers specialize in publishing and selling book or booklet versions of plays. These publishers also handle the licensing of plays to professional and amateur theatre groups. Two of the better known play publishers are Dramatist Play Service and Samuel French. If your play is successful, you may be able to get your play published, and as part of the agreement the publisher may offer you some money as an advance against future royalties.

One advantage of having your play published is that these publishers market and distribute the plays widely, more easily getting your play into the hands of producers for production consideration. Though the specifics vary, the publishers charge the producing theatre a licensing fee ($100, for example) per performance. The publishers keep 10 percent of the fees from professional productions and 20 percent from amateur shows, and the rest comes back to you as royalties.

Dealing with contracts and legal issues

The royalty arrangement and other production issues can get complicated, which is why you should have representation of some sort when it comes to contract negotiations.

If you are well versed in the minutia of production contracts, you have every right to do your own negotiating. At least one of my playwright colleagues does that. However, because your understandable eagerness to get your play produced may cause you to settle for less than you could otherwise get, getting assistance from someone experienced at playing hardball is the smart thing. The two common options for playwright representation are the much-maligned agent and an attorney. (My "much-maligned" comment refers to the perennial lament of all writers: "My agent doesn't do a thing for me.")

Agents

Getting an agent to represent your show can be a Catch-22 situation: To get a script to certain producers and theatres, you need an agent, but to attract the interest of an agent, you usually need to have had a production — some success under your belt.

The role of an agent is to get your script into the hands of producers or theatres that are likely to want to do a show like yours. Part of the job of an agent is to know who's who in theatre throughout the country and what kinds of plays they're looking for. When you get down to it, an agent is a salesperson doggedly working his contacts to get your play produced. When your agent hooks one, he negotiates the contract for you. For this, an agent takes 10 percent of the royalties the play earns and represents the play forever.

Relationships and trust built up over time are key for agents to gain access to the movers and shakers. But don't expect an agent to do all your promotion. If you're smart, you'll stoke up interest in your play on your own. (See Chapter 17 for more on promoting your work and using an agent.)

In my case, I got my agent through a playwright friend, who recommended me and my work to his agent. I had some modest productions on my résumé, and, based on the recommendation and my meager accomplishments at the time, the agent was willing to read the play I was pushing, *A Heart of Flesh*. (The agent liked the play but not the title, drawn from a Biblical quotation, so I renamed it *Journey of the Heart*. He felt the new title was more catchy and marketable.)

Lawyers

One of my mentors, the Obie-winning playwright Jack Gelber, disdained agents. He negotiated his own contracts and then ran them past a lawyer to be sure they didn't have any loose ends and everything was kosher. Jack was somewhat of a nonconformist, so it was a formula that worked for him.

Some lawyers will handle contract negotiations for you for a one-time fee. This arrangement costs you money upfront but possibly saves you money in the long run by avoiding ongoing agent fees. The trick is to locate a lawyer who's experienced in theatre. You don't want well-intentioned Uncle Jack, the real estate attorney, mucking up your first play deal.

If you feel a bit at sea over the question of agents and lawyers and contracts, don't despair. Join the Dramatists Guild (www.dramatistsguild.com). To qualify for an associate membership, all you need to show is a copy of a script you wrote or a program from a reading or workshop of your play (and pay a $90 fee). Membership in the DG gives you access to sample contracts, review of contracts offered to you, seminars and workshops, *The Dramatist* magazine, and the annual *Dramatists Guild Directory*. The last item provides lists of theatres, producers, competitions, and agents and other indispensible information. The cost of associate membership is more than worth it for the resources and peace of mind you get in knowing you have someplace to go if you need advice.

Whatever you do, never go into a ticket-selling production without a contract. Oral agreements and handshakes are worthless, even with good friends. A potentially fine production experience can be ruined when tickets start selling and you find that there's a "misunderstanding" between you and your producer buddy over the royalty or control of the work or a hundred other things that can surface when money becomes involved. I've heard theatre people say, "We're all friends; what do we need a contract (or collaboration agreement) for?" My answer: so that you stay friends. If these folks who want to do your play are such good friends, then what's the problem with signing a production contract? Seller beware.

Selling the movie rights: A dream come true?

Many playwrights dream of the day when a play of theirs will find its way to the big screen: *"The Great American Story,* based on the stage play by (your name)." If you have even modest success with a play, don't be surprised if you attract the attention of practiced and would-be movie producers.

A number of years ago, a play of mine was produced three times in California: a small production in Altadena, a medium-sized production in Pasadena, and a college production at UC San Diego. Gratifying for me, but hardly anything registering on the Richter scale. Nevertheless, I was approached by two California producers who'd seen the show. Both wanted the exclusive rights to shop the play around Hollywood as a potential film. Exciting? Absolutely. One problem, though. Neither of the interested parties was willing to put up any money for the requested privilege. (See the next section, "Exercising your options.") Reluctantly, I declined the offers.

Many books are written on the business side of movies, so I'll only touch on two aspects of it — options and the film sale. (These sections are not intended to be legal or business advice, only food for thought.)

Exercising your options

When a producer wants the exclusive right to market your play as a movie, what he is asking for is an *option.* You can grant a producer (or a director or anyone else) an exclusive option for a specified time, usually one to two years, to make a movie deal. During that option period, you have no control over the film rights. If you're going to give up the right to make any kind of deal yourself for a year or two, then you should get some money for that sacrifice/risk. It usually won't be much — a few hundred to a few thousand dollars — but it's money. And if a producer has invested money in the project, it makes the producer a little more serious about pushing it.

Beware of the producer who befriends and flatters you, and then asks you to grant an exclusive option on the basis of friendship. "After all," he will point out amiably, "no one else has been expressing interest in your play." Thanks, but no thanks. There are too many so-called producers running around collecting free options and doing little or nothing with the projects. Again, seller beware.

Selling the film rights

If someone wants to make a movie version of your play, you're being asked to sell the film rights to that person. Depending on who you are and the success of the play, you can get anything from several thousand dollars to hundreds of thousands for selling the right to make a film based on your play. If your play just won the Tony Award for best play, you're going to be able to command a great deal more money for your play than for a play that's been produced in Altadena, Pasadena, and UCSD. If you're Aaron Sorkin (*A Few Good Men, The West Wing,* along with other hit films and TV shows), you're going probably going to be able to make a six- or seven-figure deal.

Two things to keep in mind when selling the film rights:

✔ **Decide if you're interested in writing the screenplay yourself.** If so, you'll need to negotiate hard for that (and for what you will be paid as screenwriter). Most veteran movie producers have relationships with lots of professional screenwriters, and most likely the producer will want to give the project to a trusted screenwriter. If writing the screenplay is extremely important to you, you may have to be willing to walk away from the deal in order to win that concession. Even so, you may only be able to negotiate the right to write a first draft of the screenplay, after which the producer can farm the film scripting out to someone else for rewriting.

✔ **Be aware that after you sell the film rights to your play, in most cases you have no control over the end product.** It's like selling a car. When the sale is done, the new owner can do whatever he wants with it. The resulting screenplay may be very faithful to your play, or it may be so different that it's unrecognizable. What's worse, the producer may lose interest in the project and let it crumble to dust on the shelf. It happens. That's Hollywood for you. If you're "fortunate" enough to sell the rights to a play to a film producer, you need to be able to take the money and run . . . without looking back.

If you choose to seize the opportunity to negotiate a film sale, get help. When you have a potential film deal in hand, you'll have no trouble attracting an agent. Choose one who has experience negotiating film contracts. Or, find a lawyer who knows the business. Whatever you do, don't go it alone. What you don't know can hurt you.

Using Playwriting Skills Outside of Theatre

The fact that much of the expertise of playwriting involves writing dialogue — the things folks say — gives you the ability to put words in the mouths of people other than theatre actors. Your playwriting skills have many practical nontheatrical uses and can even make you a buck or two.

Corporate videos and training films

One of my several freelance jobs is writing corporate video scripts and training films. The work is very much like writing a mini-play. Of course, I have the benefit of having worked in corporate communications for years. But that doesn't mean you can't seek out paid work writing video or TV commercial scripts for local businesses, big and small. Corporate videos generally involve product launches, communicating new company rules or government regulations, or demonstrating good work and/or sales practices.

After negotiating a mutually agreed-upon fee, you meet with your client to get as much information as you can concerning the topic involved. For the script, you create, in essence, a scene in which the material is played out in dialogue and action, and then you work with your client on rewrites and refinements. But don't get emotionally involved in these kinds of project. The client has final approval. Remember, this isn't art; it's paid work, and the customer is always right.

Speeches and sermons

Many people — from corporate executives to politicians to club officers to preachers — need to stand up in front of groups to speak. Some are gifted enough to write their own presentations. Others need help, and that's where you can enter the picture.

The process of writing a speech for a client is similar to that with corporate work described above. The one difference is personality. In writing a speech, you need to meet with your client often and long enough to get a good feel, not only for the information to be communicated but also for your client's style. Is the person funny or serious? Casual or formal? Modest or confidently assertive? You need to factor these and other traits into the words you choose for that person to speak. If you have trouble getting started, check out *Public Speaking For Dummies* (Wiley).

Religious plays and pageants

For many holidays and religious observances, churches stage religious plays reenacting landmark moments in the history of the faith for the faithful. In these kinds of productions, the story line is pretty much decided for you by tradition. What you primarily will be doing is coming up with the dialogue. One thing to keep in mind: Avoid getting long-winded and complex in your dialogue. The actors performing the piece are not likely to be Meryl Streeps or Denzel Washingtons, so they will thank you for being brief and to the point.

Reenactments, skits, and holiday shows

What is true of religious plays and pageants is also true of community reenactments and holiday shows, with one slight difference. Though many historical events and figures of the past are revered almost religiously, you probably will have a little more leeway to be original and creative in dramatizing publically observed historical moments and deeds.

The key to successful skit writing is to keep them light-hearted, simple, fast-paced, and brief. You can easily ruin an otherwise successful piece by over-writing and drawing it out. Less is more.

This kind of work can be fun. I enjoy the opportunity to research historical figures, and, using my imagination and playwriting skills, bring them back to life for an appreciative audience.

Chapter 3

What Makes a Play

The stage play, or play, is among the oldest forms of literature. No more is known about when or how the play form of storytelling originated than is known about when people first sang or danced. Plays may have started when prehistoric humans began communicating spiritual traditions. Or perhaps it was when they described fascinating events to each other while sitting around the fire. The moment a person stood to dramatically act out the moment she almost got trampled by an irritated mammoth during the day's foraging, theatre was born. Maybe.

What we do know is that performances similar to plays were part of ancient Egyptian religious ceremonies as far back as 2500 BC. By about 1000 BC, India and China had theatre. But the most extensive body of early theatre works comes from ancient Greece. A great literature of tragedies and comedies survives from that period.

If you fell into a time vortex and found yourself dropped into a Greek amphitheatre around 500 BC, you'd immediately recognize what was going on. Though you probably wouldn't understand the dialogue, you'd see a group of performers in costume reciting, or maybe chanting, the dialogue of a script, moving around in a stage area before thousands of audience members in open-air stadium-style seating. You couldn't mistake it; you'd be witnessing a play. Apart from lights, sound, and other technological enhancements, theatre hasn't changed significantly in 2,500 years.

This chapter defines what a play is and compares plays with other storytelling media. To help you hit the ground running as a playwright, I introduce you to key stage play terminology and examine the ingredients of a compelling story. In this chapter, I also consider the collaborative nature of theatre, helping to prepare you to work with your future comrades.

Shining a Light on the Magic and Simplicity of a Play

A crowd of people assembles in a room and sits. The room darkens, and a curtain rises. For the next two or so hours, these people — from all circumstances and walks of life — become one. They become an audience, watching fictional events enacted before their eyes by other people (actors) playing invented people (characters) drawn from a script. For the duration of this performed story — the play — audience members forget themselves and their cares. They become absorbed and emotionally engaged in the aspirations and actions of the imaginary characters. The audience is transported — heart and soul — into the world of the play. This experience is the magic that can be conjured by a stage play.

This section explores this magic, defining exactly what makes a play a play, detailing the relationship between plays and theatre, and comparing plays with other storytelling media.

Defining a play

A play is a story told in the form of dialogue and scripted activity by an actor or actors as the characters, intended to be performed for a live audience. Or, more simply put, a play is a story performed for a live audience. The word *play* refers to both the script and to the performance of the script.

Theatre, meaning the performance of a play, probably is the simplest of the performing arts to present. To do a play, you don't *need* costly and elaborate sets, costumes, lights, sound systems, and so on. Stripped of all its frills, all you need is a script, an actor, and an audience. Theatre can involve as few as two people, assuming an audience of one.

But a play cannot exist without a playwright. Playwriting is the process of taking an idea, thinking on it, and bending, shaping, and molding it to turn out a finished work of dialogue and action for the stage.

Exploring the relationship of plays to theatre

To crudely paraphrase a Shakespearean line, plays are such stuff as theatre is made on. In other words, theatre begins and ends with the play.

Many months and often years before a production can take place, a person — the playwright — sits at a keyboard or picks up a pen and writes the play. She is moved by an idea or an interesting character to concoct a story that puts a character on a journey of some sort. Obstacles are thrown in the way of the character, and before the final page the character either achieves her goal or heroically goes down in flames.

When the script is completed, theatre practitioners (a producer, a director, actors, designers, and others) are assembled, investing their time, talent, skills, and financial resources in creating the theatrical experience — using the script as the blueprint.

Theatre involves three underpinnings that allow audiences to simultaneously participate in and stay removed from the play:

- **Willing suspension of disbelief:** This process allows the audience to put aside the knowledge that what they're watching is not reality but actors performing a script. Without thinking about it, while watching a play you forget that mundane fact and go for the ride. Suspension of disbelief enables audiences to identify with the characters and feel their pain (or joy).

- **Immediacy:** Theatre performances have *immediacy,* which means the story takes place before your eyes, in three-dimensional flesh and blood. It's not on a screen or on a page. You're watching real people only yards away from you. You're the fly on the wall — the *fourth wall* — watching the action, unnoticed by the characters involved.

- **Aesthetic distance:** Another unconscious process, aesthetic distance, enables you to get emotionally involved in the unfolding events without any attempt to participate or intervene. *Aesthetic distance* means you're involved in the story but not in the action of the play, so when a character pulls out a knife, you don't dash out of the theatre to find a police officer.

Comparing the storytelling media

Stage plays, fiction (novels and short stories), and screenplays are powerful and time-honored forms of storytelling. And though they have similarities — the use of words to present characters and relate events — they also have some very significant differences. *Vive la différence!*

Plays

Stage plays deal with what an audience can see and hear *on a stage* by means of actors performing live. In plays, the audience sees and hears live people, voices, music, and sounds as determined by the script of the play. Because performances of plays are live, no two performances are ever exactly identical.

In plays, dialogue — what the characters say to each other — reveals the intentions of characters, rather than cerebral musings (as in a novel) or large physical actions, like chases (as in a film). In a screenplay, the camera (and therefore the audience) can zoom in on one aspect of the setting, such as a ticking clock, a smoldering cigarette, or a character's facial expression, to highlight its significance to the overall plot. However, close-ups are not possible on a stage. For the writer of a play to draw attention to a clock, or cigarette, or facial expression, a character must mention the object to focus the audience on it. A character may say something like the following:

PETER

Is that clock right? It can't be eight already.

In a novel, the audience can't see the clock on the wall, and, therefore, the clock, the time, and its meaning must be filtered through a character's or a narrator's thinking. For example, "Peter grew anxious as the clock raced toward eight o'clock."

Stage plays unfold their stories in *real time* (time that passes equally in the story and for the audience) in a live environment. In movies, the director can begin a scene about a meal at the start of, say, dinner, and cut to a conversation in the middle of the meal, and then cut again to the diners getting up and leaving. The whole scene in a movie can take place in minutes. While in theatre, when a scene is set for a meal, you likely will be following the entire meal (or most of it) in real time — the time it would take to actually have dinner, more or less.

Plays only need to present a suggestion of reality. A table and two chairs are understood to be a kitchen, for example, even without the presence of a kitchen sink or refrigerator. In theatre, audiences are more conditioned and willing to mentally fill in the blanks. It's part of that magical willing suspension of disbelief mentioned in the preceding section.

In play scripts, all the story's information needs to be conveyed through the dialogue and onstage actions in fully developed scenes. One of the hardest scriptwriting patterns for new playwrights to break is the tendency to write short, scantily developed scenes à la film and TV. Most new playwrights have had much more exposure to movies and television than they have to theatre. It sometimes takes a while to appreciate the differences between the techniques of movies and TV and the conventions of theatre.

Screenplays

Screenplays (scripts for TV shows and movies) can present detailed, true-to-life re-creations of almost anything that can exist in the real world or in any world or time that can be imagined. Movies have the ability to easily move the story from place to place and back and forth in time. All of which normally is beyond the ability and practicality of plays on stage.

Screenplays (and teleplays) are written for a visual medium. Screenplays deal primarily with what an audience *sees* characters doing on a screen in permanently recorded performances. In film (and television), visual images — the pictures conveyed on screen — are the most powerful elements in the storytelling. The camera is the audience's eyes and ears. In other words, a movie tells its story by controlling the visual perspective of the audience; you see and experience only what the screenwriter and the director want you to see and experience.

In contrast, stage plays are an intimate medium. Yes, you have, of course, the visual element of seeing the play taking place on a stage before your eyes. But the emphasis is not on visual input. From its distance, the audience can't see actors' facial expressions very well. And movie-style, large-scale action scenes — car chases, battles, explosions — are not as convincingly rendered on a stage as they are on film. Plays focus on relationships, person-versus-person conflict, and what people do and say to each other in relationships.

Another major difference between screen storytelling and stage storytelling is the nature of scenes in each. Scenes in movies are very short. Usually a few seconds to a few minutes long. A full-length movie can easily have 60 to 90 scenes. Next time you watch a film, count the scenes if you can. On the other hand, stage storytelling is characterized by far fewer and more extensively developed scenes. A full-length, two-act play may have three or four scenes in each act, often fewer, seldom more. Unlike action-oriented film, plays focus on relationships and conflicts within these relationships, which are developed more efficiently and more naturally in longer scenes. And the practicalities and expense of multiple sets and costume changes keep the number of play scenes to a minimum in theatre.

Novels

Novels are strongest in dealing with the inner life of a character. The reader of a book usually knows precisely what the characters are feeling and thinking, because the author can express these things directly. For example, "No matter what I do, I'm never going to measure up to Peter's standards, Mary thought."

With a stage play, the audience watches a performance by actors of a story; the audience does not read the script. Therefore, for the audience to know what Mary is thinking, the thought needs to be conveyed through some action on Mary's part or through lines said to another character.

MARY

No matter what I do, Sue, I'm never going to live up to Peter's standards.

MARY tears up her photo of PETER.

Determining whether your story is a novel, play, or screenplay

Which medium best tells the story you have in mind depends, in large part, on the nature of the story. If, for example, your story tends toward the cerebral — meaning the characters' thoughts are central to the story — then the story may best be told as a novel. In a novel, as mentioned in the preceding section, the author can simply write what the characters are thinking at any and all moments.

If your story involves lots of physical action, like fights and car chases, or needs to take place in many locations, like starting in New York and going to the center of the earth and to outer space and on to Tokyo, then a screenplay may be your best bet. Conveying strong visual images is what movies do well.

If your story tends to be a human drama, dealing with relationships between people on a very personal level, then a play may be right.

And yes, though some stories start out as novels and then move to the stage and on to the screen, if you study how the story is told in each of the different media, you see that different aspects of the story are emphasized. In the novel, the interior lives of the characters are explored. On the screen, the action and locales of the story take precedence. And in a play, the personal relationships between the characters are stressed.

Understanding Playwriting Lingo

When you move into any new sphere, be it a new occupation or a foreign location, you're likely to find that the denizens of that new place have their own language and ways of thinking.

If you decide to enter a healthcare profession, when describing the injuries due to a bicycle spill, for instance, you would speak of contusions, abrasions, and fractures rather than bruises, scrapes, and broken bones. Similarly, as you enter into the world of stage storytelling, you need to acquire a new lingo. You want to be comfortable using appropriate terms and jargon when talking about plays so that you can speak the same language as other theatre people do. It'll enable you to be understood by your new colleagues and, not incidentally, help you sound like you belong.

In this section, I detail some maybe familiar terms and some that likely will be new to you. You don't necessarily need to memorize these words and phrases; you can always use this section as a reference.

- ✔ **Protagonist:** The main character of your story; the character with a mission, an objective, a goal toward which she is actively working/struggling. (Don't substitute *heroine* or *hero* for the word *protagonist*. Many main characters in contemporary stories are hardly heroic types. Seedy main characters — like gangsters or gun-toting outlaws — are referred to as *antiheros*. So stick with *protagonist*.)

- ✔ **Antagonist:** A character with opposing objectives who presents obstacles or roadblocks to the achievement of the protagonist's objectives. The antagonist can be a person; a thing or force, like a great white shark or a tornado; or something within the antagonist herself, like cowardice or laziness. (Don't think of the antagonist as a villain. It ain't necessarily so. Sometimes two honorable people, both trying to do the right thing, come into conflict.)

- ✔ **Conflict:** Two characters — protagonist and antagonist — having opposing objectives, each struggling to come out on top. Conflict is the essence of compelling writing, so the more evenly matched the opponents are, the more engaging and suspenseful your story will be.

Argument alone is not conflict; two people who want the same thing can argue about the best way to do it. That's hardly dramatic conflict. Real conflict is a clash between two people, or two groups of people, who have opposing goals that are of paramount importance to both.

- ✔ **Spine, arc, or through-line:** The primary story line, the protagonist's journey toward her objective, the basic question of the story that keeps audience members in their seats.

You should be able to articulate the spine of your story in one sentence that includes the protagonist as the focal point. For example, the spine of *Hamlet* is: Will Hamlet be able to avenge the murder of his father or not?

- ✔ **Stakes:** The importance and urgency of the protagonist's mission or goal. The more urgent and important the objective is to the protagonist, the more the audience will understand and care. The audience tends to go on an emotional journey with the protagonist when the stakes are high. What's at stake in *Hamlet*? Only justice, the throne of Denmark, and the lives of Hamlet and the fratricidal new king, Claudius.

✔ **Inciting incident or precipitating event:** The event that gets the story started, that launches the journey; it upsets the world of the protagonist so that she must do something to right her world. In *Hamlet,* the inciting incident is the appearance of the ghost of Hamlet's father. The ghost tells Hamlet that it was murder, not accidental death, that took his life. Now Hamlet, like it or not, has a mission to avenge his father's death.

✔ **Backstory:** Events that have taken place before the audience joins the story; past events that impact the story that's unfolding. Shortly after *Hamlet* opens, the audience learns the backstory: Hamlet's father, the former king, is dead, and Hamlet's mother quickly married again, this time to her brother-in law, Claudius. All this happened before the play begins.

✔ **Exposition:** The skillful revelation of the elements of the backstory that are absolutely necessary to make the characters' motivations, stakes, and objectives understood. The best strategy when it comes to revealing backstory is *exposition as ammunition* — that is, use the information to achieve a purpose, not just to get the audience up to speed. Have the backstory come up in the dialogue when it's absolutely necessary for the characters to discuss it. For example, the ghost of the old king speaks of his murder to young Hamlet for the purpose of inciting Hamlet to action.

✔ **Actions:** Things done by the characters that directly or indirectly help them achieve their objectives. As mentioned just above, the ghost telling Hamlet about his murder is an action on the part of the ghost to get a reaction from young Hamlet. It works.

✔ **Rising action:** An escalating climb involving alternating victories and setbacks as the protagonist pursues his objective, rising to the climax. Put simply, for every two steps your protagonist takes toward her goal, events should force her a step back.

✔ **Climax:** The scene or moment of the story, usually at the end, when the conclusion of the protagonist's journey is reached; the climax is usually the final confrontation between the protagonist and the antagonist. Only one of the two will be left standing. When the final battle is over, you know how the protagonist's journey ends. You know what you were waiting to find out. In *A Streetcar Named Desire,* protagonist Blanche DuBois's journey to find a safe haven, a place of respite, is opposed by the antagonist, her brother-in-law, Stanley Kowalski, whom she has alienated. In the climactic scene Blanche is brutally ravished by Stanley, which pushes Blanche over the edge into madness. In this play, the protagonist fails.

✔ **Resolution or dénouement:** The aftermath of the climax; how the dust settles. In *A Streetcar Named Desire,* after the climactic scene, Blanche is sent to a mental institution while Stanley and his wife, Stella, Blanche's sister, resume their volatile lives together. The resolution also is the moment that any loose ends — unanswered questions — are dealt with.

✔ **Voice:** Not necessarily the character's dialect and manner of speech, but what she thinks and has to say. Each character should be distinct, with different personas, points of view, motivations, and methods. With the number of actors used in straight (nonmusical) plays shrinking to four or fewer, you want to avoid characters that are similar in what they say, do, and want.

Following the Formula for Engaging and Compelling Plays

A number of ingredients are involved in the making of an engaging and compelling play. These elements come together to create a successful work for the stage. Ignore any of these fundamentals and you risk creating a play that doesn't satisfy the expectations of an audience. This section presents some of the basics that help you turn out an effective and absorbing stage story, a play that draws your audience in and takes it for a ride.

Creating characters the audience can care about

A crucial element of the theatrical experience is that audience members come to care about the characters, particularly the protagonist. You want the audience to pull for your protagonist, to hope that she will succeed in the quest, and to be emotionally invested in the outcome. You want the audience to experience a degree of sadness during the heartbreaking moments of your play, to gasp at your startling revelations, and to rejoice at the protagonist's ultimate success or choke back the tears if at the journey's end the protagonist is heroic but unsuccessful.

Inspiring empathy

The key to making this connection is empathy. Empathy is sharing in the sadness or happiness of another. Empathy is identifying with the character and her situation and experiencing vicariously what the character is experiencing.

An audience empathizes with a character when it buys into the character's quest and agrees, to one extent or another, with the character's goals and objectives.

Empathy is evoked when you give the audience:

- ✔ A protagonist with engaging qualities and characteristics whom the audience can root for

- ✔ A character with an objective that's perfectly understandable and that the audience can endorse, even if it's not necessarily admirable

- ✔ High stakes, consequences of importance to the protagonist if she should succeed or if she should fail

- ✔ A character with an urgent and passionate need to achieve her objective

At the beginning of Shakespeare's *Hamlet,* Hamlet is heartbroken over the death of his father, the former and much admired king. Hamlet is also depressed over the rapid remarriage of his mother to the new king, his much-less-admired Uncle Claudius. The death of a parent is a sad occurrence. And the audience can imagine how disappointing it is to Hamlet that his mother was so quickly remarried, and to his uncle, no less. Understanding and feeling Hamlet's pain is no stretch.

Raising the stakes

High stakes also help the audience care about characters. When something is vitally important to a character — and when the audience buys in to the reasons why — the audience almost automatically hopes that the character will achieve what's so important to her. They're on her side.

Say your story is about a man playing poker, and the player hopes to win a lot of money. Well, every card player wants to win. Where's the beef? Though getting an audience behind an individual who desperately wants to win is possible, who really cares if a guy wins money at Texas Hold 'Em or not? The stakes, no pun intended, are low and only marginally interesting.

However, if that same man wants to win a lot of money at poker so that he can pay for medical care needed by his critically ill little girl, the stakes are much higher, and, all of a sudden, sympathy lies with the man. You can easily empathize with the desperation of a man reduced to gambling to save his daughter.

After Hamlet learns that his estimable father was murdered by Uncle Claudius, Hamlet is on a quest to avenge his father's death. Hamlet intends to murder the murderer and usurper of the throne of Denmark. Putting aside the modern sensibility that one shouldn't take the law into one's own hands, you see Hamlet's quest to punish the evildoer as legitimate, and you care and hope that Hamlet achieves his rough justice.

Concocting stories that keep 'em guessing

Another element in keeping an audience engaged and locked into your story is suspense. Suspense in literature is a growing interest, excitement, and anxiety concerning the outcome of a story. Will the protagonist succeed or fail? What price will the protagonist need to pay to attain her objective? Will it be a sad or happy ending?

Assuming high stakes and a character with whom your audience can empathize, the suspense factor can be ratcheted up via an escalating series of successes and setbacks. The protagonist's journey — spine — should not be a smooth road. Every step of progress toward the goal should be followed by a setback of some sort so that the protagonist's journey is a seesaw of emotions. Finally, just before the climax of the play, the protagonist should face her greatest setback of all.

In *The Wonderful Wizard of Oz,* as Dorothy makes her way toward Emerald City and the Wizard, who she hopes will send her home to Kansas, she encounters a setback on almost every leg of her journey. Her obstacles include a battle with fighting trees, assaults by a seriously irritated witch, a field of noxious poppies, an attack by flying monkeys, and the order by the Wizard to whack the Wicked Witch of the West. Dorothy returns to the Wizard after the hit on the Wicked Witch, expecting him to keep his promise to help her get home, and instead he turns out to be a powerless fraud. Setback. Nevertheless, he promises to give Dorothy a lift back to Kansas in his hot air balloon. Progress. When the moment of departure comes, Dorothy encounters the biggest setback of all: The balloon comes loose and the Wizard leaves without her. All appears to be lost, until Glinda, the Good Witch, arrives with the solution to Dorothy's dilemma.

How do you accomplish this swinging pendulum of progress and setback? Each step of the way, ask yourself, "What's the worst thing that can happen to the protagonist at this moment?" And then make it happen. After your protagonist triumphs over that particular obstacle, think of the next setback that can befall your main character, and so on. By doing this, you'll have your audience breathless, wondering if your protagonist will ever achieve her objective.

Employing specificity: The angel in the details

Playwriting involves a number of paradoxes, and one of them deals with specificity and details.

New writers sometimes think they ought to keep their stories and characters as general (unspecific) as possible so that audiences will more easily be able to identify with the characters and story. The idea is, if you don't mention the character's race or religion or what she had for breakfast, audience members will have an easier time seeing themselves in the character.

Oddly enough, the truth is that it's the other way around: The more specific you are, the more universal your play is.

Years ago I wrote a play, *Song of the Coquí,* based on the experiences of my parents as a young married couple in Spanish Harlem, a Hispanic neighborhood in upper Manhattan, and their later lives in the Bronx. It dealt with many of the challenges facing minorities, including the eagerness, right or wrong, to give up one's own culture — language, customs, foods, and manner of dress — to blend in and pursue the "American dream." The play is very specific to these characters and their experiences — from food to dance to language.

After a developmental public reading (see Chapter 15) of *Song of the Coquí,* an African American man stood to offer his feedback. "I listened to this play with my eyes closed," he said, "and this could have been the story of my family." Another audience member raised her hand and said, "My family came from Italy, and they went through the same thing. I never thought about Hispanic families going through the immigrant thing."

I was astonished. And for me, those comments drove home this point: Specificity is to be embraced, not avoided. Specificity in the details of your play and its characters is what brings them alive and enables audiences to identify with your story. In playwriting, it's not the devil in the details, but angels.

Creating simplicity with an unambiguous story line

Simplicity is a virtue in playwriting. When audiences watch a play unfold, they need to "get it" the first time. An audience member can't rewind to hear the line again or to review an important moment. She can't flip back to reread a couple of pages to make sense of a complicated scene.

Simplicity in this context does not mean dumbing down your story. It means telling the story with clarity. Your spine should be clear and unambiguous if you don't want to lose your audience. Keep in mind that no one is stapled to the seat. People do leave theatres during intermission. (It's the equivalent of switching channels away from a dull TV show.) Some people don't even wait for intermission to slip out of a confusing or muddled play. If you don't want the lights to come on in a half-empty auditorium at the end of the play, you need to make sure your audience can follow the story the whole time.

You never want to make your audience feel stupid by presenting material that's so complicated it alienates your audience. The last thing you want your audience to be thinking is "I don't get it. This is embarrassing. I don't understand what's going on here."

This is not to say you shouldn't deal with complex issues or subject. You just need to find a way to present your material so that it's straightforward and accessible to audiences that don't know anything about the subject.

The Tony Award–winning play *Copenhagen,* by Michael Frayn, deals with nuclear physics and the development of the atomic bomb. You can't find a subject more esoteric than that. But at its core is simplicity; the play is really about people — people deciding about the morality of developing a weapon of mass destruction. It tantalizes audience members with the question, "What would you have done?"

Audiences don't come to theatre to learn about complex subject matter. They come to see plays in which people struggle against other people to achieve some objective, lofty or mundane. No matter how intricate the backdrop of the play, at its center should be a simple story line. If cleanliness is next to godliness, then, in playwriting, simplicity is next to divinity.

Debunking the overrated concept of originality

Often writers tie themselves in knots trying to come up with an "original" idea for a play. They're looking to make their mark by writing a story that's never been done before. Well, lotsa luck.

The fact of the matter is that new ideas for stories are few and far between. Some people espouse the notion that there's only one story line: Boy meets girl; boy loses girl; boy gets girl back. Everything else, they say, is a variation of that universal plot. Apart from coming across as sexist, that theory is far too limiting to be of any use in this discussion.

A broader but still reductive approach offers the following seven common story lines:

- Man versus nature
- Man versus man
- Man versus the environment

- Man versus machines/technology
- Man versus the supernatural
- Man versus self
- Man versus God/religion

In the place of *man,* you can, of course, substitute *woman* or *mankind.* Here's another version of the seven-plot concept:

- Overcoming the monster
- Rags to riches
- The quest
- Voyage and return
- Rebirth
- Comedy
- Tragedy

Even these lists are wide-ranging and general. I use them here to make the point that in a broad sense, when it comes to creating stories, there's nothing new under the sun.

So where does originality manifest itself? In the execution of these ideas. You can be original in the way you tell these stories and in the characters you create to populate your play. What do I mean? Take a look at two stage pieces using the same story line: Boy meets girl; boy loses girl; boy . . . well, boy loses girl forever. I'm talking about Shakespeare's *Romeo and Juliet* and the Broadway musical *West Side Story.*

Romeo and Juliet is, of course, the story of two young lovers from rival families who are destroyed in a crossfire of hatred. *West Side Story* is about two young lovers from rival gangs who are destroyed in a crossfire of hatred. Hmmm. Identical plot (because *West Side Story* is an updated adaptation of *Romeo and Juliet*). So where's the originality?

First, you should know that Shakespeare likely drew inspiration for his *Romeo and Juliet* from a 1562 narrative poem called *The Tragical History of Romeus and Juliet* by Arthur Brooke. That, in turn, was probably translated from an Italian novella, and so on and so forth back through time. So much for originality.

What was original in Shakespeare's play and in versions all the way up to *West Side Story* is the treatment of the subject matter. Shakespeare's telling of the story features the magnificent and timeless poetry and poetic turns of phrase that, as a whole, have never been equaled. *West Side Story* changes Romeo and Juliet into Tony and Maria and places the "star-cross'd lovers" in the West Side of Manhattan in the late 1950s, a period of gang warfare in New York City. The originality, therefore, is in the new context for the story, the updated characters, and the fresh dialogue (and, in this case, songs).

In other words, originality is putting your personal spin on a story and creating your own dialogue, no matter how traditional the story may be. So don't sweat "originality." You have larger fish to fry.

Writing what you're passionate about

My final thought on writing an engaging and compelling play is that you need to write about a story *you* find engaging and compelling — for two big reasons.

One, if you yourself don't find your plot and characters engaging and compelling, how can you expect audiences to find your play engaging and compelling? You need to be your own first *dramaturg* (dramatic advisor; see "Dramaturgs" later for more info). You need to be frank and unflinching in your own assessment of your project. Yes, it can be dicey to make definitive pronouncements on the embryo of an idea; the concept may need time to mature and fill out. But be as honest with yourself as possible. If *you* don't believe, how can you expect others to follow you?

Two, because you'll be working on the play for a good while, you'd better like the topic. In the normal course of events, a play can take a year or two from inspiration to paper to the stage. Though you may be able to draft a play in a matter of days — it has been done — usually you'll spend months working on the first draft and many more months developing and refining the play. You don't want to find yourself working on a subject you have little or no emotional connection to after you've invested six months or more. That's like living in a bad marriage. No fun.

Looking at How Scenes Work

Scenes are the building blocks of plays. They're the discrete segments of a play within which the events of the story are played out. The sequence of the scenes in a play has causality; one scene should inevitably lead to the next. If you can shuffle the scenes in your play without affecting the outcome of the play, the sequence of scenes lacks causality (and you have some revising to do).

Usually one or more scenes make up an act. Until the mid-to-late-20th century, most modern plays were organized into three acts. The majority of full-length plays today are composed of two acts. The play doesn't need to be divided exactly in half; one act, more often than not the first act, can be longer than the other.

In the standard two-act play, the act break — the intermission — gives audiences the opportunity to stretch their legs, grab a snack, use the facilities, or, alas, if a play is greatly flawed, slip out and head home. (See Chapter 11 for strategies to avoid intermission defections.)

Telling a story within the story

Within an act, when one scene ends, another begins; this continues to the end of the act. A scene can be viewed as a mini-play within the play itself. It should have a beginning, middle, and an end — a spine of its own.

To tell a story within each scene, make sure that you keep in mind these guidelines:

- ✓ **All scenes should contain movement.** The characters or situation at the start of the scene should be changed in some significant way by the events in the scene by the time it ends. A scene that begins in a positive condition should end up in a negative state, and vice versa, or the circumstances can go from bad to worse. In this construct, a scene that goes from good to bad or from bad to good, and so on, either improves or deteriorates the state of affairs for the character(s) in the scene.

- ✓ **All scenes should be indispensible.** Every scene should serve an important purpose; it should be a necessary part of the route that gets your protagonist from the inciting incident to the climactic moment. Removing a rung from a ladder probably makes ascent on it impossible. And like the rungs on a ladder, each scene in your play should be necessary in your protagonist's climb toward her objective.

 If you can remove a scene from your play and it makes little or no difference to the logic and flow of the play, then that scene probably should be deleted. If a scene isn't carrying its weight, then it's dead weight and should be shed.

- ✓ **Every scene should include objectives for the characters.** Just as all characters ought to have overall objectives for the entire play, they should be trying to accomplish something in each scene.

A scene near the beginning of Act II of Ibsen's *A Doll House* illustrates all three points. Dr. Rank, a longtime friend of Nora and Torvald, drops in.

Because Torvald is busy, Dr. Rank visits with Nora. In the scene that ensues, Dr. Rank, who is dying from a disease, decides to grab what's perhaps his last opportunity to tell Nora that he's always been in love with her. Nora, on the other hand, has the objective in this scene to ask Dr. Rank for help in dealing with Nils Krogstad, who is blackmailing her. But after Dr. Rank divulges his feelings for Nora, the situation becomes awkward and uncomfortable for her, and she decides not to confide in Dr. Rank. She can't bring herself to ask anything of him, even though Dr. Rank is eager to be of service.

Both characters in Ibsen's heart-wrenching scene have objectives, and, unfortunately for Nora (but fortunately for the play), their objectives conflict. Dr. Rank achieves his goal, but Nora does not. The situation for Nora in this scene has deteriorated, so the movement is from bad to worse. This scene illustrates the points above in that the situation gets significantly worse for Nora, and the characters clearly have objectives in the scene. In addition, the scene serves the crucial purpose of heightening Nora's dilemma by removing Dr. Rank as a possible source of help.

Keeping an eye open for obligatory scenes

Sometimes a play is structured such that it leads to a moment the audience is expecting to experience. This anticipated scene that the play appears to be heading for is referred to as the *obligatory scene.* And if you've led up to it, intentionally or not, you don't want to frustrate your audience. You're obliged to include that scene.

If, for instance, you're writing a play that dramatizes the careers and rivalries of two prizefighters, naturally the audience is going to believe that, sooner or later, they'll see a scene in which these two boxers meet in the ring. If you were to finish your play without that scene, the audience would feel cheated and disappointed. You will have frustrated the expectation that, ultimately, the rivals would clash.

The nature of the subject and how it's dealt with creates, or does not create, an obligatory scene. In *Hamlet,* the entire plot involves Hamlet's clumsy pursuit of his "almost blunted purpose" — to kill King Claudius, the man who murdered his father. After all Hamlet goes through and puts others through, if had Claudius died choking on a pheasant bone, millions of students through the centuries would have been spared the effort of reading the play. What I mean is, without the obligatory scene in which Hamlet goes *mano a mano* with the corrupt king, the play would have fizzled out and audiences would have felt cheated of the highly anticipated moment.

Not all plays have an obligatory scene, because not all plays are structured in a way that audiences have an inkling of the moment that's coming. In reading, or preferably seeing, *A Doll House* or *A Raisin in the Sun* or *Twelve Angry Men,* you don't experience a sense that you know what's coming. The plays will, of course, have a climactic scene, but they don't strongly suggest the nature of the approaching climax.

Determining whether your play is leading to an obligatory scene or not isn't always easy. Consider whether your play deals with an element that's naturally competitive or confrontational. If so, that's a clue that you may have an obligatory scene on your hands. In the example above, the fact that the characters are boxers is the element which indicates a coming clash. If your play is set in a house full of guns, because a gun is a powerful implement of conflict, the audience naturally will assume that guns somehow will be involved in the final outcome of the play. (See Chapter 12 to find out more about this idea, called *Chekhov's gun.*)

In the hit musical *Les Misérables,* the policeman, Javert, vows to track down and capture an escaped prisoner, Jean Valjean. This fierce commitment and the natural conflict between criminal and law enforcement clearly lead the audience to suspect that ultimately there will be a showdown between Javert and Valjean. If Valjean had been saved by Javert's death in the fighting of the French Revolution, the audience would have felt cheated of a final head-to-head confrontation.

Structuring scenes

Scenes don't have a prescribed length. A scene can be as short as a few minutes (which is more like screenwriting than playwriting) to as long as the entire length of the act. Writing longer scenes allows you more time in the play to develop the characters and story organically, and it also helps keep down the number of scenes.

Though any number of scenes can be in an act, too many scenes can give a play a choppy, start-and-stop feel that's distracting to the audience. The starting and stopping can *take the audience out of the play,* which means the magic of theatre evaporates and audience members remember where they are and that they're watching actors on a stage. Frequent interruptions of the action can defeat all the work you, the actors, the director, and the stagecraft people put in to involve the audience intellectually and emotionally in your play.

Scene breaks generally are used to indicate the passage of time or the transfer of the play's action to another location. Scenes can be separated visually by dimming the lights briefly or having a full blackout in which the stage goes completely dark, followed by the re-illumination of the stage for the next scene.

During the period between scenes, which should be as brief as possible (an interval counted in seconds, not minutes), actors can exit and enter and the set can be rearranged for the next scene. If no set change is required, scenes can be separated by only a dimming of the lights, allowing the actors to exit or enter and/or props to be reset for the next scene in the somewhat darkened view of the audience. If nothing on stage changes, scenes can be separated by a brief musical interlude to indicate the passage of time. However, though all this is important to know, these staging decisions are best left to the director.

Discovering that It Takes a Village to Bring a Play to Life

When the day comes that you judge your play to be finished, you'll find that you've completed only the first part of the journey. One of the biggest and perhaps most taxing aspect of writing plays for the stage is actually *getting* your play to the stage. Many factors facilitate or impede the progress of your play — some in your control and some not. (See Chapter 17 for more information on the challenges involved in getting your play produced.)

However, even when you're fortunate enough to have a producer or producing theatre to round up the resources to do your show, the journey's still not over. At that point, you're facing the prospect of collaboration.

Working with directors, actors, producers, and dramaturgs

Unlike writing a novel, the realization of a play isn't a one-person enterprise. Far from it. Modern theatre brings together the skills of a wide variety of theatre artists, including the director, actors, and stagecraft people. At times you may feel like an army of theatre people are marching through your play. "My" play — like it or not — becomes "our" play. This shift in perspective is due to the collaborative nature of theatre.

When you worry about losing control, try to remember that every one of the theatre professionals involved has something to contribute to the production of your play. Every one of them has a stake in the success of the play, and everyone is doing his or her best. No one wants to be associated with a flop; it doesn't look good on the résumé.

Because theatre is a collaborative medium, the production of a play is the work of many hands. If you're a control freak, learning to collaborate may be a trying experience for you. If you absolutely can't abide the thought of anyone else's paws on your work, you may want to think about writing a novel rather than a play.

Directors

After you make the script available for the production, usually the first person, after the producer(s), to read and study the play is the director. Your director must know and understand your play as well as you do. Perhaps even better. The director needs to be able to answer questions thrown at him by the actors and the stagecraft people. The director may also have to field questions from the producer(s) or even from you. Everyone looks to the director for leadership, advice, inspiration, information, and problem resolution. Widespread nervousness is common at the beginning of any production, and the director needs to be (or appear to be) in control. The director is the conductor of this orchestra, the captain of the ship, and if she's clueless, chaos will ensue.

The director formulates a vision of the play, a stage picture in her mind. The director does a huge amount of preparation before the first day of rehearsal, including studying the play line by line, character by character, and making copious notes detailing her vision.

You need to meet with your director to discuss the play while she is engaged in this process. Allow plenty of time to go through the play together, scene by scene. You both need to be on the same general wavelength concerning how you conceptualize the play. You don't want to find out well into rehearsals that in a crucial scene you see your character in a neatly tailored business suit and the director sees the character in a clown suit. (That exact situation happened to me.) Be sure to be open and collaborative in these talks.

In this dialogue with your director, be prepared to allow the director some elbow room in which to work creatively. Neither the director nor the actors are your employees or servants. They are people with specific talents and skills that they enthusiastically put to work for the production. Give them space to work. If you have a hard time doing that, stay away from the early rehearsals and let the director and actors do what they need to do.

Playwrights have veto power over the selection of directors and actors. Normally, you don't get to choose your director or the cast, but you can veto a selection if you feel a person is absolutely, positively wrong for your play. In my 25 years in theatre, I've never even thought about exercising that right. It's a weapon of mass destruction that can take the spirit out of a project. But it may comfort you to know that that authority is there. (You can find out more about your relationship with a director in Chapter 16.)

Actors

Actors, too, are an important part of the collaboration. (Today the word *actor* means both men and women.) Talented and hardworking actors often can pleasantly surprise you with the choices they make for their characters, interpreting the script in ways that exceed even what you expected. Or sometimes actors play your characters in ways that are just different, though not necessarily any better or worse, than what you envisioned.

Let the actors have input, particularly if their take doesn't make much difference to the play either way. Standing back and letting your actors do their creative thing allows them to become invested in the work and take pride in it. Give them space to exercise their creativity as they rehearse themselves into the roles.

Experienced actors also can help you refine your script. During rehearsals for a play of mine, *Casino* (no relation to the film of the same name), an actor provided me with valuable assistance I didn't want. He played the role of a casino security guard who had what I thought was a great monologue about the character's earlier experience in the military. In rehearsal, every time the scene got to the monologue, the actor looked lost. Finally, he turned to me and explained that he didn't know why his character would be saying these things at this time. I wasn't pleased with the feedback, but I cut the monologue down significantly. In the next rehearsal, the actor was still stuck. Fortunately, I knew he was a fine, meticulous actor whose comments were not to be ignored. (And very few actors ever want to have fewer lines in a play.) As much as I liked the monologue, I cut it out entirely, and the play was no worse for the deletion. In fact, the play won me my first New York Foundation for the Arts Fellowship. As novelist William Faulkner said, sometimes you've got to "kill your little darlings."

Producers

The primary work of a producer is to handle the business of making a play happen. First and foremost, that means raising the money to finance the production. The money can come from the producer himself or, more likely, from a group of investors. Theatre is expensive; getting a major production of a play up and running can cost many thousands of dollars and run well into the millions.

"Don't tickets pay for the expense of putting on a play?" you ask. Not really. To begin with, many expenses need to be covered before the producer sells any tickets, including the following:

- ✔ Renting rehearsal space
- ✔ Renting the theatre
- ✔ Paying actors, the director, and a stage manager during rehearsals
- ✔ Designing and building the set

✔ Designing and installing lights and sound

✔ Making or acquiring costumes

✔ Making or acquiring props

✔ Launching an advertising and marketing campaign (one of the biggest expenses)

What makes the work of a producer even more challenging is the fact that most productions lose money. Unless a producer is lucky enough to invest in what becomes a hit, she's probably not going to see a financial return on her investment. Hoping to make money in theatre is like hoping to make money at the racetrack.

So why do producers put up money if they're likely not to make it back? For many reasons. Some do it to support that art form they love. They look for a play they believe in and make it happen, helping make the world a better place. Some producers do it to be part of the theatre scene; they like to see their names in the playbill and enjoy hobnobbing with the cast at the opening night party. And, of course, some producers hope against hope to catch the next megahit that will make them wealthy. There are probably as many reasons for helping to fund a play as there are producers.

Problems can arise when producers — the people picking up the tab — decide to make artistic suggestions. The playwright can be very uncomfortable when a producer suggests this or that change in the script. In some cases, an experienced producer is giving you some very good advice. Other times, the producer simply has her own opinion of the play and wants to make some modifications to suit her sensibilities.

This situation can become very awkward because you don't want to alienate your producer(s). Without the money people, your play will go nowhere fast. What you may need to do is agree to the minor changes and discuss and compromise on any major issues. (For more on this dilemma, see the "Knowing when to compromise (and not)" section below.)

Dramaturgs

A *dramaturg* is a dramatic adviser, serving as an "editor" or artistic coordinator for the theatre company by helping select plays, assisting playwrights in refining their work, and acting as liaison between the theatre company and the playwright, director, and the other theatre professionals. The dramaturg also can advise the theatre company on the suitability of a play to the theatre's artistic mission and audience. Most theatre companies have someone who functions as either a dramaturg or literary manager. (The distinction between a dramaturg and a literary manager is not always clear, because they perform some of the same functions.)

Though a dramaturg's responsibilities vary, they're also usually involved in guiding plays through production process. The dramaturg must be knowledgeable enough about the play and the story's historical or social background to provide information to the playwright and director that can enhance the script and production.

New play dramaturgy focuses on helping the playwright get her script to final form. *Production dramaturgy* supports the script as it moves through the paces toward opening night. In either case, the overall role of the dramaturg is to ensure that all elements of the production, including the script, are relevant, appropriate, and consistent. A dramaturg, as a theatre specialist and objective researcher, can be a valuable contributor to the enrichment of your script and the production.

Getting to know stagecraft people

For theatre to take place, all you need is the work (a play), a performer (the actor), and an audience. But a number of creative crafts can immeasurably enhance the experience of a play. The people who lend their design and construction expertise to a theatrical production are referred to as *stagecraft people.*

Stagecraft people include

- ✔ Set designers and builders
- ✔ Lighting plot designers and technicians
- ✔ Costume designers and builders
- ✔ Sound designers and technicians
- ✔ Prop masters who construct and/or acquire props
- ✔ A choreographer (if your show includes dance)
- ✔ A composer and/or arranger (if your show has music)

All these and other stagecraft personnel work very closely with the director. They study your script and bring to the director sketches or plans for the set, lighting, sound effects, costumes, props, dance, music, and so on. Respect and appreciate the artistry of these specialists, because their work greatly augments the magic of the theatrical experience.

Knowing when to compromise

Because theatre is a collaborative medium, you want to allow all the players — director, actors, stagecraft professionals — to be creative and inventive in the staging of your play. You want them to buy into the project and take pride in what they're doing. But chances are they won't see your play exactly the way you saw it in your mind. On occasion, you may find yourself disagreeing with what a director sees in a moment of your play or how an actor plays a scene. And knowing when to compromise (accept someone else's interpretation) and when to stand your ground can be difficult.

When you're confronted with an idea for your play that's different from what you had in mind, ask yourself — and *honestly* answer — a fundamental question: Is this contrary suggestion or interpretation made by the director, actor, or stagecraft person going to take my play in a wrong direction and create problems for the play or the audience? If you believe the answer is yes, talk the matter over with the director privately. Perhaps the director missed a connection or overlooked something that happens later in the play. Even the best of directors can make an oversight, and if you discuss the issue in a calm, reasonable way, you should be able to work it out.

However, if this different interpretation of a moment boils down only to a matter of preference — your preference versus theirs — then let it go. Let your collaborators have their input and, yes, make their mark on the production. Save your objections for when they really matter. You don't want to micromanage the production or develop a reputation for being a picky pain in the butt. I've seen playwrights make a nuisance of themselves, and it ain't pretty. Producers, directors, actors, and stagecraft people start working around the intrusive playwright rather than working with her.

Educating yourself about everyone's roles

If you plan to make playwriting a big part of your life, think about taking a course or two in directing and acting. I studied acting for more than four years with two professional acting teachers and studied directing for two years at a theatre studio in Manhattan. I never intended to go into directing or acting — my focus is on playwriting — but I wanted to find out more about those fields so that I could be more effective at what I do.

I studied acting so that I could understand how an actor works. I wanted to experience in a small way what it's like to stand on stage and deliver lines with dramatic intentions. If you've never worn a pair of shoes, you probably wouldn't be the best of shoemakers, and if you've never acted, you may have trouble writing dialogue that's not only theatrical but practical and realistic for an actor to work with.

Also, playwrights benefit from knowing how to precisely and productively speak to actors rather than confusing or accidentally frustrating them. Directors and actors speak a particular language, and if you're going to give actors suggestions (adjustments), you need to do it in a specific way. ***Note:*** Normally, any performing notes you want to give actors should go through the director. In other words, you shouldn't speak to the actors directly about their work. However, if the director has allowed you, or even asked you, to provide your thoughts directly to the actors, you want to do it the right way.

If, for example, you have in mind the character weeping over the loss of a ring that was a family heirloom, you don't say to the actor, "You need to be crying here." That's called *asking for a result,* and it's a no-no. Instead, you might say to the actor, "Your character has just realized that the irreplaceable ring has been lost. It's been in the family for generations. It's a personal loss and the character is blaming herself. It's a huge blow to her. It's almost as if a family member has been lost." A savvy actor will take this in, explore the emotions connected with those adjustments, and very likely will become teary-eyed in that moment. It takes time and thought to come up with just the right way of saying things to actors, but, hey, isn't that what playwrights do — find just the right words for the moment?

I studied directing because I wanted to know what appeals to a director in a script and how a director prepares and works. Having a feel for the process of directing a play helps me understand and trust in what a director is doing in rehearsals, particularly early in the process. Understanding how a director approaches a script also made me more confident in discussing my ideas with a director. (See Chapter 16 for more about working with a director in rehearsals.)

They say a little bit of knowledge is a dangerous thing. That's true only when you assume that your limited exposure to a subject makes you an expert. Courses in acting and directing can give you an appreciation and some insight into what actors and directors deal with, but never give in to the temptation of thinking that you know better than they do. A little humility goes a long way in a collaborative process.

Chapter 4

Starting with an Idea

*H*ow ideas occur and where they come from are two of the many mysteries of the inscrutable human mind. Just where does imaginative insight come from? It certainly would be convenient if you could locate the fountain of inspiration, wherever it is, and access it when needed, like reaching into the fridge for a soft drink when thirsty.

Some people have tried coaxing out inventiveness through worship. The ancient Greeks, who pondered inspiration (and just about everything else under the sun), attributed the creative spark to the goddesses known as the Muses. The Greeks had Muses for almost everything innovative, from astronomy to erotic poetry. Those who wrote for theatre could pray for the cooperation of not one but two Muses: Melpomene, the Muse of tragedy, and Thalia, the Muse of comedy. More than two millennia later, people tend to look less to the heavens for the elusive stroke of genius and more to themselves. The great inventor Thomas Edison said, "Genius is 1 percent inspiration and 99 percent perspiration." Put in the time and hard work, he believed, and the creative spark will come.

But you don't need to be a disciple of the Muses or a sweating genius like Thomas Edison to come up with ideas for your plays. You can look to a number of everyday, down-to-earth sources of inspiration. This chapter introduces you to sources of story ideas, suggests how to keep track of story ideas, and discusses the real and imagined consequences of using true personal stories as play ideas.

Where Winning Story Ideas Come From: Observing Life

A Native American proverb points out: "Don't criticize a man until you've walked two moons in his moccasins." That saying has a number of variations, but the meaning is always that you shouldn't be quick to judge another until you've experienced what he has. Every person's experiences and motivations are unique to him.

Writing is sharing with the world your unique experiences and thinking. Your life is a one-of-a-kind source of inspiration. Although other people may witness the same events you do, your personal interpretation, your processing, and your spin on those events are what make them your own.

So don't overlook or underestimate what valuable material your day-to-day experiences and observations can provide. Anyone can learn playwriting technique; your use of playwriting to share yourself and your vision with the world is what makes you a playwright. The following sections give you ideas of some everyday sources of ideas and inspiration.

Mining your personal life

When it comes to finding ideas for plays, things that have happened to you are a no-brainer. In fact, the conventional wisdom meted out to new writers has always been to write about something you know, something you've experienced personally. Writing a play based on a personal event — a love affair, divorce, near-death experience, success, failure, confrontation, celebration, or job loss — allows you the confidence of knowing what actually happened. When you write from personal experience, you'll feel grounded in reality.

Many years ago, I was jumped and knocked to the floor of a Atlantic City casino by an enraged patron who accused me of stealing his gambling chips. It took two of the longest and most upsetting hours of my life for the police to become convinced it was a case of mistaken identity. The disturbing experience of being treated like a criminal became the idea behind my first successful and award-winning play, *Casino*.

Writing from experience comes with an important caveat. Events in life, however profound or inspiring to you, are seldom complete stories in and of themselves. A stage story, or any story for that matter, needs a beginning, middle, and an end; it needs a strong protagonist and antagonist; it needs a spine (story line); and it needs a climactic moment. In short, you can use a personal occurrence as the core of the story, but you still need to write a story. Don't be reluctant to make things up to fill in the blanks or to strengthen the story.

Plays don't get produced because they're absolutely accurate concerning what took place. Plays get produced because they have a strong and engaging story and intriguing characters.

Drawing on events witnessed

Events you've witnessed — things seen that moved, angered, elated, saddened, puzzled, intrigued, or otherwise personally impacted you — are another primary source of story ideas. These moments can be big, like a family's reaction to a son's decision to enlist for military service, or relatively small, like a couple's increasingly testy dispute over which restaurant to go to for their first anniversary.

Years ago, in my freelance writing work for a pharmaceutical company, I had the opportunity to sit in on a meeting of a hospital committee choosing which of two very ill patients would get a heart that had just become available for transplant. The members of this board — people from all walks of life — were making what was literally a life-or-death decision. This eye-opening and profoundly sobering experience became the basis for my play *Journey of the Heart*.

Recalling things told

People relate experiences to each other constantly. "Guess what I did," or "You wouldn't believe what just happened," or "Did you hear about . . . ?" Tales people tell you certainly can inspire stories for the stage. Listen and imagine. Feel free to grab a bit of gossip and run with it. Elaborate on and develop the raw idea. Ideas cannot be owned or copyrighted.

For a time I lived in Park Slope, a gentrified neighborhood of Brooklyn, and, while on my way to the grocery one day, I was stopped by a woman who was handing out flyers announcing a public gathering. She told me that the rally was in support of a woman who, as she left nearby Prospect Park, had been assaulted because she was a lesbian. The victim wound up in the hospital. The hate crime enraged me. "Why can't people just leave other people alone?" I fumed. I didn't go to the protest meeting, but I did what playwrights do. Spurred by that bit of information told to me and by my reaction to it, I composed a one-act play, *The Slope*. The play has been produced several times, from Chicago to Edinburgh, Scotland, and has won a couple of awards.

Finding inspiration in things read

Books and stories by others are a traditional source of story inspiration. Even Shakespeare relied on them for inspiration; *Hamlet* was drawn from a preexisting Hamlet legend, and *Romeo and Juliet* was based on a poem,

The Tragical History of Romeus and Juliet. Musicals more often than not are drawn from preexisting source material. Lerner and Lowe's *My Fair Lady* is an adaptation of George Bernard Shaw's play *Pygmalion.* The international blockbuster hit *Les Misérables* is based on the Victor Hugo novel of the same name. Shows from *South Pacific* to *Phantom of the Opera* to *Wicked* are based on published books. (See Chapter 14 for information on musicals.)

At some time or other, when reading a book or short story, you likely have found yourself thinking, "I can see this scene being done by actors. I'd love to do an adaptation of this story." That's the way playwrights think. Just be sure you don't infringe on anyone's rights. See the later section "Considering the protected work of others" for the copyright implications of adapting stories.

Using stories in the media

Every day dramatic stories are reported in newspapers and magazines, on TV and radio, and on the Internet. If some news event makes you happy, angry, sad, or just curious, it may be something to work with. Research the incident to see if it inspires you.

Topical subjects have long been the stuff of great theatre. In 1953, the American playwright Arthur Miller wrote the now-classic, Tony-winning play *The Crucible,* dramatizing the hysteria surrounding the Salem, Massachusetts, witch hunt and trials (1692–1693). But the play is much more than that. Through the 1950s, Senator Joe McCarthy conducted a shrill and merciless campaign to root out alleged communism and disloyalty in American government. Miller's play is an allegory intended to condemn the "witch hunt" hysteria and character assassination McCarthy employed. In other words, Miller used a historical event to comment on the contemporary event.

The popular play *Inherit the Wind* (1955), by Jerome Lawrence and Robert E. Lee, is a lightly fictionalized version of the famous 1925 Scopes trial in Tennessee. The real story began when a young science teacher was arrested for teaching the theory of evolution in violation of state law. The controversial trial made sensational headlines throughout the country, and the theory of evolution versus creationism was still topical 30 years later when *Inherit the Wind* premiered.

The devastating emergence of AIDS was the topical backdrop to the relationship struggles of two couples in Tony Kushner's astonishing Pulitzer Prize– and Tony-winning two-part play, *Angels in America: Millennium Approaches* (1991) and *Perestroika* (1992). The play is unflinching in its portrayal of the devastation wrought by a combination of the disease, politics, drugs, homophobia, self-deception, and fear in the 1980s in the U.S.

Adapting your dreams

Dreams, the stage upon which the unconscious plays out its own fascinating and sometimes frightening story lines, are a bounteous source of ideas. If nothing else, dreams can be significant clues to what interests, moves, worries, scares, or angers you.

Keep a pen and pad near your bed. (And, if you share your bed with someone, have a small flashlight nearby.) When you wake up in the middle of the night reeling from the emotional impact of a dream, make notes on the content *immediately,* while the details are fresh in your mind. Don't give in to the temptation to promise yourself you'll do it when you wake up in the morning. If you're anything like me, the dream will be gone by morning or so faded as to be worthless.

Jumping on ideas that just pop up

Ideas simply can occur to you, the playwright, out of a clear blue sky. It's nice when that happens. Sometimes a serendipitous idea may roar at you like a lion demanding acknowledgment, or sometimes a promising thought may simply enter your consciousness like a housecat slipping unnoticed into a room and jumping up onto your lap.

In the early 1970s, it occurred to veteran dancer/choreographer Michael Bennett that the personal stories behind the careers of Broadway show dancers might make for an interesting musical. He gathered a number of dancers in a room and, with their permission, tape recorded them discussing their memories and aspirations. This was the origin of the 1975 mega-hit show *A Chorus Line,* which broke all box-office records at the time and still is longest-running Broadway musical originally produced in the United States.

Be open to any and all ideas, no matter where they come from. Try not to judge your ideas right away. Make note of them immediately (see "Never Trust Your Memory: Preserving Your Ideas" later in this chapter) and allow the ideas to percolate through your mind. Some ideas will fall by the wayside, but among the others may be the gem that will become the basis of a terrific play.

Giving Up the Fear of Self-Revelation

Playwrights who use the events of their lives as a resource sometimes fear revealing too much about themselves. "If I have a character do [such and such action], people will think that I myself have done that same thing." Or "audiences may believe that my protagonist's outlandish opinions are my opinions." Or "writing about this subject would be embarrassing for me."

These concerns can prompt playwrights to omit things from their plays and to be less than truthful in their depiction of a character or moment in their plays.

Though this advice may seem contradictory, as a playwright you want to be unafraid to use your life, aspirations, hopes, fears, and beliefs as resources while, at the same time, keeping all them to yourself. When your play is truthful, people hardly ever wonder how autobiographical the work is. And as I discuss in the following sections, volunteering that information is seldom a good idea.

Keeping the inspiration a mystery

As a playwright who frequently uses his own life as grist for the mill, my experience has been that audiences don't think about where a story or a character's behavior comes from. If you provide a compelling story and engaging characters pushing toward some clear objective, audiences get involved in the story and eagerly anticipate the outcome. They aren't concerned about the story's inspiration.

I can count on one hand the number of times in 25 years that I've been asked about the origin of a moment or an event in my plays. One such instance that comes to mind relates to some dialogue in a play *(Casino)* referring to racist behavior on the part a nun. After a performance of the play, I was approached by two women who turned out to be plain-clothes nuns. (I don't recall how they knew me to be the author of the play.) They asked if it was true that a nun had engaged in the referred-to discriminatory act. I nodded. The nuns, bless their hearts, were mortified and embarrassed, and profusely apologized for something for which they themselves had no responsibility. But even in that situation, the inquiry had nothing really to do with me or the character based on me.

Here's a scriptwriting paradox: Audiences seldom wonder about the source of a well-presented stage story, but they do ask questions if the playwright has backed off something. If the story line is clearly leading to a certain moment but then veers away from the obvious, if discomforting, scene that should come next, the audience senses that the playwright shrunk from the moment or wasn't truthful to his story. And that, oddly enough, is when audiences grow suspicious and begin to think about the playwright's relationship to the story, asking themselves, "What's the playwright afraid of? Why did he avoid that issue? What's the author trying to hide?"

Look at it this way: If you're shown a crystal-clear, well-cut diamond, you'd likely enjoy its beauty, but you probably wouldn't ask who made it or where it was mined. Those issues would be irrelevant as you take pleasure from the luster of the attractive stone. On the other hand, if you're shown a cloudy and clumsily cut diamond, you very well may wonder who made such a mess of it and where such an inferior stone could have come from.

If you feel a need to hide yourself (and in this business, you shouldn't), the best place to hide is out in the open.

Protecting your secret identity

Don't ever tell people that a play is based on you or your experience. (Well, except if you're writing a book about being a playwright.) It serves no good purpose, and it definitely has a couple of downsides.

When receiving problematic feedback on a draft of a new play — being told, for example, that a character's behavior doesn't seem to make sense or that a moment in the play doesn't seem probable — new playwrights sometimes instinctively respond with the plea, "But it's true! That's the way it happened to me." That knee-jerk response, though totally understandable, excuses or explains nothing. What you're hearing in the feedback is that the character's behavior, fact-based or not, isn't coming across as appropriate to the situation. Or the activity of a scene hasn't been properly set up so that it's believable. In other words, you haven't yet gotten across the inevitability of the character's behavior or the necessity of action in the scene, which means you have more work to do.

By way of comparison, suppose you painted a portrait in oils and asked someone's opinion of the painting. If the person responds, "Sorry; I can't tell who that is," it would do you no good to protest, "But it's a famous person, a real person!" That fact is irrelevant. The real issue is how well you depicted the subject.

So rather than arguing or protesting against feedback your play gets, try to understand the input. Ask questions if the comments you're getting aren't clear to you. Maybe somewhere in the observations and suggestions you're hearing is the thought that will click on the light for you. Listen for the tip that clarifies the problem or points you to a solution for your next draft of the play.

Another reason for keeping your secret identity (the character as you) to yourself is that that knowledge can inhibit the cast. I found this out this the hard way. One of the first steps in mounting a production is a table reading of the script. The director assembles the entire cast, probably for the first time, to sit around a table and read aloud the script, with each actor reading his or her part. This reading is generally followed by an open discussion of the play. The playwright's presence, if he is available and willing to be there, is optional. In 1988, I attended the table reading of my play *Casino* for its first production in New York. Beaming with pride and excitement, I let it be known that the story was based on a traumatic event I had experienced in Atlantic City.

After the reading was completed, I was thrilled to witness the cast explode into an animated free flow of ideas and enthusiasm. Then one of the actors commented that he thought the behavior of the character Joe, at one point in the story, was stupid. Suddenly the room went absolutely silent. The spontaneity had been quashed because the cast remembered that the character of Joe was based on me, and, by extension, the playwright had just been called stupid. I quickly assured the actors that I wasn't at all offended and that they should continue their exploration and brainstorming without concern about me. The discussion resumed, but it was clear some of the cast felt the need to tiptoe around the playwright. Not a good thing.

Avoiding Stories from the Wrong Sources

Inspiration for stage stories can come from almost anywhere, and most of the time your ideas are fully suitable for scrutiny and development. Sometimes, however, they have strings attached, known or unknown to you, or pitfalls to be avoided. This section addresses some potential sources to deal with cautiously so that you don't put in a lot of time and effort working on a project only to discover a hitch with the core idea.

Considering the protected work of others

Plays commonly are based on preexisting stories of one sort or other. Keep in mind, however, that if you want to write a play based on preexisting material, you need to make sure the source material isn't copyrighted. (Copyright laws are complex and are amended every now and then, so you may need to get some legal advice in determining whether a work is still under copyright protection.)

If a work you'd like to use is under copyright protection, you'll have to get the owner's written permission (and probably need to negotiate some financial compensation) in order to use the material.

Eschewing that whispered "great idea"

Inevitably, when you're known to be playwright, people will seek you out to bring to you ideas. Someone will approach you at a party, take you aside, and say something like this:

"[Your name], I've got this great idea for a play; it can't lose. But I'm not a writer and you are. So I'll tell you my idea, you write it out, and we'll go 50-50 on the money it makes."

Very generous. But my standard — and respectful — response in these situations is to say:

"Thank you very much, [name], but I have a long list of ideas of my own pinned up on my bulletin board. More ideas than I have time for. But thanks anyway; I appreciate your confidence in me."

Or something like that. What these well-meaning folks don't realize is that ideas are, comparatively speaking, the easy part; writing is the hard part.

Copyrights and copy wrongs

Copyright is a form of protection provided by the laws of the United States to the authors of "original works of authorship," including literary, dramatic, musical, artistic, and certain other intellectual works, according to the United States Copyright Office. This protection is available to both published and unpublished works and extends to countries with which the U.S. has mutual copyright agreements.

This protection means that the person who creates a work owns that work and controls all the rights to that work, whether he has taken the time to formally copyright the work or not. However, obtaining a formal copyright can save you some possible headaches, and the process is so simple a playwright can do it. It involves

✔ Completing a relatively straightforward if lengthy (seven-page) form (which can be downloaded from the United States Copyright Office website: www. copyright.gov/forms/ formco2d.pdf)

✔ Appending a copy of the play

✔ Paying the fee of $35 if filed online or $50 if filed via snail mail

Copyright laws are complicated, but, generally speaking, when it comes to playwrights, a copyright generally gives you the *exclusive* right to, and/or authorize others to

✔ Reproduce and disseminate your play

✔ Prepare or authorize derivative works (adaptations) based on your play

✔ Distribute copies of the play to the public by sale, rental, lease, or loan

✔ Have the work performed publicly

✔ Disseminate individual images (like photos and posters) of the work

Further information on copyright protection and copyright duration, along with copyright application forms, is available at the United States Copyright Office website: www.copyright. gov.

Accepting someone else's idea also puts you in danger of lawsuits. If you listen to Joe Smith's idea and later you write a play that Joe Smith thinks is based on that idea, don't be surprised if you get a letter from Joe's lawyer. An idea can't be copyrighted or owned by anyone, but that doesn't mean someone can't sue you. A lawsuit puts you to the time and expense of having to defend yourself in court. Lawsuits happen more in the movie industry where the monies involved are vastly bigger and where a gadfly like Joe Smith might be offered a cash settlement to go away.

However, that warning is not to suggest you should never listen to an idea being pitched to you. If the person approaching you is an accomplished director or producer who can make a production happen, or if the person is a published author looking for someone to work on a play adaptation, or if the person is willing to pay you to write the play, in these and other cases a proposal can be worth entertaining. My most successful play, *The Devil's Music: The Life and Blues of Bessie Smith,* grew out of a concept brought to me by Joe Brancato, artistic director of Penguin Rep Theatre, in Stony Point, New York.

Of course, only accept an idea if the subject of the proposed play is of interest to you. Few things are more demotivating to a writer than spending many weeks and months of your valuable time working on a project you find boring or have no faith in. In such a situation, you'd quickly come to understand that money isn't everything.

In general, the best strategy is to come up with your own ideas. Avoid the suggestions of others unless someone makes you an offer you can't refuse.

Never Trust Your Memory: Preserving Your Ideas

Ideas — precious inspiration — are not to be taken for granted or haphazardly handled. Remember that your playwriting technique and script formatting prowess don't make you distinctive as a playwright; your personal vision of life and its events does. So you don't want to squander your unique resource by unnecessarily letting ideas and story possibilities slip through your fingers.

Memory is a fickle thing. Some folks have a great memory and can recall people, places, and concepts with great accuracy. Others, including me, have a memory like a sieve trying to hold water. It's just not to be relied on.

But in either case, a surefire way to keep those potential Tony-winning ideas from evaporating away is to make notes. In other words, somehow record the thought for future consideration. Never trust your memory. If you find yourself thinking, "I'll remember that later," you may be kidding yourself. Worse than that, you may be risking losing a great story concept forever. Make notes for yourself using one or more of the techniques in the following sections.

Carrying a pen and pad

Probably the simplest way to record ideas is to carry a pad and pen with you at all times. For women who carry purses, this poses little problem. Men, on the other hand, have to rely on pockets large enough to comfortably carry a notepad and pen. When one of the Muses deigns to confer upon you a brilliant idea, you can whip out your pad and pen to jot down the inspiration. With it safely noted, you can relax and confidently recite to yourself the immortal words of Scarlett O'Hara: "I won't think about that now; I'll think about that tomorrow." And you will, because the thought will *be* there for you tomorrow.

Even when I'm tapping away at my computer keyboard in my home office, I frequently resort to handwriting in a notebook if an idea comes to me that's not related to the project on my computer screen. (Yes, I know I could open another document and key in the idea. But I don't, okay? Old habits are hard to break.) When a story idea, or a clever line, or a solution to a problem in play occurs to me, I swivel my office chair around to my red-covered spiral notebook titled "Ideas," open to a clean page, and write it down. It never fails me. And I always know where to find that brainstorm when I'm ready to work with it.

Also, a pen and pad at your bedside are handy when making a note about a dream. When you surface from an fascinating dream, you're not likely to want to climb out from under your cozy blanket to turn on the laptop. Use a pen and pad. And don't put it off until morning or later. Make those notations immediately before your dream fades away.

Keeping a diary or journal

One of the most important things a playwright can do to preserve ideas and incidents as a resource for writing is to keep a diary or journal. You can think about it as storing away gold deep in a cave to be mined later. A journal can contain anything you like, from daily occurrences — trivial or crucial — to the progression of a great love to your raw thoughts on events you witness and participate in. When you keep a diary or journal, you can go back to an event in your life and review it and its emotional impact as material for a stage story. Why chance trusting important occurrences and musings to your memory when you can record the facts and your impressions just before bedtime?

Consider this: Perhaps your playwriting career will be so successful that a biography or autobiography will be in great demand some day. The writing of such a book would be a heck of a lot easier if you have, in essence, in-depth and ongoing notes on your life.

Switching on sound-recording devices

Murphy's Law states that if something can go wrong, it will . . . and at the worst possible time. Parra's Principle states that if something can go right, it will . . . at the worst possible time. When the Muses drop an idea on you, they don't ask, "Is this a good time?" You take it or leave it.

Ideas have a tendency to materialize in situations that are positively inconvenient for writing, like while driving, riding a bicycle, jogging, or enjoying a hot soak in the bathtub. The solitary and contemplative nature of these activities is probably what facilitates the birth of ideas. If you have this experience, you can deal with it in several ways.

First of all, never attempt to jot down anything while driving. Period. At least wait until you're stopped at a traffic light. A safer alternative to writing when your eyes are busy is a voice recorder. In addition to a dedicated voice recorder, almost every electronic device — from laptops to cellphones — can be used to record a message to yourself. You can use any of these devices to record a few words as a reminder about an idea that you can flesh out later. I keep a microcassette recorder in my car's glove compartment (along with a pepper mill and a bottle of ibuprofen). And when I bike or jog, I wear a fanny pack large enough to hold my cellphone so that I can stop and make a vocal notation if an idea should come to me while exercising. (Yes, for running purists that's a lot of additional weight, but this isn't *Running For Dummies.*)

Although taking a hand off the steering wheel to turn on a recording device isn't the safest thing to do, it beats by far taking both hands off the wheel to hold a pad with one hand and write with the other. I've seen drivers leaning forward to steer with their elbows as they write something, dial a phone call, blow their noses into a tissue, or scoop a spoonful of yogurt from the container into their mouths. Don't be the nut who does anything like that. No idea is worth risking your life or endangering the lives of others. Use good judgment when employing electronics behind the wheel.

Chapter 5

Finding Your Play's Theme

• •

• •

The *theme* of a play is the point of the story — the moral or philosophical statement or social commentary put forth by the play. It's what the show has to say to the audience. You can think of the theme as the playwright's agenda, the message you want audience members to talk about, even argue over, on the way home. Often explorations of timeless and universal concepts, themes can offer powerful observations on life, human nature and behavior, society, religious beliefs, relationships, and so on. And themes are most often implied rather than stated outright; the audience usually needs to "read between the lines" to get it.

Theme is considered by some writers to be as important a component in writing a play as are story line, characters, and setting. As your experience grows and your playwriting style develops, you'll discover for yourself whether theme in your writing is on a front or back burner.

This chapter explores theme as a component of playwriting and discusses the advantages and possible drawbacks of thematic consideration. In examining the concept of theme, my goal is to help you identify and underscore the message or meaning of your play.

Deciding on a Theme

Not all plays are thematic. Some plays are meant to be taken at face value. The very successful *And Then There Were None* is a murder mystery play adapted by Agatha Christie from her novel *Ten Little Indians*. The play is exactly what it was intended to be: an entertaining and suspenseful staged whodunit. No real theme or take-home message is embedded in the story. It's basically a straightforward, fun evening of theatre.

On the other hand, other plays are unambiguously thematic. Perhaps the granddaddy of all thematic plays of the last century is *Mother Courage and Her Children,* by the illustrious German playwright and poet Berthold Brecht. Written in a fury over the Nazi invasion of Poland, the play is set during the Thirty Years' War (1618–1648) and dramatizes very pointedly the cruelty, death, and destruction wrought by war. *Mother Courage,* considered the greatest of all anti-war plays, was very much intended by Brecht to be a play with a potent message. Clearly some plays are more message driven than others.

This section covers how your theme can best emerge in your play and how you can identify for yourself the themes that move you.

Letting your theme reveal itself

Some playwrights don't consciously consider theme when writing, preferring to leave the determination of the play's theme to the interpretation of the audience. For the sake of convenience, I call these writers *non-themers.*

When you're telling a story that resonates with you — the characters and events have a deep meaning for you — some of your thematic convictions are already rooted in the idea. You wouldn't have chosen, consciously or unconsciously, this subject or story to write about if some of your perspectives and beliefs — themes — weren't embedded in it. And if you handle the story well, audiences will discover those themes for themselves.

Playwright Barbara Lebow was interviewed about one of her plays, *Plumfield, Iraq,* a piece that dramatizes the toll war takes on individuals. When Lebow was asked if her show was an anti-war play, she replied, "It's not a marching, yelling, anti-war play. I never consciously write a message play. I don't like being hit over the head with a message. I can't start with an idea. I start with a feeling, and then the way to express the feeling somehow emerges."

For whatever it's worth, I'm in Lebow's camp. When I've tried to write a play based on some theme or message I'd like to deliver, I end up concocting events and characters to illustrate the point I want to make rather than composing events and characters to construct a compelling story. And that's not good. The characters come off as two-dimensional because they were born not of the need to tell an enthralling story but of the desire to use the play to spout off my philosophical agenda.

On the other hand, when I write a play involving fully developed characters struggling with obstacles in the urgent pursuit of an important (to them) objective, evocative themes usually emerge on their own.

Making your theme obvious to the audience

Other playwrights deliberately use theme as a launching pad and focal point for their writing. I call these writers *themers*. Those who actively use theme as motivation and as one of the building blocks of a play often start with their theme, as Brecht did with *Mother Courage*. These playwrights are inspired to write by their responses to an event or their passionate beliefs on an issue. These responses and beliefs comprise the springboard for the play.

The critically acclaimed *Laramie Project* was written by Moisés Kaufman in reaction to the 1998 murder of Matthew Shepard, a gay student at the University of Wyoming in Laramie. The murder was a hate crime motivated by homophobia. Kaufman's celebrated and widely produced play poignantly and powerfully brings home the message of the horrors that can arise from unreasoning prejudice, hate, and intolerance.

The degree to which theme motivates you to write a play, or is explicitly stated in the story of your play, probably will be more a reflection of your philosophical makeup and writing style than a result of conscious choice. Also, whether a playwright is influenced heavily by theme or by story can be, to some extent, a matter of interpretation. Elsewhere in this book I mention that I was impelled to write a play after learning of an incident of gay bashing. Some people familiar with the play have suggested that I was motivated to write it by themes of bigotry and intolerance. Maybe so, but that wasn't the way I saw it. I found the assault enraging. The play I wrote, *The Slope,* is about the aftermath of the barbarity. To me, the play is a gritty and straightforward exploration of how a couple of the victim's friends and family deal with the brutality; the play focuses on the collateral damage an outrage like that brings about. But themes do have a way of making themselves evident.

Whether your play is more or less a message play, theme is only inherently problematic if your play becomes didactic — if the message is the main thing audiences notice. What separates an effective message play from an unsuccessful one is whether or not the audience cares about the characters and is engaged in the story.

A play that very conspicuously derives from a theme is sometimes referred to as a *message play.* The main purpose of such a play is to call attention to its theme and drive home a message. Though the objective of your play may be to speak on an important theme, you probably don't want your work to be labeled a "message play"; some theatregoers avoid message plays for fear they'll be preachy, cerebral, talky, undramatic, and, in short, tedious. But then again, *Mother Courage and Her Children,* decidedly a message play, is powerful and heart wrenching. So, like many other aspects of playwriting, how skillfully an element is handled may make all the difference.

Identifying a theme

Themes choose themselves for you; they arise from what you're passionate about and what moves you, positively or negatively. The themes of your work reflect who you are and how you think. Normally, themers don't have to go looking for themes to write on, but they do have to choose from among the multitude of themes and topics crying for their attention and writing time.

If you need some help focusing your feelings to identify themes for yourself, ask yourself these questions:

- ✔ If you could snap your fingers and instantly change anything in the world around you, what would it be? Why?

- ✔ What makes you angry or unhappy when you read newspapers or watch or listen to the news? Why do you feel that way?

- ✔ Are you happy? Why (or why not)? What could change that?

- ✔ Do you feel that something is terribly unfair? Whom does it affect, why does it matter, and can anything be done about it?

- ✔ Do you have zealous political views? About what?

- ✔ What is your personal strongest belief? How far would you go to abide by that credo?

When you zero in on something you feel strongly about, put a character in a situation where she has to deal with that issue or belief in a tangible, concrete way. Create another character who, for good reasons, represents the opposition. Then give the characters a reason why they urgently need to resolve this issue, or act on their beliefs, immediately. And you're off!

For example, during the Great Depression, actor Clifford Odets was appalled by what he saw as the callous exploitation of the working class by business (a theme). The only protection workers had were unions and the right to strike. Unionization was still relatively new, and employers were trying their best to label the unions as subversive and strikes as anti-American in an attempt to destroy the unions.

In response to this, Odets wrote the play *Waiting for Lefty*. Based on a strike of taxi drivers the year before, the play is a series of vignettes dramatizing how the lives of working class people were devastated by profit-mongering business interests. So on-target was the message of the play that, at the end the premiere performance, the audience was on its feet cheering in support of the downtrodden and chanting, "Strike!" The thin line between theatre and the real world had vanished. Odets's point of view had been communicated.

Conveying Your Theme without Losing Your Audience

For those of you who have themes burning a hole in your souls and messages you feel bound to disseminate, you need to keep in mind several factors for your play to be successful. And they all come down to holding the attention and interest of your audience.

Following the golden rule: Thou shalt entertain

When you pick up the pen or take your seat at the computer keyboard aflame with a desire to set the world right on some topic or occurrence, it is of paramount importance that you faithfully abide by playwriting's golden rule: *Thou shalt entertain.* By far, the most important purpose of playwriting is to entertain.

The term *entertainment* as it's used here covers more than amusement. An entertaining play interests, intrigues, engages, and otherwise captures the imagination of the audience. When people are entertained, they forget themselves and where they are for a while. Their personal cares and responsibilities fade away as your work and the efforts of the actors and director draw their minds and emotions into the world of the play. It's no coincidence that a synonym for entertainment is "diversion." When audiences are entertained, their attention is diverted from their lives and personal challenges onto the lives and challenges of the characters on stage. This psychological breather is referred to as *escapism.*

When you entertain your audiences, they will sit for almost anything you have to say or show them. The magic of theatre and your play enthrall audience members, and entertainment is the spoonful of sugar that helps your medicine go down.

However, if the opposite occurs — if your play fails to entertain — no matter how lofty and sacrosanct your themes and messages are, they will be wasted on inattentive audiences. Folks will be looking at watches, wondering how many tweets await them, thinking about where to go for a late bite afterwards, or trying to recall if they set the DVR before they left home. Without entertainment value, your themes and messages will fall on distracted ears.

Avoiding the temptation to teach

When you decide to go to the theatre, you first need to select the play you want to see. And in considering a particular play, you ask yourself a number of questions: Is it a genre of play I like? Does it deal with a subject that interests me? Was the play well reviewed? Has the playwright written anything else of merit? And so forth. Because theatregoing involves spending significant money on tickets, you usually want to have satisfactory answers to these and other questions before you open your wallet.

But when considering a play to go to, you probably *don't* ask yourself questions like: Does the play have a message or moral for me? Will I be lectured to? Is the play going to teach me something? Theatregoers normally don't see plays to be educated. And if you believe a show to be the dreaded *message play* — if you've heard the play is longwinded and preachy; if you conclude that the play is a propaganda piece pontificating on the pet-peeves of the playwright — you probably won't buy tickets.

In short, when people want to be taught, they go to a classroom. And when they desire entertainment, they go to the theatre. The wise playwright does not mistake one for the other.

All that being said, a few remarkable playwrights have gotten away with being didactic and overtly intellectual. One of them, George Bernard Shaw, embraced his penchant for edifying and moralizing in his writing. The dialogue in his lengthy plays is unabashedly filled with witty but sermonizing social criticism.

A Nobel Prize winner, Shaw wrote more than 60 plays. Many of his plays, including *Mrs. Warren's Profession, Arms and the Man, Major Barbara, Pygmalion,* and *Heartbreak House,* are still performed all over the world. They deal with social issues, like class distinctions, education, marriage, poverty, prostitution, religion, government, healthcare, and war. His lengthy (by today's standards) and dialogue-heavy plays are witty and urbanely comedic, which helps make his message plays popular despite their blatant moralizing.

If you want to impart your perspectives and convictions to the world through your plays, you may want to explore the works of Shaw, as well as the works of Oscar Wilde and Noël Coward, two other playwrights who successfully integrated entertainment with social criticism using humor and clever wordplay. As much as their works were intended to instruct and correct society, these writers never forgot that, in playwriting, entertainment comes before all else.

Telling the truth

In Shakespeare's *Hamlet,* the title character explains:

> . . . *the purpose of playing* [performing a show] . . . *was and is to hold, as 'twere, the mirror up to nature* . . .

Hamlet (and by extension Shakespeare) was suggesting that plays should be more than a form of entertainment; they should be a vehicle for communicating truth. To the Bard of Avon's celebrated character, theatre should act as a mirror in which society can glimpse its virtues and vices truthfully reflected.

Theatre often is on the cutting edge of social movements and is a leader in recognizing and putting up for consideration the ills and vexing issues of society. Plays can give voice to the voiceless, espouse marginalized causes, and champion the underdog. Maybe more than any other art form, theatre pushes the envelope in daring to hold that metaphorical mirror up to society. It is no accident that when a dictatorship or any repressive regime takes control of a country, among the first things it does is to shut down or heavily censor the news media and the arts, principally theatre. The truth is something tyrannical governments have no interest in seeing communicated or reflected.

As a playwright, you have the extraordinary opportunity to share your most powerful and deeply held convictions (themes) through the medium of stage storytelling. Be unafraid to tell it like it is, or, more accurately, tell it like *you* see it. Great plays are not made by writers who hold back, play it safe, or worry what others may think. Because truth can be subjective, truthfulness in writing means being courageous in your choice of material and candid in its presentation in your play. If you censor yourself by backing off of or soft-pedaling your story and its themes, you squander the precious opportunity playwriting gives you to make your mark.

Keeping your convictions out of sight

Whether you consider yourself a themer or a non-themer, you want to take care to keep your convictions and causes out of sight. Or to be more specific, you want to keep your agenda out of the dialogue. Audiences should infer your themes primarily from what the characters *do,* not so much from what the characters explicitly *say.*

Few experiences are more mind-numbing in theatre than having to listen to a character whose dialogue is essentially a speech or sermon aimed at educating the audience. Dialogue that's too centered on the message you want to convey loses its natural conversational tone and rhythm and becomes a lecture or diatribe.

How do you know when a character's dialogue is getting blatantly and tediously preachy? The answer lies, in part, in the nature of theatrical dialogue. Theoretically, a character should speak only when clearly motivated to do so. Both when a character speaks and what she says should be directly or indirectly related to her efforts to achieve her objectives. Dialogue should be part of the character's actions and intentions. In other words, dialogue always should be overtly or covertly goal-focused for the character who speaks it. Therefore, alarm bells should go off

✔ When your dialogue strays from being purposeful for the character

✔ When dialogue begins to sound long-winded and pompous

✔ When you begin to hear your own opinions in the dialogue you write

Ask yourself, is the character speaking these lines because *she* needs to, or is she saying these things because *you* need her to? If it's the latter, your naked convictions may be showing, and the time has come for some judicious dialogue cutting.

Surveying Themes in Three Classic Plays

In Chapter 2, I discuss the wisdom and efficiency of learning from the triumphs and failures other playwrights. In this section, I use *Hamlet, A Doll House,* and *A Raisin in the Sun* as examples of the playwriting topics that I explore in this chapter. Read on for a glimpse at how themes are handled in these plays.

Hamlet

Themes, somewhat like beauty, are in the eyes of the beholder. A challenge in appreciating the works of William Shakespeare is not finding themes but isolating the major themes in any given work of his. Nevertheless, part of Shakespeare's genius is his variety of themes: He dealt with just about every human emotion and motivation, from ambition to racism to vengeance, in his 37 or so plays.

Hamlet, perhaps Shakespeare's most famous and psychologically complex play, is seething with themes involving justice and vengeance, filial duty, ambition and treachery, and incest and love.

✔ **Justice/vengeance:** The ghost of Hamlet's father appears to Hamlet and says he was murdered by his brother, Claudius, the new king of Denmark. The ghost commands Hamlet to avenge his murder, launching Hamlet on a mission of revenge. What's at stake? Justice. The new king must be punished for the crime of fratricide. Also at stake is the throne of Denmark, which, in the normal course of events, would have come to Hamlet. When Hamlet finally makes Claudius pay for his crime with his life, the collateral damage is extensive. At least eight characters are dead, including Hamlet himself. Vengeance, it can be said, consumes all involved.

✔ **Filial duty:** When told of his father's murder by his father's ghost, Hamlet immediately agrees to embark on his quest of revenge. In addition to his love of his father and his hatred of Claudius, Hamlet's duty to his father, to whom he was devoted, is not to be shirked.

✔ **Ambition/treachery:** Claudius, his eye on the throne, willfully murders his brother, the old King Hamlet, with poison. His ambition to be king and to possess the Queen of Denmark, Gertrude, Hamlet's mother, leads him to treachery, to "murder most foul." And in the end, Claudius, owing to his own conniving, watches his beloved Gertrude die and suffers death by poison and stabbing at the hands of his brother's son. Cheaters never prosper.

✔ **Incest/love:** Hamlet is bitter and inconsolable over his mother's "o'erhasty" remarriage — in only a matter of weeks — to her brother-in-law. Hamlet sees this as incestuous. It gives Hamlet pause to consider the nature of love, love versus lust, and, in a somewhat misogynistic vein, the fidelity of women.

A Doll House

The primary theme of Henrik Ibsen's play *A Doll House* — the question of a woman's role in society — is about as easy to miss as a ton of bricks landing on your head. The inspiration for the play came from events in the marriage of two of Ibsen's friends, Laura and Victor Kieler. A secret loan secured by Laura outraged Victor sufficiently to divorce Laura and have her committed to an insane asylum. Years later the two reconciled, but the shock and distress the incident caused Ibsen inspired him to write the landmark play.

The main character, Nora Helmer, is a dutiful mother, wife, and homemaker, who, in dealing with blackmail and betrayal, begins to question the established and limited role of women in society. She realizes she needs to know and understand herself as an individual person before she can know where she fits in.

In *A Doll House,* Ibsen challenged the complacency of the male-dominated society of the late 19th century. The ending of his play, when Nora has audacity to leave behind her husband and children to find herself, stunned theatre audiences and sent shockwaves throughout the Western world. Ibsen's play articulated the frustrations, hopes, and aspirations of millions of women, who, whether they liked it or not, were consigned to traditional roles in the conventional home.

Though *A Doll House* has been called the first women's rights play, Ibsen denied he had a feminist motive. His objective was to tell a compelling story about a husband and wife trapped in the rigid roles imposed on them by tradition, by an entrenched, male-dominated social system that cared not at all about fairness or the possibility that a woman might dare to want something else for herself. Despite Ibsen's conscious motivation in writing the play, themes that today are identified as feminist nonetheless emerge from the play.

A Raisin in the Sun

Lorraine Hansberry's groundbreaking play *A Raisin in the Sun* is the story of an African American family — three generations living in a cramped tenement apartment — and the pursuit of the American dream. This includes chauffeur Walter Lee Younger's aspirations to have a business of his own, his sister's hope of attending medical school, and matriarch Mama Younger's dream of exchanging tenement life for a home in the suburbs.

The major theme of the play, roughly based on the experiences of the author's family, is the damage and pain that bigotry can cause and one family's valiant efforts to overcome the limitations imposed by racist housing policies.

But thematically the play is as rich as it is emotionally powerful. In addition to racism, themes that are powerfully yet subtly explored include self-fulfillment, the pursuit of the "American dream," the appreciation of racial heritage, the necessity of education, and family structure and the importance of familial love and support. One of the reasons *A Raisin in the Sun* remains so beloved more than a half century after its premiere is that anyone can identify with the themes in the play.

Part II

Creating a Blueprint for Your Play

In this part . . .

*I*n addition to telling an entertaining story, plays have another crucial requirement: They must function to hold the attention and interest of the audience from start to finish. A play is a storytelling machine with parts that work together to take audiences for a ride. And to build this machine, you need a blueprint, a plan. The plan involves mapping out your story, creating believable characters to populate your play, and writing dialogue that suits the characters and serves the play. You explore all these elements in Part II so that you'll be able to quickly get down to business crafting that play you've been dreaming about.

Chapter 6

Putting Your Story in Focus

To get to the heart of any subject or issue, writers can use the formula commonly known as the "five Ws": *who, what, when, where,* and *why.* Some writers allow the question *how* to tag along; I include the *how* question in my planning and writing because it helps address the further questions of *in what way* and *by what means.*

As a playwright, you can use the five Ws to ensure that you include all the essential information needed by audience members to follow and get involved in the story taking place before their eyes. Ask yourself the questions to help you structure your story and prevent overlooking fundamental elements.

While developing your play, you want to answer the five Ws in such a way that the stakes are high. High stakes invite your audience to care about your characters. When the objective of your protagonist's quest is of urgent and paramount importance to him, the audience naturally takes his side and pulls for him to get it done. This emotional investment in the story adds power to the play.

After the story of your play has been formed in your mind, you can begin to consider what type of format is best. You may think that you need to make foundational decisions (such as comedy or tragedy, short or long, and many characters or one) even before you put pen to paper or fingers to keyboard, but it's the other way around. The story determines the storytelling form.

This chapter details how you can use the five Ws to focus your play, how high stakes add power to your stage story, and how it's the story, not you, that determines the form your play will take.

Asking Yourself the Five Ws (and an H)

The questions *who, what, when, where, why,* and *how* are indispensable to playwrights. This checklist is vital in helping you clarify and focus for yourself the story you plan to tell. It's a convenient and easy way to make sure you don't unintentionally omit or neglect any essential components in the structure of your play.

How do these Ws — *who, what, where, when, why,* and *how* — work for you as a playwright? Easy. Just answer the questions they ask.

Who is your play about?

Who is the first question to ask yourself. Who is your play about? This question requires you to identify your main character, the protagonist, the character whose mission you want the audience to follow, the character who's taking the initiative. (See Chapters 3 and 7 for more about the protagonist.)

Most plays have one central character whose story you're telling. This character is launched into a journey by the circumstances of the play, and the audience watches eagerly to see whether he can overcome the hurdles and succeed.

But at times, identifying the main character of a play is challenging. The following sections detail a couple of tests that you can apply to help you zero in on your "who," the protagonist.

Who's on first?

One test asks the question, whom does the audience meet first? Usually, but not always, the major character met the soonest is the protagonist. By *met* I don't necessarily mean a character who happens to enter first. I'm talking about the first character the audience gets to know significantly.

For example, in *A Raisin in the Sun,* by Lorraine Hansberry, the first character who enters is the harried Ruth. She's just dragged herself out of bed to wake up for school her young son, asleep on the sofa. But when her husband, Walter Lee Younger, enters the scene, the sparks begin to fly. The audience immediately finds out he is anxiously awaiting the arrival of a big check, he had an important meeting with some friends the night before, and his relationship with Ruth is strained. His dream, revealed shortly after, is to be part-owner of a liquor store. Walter Lee is the play's protagonist; his desperate and stubborn pursuit of his dream is what the audience tracks.

Finding the protagonist in an ensemble cast

Occasionally a play features what's referred to as an *ensemble cast* featuring numerous major characters, all of whom get significant stage time. But even in an ensemble piece in which all characters are roughly equal, almost inevitably a character emerges as the leader or as the character who drives of the events of the play.

Twelve Angry Men, by Reginald Rose, is an example of an ensemble show. The setting of the play is a jury room in which a dozen men struggle, sometimes heatedly, to arrive at a verdict in a murder case. As the deliberations proceed, the audience learns a detail or two about each juror — what he does for a living,

what family he has, what his personal interests are, and so on. And each character, identified only by jury number, has his moment to speak his mind about the evidence and the accused. Yet Juror #8 stands out because he drives the story by insisting his fellow jurors take a close look at the evidence rather than jumping to a quick verdict.

Other examples of plays that can be seen as ensemble pieces include the much-loved *Our Town,* by Thornton Wilder, Tony Kushner's *Angels in America* plays, and Michael Bennett's long-running Broadway musical, *A Chorus Line* — all Tony Award winners.

Last man standing . . . or not

The second test you can apply in picking out the protagonist in a story is to look at the climactic moment. It's the scene, close to the end of the play, when the protagonist and the antagonist come up against each other in a final confrontation. Only one will remain standing. If your candidate for main character is not one of the contestants at the climax, then he probably isn't the protagonist.

The great actor Sydney Poitier, who played Walter Lee Younger on Broadway and in the first film version of *A Raisin in the Sun,* relates that he and actress Claudia McNeil, who played his mother, Lena (Mama) Younger, the family matriarch, were continually at odds with each other over whom the play's main character — the protagonist — is. McNeil believed it was her character. And Mama does drive certain crucial events of the play. But Walter Lee's catharsis and resurgent triumph over the crash of his dream and the demeaning effects of racism is what provides the play's moving climactic moment.

What is the protagonist's problem?

What is the next question you ask yourself: What is your play about, or, more specifically, what is the protagonist's problem? Close to the beginning of your play, something occurs that disturbs the world of your protagonist. Referred to as the *inciting incident,* this event upsets the status quo, sets events in motion, and forces your protagonist to do something to fix the problem, right the wrong, and restore order. In other words, something happens that creates an urgent and unavoidable need for the protagonist.

Ibsen's *A Doll House* opens on the apparently tranquil late-19th-century domesticity of Nora Helmer, who seems to be thriving in her conventional role as homemaker, wife, and mother. She lives in a comfortable home, has a doting husband, Torvald, and has beautiful children cared for by a live-in nanny. This picture of idyllic home life is the status quo, the routine circumstances of Nora's life.

Then something happens. Nils Krogstad, one of Torvald's employees, arrives uninvited. He fears he's about to lose his job and puts pressure on Nora to speak with Torvald on his behalf. Years earlier, Nora, unknown to her husband, Torvald, borrowed money from Krogstad to provide care for Torvald, who had been very ill. Because she had no significant income of her own, Nora succeeded in getting the loan from Krogstad only by forging the signature of her father as loan cosigner. Unfortunately, Krogstad discovers that Nora's father was dead at the time the loan papers were signed.

Krogstad uses his knowledge of her illegal act to blackmail Nora into helping him keep his job. Nora now has an agonizing problem. To avoid disgracing her family and even going to jail, she must somehow convince Torvald to keep Krogstad on the payroll. And she must do so without letting her rigid and moralistic husband know that she is a criminal. This scenario is what the play is about.

Where is this all going on?

An adage in real estate suggests that the three most important factors in determining the desirability of a property are "location, location, and location." Though location is not the most important factor in structuring your play, it can have a huge impact on how your story plays out.

Location, or the *where* of a play, is not something to be decided lightly. The venue of your story can be as important as any character you create. Location of your play can very profoundly impact the behavior of the characters, the choices they make, and the reasons for their behaviors and actions.

The great Tennessee Williams was a master at maximizing the impact of location in his plays. Williams set many of his plays in the southern United States, where the climate can be unrelentingly hot and humid. *A Streetcar Named Desire* takes place in a sizzling, seedy, noisy section of New Orleans. The clothes of the characters are constantly wet with perspiration. The play's mentally and physically frail protagonist, Blanche DuBois, resorts to frequent baths for relief from the humidity, a practice that irritates Stanley, her brother-in-law. At a point in the play, Stanley peels off a sweat-stained T-shirt, provocatively baring his chest to his flustered sister-in-law, Blanche.

Most importantly, the merciless heat and humidity characteristic of the New Orleans location ignite outbursts of temper and violence in Stanley and in other characters. Volatile behavior is not uncommon when people are over-heated, sticky, and uncomfortable.

In addition, Blanche is frequently startled and shaken by shouting, screeching cats, train whistles and rumblings, and the plaintive cry, emanating from the chaotic surroundings, of an ethereal street vendor selling *flores para los muertos* (flowers for the dead). These environmental jolts, in conjunction with her continual wrangling with the short-tempered Stanley, exacerbate the decline of her already fragile psyche. The torrid and tumultuous location *Streetcar* clearly works to intensify the peril for Blanche.

When does the story take place?

The *when* of a play encompasses everything from something as simple as the time of day to the complexity of the period of history in which the play is set. Factoring into your play the influence of the time and the time period can enrich the landscape of your play and help ground and drive the behavior of your characters.

In *Twelve Angry Men,* the time of day comes into play. When the trials ends and the deliberations begin in late afternoon, the jurors are anxious to return a quick verdict so that they can go home for the evening, or, in the case of Juror #7, to a baseball game that night. However, one man, Juror #8, fights against the time concerns. He struggles to get his fellow jurors to take their time and look closely at the evidence, because a life hangs in the balance.

Knowledge of the historical/societal backdrop of your play is essential, particu-larly with a play that takes place in the past. If you must know your characters as well as you know your best friends — and you should (see Chapter 7), you also should know the time period of your play almost as well as if you lived in it.

My musical play, *The Devil's Music: The Life and Blues of Bessie Smith,* is set in Tennessee in September, 1937, the night before Bessie Smith's death. In writing the play, I researched the "when" of Bessie's life. Three factors of the time period affected the way I told her story:

- ✔ **The Great Depression:** In 1937, the U.S. was still immersed in the Great Depression. Millions were out of work and had little or no money, which gave me a deeper understanding of the monetary success Bessie achieved — at one point, she was grossing $2,000 a week, an enormous sum back then, particularly astonishing when you consider that the blues were the anthem, not of the well-to-do, but of the down-and-out for whom buying a show ticket or record was a major expense.

✔ **Racial bigotry:** Born in Tennessee, Bessie was very much a target of racial bigotry, including an attempted attack by the Ku Klux Klan. African Americans had great difficulty traveling back then. Seating in public transportation could be segregated, and lodging and many restaurants were closed to blacks — in the North as well as the South. Recognition of this helped me grasp why Bessie avoided the humiliation of being turned away from public facilities by arranging to have her own railroad car for sleeping and transporting the cast and crew of her show. It was not a matter of vanity but necessity.

✔ **Changing musical styles:** In that period, the blues, the music Bessie performed, was beginning to decrease in popularity. Emerging to take its place was swing, music Bessie had little interest in. Awareness of this transition in the American music scene helped me comprehend why Bessie's star began to fade, even though she could sing and wow audiences as well as ever.

Why is the situation important?

The importance of the situation to your main character is usually fairly straightforward, and this *why* of a play is arguably the most important of the five Ws to the functioning of the script. As the playwright, you must be clear on why the situation is vital to your protagonist, and it better be. The audience, in turn, must be able to recognize quickly why the situation is crucial to the protagonist. This *why* invites the audience to care.

In *A Raisin in the Sun,* Walter Lee Younger, a chauffeur for a wealthy white man, sees the arriving insurance check as means to finance his share of a partnership in a liquor store. Walter Lee sees this as a once-in-a-lifetime opportunity to ditch the job he feels is humiliating and become an independent man of business. In addition, the audience quickly comes to understand that, for Walter Lee, being his own boss also means stepping out from under the large shadow cast by his well-intentioned but domineering mother, Lena. As Walter Lee sees it, ownership of the liquor store will allow him to provide a better way of life for his wife and son, and, in the process, allow him to stand on his own two feet as a man.

For your play to be fully effective, the importance to the situation needs to be evident and clear. The audience will empathize and sympathize with the protagonist if they understand why the protagonist needs to succeed in his quest.

How is the problem being solved?

The last of the Ws is the *how* question: How is your protagonist trying to solve his problem(s)? Or how far will your protagonist go to achieve his solution? The more important the objective, the more resolute and even desperate your protagonist will be to achieve it. Desperation often leads to inappropriate measures and unsavory behavior.

The stature of a challenge

Very few people would be interested in or impressed by a college baseball team taking on a Little League team. There's no challenge in that. But if the college team faces the New York Yankees, the challenge is huge and attention-getting. In other words, the stature of the challenge your protagonist faces should be worthy of him. It should be daunting and maybe even seemingly impossible. Audiences naturally root for the underdog.

A clever moment in the great courtroom play by Jerome Lawrence and Robert Edwin Lee, *Inherit*

the Wind, refers to the stature of a challenge. The play's somewhat pompous prosecutor, Matthew Harrison Brady, when told he would be opposed in the courtroom by a formidable, nationally known defense lawyer, scoffs: "If the enemy sends its Goliath into battle, it magnifies our cause." And referring to the legend of the slaying of a dragon by St. George, Brady adds: "If St. George had slain a dragon*fly,* who would remember him?"

How your protagonist goes about reaching his goal — revenge, safety, independence, or whatever the objective is for the character — should reflect a high degree of importance and high stakes. If your character will stop at nothing, or close to it, to solve his problem or meet a challenge, you'll likely have audience members at the edge of their seats. (The next section discusses high stakes in more detail.)

In *A Streetcar Named Desire,* Blanche DuBois, in a frantic attempt to find a place of safety and security for herself, is grasping at straws. She concocts false stories to cover up a past of sexual indiscretions. In the hope of having Stella's nurturing all to herself, she's mercilessly critical of Stanley, trying to drive a wedge between him and Stella. Blanche plays the role of the innocent and charming Southern belle with Mitch, Stanley's best friend, attempting to entice the inexperienced man into marriage. All of these scandalous and ultimately self-defeating behaviors arise from Blanche's increasing fear, panic, and desperate struggle for self-preservation.

Keeping the Stakes High

High stakes help audiences care about your protagonist. If they can see that the object of the protagonist's journey is critically important to him, they automatically hope for him to succeed. People naturally sympathize with and emotionally pull for a character who's on a mission with momentous consequences. It's human nature and part of the magic of storytelling.

The audience's natural sympathy for a protagonist with a lot to lose even comes into play when the characters are less than admirable. Recently I read James M. Cain's classic noir crime novel, *Double Indemnity.* In it, insurance agent Walter Huff is attracted to a married woman who comes to him about a life insurance policy for her husband. In short order, he and she are plotting to murder her husband for the insurance money. And they do it. The question of the story then becomes, will they be caught or will they get away with the killing and insurance swindle? What's at stake? Justice, as well as the very lives of Huff and the "femme fatale," hangs in the balance.

I won't reveal the novel's clever twists and turns, but, as the narrative continued, I found myself increasingly anxious for Huff, hoping he wouldn't make some blunder that would lead to his apprehension. "Wait a minute!" I thought as I read. "Huff just orchestrated a cold-blooded, premeditated murder. I should *want* him to be caught and to get what's coming to him." But no. I was hooked and pulling for this very flawed protagonist — an antihero — to safely make his getaway and live happily ever after with his accomplice. My reaction to this character illustrates that the more the protagonist has to gain or lose, the more the reader (or audience) is drawn in.

If the objective of the protagonist's struggle is not all that important to him — if it hardly matters one way or the other to the protagonist how things turn out — the audience likewise is not going to be very much invested in the outcome.

The antihero

The protagonist of a play or any story doesn't need to be a "good guy." Although most often a protagonist is an admirable character out to achieve a worthwhile goal, that's not always the case. For that reason, avoid referring to your main character as the hero (or heroine) of your play.

A *hero* is a person who is praiseworthy and embarks on a noble mission. He possesses character traits the audience members can admire, and he behaves in ways they would like to emulate. Sometimes a hero succeeds, and sometimes he goes down in a blaze of glory, but he's always a good bloke.

In some stories, the main character is anything but a hero. Sweeney Todd, the title character of Stephen Sondheim's dark and violent musical *Sweeney Todd, the Demon Barber of Fleet Street,* is clearly the main character of the story, but he's far from anyone the

viewers would want to be like. Todd is on a mission to revenge a gross injustice done to him, and he goes about murdering those responsible. Audiences can sympathize with Sweeney Todd, whose life and family were unfairly taken from him, but they don't admire or want to emulate his ruthless ways. Sweeney Todd is what's referred to as an antihero.

An *antihero* is a protagonist who lacks virtue or courage or conscience, and whose behavior, goals, and methods may be ignominious. Sometimes an antihero is redeemed by the end of the journey, and sometimes he pays in some ironic and terrible way for his transgressions.

Nevertheless, even when the audience members shudder at the antihero's nefarious methods and actions, they often find themselves hoping the he succeeds in whatever he's doing. Even if he's no hero, he's still the protagonist.

What if the protagonist succeeds?

The higher the stakes for your protagonist, the more motivated, even desperate, he will be to achieve the objective. The higher the stakes, the more involved your audience will be. However, sometimes you may have to dig a little to identify the stakes for a protagonist; they may not always be clear cut and obvious.

For example, in Arthur Miller's classic play *Death of a Salesman,* the stakes for the protagonist, Willy Loman, are relatively subtle. Willy is an aging traveling salesman who struggles to maintain the façade of the top-notch salesman he never was. In fact, he's a failure and borrows money from a neighbor to get by. His values are a bit twisted; he proclaims that being "well liked" is the key to success in life. He instills this superficial philosophy in his two sons whom, ultimately, he alienates. Their lives also are shipwrecks. Furthermore, Willy's mind slips in and out of reality, alternating with a recurring daydream of the life he might have had if he'd partnered and traveled with his more adventurous brother.

What's at stake, then, for Willy Loman? Fame, fortune, romance? Nothing so obvious. So how do you measure the stakes for a protagonist like Willy? One way is to ask yourself this: What happens if the protagonist succeeds? What can he gain?

In the case of Willy Loman, if he's successful at convincing everyone that his career has been a success and his sons are chips off the old first-rate businessman block, he will, as he sees it, get the credit he feels he deserves. He'll be popular and well liked by his sons, he'll appear financially sound, and his life will have had meaning. In short, if he succeeds, he is sure he'll be able to hold his head high. Therefore, Willy's self-esteem and slender hold on reality — his sanity — are at stake. And these are high stakes indeed.

What's to be lost if the protagonist fails?

Looking at what a character has to gain from his journey can help you ascertain the stakes for that character. But the opposite question, what a character has to lose, can also help you define the stakes for your protagonist.

This second questions often is the easier of the two to answer. It usually directly relates to the inciting incident, the event that upsets the status quo and launches the protagonist on a mission to, one way or another, right things.

In *A Raisin in the Sun,* Walter Lee is on a mission to convince his mother to let him use the arriving insurance check to buy into a liquor store partnership. What if he fails? He will lose what he believes is his one and only chance to escape the job he sees as servile, he'll miss the opportunity to rise to the stature of businessman, he'll not be able to provide a better life for his wife and son, and he won't take his place as head of the family. And when his mother entrusts the money to Walter Lee, he stands to lose the money that could send his sister to medical school. And he would no longer be able to hang on to the belief that, given half a chance, he could take the world by storm. The stakes for Walter Lee that emerge from all this are self-respect, financial independence, a better future for his family, and, as it's stated in the play, his manhood. Nothing trivial here.

Careful consideration of what your protagonist has to gain or lose if he succeeds or fails to achieve his objective should reveal or reinforce for you what's at stake for the character. An appreciation and understanding of the gravity and urgency of those stakes will help you envision the lengths to which your protagonist will go to complete his mission.

Hearing Aristotle out: Aristotelian unities

The ancient Greeks had something to say about pretty much everything, and playwriting was no exception. The granddaddy of all pronouncements on dramatic composition can be found in Aristotle's treatise *Poetics,* written around 335 BC. In that work, Aristotle laid out the fundamentals, as he saw them, of the well-made play. According to Aristotle, the formula for a successful drama included observing what today are referred to as the *Aristotelian unities.* The Greek philosopher expounded the belief that the well-made drama, tragedy in particular, involved unities:

✔ **Unity of action:** A play should have one main action — plot, story line, or spine — that it follows. The plot should be constructed with causation; the events in one scene of the story should inevitably lead to the events in the next scene. If any event is removed, the disconnect or gap in the story will break the logic and causality of the play; the play won't make sense. If an event or moment or character in your play can be removed without making any difference to the play, then, according to Aristotle, that event or moment or character is not organic to your play and should be done away with.

✔ **Unity of time:** The events of a play should take place in one day. And the closer you can get to real time, the better.

Unity of place is also generally attributed to Aristotle but was actually concocted much later. It specifies that the events of a play should occur in one place. A play is presented on a stage in a theatre in front of an audience of real people, and whatever occurs in the play is limited to what can be done on a stage. Frequent changes in costumes and sets for multiple scenes can feel disruptive to the flow of the play. Therefore, in general, the fewer the scenes and set changes involved in a play, the better.

In contemporary theatre, Aristotle's unities are viewed as an unnecessary set of restrictions that are passé. In today's playwriting, anything goes, so long as it entertains the audience and holds the audience's interest. Does that make the three unities irrelevant? Not entirely. The unities reflect a precision and discipline in playwriting that are instructive even if ultimately considered needlessly restraining. Read Aristotle's *Poetics* (you can find it free online) for yourself. Many of the great plays and playwrights of the past were influenced by his observations and advice.

Choosing between Comedy and Drama

The symbol of theatre is the familiar conjoined masks: the mask of comedy and the mask of tragedy. Originating in the Greek Muses of comedy and tragedy, these masks exemplify the two most fundamental genres of theatre. Today, theatre people more commonly refer to the two broad classifications as comedy and drama. And when evaluating an idea for a play, determining which genre to use is one of the most important questions.

You can deal with almost any issue or story line as either a comedy or drama. Take, for instance, the story of a man's startling discovery that his old-maid aunts have poisoned a dozen or so lonely old men and had their bodies buried in the basement of their home. Mass murder hardly seems like the subject of humor; drama would appear to be the right genre for this material. Yet the preceding is the story line of one of the funniest stage comedies ever written, *Arsenic and Old Lace,* by Joseph Kesselring.

When it came to comedy and tragedy, in ancient Greece the twain never met. A play was either a tragedy or a comedy, never a mix. Today, however, plays are rarely all one or the other. Most strong and enduring comedies have their dramatic moments, and most dramas have at least a moment or two of levity. Even Shakespeare's stunning and heartbreaking tragedies, like *Hamlet* and *Romeo and Juliet,* have comic characters and humorous scenes referred to as *comic relief* (the use of humor to give the audience a bit of a breather from the otherwise heavy drama unfolding before them).

My comfort zone as a playwright is somewhere in between drama and comedy, but closer to drama. To date, though I fancy myself as having a robust sense of humor, I've not been able to write an out-and-out comedy. Because I tend to see life as a mixture of dramatic situations and humorous moments (hardly a philosophical breakthrough), when I've tried to write a pure comedy, the play inevitably ends up drifting back into the sphere that comes naturally to me — the drama with humor, or *dramedy,* as the hybrid is sometimes called.

The choice between comedic or dramatic treatment of your idea largely rests on the slant of your story. Is your exploration of the idea primarily serious in nature, or do you see it as mostly ironic and funny?

Another important factor is your particular gift as a writer. Do you have an inclination toward envisioning and creating dramatic situations, or do you have a unrelenting sense of humor and the knack for writing witty lines? The subject matter and your writing skills and propensity will take you in one direction or the other.

Picking the Right Form for Your Story

A principle in architecture and engineering posits that form follows function. This concept means that the form or shape of a building or any other object should be based, first and foremost, on its ability to facilitate the intended function or purpose. The item being designed needs to work, and the form it's given must not get in the way. If, on the other hand, form is your priority, you may find that the form you choose, though appealing to you, isn't best for the intended functionality.

The following sections explore this concept in terms of playwriting. The nature of the idea or the characteristics of the topic you're working with — your play's function, if you will — should determine the form of your play.

Sticking to one-act plays for short subjects

A *one-act* play is performed from start to finish without an intermission, usually running anywhere from ten minutes to an hour. Some one-act plays are longer, going as long as 90 minutes. However, I consider a 90-minute play, even if it doesn't have a break, a full-length play. (See the next section, "Staging full-length plays for multifaceted ideas.")

Some one-act plays are shorter than ten minutes. I've seen contests for *one-minute* plays that use approximately one page of script. (Personally, I have no idea what can be accomplished with one-page plays, other than enriching the sponsoring organization with the entry fees.)

Because they are short in duration, probably averaging 20 to 30 minutes, one-act plays have to involve few characters, relatively uncomplicated story lines, and usually one set. With a one-act play, you need to get to the heart of the matter — the climactic scene — almost immediately. You don't have the time to gradually build to the pivotal scene.

If the story you want to stage is simple and straightforward and requires only a scene (or maybe two) to play out — in other words, it's short and sweet — then the one-act play may be the best way to tell your story.

Because most one-act plays are too short to stand on their own as an "evening of entertainment" (see the next section), you can pair the play with another one-act (or more) play, perhaps thematically related, for an evening of your work.

I've seen and enjoyed programs of one-act plays both by a mix of writers and all by one writer. Neil Simon's play *Plaza Suite* is a collection of three one-act plays that all take place in the same suite of the Plaza Hotel in New York. His play *California Suite* features four one-act plays in the Beverly Hills Hotel. The location is the glue that binds these one-act plays, each with different characters and issues, into an evening of theatre.

In the playwriting courses I teach, I suggest — but I don't insist — that new playwrights initially work in the one-act form rather than on a full-length play. To me, writing a full-length play your first time out is like running a marathon without having run shorter races first. It can be done, but the shorter form is a good learning instrument and helps you understand and appreciate the inherent challenges of the longer form. And I myself am never hesitant about writing one-act plays; most of my successful plays are one-acts. The first award I ever won was for my 40-minute one-act play, *Casino*.

Staging full-length plays for multifaceted ideas

Roughly speaking, a *full-length* play is one that provides "an evening of theatre." But what's considered an evening of theatre has evolved — or maybe devolved is a more accurate description — over the centuries. Today, full-length plays average two hours, but they can run from around 90 minutes to three hours.

Until the 18th century, most plays were divided into five acts. Each act could go anywhere from 30 to 90 minutes. A play could easily run five hours. Although five hours in a theatre may feel like an eternity to you, it was fine with audiences of bygone eras. They didn't have television or the Internet to rush home to. Audiences back then wanted a *full* evening of entertainment, and the five-act play gave it to them. Eventually, the five-act play gave way to the three-act play (a play lasting about three hours with two intermissions), which was the standard into the late 20th century when the two-act full-length play (a play about two hours in length with one intermission) became the norm.

But whatever the duration, the full-length play affords the playwright a larger playing field in which to execute his game plan. The additional length, as compared with a one-act play, allows time for more scenes in which deeper character and conflict development and all the potential complexities of the story can be explored.

In addition, the full-length play accommodates subplots more efficiently than its shorter brother, the one act. Subplots are secondary stories within the main story that impact the main story. Subplots can complicate the protagonists journey and heighten the stakes. For example, in *Hamlet*, Hamlet's heartbreaking relationship with Ophelia is a subplot — a story within the main story. Another subplot is Hamlet's ill-fated friendship with Rosencrantz and Guildenstern. The death of Ophelia and what Hamlet sees as his betrayal by his childhood buddies hurt and enrage Hamlet, further propelling him toward his goal — revenge.

When is the full-length play your better choice? The full-length format serves your purposes well if your story is, well, lengthy — lots of events, twists, and turns. Or if your story features several primary characters, each of whom requires significant character development, a full-length may be best. The bottom line is, if in your honest opinion you've got a story to tell that's too big for a one act, then go the full-length route.

Playwrights often have the temptation to take a solid one-act play idea and stretch it into a full-length play. This temptation tends to arise when you've written a successful one-act play and you get audience praise and input urging you to make a full-length play out of it. Accept the compliment but not the advice. That well-intentioned feedback can be counterproductive. I've seen fine one-act plays ruined by attempting to stretch it into a full-length. Better to have a fast-paced and gripping one-act play than a slow and watered-down full-length.

That being said, as with all guidelines, this one has exceptions. If you're confident you can bring more material and fresh angles to the story, then give it a shot. But proceed with caution, keeping in mind that if there had been more to the story when you started the project, you likely would have written a full-length to begin with.

Exploring the 90-minute full-length play

In recent years, a trend toward full-length plays that are only 90 minutes long has developed. They're usually played straight through without an intermission. (Any longer than 90 minutes without a break and you risk the disruption caused by audience members climbing over each other to slip out for a potty trip.)

One theory about why some artistic directors find these shorter plays attractive is that audiences today are accustomed to seeing stories played out in an hour — the length of most dramatic TV shows. Audiences have been acculturated to drama in small doses, and some theatre people believe that any script much longer than 90 minutes tries the patience of contemporary audiences.

Maybe so, but when you're enthralled by a story, emotionally involved and excited to see how it ends, you tend to lose all track of time. How many times have you emerged from a terrific play or movie thinking, "Boy, that didn't seem like two and a half hours"? When you're totally engaged in a story, you don't care about time. In fact, you sometimes wish the story could have gone on even longer. On the other hand, when you're witnessing a dud, 30 minutes can seem like an eternity. Perhaps it's just that much writing today isn't good enough to sustain the attention of audiences for more than 90 minutes.

Another possible explanation for the proliferation of the 90-minute full-length play is that a shorter show tends to be simpler to produce than a show that runs two or more hours. As a general rule, the shorter the play, the fewer actors and scenes (scene changes) the play requires. And the fewer the elements in staging a play, the less expensive the play is to produce.

Lastly, artistic directors and theatre staffs are people, too, people who wouldn't mind getting home earlier. With a 90-minute full-length, if you have an 8 p.m. curtain, you could be heading to the parking lot by 9:30 and home in plenty of time to catch Jay Leno.

This trend toward shorter full-length plays, as observed earlier, is not new, but if short "full lengths" becomes the norm, it will mean that playwrights will have smaller canvases upon which to create their art. And some stories simply need more space and time. How memorable would Michelangelo's *Creation of Adam* on the ceiling of the Sistine Chapel be, or how much would Pablo Picasso's *Guernica* impress, if these works were restricted to canvases 4 feet by 3 feet?

The way Gustav Freytag sliced it

For much of theatre history, full-length plays were composed of five acts. According to the landmark play dissection performed by novelist and playwright Gustav Freytag in *Die Technik des Dramas (Dramatic Techniques)* in 1863, theoretically, each act had a specific function.

Freytag suggested that the overall structure of a play consisted of five steps corresponding to the five acts: exposition, rising action, climax, falling action, and dénouement.

✓ **Exposition:** The act in which the characters, setting, and any necessary background are laid out for the audience. It sets the stage and ends with the inciting incident, the happening that sets events (the plot) in motion.

✓ **Rising action:** The act in which the protagonist, in conflict with the antagonist, wages an uphill battle to reach his objective. This act is usually characterized by alternating gains and setbacks for the protagonist.

✓ **Climax:** The act in which things go from bad to good for the protagonist (in a comedy) or from good to bad (in a tragedy). This act is referred to as the turning point of the play.

✓ **Falling action:** The act in which conflict between the protagonist and the antagonist unravels, with the protagonist winning or losing against the antagonist. In short, you're heading downhill to the conclusion.

✓ **Dénouement:** The act in which the audience sees how the dust settles and what the new landscape is like. Is the protagonist better or worse off? How has the protagonist changed? What has been learned or achieved? The act ends with a new status quo.

Considering the one-person show

The one-person show is a form that has proliferated in recent years. Sometimes called a *one-man show, solo show,* or *solo performance,* the one-person show seems to polarize theatre people and audiences: It's either loved and appreciated or hated and shunned.

Essentially, a one-person show is an extended monologue that usually breaks the *fourth wall,* the imaginary wall between the performer and the audience. In one-person shows, the performer either addresses the audience as an audience or speaks toward the audience as representing an unseen character on stage with the performer's character.

One-person performances encompass everything from stand-up comedy to poetry recitals to magic shows to cabaret to plays performed by one person. In some theatrical one-person shows, the performer plays one character throughout. A striking example is the Drama Desk Award–winning one-person show *Tru,* by Jay Presson Allen, in which the accomplished author and notorious celebrity Truman Capote examines his life after alienating many friends and confidants with the publication of his thinly veiled tell-all book.

At the other end of the spectrum, the performer can play more than one character in one-person shows. The Obie Award–winning *Mambo Mouth,* written (and sometimes performed) by actor John Leguizamo, is a series of comedic and often touching vignettes in which the lone actor plays seven different characters. (I had the pleasure of providing John with some feedback as he worked on the script.)

Pros

One-person shows have many proponents because these shows offer certain advantages, one of which is that they're relatively simple and inexpensive to produce. Usually a one-person show involves one set, sometimes as rudimentary as a chair and table. And by definition, these shows feature only one actor. That's about as barebones and cheap as any show can be, and lots of producers (the money people) love that sort of economy in theatre.

One-person shows also can be popular with actors. For one thing, performing in a one-person show means the actor need not share the spotlight with anyone else. The actor carries the entire burden of the performance, but the stage is exclusively his for the duration.

Audiences tend to enjoy one-person show most when they star a well-known performer. Tickets are snapped up by a public eager to spend 90 minutes to two hours with the likes of Patrick Stewart, Lily Tomlin, Whoopi Goldberg, or Carrie Fisher (all of whom have done one-person shows).

Cons

Some audience members feel the same way about one-person shows as vampires do about garlic cloves: The distance between them can't be large enough.

One reason one-person shows can be unpopular is that few of them provide the essence of drama — conflict. Conflict between characters is what draws in audiences. But maintaining the illusion of conflict is difficult when there's only one person on stage.

Admittedly, one-person shows don't always lack dramatic conflict; the piece could, for example, deal with a character battling his demons (as in *Tru*). But a considerable amount of playwriting finesse and acting skill are needed to pull it off. You may be thinking, "How hard can it be to write dialogue for one character?" But as challenging as it is to write a conventional play with a strong protagonist and determined antagonist struggling to emerge ahead in an important and urgent journey, doing that with only one actor at your disposal is even more difficult.

Another problem with one-person plays is that often they're written by actors looking to create work for themselves, and being a fine actor doesn't automatically make someone a good playwright. Playwriting skills and acting skills are, of course, related, but they are far from identical. Consequently, many actor-written one-person plays deal with the frustrations in their lives and careers and come across as confessional and self-indulgent. Ticket buyers need be burned only once by a self-aggrandizing vanity piece to have the one-person show become a dirty word.

Making it work for you

In my estimation, the one-person form works as a stage storytelling vehicle only for practical, seldom artistic, reasons. In other words, if your objective is to stage a play minimally and cheaply, for whatever reason, the one-person show fits those parameters.

So if you're going to write a one-person show, the trick to doing it well, apart from intimately knowing the subject of the piece, is to have well-grounded answers to these three questions: Who is he talking to? What does he want? And why is he saying these things? The answers to these questions need to be pinpoint specific, and they need to make sense to you, the actor, and the audience.

Thinking of your character as just speaking out to the air, to no one in particular or to some vague or generic person, is a decidedly strong step in the wrong direction. The resulting dialogue may tend to meander unintentionally, or you may have trouble finding an appropriate and consistent tone for your character's dialogue.

Having in mind a clear image of whom your character is addressing defines what the character says and how he says it. If your character is talking to a child, for example, what he brings up and how he characterizes it are very different than if he is speaking with a reporter, police officer, his significant other, or even his dog.

Equally important to composing a serviceable one-person script is to be clear on what your character wants and why your character is saying what he's saying. Just as in a standard play, your lone character's goal determines what he says and how he behaves. Is the character seeking forgiveness? Is he trying to vindicate himself in some way? If he's telling a story, what is his reason for doing so? What's your character trying to prove?

Don't make the mistake of thinking that the charisma of your character and the entertainment he will provide are enough. Maybe in stand-up comedy or in a celebrity tell-all piece, but not in theatre. When you take on the form of a play, you need to tell an engaging and structured story — a tale with a character who has an objective playing out a story with a beginning, middle, and end — whether the characters in your piece number one or a dozen.

Chapter 7

Creating Full and Rich Characters

- -

In This Chapter

▶ Writing mini-biographies of your characters

▶ Deciding whether you can write about people you know

▶ Eliminating marginal characters and letting strong characters guide the play

- -

During the 1992 presidential election, Arkansas Governor Bill Clinton campaigned with a somewhat irreverent but laser-beam focused campaign slogan: "It's the economy, stupid." The catchphrase emphasized the candidate's position that nothing was more urgent or consequential to the country than repairing the nation's economy.

In the art and craft of playwriting, it can be said: "It's the characters, stupid." Richly drawn and powerfully motivated characters are the most consequential factor in any play. The success of stage play storytelling relies in large measure on whether it has engaging characters the audience can sympathize with, care about, and pull for.

This connection between the audience and a play's characters occurs on a gut level, and it's unconscious. Given vivid and strong characters — who face a suitably challenging dilemma the audience can identify with — the audience-character relationship forms automatically. Hearts go out to the protagonist, and the audience hopes for an agreeable solution to her quandary — a happy ending. This unconscious emotional connection is vital. Without it, audiences don't come along for the ride and don't participate emotionally; they sit back detached and only observe (or maybe even — gasp! — depart during intermission).

This chapter focuses on creating fully developed, lifelike characters. Your active and motivated characters will drive the events of the play and make your audiences care.

Creating Lifelike People

A big factor in creating characters audiences care about is making them "real," or lifelike. As a playwright, you should strive to create characters as close to actual people as is possible. And the key to doing that can be summed up in one word: detail.

The more specific you make your characters, the more lifelike they will be for you and the audience. Know *all* the details of the lives of the characters you create, not just details that explicitly appear in the script. Put another way, you should know your characters as well as you know your best friends. And, when you think about it, you'll realize that you know quite a bit about your close friends.

Visualize the person you consider to be your best friend. Now, if I were to offer your friend two tickets to an opera, would that person's response be "yes"? You very likely know whether that person would enjoy going to the opera or not. Even someone you know well may surprise you, but you can be 99 percent sure you know what her answer would be to that invitation.

The bottom line is, because you know that person and the details of her life intimately, you can predict with a high degree of accuracy your best friend's choices and behaviors under given circumstances. You should know all your characters just as thoroughly.

In the following sections, you explore key questions about your characters, use that information to create their life stories, and listen to what your individual characters tell you.

Answering key character-building questions

To create characters that are as specific and real as fictional characters can get, you need to know them intimately. Up close and personal. Following are only some of the features and traits you should know about your characters. For example, imagine that you're constructing a character named Pat.

✔ **Sex:** Is Pat a man or woman? You don't have to read a book about the different "planets" men and women are from to know that men and women react to life's events in very different ways. For instance, in the Broadway musical *Grease*, Danny boasts to the guys of a girl he met,

Sandy, as a summer conquest. Meanwhile Sandy recalls her time with Danny as "Summer Nights" of hand-holding romance.

- **Early life:** When and where was Pat born? Where did Pat grow up? Did Pat live in a poor or wealthy neighborhood? Did Pat have lots of friends or was Pat a loner? It's a no-brainer that Pat's childhood, happy or sad, can have a big impact on how Pat behaves later in life.

- **Parents:** What are the names of Pat's parents? Are they still alive? What do (did) they do for a living? Was Pat close to them? Were they support-ive of Pat? Plays, novels, and movies are filled with characters working out (and acting out) issues with their parents. Parents, even absent ones, have a profound influence on a person's life.

- **Siblings:** Does Pat have brothers or sisters? Or is she an only child? The development of social skills and relationships later in life can be influ-enced by experiences with siblings . . . or by their absence.

- **Schooling:** Did Pat graduate high school or drop out? Did Pat go to col-lege? Did Pat graduate? What was Pat's major area of study? Education, or the lack of it, can influence a person's self-esteem and grasp of the issues faced in everyday life.

- **Work:** Assuming Pat is an adult, what does Pat do for a living? Is Pat happy and fulfilled doing it? Is it blue-collar or office work? Does it pay well or not? For good or ill, people often measure their worth and status by the work they do and how much they earn.

- **Marital status:** Is Pat married or in a committed relationship? Is Pat happy in that relationship? Has Pat been faithful? Has Pat been treated well in the relationship? The significance of relationships in our lives is evidenced by the oodles of plays, novels, and movies written about per-sonal relationships and their ups and downs.

- **Religion:** What is Pat's religious background, if any? Is religion relevant to Pat's life? Given the aftermath of 9/11, it's well substantiated that peo-ple's choices and behaviors can be powerfully influenced by religious rationales, incomprehensible or not.

- **Race/ethnicity:** What is Pat's heritage? Unfortunately, some parts of the world are not always friendly places to people of color. Consequently, people of minority races and ethnic backgrounds, when under pressure, may make different choices and behave differently than others under similar circumstances.

- **Politics:** Is Pat a Democrat? Republican? Independent? Other? A person's political beliefs can very strongly affect what that person chooses to believe and how she behaves in society.

You probably can answer most, if not all, of the questions above about your best friend, which is why you can predict very accurately her choices and behaviors. Answering these questions for your characters helps you write specific and relevant dialogue and action. But remember, this list is only a sampling of the questions you should be able to answer about all your characters. The more detailed you are, the better off you'll be down the road.

As a shortcut, many writers base characters on people they know personally. "Borrowing" details from people you're acquainted with saves having to make up characteristics and life stories. For more on this approach, turn to the section "Weighing Storytelling versus the Privacy of Friends and Family" later in this chapter.

Keep in mind that most of the qualities and traits you devise for your characters may not be mentioned specifically in your play. But because you know all these things about your characters, you'll have a very good idea what these characters will do and say under the circumstances into which you put them.

Giving imaginary people detailed histories

Just because you know the answers to the questions in the preceding section about your characters, they're not going to walk up and shake your hand. But your characters will be almost as alive and vivid for you as any of your flesh-and-blood friends. You will feel that they've taken on lives of their own. And, when that happens, you're cookin' with gas.

Many writers, in imagining or creating their characters, find that writing brief biographies of each of their characters is advantageous. These mini-biographies, ranging from a few paragraphs to several pages in length, assemble and focus the essential facts about your characters and can serve to refresh your memory when you return to work on the play. Here's an example:

> **Romeo Montague** is a young nobleman and the heir of the Montague family of Verona in northern Italy. He is the son of the very wealthy head of the family, Montague. Romeo's mother, Lady Montague, is the matriarch of the house of Montague, and is very protective of her son. The Montague family has a bitter and long-standing feud with the rival Capulet family.
>
> Romeo, who is passionate, moody, romantic, and somewhat impulsive and reckless, is about 16 years old. A handsome fellow, Romeo is infatuated with a young lady named Rosaline, who happens to be a niece of Capulet, the head of the rival family.

Romeo is skilled with a sword. He has several close and loyal friends and family members, including Mercutio, Benvolio, and Tybalt. And he has a personal servant, Balthasar, and a confidant — a priest, Friar Lawrence, who is highly skilled in herbs and potions.

This, of course, is a reconstruction of a biography William Shakespeare might have written for his character Romeo in his great and timeless play, *Romeo and Juliet.* The bio was culled from the scant information about Romeo that can be found in the play. But when you write original character biographies, you're able to make them more detailed and thorough than was possible with this reconstructed biography of Romeo. (And, yes, it's correct that Romeo begins the play obsessed with another Capulet, Rosaline, and not Juliet Capulet, whom Romeo meets later.)

To get a feel for constructing character bios, do a couple for practice. Begin with a biography of yourself as a character. Giving this self-character a fictional name may help you by providing the distance you need to be objective. Using the list of features and traits in the preceding section as a starting point, write a biography of a page or two on yourself as a character. Take your time and be as detailed as you can. And don't include just your positive characteristics. Flaws and foibles help make a character human and interesting.

When you complete the self-character bio, try one on your best friend as a character. Again, use a fictional name for that friend if you feel it will help you describe the person objectively. See if you can come up with as much detail about this friend-character as you did for your self-character.

When you've finished the two biographies, look them over a couple of times. I suspect you'll conclude that you know these "characters" well and can easily predict what they would do under most circumstances. Certainly these characters are clear, consistent, and very much alive for you.

You may have to fight the temptation to skip the step of writing character biographies, particularly when you're hot on an idea and eager to get started writing your play. In the long run, though, the time you invest creating and fleshing out your characters in mini-bios actually saves time down the road. If you have bios for your people, you're much less likely to have to stop writing to figure something out about your character(s).

You will possibly — even probably — have to refine and change the details of your character biographies as you go along. But having a clear picture of your characters at the start helps you stay focused, gives your story clear and consistent direction, and helps you avoid the dreaded writer's block.

Yes, your characters will speak to you

You've probably heard or read about writers saying that their characters took on "lives of their own." "The characters took over the story." "My characters spoke." This all sounds like demonic possession or booze talking, but the fact is that it's true. It happens. Your characters *will* do all those things. And it's nothing to fear. The phenomenon occurs as a result of endowing your characters with plentiful detail and individuality.

Some scientists posit that, eons ago, the earth was covered in a lifeless, watery soup of chemicals, amino acids, and who knows what else. And it took a spark, perhaps bolt of lightning, to jumpstart life by bonding elements in this chemical soup into something alive. This phenomenon parallels the creative process of bringing characters to life. When you create a literary soup of well-thought-through and fully dimensional characters, all that's needed is the spark — an event that ignites the conflict — for your characters to begin speaking and virtually acting on their own to achieve their goals.

In other words, if you've done your homework, if you've fleshed out your characters with abundant detail and individuality, they will seem to come to life for you. In your mind's eye, you will begin to *see* your well-rounded and detail-rich characters doing and behaving. In your mind's ear, you will *hear* what they say to each other. You may experience the sense that you're eavesdropping or taking dictation, watching the scene unfold as you race to get it all down on paper (or keyed into the computer). It's a heady experience. And there's nothing magical or spooky about it.

Individualizing your characters

As you begin creating the people of your play — writing their biographies — in addition to detail and specificity, another important goal to shoot for is individuality. You want to make the characters of your play as individual — different from each other — as possible. *The essence of strong storytelling is conflict;* different characters wanting opposing things are usually on a collision course. And the more individual you make your characters, the easier it is to stoke up the conflict. This fundamental goal of dramatic individuality even applies to characters who are the members of the same family.

Consider a cast of three characters — Mom, Dad, and your newly created character, Pat. As far back as anyone can remember, this family has lived in New York City and has always voted Democrat. And as a presidential election approaches, Mom, Dad, and Pat — all Democrats — find themselves sitting around their kitchen table, praising the Democratic candidate and heaping abuse upon the Republican candidate. Realistic? Yes. Dramatic? Hardly — this scene has no conflict. The characters all agree.

Allow me to make a slight adjustment in the partisan landscape of our politically astute family. Mom now comes from a clan of Boston Democrats, Dad from a family of Atlanta Republicans, and Pat, well, Pat's an independent. As the presidential election approaches, there are likely to be fireworks between Mom and Dad, both of whom detest the other's presidential candidate. And depending on other characteristics you've given these two, the debate can easily turn nasty and even get personal. However, Mom and Dad are in sync about one thing; they both want Pat's vote. That easily can decay from a political debate to a personal battle for Pat's loyalty. Pat can become the emotional equivalent of a tennis ball at Wimbledon. Unlike the first scenario, this situation has the makings of drama. Why? The three characters are very much individual when it comes to politics. Ergo conflict.

When "borrowing" details from the lives of people you know to create characters, be sure that your characters have individuality. That may entail amending some of the details you're borrowing. You may have to make things up. That's okay. A playwright is a *creative* writer. Always feel free to embellish your characters, whether totally imaginary or based on people you know. You don't want to become a slave to "facts." As the saying goes, never let the truth get in the way of a good story.

Finding your character's motivation

"What's my motivation?" has become a standard gag line uttered melodramatically in comic stage, movie, or TV scenes by characters who are pretentious, would-be actors. But for the playwright striving to create lifelike characters, it's no laughing matter.

This now-cliché question — "what's my motivation" — implies that the actor, in preparing for her given role, needs to know what is propelling the character forward and what the character is after. To know what a character wants is to know how to play that character.

Similarly, knowing what the character wants is a crucial element in creating lifelike characters. Simply put, the character's motivation is what the character is after; what the character desperately needs; what the character will stop at nothing to achieve or obtain. And the more important and powerful the motivation, the more dramatic, and possibly extreme, the character's actions will be.

For example, Hamlet, the title character in Shakespeare's classic play, needs to avenge the murder of his father. His motivation is revenge and, in its peculiar way, justice. In the end, he achieves his goal, but at a terrible cost — a body count rivaling today's shoot-'em-up action films.

In addition to a quest for vengeance and justice, powerful motivations that enliven characters and launch their quests can involve love, hate, greed, ambition, shame, fear, and so on. Any powerful human emotion can fuel a character's motivation to go after something.

So when contemplating what makes your character tick, be sure you know what her motivation is. To know what your character wants and what lengths she will go to to get it is to understand what drives your character (and, therefore, your play).

Making all your characters more than types

Making sure your main characters are fully developed is one thing, but you need to make sure that *none* of your precious people are "types." The temptation to see characters as a type may be stronger in comedy than in drama. But don't make the mistake of relegating your secondary characters to typedom.

What am I talking about? I'm referring to characters that may be labeled the klutzy type, nerdy type, bully type, promiscuous type, treacherous type, or miserly type. Certainly a character can be a klutz or a nerd or a bully and so on, but your characters should be much more than any of those traits.

How does one create a type? By skimping on the detail and depth. A type character is defined by a large and superficial characteristic — like klutziness, nerdiness, or miserliness — rather than the extensive and specific detail that would make that character a three-dimensional person. You avoid creating a type when you give a character a rich life story, individual idiosyncrasies, personal hopes and dreams, and a meaningful objective.

All your characters — main characters or secondary — should be fully drawn and have strong legitimacy (as discussed previously in "Answering key character-building questions" and later in "Legitimizing all your characters"). All your characters must be robustly motivated and solidly grounded in the reasons they do the things they do. Populate your play with wholly fleshed-out "real" people, rather than types, and your play will be off to a sturdy start.

Weighing Storytelling versus the Privacy of Friends and Family

The classic advice given to beginning writers is to write what you know. In other words, write about people, places, and things you have experience with. The result often is truthful and powerful. Probably every writer at one time or another comes up with a story based on personal experiences involving friends and/or family. But using people you know can pose problems.

Think of it this way: Do you have a right to write plays that mirror the strengths and weaknesses of people you know, particularly those near and dear to you? They likely will recognize themselves in your work, even if no one else does. Will they be pleased or embarrassed or angry? Do you risk alienating people close to you by basing characters on them?

Your life and how you process the world around you comprise your unique gift to the world, so you may feel an artistic obligation to tell truthfully the stories that move you, no matter whom they involve. But are you invading the privacy of your loved ones and holding them up to scrutiny they did not seek? Probably. Of course, you can always ask permission from the people involved. But what happens if you get no for an answer? This dilemma has no easy solution. You'll need to arrive at your own answer. But know you are not alone. It's a predicament faced by writers since storytelling began.

One of the best-known examples of this predicament involves the great play *Long Day's Journey into Night,* written by Eugene O'Neill. The drama, completed in 1942 and considered by many to be O'Neill's masterpiece, won a Tony Award for Best Play and a Pulitzer Prize for drama in 1957, 15 years later. But why the 15-year gap in time? Because the play, which starkly depicts alcoholism and drug addiction in a family closely based on his own, was locked away until after O'Neill's death. The story was so nakedly truthful and personally agonizing that he instructed that it not be published or produced until after his death. As a result, he neither saw the play done nor got to enjoy the applause and the many prestigious honors the play earned.

O'Neill's decision may have been to save himself the ache of seeing the painful story staged as well as to protect the reputation of his parents, who had been prominent theatre people. This story shows how awkward and self-conscious the behavior of a writer can be when material is drawn from the lives of those near and dear.

Setting Up Your Characters to Drive the Play

Movies excel at depicting action, whereas novels and short stories are strong at exploring the cerebral, interior lives of their characters. But plays work best when characters are trying desperately to achieve some objective in defiance of another character. In other words, most plays are about people versus people. Plays are character driven. And because characters are king in theatre, beyond being detailed, specific, and individual, characters need to work well. They need to function.

As an analogy, consider the automobile. The fundamental purpose of a car is to take you for a ride somewhere. The principal components that enable the vehicle to achieve that end are the engine and fuel. Without fuel, an engine doesn't run, and without a functioning engine, the car goes nowhere. No matter how stylish or spacious the car, if it doesn't get you from point A to point B, the contraption is essentially useless.

Similarly, the fundamental purpose of a play is to take the audience for an absorbing and dramatic ride. And the principle components that enable this vehicle to achieve that end are the story and the characters. And without engaging characters to fuel the engine — to drive the story — the play stalls, and the audience is left high and dry. Perhaps this is driving the car metaphor too far (pun intended), but the bottom line is that characters must work.

In this section, you explore a number of factors involved in creating effective characters that are fully functional and effectively drive the play. These factors include giving your characters legitimacy, facilitating their behavior, and eliminating unnecessary characters.

Knowing — and loving — all your characters

Writing a play is an act of creation. You are the creator of the world of your play, of the events that take place in it, and the people who inhabit it. Some of the characters you create will have objectives that are noble and inspiring, while others will have goals that appear deceitful and shameful. Some of your people will behave gallantly and heroically; others will act in ways that seem scandalous and cowardly. But whatever your characters are and no matter what they do, as creator of their world, *you must love them all.*

In a way, you're the parent of your characters. And like a parent, you must love the child who is mischievous in school and consistently disobeys just as much as you love the child who consistently gets straight As in school and helps an elderly neighbor carry groceries. Loving all your creations enables you to create characters who are well rounded and interesting to the audience, even if some of the things your characters do are dreadful.

If you don't love all your characters, including your antagonists, you're likely to put emotional and psychic distance between yourself and those characters. You will tend to invent two-dimensional characters, stereotypes, straw men (and straw women) put up on stage only to be knocked down. Without your tender loving care, some of your characters won't be "real" people. And "real," fully empowered people on stage, duking it out — comedically or dramatically — over some important object or issue, is what theatre audiences crave.

Legitimizing all your characters

Closely aligned with loving all your characters is legitimizing them. Give all your characters motivations that are powerful and clear. Even if the audience isn't rooting for a character (the antagonist, for example) to achieve her objective, the audience should be able to see why the character sees her actions as legitimate — meaning valid and justifiable — to that character. In other words, the audience may not be able to agree with what a character is doing, but the audience should be able to understand why the character thinks she's right.

Giving legitimacy to your *protagonist,* the main character of your story, is a relatively uncomplicated thing to do. Here are some examples of legitimately motivated characters:

✔ Romeo meets Juliet, and, despite their feuding families, he determines to make her his. Boys meeting and wanting girls, and vice versa, happens all the time. Simple and legitimate. We can get behind that. (*Romeo and Juliet,* William Shakespeare)

✔ Dorothy finds herself in a strange land filled with odd little people and bizarre creatures. She realizes how much home means to her, and she strives to get back to her Kansas farm. Appreciating and wanting what you had after it's taken from you is straightforward and legitimate. The audience can easily sympathize with her desire to get home. (*The Wizard of Oz,* L. Frank Baum)

✔ Juror #8 strives to get fellow jurors to take a close look at the evidence in a murder trial, rather than jumping to a quick verdict. A boy's life is at stake. You can hardly come up with a clearer and more legitimate motivation than preventing a miscarriage of justice. We're with Juror #8 100 percent. (*Twelve Angry Men,* Reginald Rose)

Giving legitimacy to your *antagonist,* the person or thing that stands in the way of your protagonist, is not easy to do. Just as in life, our instinct is to shun the troublemaker, give her short shrift, and focus on more pleasant people and places. As a playwright, you can't give in to that natural but counterproductive inclination.

Your antagonist, if she is to be believed and fully functional, must have legitimate motivations, too. A battle is much more fascinating when the foes are equally motivated and evenly matched. When the antagonist has a logical and understandable reason for what she does, the tension tends to be high and the audience just may find its loyalties torn: "Who do we root for? There's right on both sides." When you get that to happen, you've hit theatrical pay dirt.

✔ Javert, the antagonist, is an excellent policeman. The protagonist, Jean Valjean, is jailed for stealing a loaf of bread, knocks Javert out, and escapes so that he can keep a promise to find and care for an orphan girl. Keeping a promise is a good thing, particularly when it concerns a neglected child. Officer Javert vows to capture Valjean and return him to prison, no matter what it takes. Capturing an escaped prisoner is a good thing, too! So the protagonist and antagonist both have legitimate goals. Cool! (*Les Misérables,* Claude-Michel Schonberg, Herbert Kretzmer, Alain Boublil, from the Victor Hugo novel)

✔ Iago is intent on sowing the seeds of marital jealously in Othello even though Othello's wife, Desdemona, is loving and blameless. Nasty thing to do. But Iago was passed up by Othello for a military promotion that Iago feels was due him; therefore, he's got what he thinks is a good reason for his ruthless behavior. The audience can't condone Iago's actions, but it can understand his disappointment and frustration. As a character, Iago has a clear rationale, even if twisted, and, therefore, he has legitimacy. (*Othello,* William Shakespeare)

By now I hope the direction I'm heading in is clear: No moustache-twirling "bad guys" allowed. If, as playwright, you love all your characters and you give them all — even the antagonists — legitimacy, you'll find your play has no room for the formulaic bad guy (or girl).

Antagonists lacking legitimacy and displaying few, if any, redeeming qualities are two-dimensional and relatively uninteresting. Easy-to-boo-and-hiss-at characters are the kind of antagonists you find in cartoons, comic books, silent movie melodramas, superhero movies, and passé and inferior plays. Fun, maybe, but far from the lifelike characters you should be striving for.

So in your playwriting, shoot for an antagonist who will conflict your audience. Give your antagonist the complexity and legitimacy that will make your audience pause to think before choosing sides and send the audience home thinking about the dilemma and legitimacy of your characters.

I have a friend who has a hard time watching sports events. She can exult with the winner of the game, but she also keenly feels the loser's pain. Although that may not be the best temperament for a sports fan, it's great for theatregoing and playwriting.

Facilitating, not forcing, character behavior

The quickest way to stifle your characters, kill spontaneity, and dispel the magic of playwriting is to *force* your characters to do what you want them to. Well, why shouldn't you give their strings a firm tug when you need your characters to behave a certain way or say something? After all, are you not the all-powerful creator of the characters and their world? Yes and no.

As the playwright, you have a vision of the play and a plan for whatever scene you're working on. But the shrewd and confident playwright gives free rein to the imagination and allows her characters to play out the scene organically. You can think of it as creative daydreaming. In your mind's eye, let your characters behave, speak, and interact as the full and rich people you mean them to be. They may play out the scene exactly as you planned it. Or they may surprise you with actions and words you hadn't anticipated. A scene you planned as dramatic may take a comic turn, or a scene you envisioned as funny may turn bittersweet. These happy accidents won't happen if you're heavy handed and inflexible in your approach to the scene.

When your characters speak, listen. Be open to inspiration and modification. Don't force things. Throw away the old outline if need be and write a new one. Yes, it's more work, but it usually results in a more truthful and exciting play.

Euthanizing your marginal characters

In the middle of the last century, plays sometimes began with the curtain rising to reveal a living room in a fashionable apartment in an upscale part of town. Enter the butler and the maid. As the two clean and order the room for an impending party, they gossip about the master and mistress of the dwelling, their employers' hopes and aspirations, and the arriving visitor(s) who, of course, will throw a monkey wrench into everything. Exit the domestics, to be seen only minimally throughout the rest of the play, and enter the principal characters.

Aside from being a clunky and outdated way of bringing the audience up to speed on the *backstory* (discussed in Chapter 10), today that play would be considered overpopulated. Nowadays, the butler and the maid are considered marginal and expendable and are unceremoniously eliminated. In contemporary theatre, straight plays (meaning non-musicals) tend to have small casts. Plays with as few as four actors are not unusual, and a production requiring four or fewer actors is considered highly commercial. (Yes, like any rule, this one has exceptions, but don't bank on being that exception.)

It's a fact of theatre life that producers struggle to keep their costs down. Everything — from theatre rental to sets, costumes, lighting, sound, and props to advertising and marketing to salaries for cast and crew — is very expensive, particularly in New York City. What producers do, for better or worse (worse, actually), is to try to save money by keeping the cast size small and keeping the talent payroll down. Ironically, the cost of paying actors is not nearly the biggest expense in producing a show. (You can find more about this sad reality in Chapter 17.)

Consequently, a skill that's becoming more and more useful in playwriting is staging ingenuity. How do I tell the story I need to tell with four or fewer actors? One way is to euthanize your butlers, maids, doormen, delivery boys, and other marginal characters. Bit-part players need not apply. Your characters will have to fix their own drinks and empty their own ashtrays. One of your characters will need to exit the stage and reenter with the delivered pizza rather than having a delivery boy character carry it on stage. In early-21st-century theatre, the range of colors a playwright has available to apply to the play's canvas is, unfortunately, limited.

If you can't bear to part with marginal character or two, there is a method that allows you to eat your cake and have it too. You can get more mileage out of your small cast by having an actor double up. An actor may play butler in the first scene, the delivery boy in the next scene, the police inspector in the third scene, and so on. Taking on multiple roles requires a versatile and quick-witted actor. It also requires that you allow time in your script for your actor to change costumes between appearances on stage.

However, doubling up roles has a significant downside. It can distract the audience. When people in the audience realize that an actor is playing multiple parts, they may pay more attention to that actor's skill in playing a variety of characters than to the events of the play itself. A doubling-up actor could, as they say, steal the show. Usually, that's not what a playwright has in mind.

Chapter 8

Dialogue: The Most Important Tool in Your Toolbox

. . . .

. . . .

ialogue is the words spoken between two or more characters in a script. It's what characters are motivated to say to each other. Dialogue reveals who the characters are, what their thoughts are, and what they want. Dialogue is the primary component in playwriting, and, consequently, the most important. On average, most of what you write on the page of a script for a play is dialogue. (The rest is a smattering of *stage directions*, descriptions of the setting and what the characters are physically doing).

The principal purpose of dialogue is to advance the action of the play. Although the characters in a scene may appear to be simply talking, there is much more to good dialogue than meets the layman's eye. Like the strategic movement of pieces in a game of chess, aimed at trapping and capturing the opponent's king, a character's dialogue is calculated to achieve his objectives over those of another character. Effective dialogue, therefore, is, overtly or subtly, verbal fencing . . . with some prize at stake.

Unlike the readers of prose, theatre audiences don't read the script of the play as they watch a performance. Therefore, what the characters think and desire must be communicated through what they say and do on stage. One of the most difficult concepts for new playwrights to understand is that if you want the theatre audience to know some thought or bit of information, a character on stage has to *say* it (or do something that reveals it).

This chapter focuses on writing convincing and effective stage dialogue, the principal device for story development in stage plays. I describe the characteristics of good and not-so-good dialogue and investigate some of the more specialized forms and uses of dialogue.

Writing Purposeful Dialogue

Dialogue is purposeful speech. Every line of dialogue you write should serve a function, even though it may come across as ordinary conversation to the audience. The seemingly insignificant movement of a pawn from one square to another in a chess game ultimately can have enormous consequences to the outcome of the game. Similarly, what may pass for everyday conversation between characters in a play can foreshadow or ignite a chain of events that will have momentous consequences to the characters and their objectives.

And all this is not as hard to achieve as it may sound. If you can talk, you can write dialogue. You just put yourself in your character's shoes — keeping in mind the character's personality and goals — and then just write what you would say if you were the character in those circumstances. Piece of cake.

Well, okay, there *is* a little bit more to writing dialogue than that. You have to consider both *what* is said and *why* it's said. Here's a simple example. Bob and Mary sit in front of desktop computers in their shared office. Bob looks up at a wall clock, and he says: "It's 12:35." That's *what* is said, a simple statement of fact. Not particularly noteworthy. It's the *why* of the statement that transforms that straightforward declaration into purposeful dialogue.

Suppose that the play has already set up that Bob can't leave his computer at the moment, but he desperately needs to make a phone call that he'd rather Mary not know about. And it's been established that Mary habitually goes out to lunch at 12:30. By mentioning the time, Bob has performed a clear action intended to draw Mary's attention to the time, which should spur her to get up and scram. It's the *why* of that banal and otherwise uninspiring sentence — "It's 12:35" — that makes the dialogue purposeful and engaging. The audience will watch to see if Bob's "innocent" remark has the desired effect.

Using Dialogue to Its Full Potential

As a playwright, you occasionally will hear some non-devotee of theatre — believe it or not, they exist — make a reproving statement like "Plays are just people standing around talking. All talk and no action! Humbug!"

The truth is that good plays are filled with action — just not physical action. In plays, anything a character says or does as a step toward accomplishing his objective is called *action*. Plays feature people working other people, or trying to achieve something, or trying to get the better of other people, characters taking action through the wonderful and horrible things they say to each other.

As you construct your story, scene by scene, your protagonist or antagonist should be *doing* something to achieve his goals — to be elected president, to win someone's love, to solve a mystery, whatever. This section describes how you use dialogue to create action and fuel dynamic relationships, how to reveal the character of your characters, and how to use subtext to have characters say things without actually saying them.

Creating action through dialogue

Though a play relies on dialogue, the words a character speaks must have purpose. The words spoken by a character should be intended to have an effect on another character. The intended effect of dialogue (which should get the character closer to his own goals) is the action. For example, is the dialogue meant to *bully* another character into opening his wallet? Or is it meant to *intimidate* the other into quitting a job? Or *charm* the other character into dropping his guard?

As you construct your scenes, be sure your characters are engaging in clear and strong actions. Following are some examples of strong, clear actions (note that they're active verbs):

✔ To advise	✔ To dominate
✔ To attack	✔ To embarrass
✔ To bait	✔ To enchant
✔ To beg	✔ To enforce
✔ To belittle	✔ To flirt
✔ To blackmail	✔ To guilt someone
✔ To bully	✔ To harass
✔ To challenge	✔ To humiliate
✔ To clarify	✔ To ingratiate oneself
✔ To coax	✔ To insult
✔ To coerce	✔ To intimidate
✔ To comfort	✔ To irritate
✔ To deceive	✔ To pacify
✔ To defeat	✔ To praise
✔ To demand	✔ To probe
✔ To dig out	✔ To punish
✔ To disillusion	✔ To quiz

- ✔ To reprimand
- ✔ To seduce
- ✔ To show off
- ✔ To spoil
- ✔ To teach

- ✔ To tease
- ✔ To test
- ✔ To threaten
- ✔ To warn

Actions are the weapons used between the protagonist and the antagonist as the protagonist struggles to achieve his goal. As you search for or refine an idea for a play, you won't have to go very far to find relationships that have a natural protagonist/antagonist dynamic.

Don't lose sight of who's who in your play. Your protagonist is the character who's on a mission, the character whose journey the audience is tracking. And the antagonist is the person or thing with opposing objectives, presenting obstacles to the protagonist. Also keep in mind that the antagonist of your play need not be "the bad guy" or a villain of any sort. Your antagonist can simply be someone who has legitimate reasons to oppose the protagonist. A police officer pursuing the protagonist of a story, even if we know the protagonist to be innocent of any crime, is not an evil person. The cop is simply doing his duty.

Make sure that the characters you come up with are at odds with each other through a natural dynamic or through some conflict of your own creation. Table 8-1 is a list of relationships with built-in conflict, any of which provide a jumping-off point when devising a story line or plot. Note that in many of the relationships in the table, the roles can be switched. The child, for example, can be the protagonist and the parents the antagonist, or the student can be the protagonist and the teacher the antagonist. The point is that the pairings have a natural tension that can be exploited in your play.

Table 8-1   Natural Protagonist/Antagonist Relationships

Protagonist	Antagonist	Protagonist	Antagonist
Parent	Child	Spouse	In-laws
Teacher	Student	Cat	Mouse
Seller	Buyer	Minister	Sinner
Criminal	Victim	Popular person (extrovert)	Wallflower (introvert)
Law officer	Criminal	Beggar	Benefactor
Man or woman	Nature	Therapist	Client

Protagonist	Antagonist	Protagonist	Antagonist
Servant	Master	Substance abuser	Clean and sober individual
Avenger	Evildoer	Hunter	Prey
Star	Fan	Driver	Passenger
Employee	Employer	Spy or snoop	Target
Husband	Wife	Business rivals	
Doctor	Patient	Siblings	
Prisoner	Jailor	Co-conspirators	
Hostage	Captor	Diplomats	
Rebel	Oppressor	Rival warriors	
The poor	The rich	Lovers	
Democrat	Republican	Ex-lovers	

So how exactly do you use dialogue as action? By writing lines of dialogue that help the character — protagonist, antagonist, or other character — achieve his goal. One of the marvelous scenes in *Hamlet* is one in which the objectives of the two characters, Hamlet and Polonius, are unmistakably in conflict, and the dialogue they speak advances their actions.

Hamlet, who is on a mission to revenge the murder of his father by the new king, Claudius, has decided to use pretended insanity as a tactic for getting to the bottom of things. Polonius, King Claudius's pompous and meddlesome advisor, has taken it upon himself to find out the cause of Hamlet's madness. Polonius encounters Hamlet reading a book. In the following exchange, Hamlet toys with Polonius, while Polonius tries his best to make sense of Hamlet's responses. (The *aside* in a couple of Polonius's lines is intended to indicate that he is thinking out loud, which, of course, shares with the audience his thoughts. The words in brackets are mine.)

POLONIUS

What do you read, my lord?

HAMLET

Words, words, words.

POLONIUS

What is the matter, my lord?

HAMLET

Between who?

POLONIUS

I mean, the matter that you read, my lord.

HAMLET

Slanders, sir: for the satirical slave says here that old men have grey beards; that their faces are wrinkled; their eyes purging thick amber and plum-tree gum; and that they have a plentiful lack of wit, together with most weak hams [legs]: all which, sir, though I most powerfully and potently believe, yet I hold it not honesty to have it thus set down; for you yourself, sir, should be old as I am, if, like a crab, you could go backward.

POLONIUS

(Aside.) Though this be madness, yet there is a method [sense] in't. — Will you walk out of the air, my lord?

HAMLET

Into my grave?

POLONIUS

Indeed, that is out o' the air. (Aside.) How pregnant [filled with meaning] sometimes his replies are! a happiness that often madness hits on, which reason and sanity could not so prosperously be delivered of. I will leave him and suddenly contrive the means of meeting between him and my daughter. — My honourable lord, I will most humbly take my leave of you.

HAMLET

You cannot, sir, take from me anything that I will more willingly part withal, — except my life, except my life, except my life.

POLONIUS

Fare you well, my lord.

In the above passage, nothing physical has occurred, but it's clear that Polonius's actions are to probe and test Hamlet, and Hamlet's action in the scene are to tease and deflect.

Revealing character through dialogue

People often reveal their personalities, beliefs, hopes, and values — directly or indirectly — through what they say as well as what they do. And when you create characters, their dialogue should be crafted so that audiences pick up clues and hints. Without thinking about it, audiences begin to formulate a picture of who the characters are and what the characters want from what they say.

In one scene of *A Streetcar Named Desire,* you find out a great deal about the protagonist, Blanche DuBois, from her own words. Down and out and with nowhere else to go, she arrives outside the seedy New Orleans apartment occupied by her sister, Stella, and Stella's husband Stanley Kowalski. The Kowalskis are out, but their landlady, Eunice, offers assistance to Blanche. Blanche explains to Eunice that she's looking for "my sister, Stella DuBois. I mean — Mrs. Stanley Kowalski." That seemingly innocent slip of the tongue actually reveals that Blanche doesn't accept that her sister is married to a man Blanche later labels as "common."

Blanche takes in the seamy conditions around her and immediately concludes she must have been given the wrong address. When Eunice informs her that she's reached her destination, Blanche blurts out, "This — can this be — her home?" The knee-jerk remark shows the audience that Blanche has the brazenness to turn her nose up at her sister's dwelling, also demonstrating a lack of tact. Eunice lets Blanche into the Kowalski flat, and Blanche rudely dismisses the accommodating and hospitable Eunice, saying, "What I meant is I'd like to be left alone." Blanche again shows herself to be ungracious and a tad ungrateful.

In only a few minutes, Blanche, through dialogue with Eunice, reveals quite a bit about herself and her personality.

Finding subtext between the lines

Sometimes what characters don't say and what you can infer by "reading between the lines" are more revealing of character or motivation than what characters do say. The information the audience can draw from what's not said in dialogue is referred to as *subtext*. Subtext may reinforce or contradict the apparent meaning of the dialogue actually spoken by the characters.

Subtext has the benefit of making audiences think a little rather than being spoon-fed the point of the scene. When audiences have to work a bit, they become more engaged as participants in the story.

In my play *Song of the Coquí,* Raymond invites his adult son, Ray, to lunch in a restaurant. The conversation, picked up here in the middle of the scene, is ostensibly about Raymond wanting to buy a ring for his wife (Ray's mother). The exchange slips into a testy discussion about her alcohol consumption.

> RAYMOND
>
> (A beat) I never told you this, Ray. (With difficulty) I . . . find empty bottles. Under the sink. In the broom closet.

> RAY
>
> (A beat) You drink, too.

> RAYMOND
>
> (Irritably) You think you know everything!

> RAY
>
> Maybe she just forgets to throw them out.

> RAYMOND
>
> You don't understand. I want to get her a ring, like you got for . . . your girlfriend. But your mother . . . might fall and knock the diamonds out.

> RAY
>
> Fall?

> RAYMOND
>
> Yes.

> RAY
>
> Dad, it's pretty hard to knock a stone out of a ring.

> RAYMOND
>
> You don't know! You gotta be realistic! Practical. You gotta think ahead, Ray. Think!

                    RAY

God, I hate when you say that.

                  RAYMOND

What? What are you talking about?

                    RAY

"Practical, realistic!" (A beat) Nothing. Never mind.

                  RAYMOND

(A beat) You gonna help me or what? You don't have to if you
don't want to. I don't want to make you do anything if you're too
busy . . . to help me.

                    RAY

How much do you want to spend?

                  RAYMOND

You want a frankfurter?

                    RAY

I'm talking about this ring you want to get Mom.

                  RAYMOND

It doesn't matter. Two, three hundred maybe.

                    RAY

(Cynically) That much?

                  RAYMOND

For your mother, yeah.

                    RAY

(A beat) You wanna go now?

                  RAYMOND

What's your hurry? You don't like sitting with your father?

RAY

I meant to a jewelry store. Do you want to go shop now?

RAYMOND

No, we got plenty time before Christmas. I gotta get back. I told your mother I was getting the oil changed. I don't want her to know. I want it to be a surprise. I'll call you.

RAY

Okay, Dad.

On the surface, the exchange is about buying a ring for mommy dearest. But at least two indications hint to the audience that the real discussion, certainly from the elder man's viewpoint, is very much about something else.

First of all, Raymond's concern about his wife falling and knocking loose stones from a ring is somewhat bizarre, and the younger man picks up on that. If Raymond is apprehensive about his wife drinking and falling, potential damage to a piece of jewelry should be the least of his worries. Secondly, Raymond's last statement indicates that Christmas, the occasion for the gift, is a good bit of time away yet. Buying a gift at this point is far from urgent. So what's up with the father character?

When later Ray considers the conversation he had with his dad, he realizes that his dad's real message was subtextual. Raymond is troubled that his wife's drinking has gotten out of hand, and he doesn't know what to do about it. He feels powerless. The entire scene is a cry for help from father to son.

 Do you absolutely need subtext in dialogue? No, not necessarily. Shakespeare never used subtext. He wrote *on the nose:* His scenes and the characters in them are always about precisely what's being said and exactly what's taking place. But Shakespeare had the advantage of being a master of plot and poetry. An advantage you can bring to your work is depth and complexity, both of which can be achieved, in part, through the use of subtext.

Making It Sound Real

With the advent of modern theatre, most playwrights endeavor to write dialogue in the vernacular (common language) of their time. Modern playwrights generally strive for a language that sounds conversational to the ear rather than writing conspicuously poetic and contrived dialogue that calls attention to itself. As with all trends and practices, you can find exceptions, but making dialogue sound like real speech is the goal of most contemporary playwrights.

Nobody speaks Shakespeare

Many students coming to the plays of William Shakespeare for the first time jump to the conclusion that the people England's Elizabethan period spoke the way Shakespeare wrote. Not so. Shakespeare didn't attempt to make his dialogue "real." Playwrights back then were referred to as *poets,* and writing natural-sounding dialogue was not one of their goals. Shakespeare's plays are written in blank verse and much of his phrasing has a poetic turn to it, far from natural speech. So even in Elizabethan England you would not likely hear a potential suicide shouting, "To be or not to be!"

Furthermore, Elizabethans had never heard of many of the words Shakespeare used. Some scholars estimate that Shakespeare introduced into the English language about a tenth of the words he used in his plays, including *accommodation, courtship, assassination, obscene, premeditated, invulnerable, remorseless, majestic,* and *radiance.*

Developing your ear for natural-sounding dialogue

The goal for most playwrights is to make dialogue sound like natural conversation. But because the dialogue you write should be purposeful (as discussed earlier in "Writing Purposeful Dialogue"), your dialogue may not necessarily be what people would actually say. The words you put in the mouths of your characters, although written to sound like conversation, are calculated to reveal character and advance the story. As the playwright, you might experience a tension between writing real language and shaping language as action.

However, you can find a comfortable middle ground. The real/purposeful language tension is resolved by striving not for realism but for *verisimilitude* (having the appearance of being real). Your dialogue is engineered with a purpose but has, for the audience, the appearance and sound of real conversation. One way to accomplish verisimilitude is to listen closely to how real people say and do the things you need your characters to say and do.

As a playwright, you want to make yourself a student of dialogue and expression. Take notes (handwritten or mental) on how people articulate their ideas and on the idioms (expressions) they use. Pay attention not only to what people say, but also to how they say it, particularly when you come across someone with an unusual way of expressing himself.

The great African American playwright August Wilson related to *The Paris Review* his awakening to the process of listening to the specific and individual ways people express themselves:

> *When I first started writing plays I couldn't write good dialogue because I didn't respect how black people talked. I thought that in order to make art out of their dialogue I had to change it, make it into something different. Once I learned to value and respect my characters, I could really hear them. I let them start talking.*

If the idiosyncratic traits of the characters you're creating don't come naturally to you, try to spend time among people who speak, think, and act like the character(s) you want to put on stage. Many actors do this in preparing to play roles, and so should you, the person who creates those roles.

In the opening of George Bernard Shaw's play *Pygmalion* (and in the musical based on that play, *My Fair Lady*), the male lead character, Henry Higgins, is discovered (first revealed to the audience) in London's busy Covent Garden, pad in hand, inconspicuously making notes on the language used by the people there. Higgins is a professor of phonetics, and he's making notes on accents and dialects for future reference.

Emulating this kind of research — paying scrupulous attention to linguistic detail and individual expression — helps you develop your ear for dialogue and create characters that speak and sound like the people you mean them to be.

Giving each character a distinctive voice

While on the subject of how characters express themselves, you need to consider character voice. In the context of playwriting, a character's *voice* is not how the character sounds but what he has to say: his point of view, his philosophical orientation, his psychology, and what he represents to himself and to the world. You can think of a character's voice as his persona.

Give every character in your play a distinct voice. Unless the circumstances of your play somehow require it, no two characters should have identical or even comparable voices, not even identical twins. If you have two characters who think alike, have concurring opinions and beliefs, and who espouse the same world view, you probably have one character too many.

In composing your play, keep in mind you don't need two characters serving the same purpose, particularly in today's theatre environment in which small cast plays are much sought-after. The solution is to delete one of the characters or combine them into one character. You get the best mileage out of your cast if each character represents distinct viewpoints and conflicting objectives.

Handling accents and dialects

When you create characters who hail from different regions of the country or different parts of the world or who speak with accents that reflect the influence of other languages, writing their dialogue isn't much of a problem.

Playwrights used to try to write out accents and dialects phonetically. For example, if a driver was pulled over by an ornery police officer in the South, in the old days the dialogue might have looked something like this:

COP

Now where's da fiah, boy? Dint nobody tell ya it ain't smart ta go speedin' through dis heeuh counteh? Yeuh, you betta be scayud. Mayun, you in a heap a trouble.

This kind of dialogue is challenging to write and sometimes confusing to read. Fortunately, it's not necessary. Actors study accents and dialects as part of their training, and when the director of your play holds auditions, he will make a point of casting an actor who can do a convincing Southern accent, if that's what you need. It ain't necessarly your jahub, mayun.

In short, you don't need to try to capture accents and regional dialects in dialogue. All you need to do is to indicate in the character descriptions on your script's second page, or in stage directions, that your character speaks with a (fill in the blank) accent.

Knowing the audience you're writing for

On some occasions, you may find yourself writing a play for a special audience with narrow interests. In this situation, you want to keep in mind and accommodate the audience your work is intended for. Different audiences bring different types of life experience and varying levels of understanding to the processing and appreciation of material in your play.

If you're writing a play for young children, for instance, use very basic subject matter and vocabulary. Your story line should be straightforward with no subplots or complex characters. With kids, the characters and your story line should be WYSIWYG (what you see is what you get).

On the other hand, if you're writing a play for high school students, you're able to deal with topics that are appropriate for relatively mature audiences. The vocabulary and language you employ can be more sophisticated, and you can layer in subplots and use characters with more complicated motivations.

If you're writing a play for church or temple members, the subject matter needs to conform to the expectations and beliefs of the congregation. Plays with religious themes usually aren't the forum for unorthodox notions and iconoclasm.

Plays for business purposes, like role-play scripts dramatizing the use of sales strategies and tactics, tend to be very, well, businesslike and to the point. I've used humor in writing corporate scripts, but you need to know the temperament of the people you're writing for. Are they conventional, no-nonsense individuals with a low tolerance for material that strays from what's expected? Or are your clients endowed with a sense of humor and willing to look at amusing ways of presenting the material? You need answers to these questions before you begin.

One interesting challenge that comes with writing for specialized audiences is deciding how much background information and fundamental knowledge you need to include in the script to be sure everyone in the audience is up to speed. Can you presume advanced knowledge? You don't want to spend a lot of time dealing with basic salesmanship if you're writing for an audience of sales managers. And neither do you want to work assuming everyone involved knows the basics when maybe they don't. Or, if writing a historical play for a religious group or elementary school, you should find out how familiar the audience is with the material. Do you need to start at square one with the subject matter, or does the intended audience already know the basics of the story? How do you get a handle on these factors? Ask.

Following Key Do's and Don'ts of Dialogue

In writing dialogue, as in any endeavor, you can improve by following tips and guidelines and avoiding counterproductive practices. The following pointers are not intended to be rigid and absolute, but if you lack a good reason to do otherwise, these tried-and-true hints about writing dialogue will be helpful.

Do use the "rule of three" for important info

In plays, there are bits of information crucial to audiences' understanding of the events that follow. Audience members may need to remember that a character has been divorced four times to later understand his reluctance to remarry. Or, in a murder mystery, the audience may need to remain conscious of the fact a gun is in the house so that a character's fear of standing up to the gun's owner makes sense.

If essential set-up information is being communicated in your play or some bit of information spoken in the dialogue has to be understood and remembered, follow *the rule of three*. It simply states that if you're providing the audience with an indispensable bit of information, say it three times. But to avoid obvious repetition, the trick is to communicate the information three different ways. With a little ingenuity, you can mention something three times without drawing distracting attention to it. For example, here's a character named Ralph, from a nonexistent play, in a job interview:

> RALPH
>
> I think I'm very qualified for the supervisor position, Mr. Vernon. I have four college degrees. I have a B.A. in journalism, an M.A. in history, and two doctorates — one in political science and the other in business. I know this might make me sound like a jack of all trades and master of none, but, Mr. Vernon, I like to think of multiple degrees as making me a quadruple threat.

You're not likely to forget during the play that Ralph has four diplomas. He said it three different ways: overtly ("four college degrees"); mathematically, ("a B.A. in journalism, an M.A. in history, and two doctorates"); and synonymicly ("quadruple threat").

In applying the rule of three, the three references you're implanting don't always need to come in the same speech, like they did above. They can be spread out over the course of a scene, but the reinforcement is less effective if they're further apart.

Don't make characters, like, talk perfectly

In life, people seldom speak in perfectly articulated and grammatically correct sentences. More often than not, they, like, make, you know, mistakes, display, eh, hesitation, and don't finish . . . They also often, sometimes anyway, usually repeat ourselves, and speak in incomplete sentences. This kind of imperfect expression, which is unsatisfactory in formal writing, is acceptable and natural in ordinary, everyday conversation. No one expects regular people to always, like, talk right.

Therefore, in composing dialogue that sounds appropriate to the character and natural to the ear — real, in other words — build imperfections and verbal ticks into the lines you write.

Playwright, screenwriter, and director David Mamet is a master at crafting idiosyncratic dialogue that's dead-on for the specific characters he creates. His Tony-nominated, Pulitzer Prize–winning play *Glengarry Glen Ross,* which dramatizes the desperation of Chicago real estate agents trying to sell undesirable property, opens with a monologue that perfectly captures the language imperfection and halting rhythms of everyday speech for this particular character. The opening scene begins with a plaintive appeal by Levene, an older salesman whose career is waning, to his manager, asking for promising sales leads.

LEVENE

John . . . John . . . John. Okay. John. John. Look: *(pause)* The Glengarry Highland's leads, you're sending Roma out. Fine. He's a good man. We know what he is. He's fine. All I'm saying, you look at the *board,* he's throwing . . . wait, wait, wait, he's throwing them *away,* he's throwing the leads away. All that I'm saying, that you're wasting your leads. I don't want to tell you your *job.* All that I'm saying, things get *set,* I know they do, you get a certain *mindset* . . . A guy gets a reputation. We know how this . . . all I'm saying, put a *closer* on the job. There's more than one man for the . . . and you watch, now *wait* a second — and you watch your *dollar* volumes . . . You start closing them for *fifty* 'stead of *twenty-five* . . . you put a closer on the . . .

Heightened by the character's stumbling and repetitious manner of speech, a powerful anxiety oozes from Levene. Mamet's brilliant dialogue defines the character and sets a tone of dysfunction and desperation for the play.

Your ability to write dialogue that suits the character can be cultivated by listening and analyzing and noting the way people speak. Do your homework.

Don't overuse run-of-the-mill clichés

A cliché is a worn-out and unimaginative phrase or idiom commonly used as a convenient, if unoriginal, way of expressing an idea. Common clichés include *raining cats and dogs, like taking candy from a baby, blowing a gasket, sink or swim, what goes around comes around, better late than never, Rome wasn't built in a day, love is blind, like father like son, lie like a rug, dog eat dog, the ball's in your court,* and, yes, *run of the mill.*

People use clichés, knowingly or not, so characters can sound natural using an occasional cliché. And you may want to write a comic character who speaks nothing but clichés. But there's a big difference between intentionally writing clichés into your dialogue and writing clichéd dialogue.

If you find that you're relying on familiar phrases and figures of speech when writing lines for your characters, take the time to explore fresher ways to express the characters' thoughts. Ask yourself: What is my character trying to say, and how would he say it? As much as possible, a character's speech and choice of words should be personal and specific to that character.

Don't wear out character names

When I was a teenager, if I wanted to display superiority over someone, when he called my name I'd disdainfully respond: "Hey, that's my name. Don't wear it out."

At the beginning of a play, the audience needs to know the names of the characters they're watching, especially if later in the play characters not present are referred to by name. You don't want one audience member elbowing another, whispering "Arnold? Who's Arnold again?" Consequently, at the outset of the play, you do want your characters to use each other's names a couple of times to let the audience know who's who. However, in using character names, there can be too much of a good thing.

When it comes to including character names in the dialogue, hey, don't wear them out. When new writers compose dialogue, they have a tendency to overuse the names of the characters. The overrepetition of names becomes obvious and begins to sound funny — unintentionally. Consider this example:

JOHN

Hello, Mary, thanks for coming over.

MARY

Anytime, John. It's always fun to visit with you.

JOHN

Did you bring the Scrabble game, Mary?

MARY

Yes, John, it's in my bag here.

JOHN

Look at the size of that thing. That bag must weigh a ton, Mary.

MARY

It's actually made of lightweight . . . I don't know what it's made of, John, but it's light as a feather.

JOHN

Get the game out, Mary, while I fix us some drinks.

MARY

Not too much scotch in my scotch and soda, John.

JOHN

How long have I been making drinks for you, Mary?

MARY

Right, John, sorry.

By the time an audience gets through something like this, you can bet the farm that there'll be some barely suppressed giggling. The overuse of names by the characters eventually becomes distracting and sounds just plain silly. But look at the same scene with a more judicious use of names.

JOHN

Hello, Mary, thanks for coming over.

MARY

Anytime. It's always fun to visit with you.

JOHN

Did you bring the Scrabble game?

MARY

Yes, John, it's in my bag here.

JOHN

Look at the size of that thing. That bag must weigh a ton.

MARY

It's actually made of lightweight . . . I don't know what it's made of, but it's light as a feather.

JOHN

Get the game out, while I fix us some drinks.

MARY

Not too much scotch in my scotch and soda.

JOHN

How long have I been making drinks for you?

MARY

Right, John, sorry.

Clearly this is a case of "less is more." The dialogue flows more smoothly when the names are used sparingly and more naturally. The inclusion two or so times of each character's name is sufficient to communicate the names, and, most likely, to reinforce them in the minds of audience members.

Don't let lines echo . . . echo . . . echo

What I call *echoing* is the tendency to write a line of dialogue that picks up the last few words of the preceding line. Following are multiple examples:

JOAN

Let's face it. This relationship is over.

PETER

What do you mean the relationship is over? As far as I'm concerned, we've only just begun.

JOAN

Just begun? We've lived together for two years now!

PETER

Two years? It hardly seems like that.

JOAN

What it seems like? You're never here!

PETER

Never here? How can you say that?

JOAN

I can say that because it's true. You've been travelling two out of the last three months.

PETER

Two out of the last three months? You're exaggerating!

JOAN

Exaggerating? You obviously aren't paying attention.

People do often echo each other in conversation, particularly when they're arguing, but what passes unnoticed in everyday conversation can become very noticeable and distracting in dialogue spoken on stage. Echoing can make dialogue sound clumsy, and it can become unintentionally funny. Additionally, echoing bogs down the pace of the dialogue, adding a lot of unnecessary words to your script. Here's the scene without the echoing.

JOAN

Let's face it. This relationship is over.

PETER

As far as I'm concerned, we've only just begun.

JOAN

We've lived together for two years now!

PETER

It hardly seems like that.

JOAN

You're never here!

PETER

How can you say that?

JOAN

You've been travelling two out of the last three months.

PETER

You're exaggerating!

JOAN

You obviously aren't paying attention.

The revised, echoless dialogue has a tautness and fast pace that adds vitality and urgency to the scene. You don't need to worry that, without some echoing, audiences are not going to follow the conversation. Audiences can put the pieces together. Little, if anything, is lost by dropping the echoing.

Do make dialogue alternate between characters

When you converse with someone in real life, you and your companion rarely take turns speaking at length. People tend to speak in short bursts, cutting each other off, speaking over each other, and struggling to get a word in edgewise, either out of enthusiasm or anger.

New playwrights tend to write dialogue that amounts to alternating monologues. This is not the way people ordinarily speak, and the artificiality of long speeches diminishes the naturalism of your lines. For example:

WILLIAM

You used to take me to hockey practice regardless of the hour. When I first started playing, the ice arenas only allowed team practicing in the wee hours. We'd start at something like 2 a.m. and we'd skate until 4 or 4:30. The darned arena had a roof but no sides; open air I guess you'd call it. It'd be freezing out, but we'd be in there skating our little butts off. And, through all this, you'd be sitting in the car outside, running the engine so you wouldn't freeze. Even if you had to go to work in a few hours. I hope I can be as self-sacrificing with my son as you were with me, Dad.

DAD

I remember that all too clearly. Sometimes I think I haven't yet thawed out from huddling up in my car in below freezing temperature. It was cold as a witch's . . . nose outside that skating rink. I used a lot of gas, keeping the car running so that I could have some heat. And the heater in the car, a big boat of an Oldsmobile, didn't work well. My hands and feet would get numb, even with thick boots and heavy gloves on. But, as I sat there miserable, not able to get warm or even to sleep, I felt it was all right. But it was all worth it if it gave you something good to do, a sport to play, and friends to play and hang out with. That was something I never had.

Sitting through a series of long speeches, even if they're well written, tries the patience of audiences. A scene with meaningful content can drag on and on if you're listening to speech after speech.

The solution to this problem is to write lines of dialogue that alternate back and forth from character to character. One character need not wait until the other has finished his speech before saying what he wants to say. Here's a revision of the scene between William and his dad.

WILLIAM

You used to take me to hockey practice regardless of the hour. When I first started playing, the ice arenas only allowed team practicing in the wee hours.

DAD

I remember that all too clearly.

WILLIAM

We'd start at something like 2 a.m. and we'd skate until 4 or 4:30.

DAD

Sometimes I think I haven't yet thawed out from huddling up in my car in below freezing temperature. It was cold as a witch's . . . nose outside that skating rink. I used a lot of gas, keeping the car running so that I could have some heat. And the heater in the car, a big boat of an Oldsmobile, didn't work well.

WILLIAM

The darned arena had a roof but no sides; open air I guess you'd call it. It'd be freezing out, but we'd be in there skating our little butts off.

DAD

My hands and feet would get numb, even with thick boots and heavy gloves on. But, as I sat there miserable, not able to get warm or even to sleep, I felt it was all right.

WILLIAM

And, through all this, you'd be sitting in the car outside, running the engine so you wouldn't freeze. Even if you had to go to work in a few hours.

DAD

But it was all worth it if it gave you something good to do, a sport to play, and friends to play and hang out with. That was something I never had.

WILLIAM

I hope I can be as self-sacrificing with my son as you were with me, Dad.

Despite the lack of conflict in this nostalgic moment, the scene has a more natural dynamic and fluidity that was lacking in the prior version. Even though both of the characters are reminiscing almost in worlds of their own, the dialogue has a feel of interaction, of communication, of reacting to each other that the first version lacks.

Occasionally new playwrights try to avoid the feel of speechifying on the part of one character, say character A, by interspersing lines, like "Go on" or "Tell me more" or "Then what happened?" interjected by character B. Nice try, but no. This kind of clumsy prodding does little to add the feel of conversation to an otherwise dull, one-sided scene.

Do keep your agenda out of the dialogue

You've likely heard the dictum that, in polite social situations, avoiding religion and politics is best. Religion and politics are personal choices, and their principles are usually strongly held. As a result, people can be highly sensitive to perceived or overt criticism of their religious or political beliefs, and unpleasant confrontations can easily ensue.

Theatre, on the other hand, rarely shies away from dealing with divisive issues. In fact, theatre is often on the cutting edge of controversy and social trends. So although you don't need to avoid hot buttons, you do need to know when you're being boorish about it.

If you're not alert, you may raise valid issues and beliefs in a play in an unintentionally intrusive, off-putting, and counterproductive way that feels out of place and distracting. This maladroit presentation of an issue or viewpoint in a play is referred to as "hearing the voice of the playwright." Usually it's not a good thing.

How do you know when you've climbed into your pulpit and are foisting your unvarnished opinions on an unsuspecting theatre audience? The following indicators can help alert you:

- **Restlessness:** When a character in your play launches into a diatribe on a pet issue of yours, watch the audience (preferably in a development reading or workshop rather than in a paid performance of the play). If you see your audience members shifting in their seats or hear a contagious rash of coughing, your audience may have tuned out.

- **Rootlessness:** If the subject of your character's harangue is not rooted in the concept of the play, or if the proffered opinions feel unrelated or only marginally related to the story being enacted, the topic of your character's monologue may feel out of place to the audience. Avoid this theatrical equivalent of "and while I have your attention" and stick to topics that spring from the motivation of the character or from the subject matter of the play.

- **On-the-nose writing:** Another bellwether of superimposed opinion or superfluous politicking is *on-the-nose writing,* in which the character says exactly what he means. If he's directly ladling out his credo with little art or artifice, you may be sermonizing to your audience.

Writing Monologues, Soliloquies, and Asides

Monologues and soliloquies are specialized forms of dialogue that both involve one person speaking. The distinction between a monologue and a soliloquy is blurry sometimes, but they are different. Asides are dialogue addressed directly at the audience. Monologues and asides should be used infrequently and with care, and soliloquies pretty much not at all.

Monologues

A *monologue* is a one-person play or, more commonly, a long stretch of dialogue in a play uttered uninterrupted by one character in the presence of another. In a monologue, the character is talking to himself at length or to another character, seen or unseen by the audience. To put the definition in plain English, a monologue is a one-sided conversation. (Monologues that are a minute or two long are used by actors for auditioning purposes.)

Monologues should be used infrequently, if at all. They are a poor substitute for dialogue and tend to slow the pace of a scene. That being said, your play may have a moment when your character needs to express a hope, dream, or ambition, or relate a meaningful moment, good or bad, in his life. But even with monologues, the rules of dialogue apply:

- ✔ The monologue should be specific to the character.

- ✔ The character should have powerful motivation to share his thoughts.

- ✔ The monologue should be a tactic, conscious or not, by the character to achieve a goal — to impress or seduce or warn or anger (and so on) whomever is listening.

Soliloquies

A *soliloquy* is a speech in a play in which a character is meant to be thinking out loud. The character is usually alone on stage. In a soliloquy, the character speaks his thoughts for no other reason than to let the audience know what he's thinking, so it's probably one of the more unnatural and artificial behaviors a character can engage in. Soliloquies are sometimes compared to talking to yourself, but in life, people who talk to themselves never speak out loud in complete sentences and in well-organized speeches. The thoughts rolling around in your head are precisely that — in your head. You may blurt out a word or two, or even a phrase, but not a whole speech. Soliloquy is a device that's simply unreal.

For Shakespeare, back when acting was about performing (with a capital P) and behavior could be larger than life, soliloquies were a staple. Will's plays are loaded with moments when the characters find themselves alone and orally ruminate on their aspirations and disappointments. Hamlet's "To be or not to be" speech is the classic example. But in our age, when audiences are accustomed to naturalism in plays, soliloquies are rarely used.

Asides

An *aside* is dialogue spoken to the audience, as if the character is taking the spectators into his confidence. It involves breaking the *fourth wall,* the imaginary wall that normally separates the characters onstage from any direct interaction with the audience.

Asides, which can be humorous, ironic, cynical, sarcastic, searching, and so on, allow the speaker to comment on the events taking place in the play. When a character addresses the audience, the other characters on stage either go into a freeze (go motionless) until the lines are concluded or they continue their behavior, unaware that a character is speaking to the audience.

Asides are more likely to be used in comedies than in dramas. Neil Simon uses asides very effectively in some of his comedies.

If you're going to use asides or any other artificial technique, do it early in the play to establish for the audience that this convention will be part of the play. You don't want to get two-thirds of the way through the play and then break the fourth wall. Audiences will be distracted and wonder what's going on.

In playwriting, showing is better than telling. In my observation, new playwrights use asides because they haven't been able to come up with a way to *dramatize* some moment or event, and so they resort to *telling* it to the audience. Try harder. Though asides are not wrong to use, they tend to remind audiences that they are watching a play, inhibiting them from getting fully involved in the story of the play.

Chapter 9

Practical Considerations: Staging, Cast, and Audience

- -

In This Chapter

▶ Writing plays that are doable

▶ Remembering the human factor in creating plays

- -

*P*lays are not movies. Plays are not novels. Although these observations are self-evident, some new playwrights have a surprisingly difficult time thinking theatrically rather than cinematically or novelistically.

Some ideas work best in movies. Film is a visual medium, and it far exceeds other media in depicting physical action, like car chases, explosions, and battles, and in transporting audiences from one exotic locale to another in the blink of an eye, literally. And with the advent of CGI (computer-generated imagery), movie makers can show onscreen virtually anything that can be imagined. Novels can describe large physical actions and activity in real or imagined places. And novels are the best medium for exploring the inner lives and psychology of characters. Novelists (and short story writers) can explicitly tell you what's going on in the hearts and minds of characters.

Stage plays have their advantages, too. Plays are best at depicting intimate stories of people emotionally interacting with other people. While watching a play in a theatre, you become the proverbial fly on the wall, the *fourth wall*. You observe and emotionally engage in the actions of flesh-and-blood human beings mere yards from where you sit. The experience of dramatic events unfolding before your eyes can be much more powerful and personal than events recorded for the screen or related in print. To make a crude comparison, seeing an automobile accident in person is much more affecting than seeing the same incident on a TV news show or reading about it in a newspaper.

The bottom line is that some things can be done well on a stage in a theatre, and some things can't. That being said, in terms of elaborate staging for plays, particularly in musicals, theatre is constantly pushing the envelope. As a playwright, you need to know what's doable and practical in the staging of a play. This chapter explores the realities and practicalities of writing for the stage and looks at some of the issues involved in working with theatre people.

Writing Plays with Staging in Mind

In a series of recollections published in 1624, the poet John Donne wrote the immortal words: "No man is an island, entire of itself, every man is a piece of the continent, a part of the main."

As a playwright, you are not an island. Theatre is, by its nature, a collaborative medium. Before your play is seen by audiences in a theatre, many hands will leave their fingerprints on the work. Your script moves from a play to a project. And many people with different skills — actors, directors, designers, and so on — are necessary to make the project a success. Therefore, if you have the naïvely romantic notion that your vision is the only creative influence to be involved in the production of your play, get over it. As the playwright, you are just one spoke in the wheel.

This section explores the practical side of theatre storytelling: some of the capabilities and limitations of the medium, what you can anticipate and factor into the preparation of your script, and what you can rely on the other inhabitants of the theatre "continent" to do.

Giving minimal stage directions

The script for a play has two primary components: the dialogue (what your characters say, covered in Chapter 8) and stage directions (what the scene looks like and what the characters are physically doing in the scene). On the script page, stage directions have their own left margin, two or two-and-a-half inches in. Interspersed with the dialogue, stage directions, like these from a conference room scene in my play *Journey of the Heart,* should look something like this:

HUNTER

Would you be so kind as to put that thing away?

TOM clicks the recorder off and returns it to his portfolio.

Fine. Linda?

LINDA

Right.

LINDA fumbles through her papers for the agenda. As she conducts the session, she also takes the minutes of the meeting.

Okay. This meeting of the Patient Review and Ethics Committee will come to order. Absent are members Peter Youngman, Betty Hawthorne, Sandra Kushner, Fred Gregory, and Eleanor Ritter.

> HUNTER

Eleanor will be joining us shortly to make a report.

> LINDA

Okay. At this time, the chair wishes to formally introduce . . .

> > LINDA is interrupted by a loud thud at the window. The pickets' chanting increases in volume for a moment. All eyes go to the window.

What was that!?

The stage directions are the indented bits of text. Stage directions should describe only what is physically present or happening onstage so that the director, the actors, and the stagecraft people know what you, the playwright, intend to be happening in the moment. The stage directions in the preceding example specify the clicking off of a tape recorder, Linda fumbling through papers and taking notes, and the thud of a stone thrown at a window of the meeting room.

Stage directions are also used at the beginning of each scene to set the stage for what follows. These stage directions let everyone know what you think the set for the scene should look like and what needs to be there. Consider this example:

> ACT I, Scene 2

> Minutes later, TOM enters a plush and spacious hospital conference room, dominated by a large semi-circular wooden table and nine chairs. The center of the table already is occupied with papers and files. There's also a side table with water pitcher, glasses, and telephone. The room has a window on the fourth wall, suggested by the acting. Speaking on a phone in a corner of the room, his back to the door is DR. HUNTER, who's not aware of TOM's presence. While HUNTER speaks, TOM puts his portfolio on the table, and takes out a pen, pad, and microcassette recorder.

Again, these scene-setting stage directions only describe what can be seen by the audience, what is doable by the actors, and/or what props — files, water pitcher, and telephone — will actually be used by the actors in the scene. In the preceding example, I didn't go further into describing the appearance of the conference room because the set designer will more than likely design a conference room superior to what I might have envisioned. (In every production of this play, I have been impressed by the creativity of the set designers.)

The rule of thumb when you're writing stage directions is to be as concise as possible. If you write too much, you risk falling into the two big traps: micromanaging and cerebralizing.

Micromanaging

The purpose of stage directions is to convey to the director, actors, and stagecraft people (set, lighting, sound, and costume designers, and so on) how you see the set, in general terms, and what happens physically in each scene. Stage directions should be short and to the point. You should restrict physical descriptions of items in the set or of people's appearances to what's relevant and required for the play.

The great American playwright Eugene O'Neill was infamous for his extraordinarily long stage directions. The opening stage directions for his masterpiece play, *Long Day's Journey into Night,* are three (single-spaced) pages long. In describing the home of the Tyrone family in these stage directions, he not only mentions the presence of bookcases — which is perfectly legitimate — but he also specifies the names of the authors of the books on the bookcase shelves — which is way too much detail because audiences won't be able read the spines of the books from their seats. O'Neill also describes Mary, the matriarch of the household, as "a trifle plump." It's not necessary to the play that Mary be any kind of plump. In fact, the great actress Katherine Hepburn played Mary in a film version of the play, and she was as thin as a rail.

On the other hand, if a character needs to speak with an Italian accent because he's recently from Italy and his heavy accent prevents him from moving freely in upper-crust New York society, then the stage directions do need to mention the accent. That detail impacts the play. But don't specify that a character is a blonde when it really doesn't make any difference to the play what her hair color is.

In other words, don't micromanage. Give your director, actors, and stagecraft professionals room to exercise their creativity. I have almost always been pleasantly surprised by the ideas and creativity brought to my plays by perceptive directors, actors, and stagecraft people. Their contributions to the production of my plays usually have been more exciting than anything I imagined. By not writing trivial details into your stage directions, you create an atmosphere in which your production colleagues feel welcome to do their magic. And if you write too much unnecessary detail into your stage directions, you run the risk of being ignored.

Cerebralizing

Some new playwrights write into their stage directions not only what characters are doing but what characters are thinking. For instance:

DAVID

What the . . . ?

> DAVID takes a gun out of the cabinet drawer and examines it. He wonders whose it is and how it got there. It reminds him of the pistol he used when he was in the Army. There's a knock at the door. DAVID quickly returns the gun to the drawer and closes the drawer. He steps away from the cabinet as CELIA enters.

The second and third sentence of the stage directions above — *He wonders whose it is and how it got there. It reminds him of the pistol he used when he was in the Army* — do not belong in stage directions. They describe what the character is *thinking* rather than doing, which I refer to as *cerebralizing* in stage directions. If you want the audience to know what a character in a play is thinking, the character either needs to either say what she's thinking or she needs to do something physically that demonstrates her thoughts. Audience members don't have the script in their hands and, therefore, can't benefit from what you put in the stage directions.

If you're tempted to cerebralize in your stage directions so that your actor will know what the character should be thinking at any given moment, don't. What the actor knows doesn't matter; what the actor is able to communicate to the audience by dialogue or by some physical activity is what counts. For example, the quick shutting of the drawer and movement away from the cabinet in the stage directions above clearly indicate that David doesn't want to be seen looking at the gun. The action speaks for itself.

Going easy on those special effects

Special effects are really the province and specialty of movies. From the stop-motion animation of an ape puppet for the film *King Kong* in the 1930s to the computer-generated race of blue beings in *Avatar,* film can do things and go places that are impossible to recreate on the stage for a live audience.

As a playwright, it's important for you to understand that when it comes to special effects, comparatively little can be done in a realistic manner onstage, and even then not without a level of expense that can be problematic. Even a simple effect, like breaking a glass or bottle, necessitates the use of special safe breakaway bottles that cost around $10 apiece. This one special effect in a two-week run can cost around $200 or more. What you write into your play can have a heavy bearing on whether or not a theatre feels your play is practical and affordable to produce.

One of the earliest theatrical special effects, believe it or not, was flying. In ancient Greece, some plays ended with the appearance of a god who solved all problems and put everything back in order. The actor playing the god was lowered by a crane into the stage area, thus simulating the deity's arrival from the heavens. (Incidentally, this special effect is the origin of the storytelling term *deus ex machina,* "god from a machine." A *deus ex machina* ending is one in which someone or something comes out of nowhere to save the day. Today, such endings are considered violations of good story structure.)

More than a century ago, a stage carpenter named George Kirby invented a practical and safe mechanism that enabled Peter Pan to fly in the first stage adaptation of the J. M. Barrie story. But making characters fly still isn't easy.

The difficulty and expense in staging convincing special effects in a theatre are illustrated by the technical problems that plagued the spectacular Broadway show *Spiderman: Turn Off the Dark.* A flying stunt actor fell during a performance of the musical and suffered serious injuries. Even with a reported budget of $60 or $65 million, the production staff struggled to make characters fly and fight safely while high over the heads of audiences.

Helping the director help you

For most of recorded theatre history, the production of plays involved little more than a script, actors, costumes, and a painted backdrop. Plays were recited more than acted. Any coordination the production needed fell to either by the playwright, the company manager, or an actor-manager. No one called a director was anywhere in sight.

In the late 1800s and early 1900s, theatre became more complex. Plays became more naturalistic (true to real life), tending to deal with everyday people and real-life issues rather than nobility and high society. Acting styles became more realistic, and actors needed coaching to develop and coordinate convincing performances. Sets became more detailed, with furniture and props, making set changes more complicated than the old painted backdrops. Technological advances, like electric theatre lighting and sound, were thrown into the mix. Staging a play had become a logistical nightmare.

Necessity being the mother of invention, enter the director. The director takes on the responsibility of coordinating all the elements of a theatre production. But in addition to being a traffic cop, the director brings a unifying vision to a production. She studies the script and brings together all the necessary pieces to stage the show as she sees it. The director also works with the cast to achieve a higher level of performance.

When you write a play, you can help the director and yourself by being cognizant of stage realities and practicalities. No matter how you see your story played out in your head, you need to remember that actors are not playing pieces on a chessboard to be moved about at will. Actors are human beings who need adequate time and space to do what's required.

When writing scenes, consider the director's perspective. If you're writing a stage adaptation of *The Three Musketeers,* for example, it might occur to you that, during a sword-fighting duel, having one of the combatants swinging across the stage on a rope would be a terrific moment. Is that stunt possible? Yes, but what may sound to you like a simple bit of staging could actually be very complicated and, what's worse, dangerous. On top of having to cast an actor who's willing and capable of doing such a stunt, the director would need to coordinate the efforts of the actor, set designer, and the rest of the cast onstage to avoid putting the brave thespian, or anyone else, in the hospital.

Upstage, downstage

The compass of a stage is simple. Like the four primary directions of a navigational compass — north, south, east, and west — actors on a stage can travel in four primary directions.

When visualizing (and writing stage directions for) the navigation of the stage by actors, the first and most important concept is that stage direction is reckoned from the actor's point of view, not the audience's.

An analysis of the playing area of a theatre begins at center stage, which is literally what it says — the center of the stage. Think of yourself as the actor standing exactly in the middle of the stage *facing the audience.* You are center stage. Following are the options for movement (as shown in Figure 9-1):

- **Downstage:** When you step toward the audience, you're heading *downstage.*
- **Stage right:** When you move to your right, toward one of the wings, you're moving *stage right.*

✔ **Stage left:** When you move to your left — toward the opposite wing — you're moving *stage left*.

✔ **Upstage:** When you turn your back and move away from the audience, you're heading *upstage*.

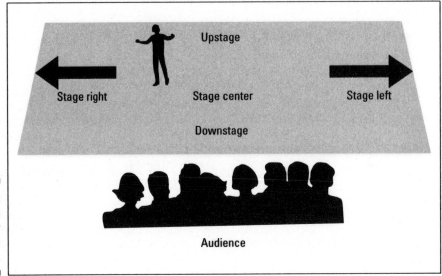

Figure 9-1: Navigating your way around the stage.

Setting up sets and props

The complexity of sets for a play ranges from a bare stage with maybe only a table and chair to the construction of an almost move-in ready home. The first play I ever saw was a production of *The Miracle Worker* done at my high school. For the show, the school stage crew built a two-story house onstage, complete with a porch, dining room, and upstairs bedrooms. And all that for just three performances on one weekend!

One of the inexplicable miracles of theatre is that audiences usually accept a bare-bones set as willingly as they do a three-sided McMansion. Put out two chairs side by side and two more chairs side by side behind the first two, and — voilà! — you have car. Few audience members question this. Unlike moviegoers and TV viewers, theatre patrons don't expect realistic detail; for your audience, the play's the thing . . . not the set.

Props, short for properties, are items an actor can pick up and use during a performance. The list of props for a show set in a living room may include ashtrays, a cigarette lighter, bottles of booze, drinking glasses and coasters, magazines, a TV remote control, someone's hat and gloves, or a pile of books — whatever the director, set designer, and prop master (or mistress) think the script calls for. Personal props are items actors carry on their persons, like watches, a pack of cigarettes, a wallet with money, a pistol, and so on.

The dividing line between what's a prop and what's part of the set varies from show to show and with the size of the theatre. In some productions, the set designer may also be responsible for the props. In a large, well-budgeted production, a prop master is a separate job.

Who determines how elaborate your set is? The following elements help shape your set and prop needs:

- ✔ **The script:** If you write a naturalistic play that takes place, for example, in the living room of a suburban home, your set is probably going to need the furniture that's common to such rooms — a sofa, end tables, coffee table, lamps, rug, TV, bookcases/shelves, hung paintings, windows with curtains, and so on — all to create a sense of realism for your play.

- ✔ **The genre of the play and the concept of the director:** The type of play and director's style can influence the degree to which you dress the set. Some plays require minimal sets or no sets and few props, like the American classic *Our Town,* by Thornton Wilder. And some directors prefer sets that are stripped down to the essentials. It's important that you and your director get in sync when it comes to the production values of your play.

- ✔ **Your budget:** How elaborate you're able to get may simply depend on how much money you have to spend on stagecraft staff and materials.

With producers clearly leaning toward plays with fewer actors and modest production values (the staging elements), you enhance your chances of getting your play done by keeping the production requirements simple. If you can manage to limit your entire play to one set in one place — an army barracks or a honeymoon suite or a cabin aboard a cruise ship, whatever — you're well ahead in the game. By doing so, you eliminate the need for set changes between acts and scenes, and, consequently, keep down the cost of the set.

The second best bet is to envision a set in which you can change scenes (locations) by moving in and out only a few set pieces. This is called the *unit set.* Recently I saw a production of *Cactus Flower* in New York City. The permanent portion of the set consisted of wood paneling on the upstage wall, which included doors and windows. When a small bed was put onstage, the room became a character's bedroom; when, between scenes, the bed was replaced with a desk, the space became a dentist's waiting room; and, when the desk was removed and a couple of padded benches were set down, the characters were in a bar.

Recognizing the Human Factor

In writing plays, you have to take into consideration a number of issues inherent in live performance. In this section, I explore the real-time nature of play performances; discuss how to deal with costume changes, naughty language, and nudity onstage; and suggest when to factor in time for audience response.

Whatever you envision your characters doing — singing, dancing, or performing a full-length monologue — avoid asking your actors to do anything that pushes them to engage in unhealthful, hazardous, or counterproductive activities. The show must go on, but not at the risk of permanently injuring an actor.

Working in real time

Because plays are performed live in front of a live audience, time onstage is the same as time for the audience. In other words, two hours of stage time equal two hours of "real" time.

One of the best examples of this is the play *Twelve Angry Men*. In the play, twelve jurors deliberate for close to two hours over the guilt or innocence of a young man accused of murdering his father. The time the jurors spend working to arrive at a verdict consumes close to two hours of the audience's time.

In a play, actions need to take approximately as much time to happen as they do in real life. Sometimes new playwrights don't allow adequate time for things to happen. For example, a husband and wife are home, and the husband tells his wife he's going for pizza and exits the stage. The couple's son enters and spends the next three minutes telling mom why he refuses to go to college. The front door opens, and hubby enters with a piping hot pizza. What's wrong with this picture? In real life, a person can't suddenly decide he wants pizza, hop in the car, purchase a freshly baked pie, and drive back in the space of three minutes. A trip like that would take at least 20 minutes.

So how do you handle actions that take too much time to show? The simplest way is to end the scene. The change of scene, similar to a cut in a movie, can indicate that time has passed. In the pizza example, you end the scene after the wife's chat with her son. The stage lights go out or maybe just dim, and a few moments later they go up again, marking the beginning of a new scene. The door opens, and in comes hubby with the piping hot pie.

If you don't allow appropriate amounts of time for things to happen in your play, it can be distracting. Audience members will whisper to each other about the impossibility. Or, worse, they will find it funny and laugh when you don't want the audience to be laughing.

Allowing for human limitations

I learned to appreciate the human factor in playwriting with my play *The Devil's Music: The Life and Blues of Bessie Smith.* In writing the script, I alternated stretches of Bessie's dialogue with 14 of the songs Bessie Smith made famous. What I didn't take into consideration was the strain 80 minutes of almost nonstop talking and singing would put on the vocal chords of the performer. Our actor was onstage for the entire show. Eight performances a week!

The director and I suggested dropping a song or two to alleviate some of the strain, but the actor playing Bessie wouldn't hear of it. She had embraced the show as it was, and very few actors willingly give up stage time; she gamely played the devil out of the role to standing ovations every show. Inevitably, after one stretch of performances, her voice gave out, and the director and I had no alternative but to tell the producer we needed to cancel a couple of performances. The producer was not a happy puppy.

After some rest and TLC, the actor returned and resumed performances. Our production and the actor almost suffered a major disaster because I hadn't considered the human factor in so demanding a performance.

Allowing time for costume changes

If your play involves scenes taking place on different occasions, the actors are probably going to need costume changes. Costume changes can involve something as simple as changing clothes, or they can include makeup changes if, for example, a character has a black eye in one scene and is healed in the next scene. If an actor tends to perspire a lot under hot stage lights, he might need a moment to wash his face. Whatever the costume changes involve, they require some amount of time.

For example, suppose your actors are in a scene set in a garden, and they're weeding in T-shirts and jeans. If the next scene calls for those same actors to be in formal clothing at a wedding, the actors are going to need time to exit the stage, get to the dressing rooms, change costumes, and get back onstage. This necessity is obvious when you think about it, but you do have to think about it.

Therefore, you have to plan your scenes so that the costume change has time to happen. Using the weeding/wedding example, you can construct the scene so that one of the two actors exits a few minutes before the scene ends. That actor then is able to change and enter the next scene at the start while the second actor changes quickly, coming onstage a few minutes later.

The last thing you want is to have your audience sitting in front of a darkened stage waiting who knows how long for the next scene to begin. It interrupts the flow of the story. It also takes audiences right out of the play; they're reminded that they're in a theatre, it's almost time for the intermission, they have a phone call to make, they're hungry, and so forth. Not what you want your audience to be thinking about.

Using naughty language and nudity

In life, people use bad language and people sometimes get naked. Profanity and nude scenes also happen all the time in film. But what about theatre? Are these things okay to do in a stage play? Yes, but very carefully.

Profanity

I wrote an award-winning play, *The Slope,* in which the male lead utters a four-letter word a half dozen times in the first minute or so of the play. Years ago, in planning a public reading of that play at a public library, I wondered whether the language might be inappropriate for library patrons. I explained the situation to the library director, a lovely woman on the verge of retirement, and she responded: "What do you think we hear when we're out in the street?" The reading went off without a hitch.

Bad language — meaning swear words, not poor syntax — can be offensive. So first of all, if you're going to use four-letter or other wicked words, do so if that manner of speech is true and natural to your character. In my play, the male lead is a construction worker and has a potty mouth; for him to use words like *darn, heck,* and *shucks* would have been laughable.

Secondly, if you're going to use profanity, do it early. The fact that my character in *The Slope* cusses a blue streak at the beginning of the play essentially tells the audience: This character is going to talk like this, so get used to it. And in the vast majority of cases, audiences do get used to it — at least for the duration of the play. Introducing toilet talk late in a play is more jarring to the unsuspecting audience and, what's worse, potentially distracting because it comes without warning. The last thing you want your audience focusing on as your play approaches its climactic moment is the disconcerting use of off-color language.

Nudity

Nudity is a whole 'nother ballgame. Nudity onstage is much more shocking than it is in movies. In movies, you're not looking at naked people but at a recorded image of naked people. That degree of distance is enough to put most people at relative ease with actors playing scenes in the buff.

However, in theatre, when actors get naked, they're real people getting naked right in front of the audience. Even people who aren't particularly uncomfortable with nakedness in life can be disturbed or embarrassed by the appearance of nude actors onstage.

The key to getting away with nudity is to establish early in the play that nudity will occur. In the grim and powerful play *Beirut,* by Alan Bowne, the characters spend much of the play naked or semi-naked. But the nakedness takes place immediately, establishing right upfront that you're gonna be seeing a lot of skin; get used to it or go home. Most people choose to brave the onslaught of bare flesh and naughty bits . . . for art's sake.

Whenever you push the boundaries, there is a potential price to pay. The major danger with nudity is that it can take over your play. Audience members can begin thinking about the "poor actor" who has to take her clothes off. "Does that bother him?" "How does she not get embarrassed?" "Does his mother know about this?" All these thoughts can be rolling around in the heads of audience members, effectively taking their minds off the story you're trying to tell.

If you write a play in which the actors need to take off their clothes, that information needs to be in the casting announcement. Actors should be warned upfront (no pun intended) so they can make a no-pressure decision as to whether they want to audition for the role or not. You don't want to put yourself in the position of going through the time and effort involved in auditioning only to find yourself at the end of the process saying, "Oh, by the way . . ." In such a situation, if your actor decides nudity is not for her, both you and she will have put in a lot of time for nothing.

Considering the audience as participant

Theatre is symbiotic. The play impacts the audience, and the audience impacts the play. Because a movie is permanently recorded, a presentation of a film is unaffected by what goes on in the audience, from snoozing to rioting. But live theatre is very different in that respect. Actors are human beings like the rest of us, and in a live stage performance, their work can be influenced by the reactions of audiences. The most obvious example is laughter in a comedy.

Actors are trained to achieve a high level of "privacy" in performing. That means an actor learns to think and behave as if he is alone in the room (or whatever the play's location is) or only with the other characters onstage at the time. In other words, actors block out the audience, visualizing a *fourth wall* between themselves and the audience. (Learning to concern themselves only with what's happening onstage is what enables actors to do nude scenes without crippling embarrassment.)

With comedy, however, actors walk a fine line, because the audience reaction impacts the timing of the actors' performances. On one hand, they need to be "private" and put out of their minds everything except the activity onstage. On the other hand, they do need to be aware of the laughter. An actor doing a Neil Simon play, for instance, needs to wait until the audience stops laughing before continuing on with her next line. If she acts as if there's no audience, she will deliver her next line while the audience is still laughing and the line won't be heard.

If you're writing a comedy, consider building into your dialogue a *throwaway line* immediately after a laugh line. A throwaway line is line of dialogue that is relatively unimportant and can be missed by the audience without harming the play. This strategy protects you from an anxious actor who continues his dialogue even though the audience hasn't finished laughing at the laugh line.

Actors inevitably pick up on the energy of an audience, especially in comedies. If the audience is low-energy and minimally responsive — mama told us there'd be days like that — the actors onstage sense it, even though they try to be private, and it can drive down the actors' energy. The opposite is true, too. A highly energized and enthusiastic audience can electrify a cast into a sparkling performance. A maxim in theatre is that no two performances are exactly alike, and the audience can be large factor in that variability.

As a playwright, avoid judging the success of any given performance of your play by the audience's reaction. At one performance of my play *Casino,* the audience was virtually silent throughout; the comedic lines got no laughter and the dramatic moments got no visible reaction whatsoever. I was mortified, sure that the audience was hating the experience. However, at the very end of that particular performance, the audience literally gave a huge, audible, collective exhale. Clearly the audience had been emotionally involved in the performance, and the suspense of the play's ending had caused the audience members to hold their breath. If you shouldn't judge a book by its cover, I learned that you shouldn't judge an audience's involvement only by what you can see and hear. So even if you don't hear or see the audience's reaction to your play, don't fret; they might still be very much, if less visibly, involved in the play.

Part III

The Nuts and Bolts of Putting Your Story Together

The 5th Wave   By Rich Tennant

"I'm not saying your play is too long, but maybe you could consolidate Acts 51 and 52."

In this part . . .

Plays have a beginning, a middle, and an end. You
may find that fact obvious, but what's less clear is
that each of these sections has particular necessities and
performs specific functions. This part explores how to
maximize the impact of each section of your play. You
find out how to get your plot and protagonist in motion,
how to provide obstacles and challenges for your main
character, how to bring the story to a final confrontation
between the protagonist and the antagonist, and, finally,
how to convey what the world of your play looks like after
all is said and done.

Chapter 10

The Beginning: Finding a Starting Point for Your Play

In This Chapter

▶ Planning your play

▶ Deciding where to begin

▶ Identifying the event that motivates your main character

▶ Providing the background info the audience needs to know

▶ Checking out how some famous plays begin

*B*eing the author of a story is as close to being a supreme being as you can get. You create a world as you see it, and you populate it with people of your own design. The world you create can be very much, for better or worse, like the one we inhabit. It can be anything from the nostalgic, early-20th-century American community of Grover's Corners in Thornton Wilder's *Our Town* to the fantastical Neverland, J. M. Barrie's island of lost boys led by a flying Peter Pan and crawling with inept pirates, Indians, and a crocodile whose internal clock is ticking. The people you create — characters — can be as normal and everyday as the collection of nameless men who comprise the jury in *Twelve Angry Men* or as outlandish as the extraordinary murderous barber of Fleet Street, London, Sweeney Todd.

This chapter surveys the preliminary steps involved in preparing to write about the world you create. When beginning a play, you have to decide where you start (the point of attack) and what fires up the protagonist (the inciting incident). In this chapter, you also see how to write exposition that unobtrusively gets your audience up to speed on past events (backstory), information necessary for the audience to know to understand what's happening. For example, in *Peter Pan,* the audience wants to know how the clock got into the belly of the crocodile. In this chapter, you find out how to use skillful exposition to convey such info in a seemingly natural way. The beginning of your play is crucial. By making strong and practical choices, you can entice, intrigue, and engage the audience quickly, getting your play off to a robust start.

Laying the Foundation Before Pen Hits Paper

To begin a project, some writers pick up a pen or sit at a keyboard and just begin to write whatever comes to them. If nothing comes to them, then they write that nothing is coming to them. Other writers tend to be a bit more planned and organized when they start a new play. They like to have a more-or-less clear picture of who their primary characters are, where the story is taking place, what the thrust of the story is, and what the climactic scene could be like.

These playwrights don't expect to know everything that they will eventually set down. Part of the excitement of writing is making little discoveries and having brainstorms along the way. It's like planning a cross-country drive. You decide where you're departing from, say New York City, and where you plan to end up, Los Angeles, and you may pick out a few stops, like the Grand Canyon, but the rest of it you intend to play it by ear. Setting some definite points along the way helps ensure you don't miss important landmarks in your play.

Even playwrights who tightly plan their work should give themselves permission — more than that, *encourage* themselves — to change the plan as they go along. Being rigid is counterproductive to the creative process, so don't chisel your plan in stone. Many a play has been enriched by a happy accident or unanticipated inspiration that the author, open to new ideas, embraced.

This section covers some of the signposts on the playwriting journey, some fundamental aspects of the plan you may consider before setting pen to paper or tapping that first key.

Getting the characters into the crosshairs

As you enter the world of the play, you should know well the people you will put there. You should know and understand your characters at least as well as you know and understand your best friends.

In Chapter 7, I suggest that you write mini-biographies of your characters, particularly your main characters. For each character, ask yourself questions like: What is his work? What are his relationships? What are his beliefs, values, ethics at peace and under pressure? Also be sure you know what motivates your characters and what's at stake for them if they succeed or fail. Know the lengths to which your characters will go to achieve their goals. The discipline involved in thinking through these details pays off in an intimate knowledge of your characters. Knowing your characters intimately means you can anticipate what your characters will do under the circumstances of the play, and that knowledge makes creating scenes much easier.

Be sure you clearly identify your protagonist, antagonist, and other primary characters. (See Chapter 6 for help determining who the protagonist and antagonist are.) Before you start writing is a good time to be sure that you're creating as few characters as possible. Like it or not, today the smaller the cast is, the better. Small casts improve your odds of having your play produced, so ask yourself whom you absolutely need to tell the story. And then axe the superfluous characters.

Using the setting as a character

A very important tool in playwriting that's often overlooked by new playwrights is the setting of the play. Where your play takes place, and what the conditions are in that setting, can powerfully influence what your characters say and do. Your setting can be as important as any character in your play.

Select a setting and conditions for your play that enrich and energize your scene. Make the choice that presents another obstacle to your protagonist. Don't overlook the power and influence location can have in the dynamic of a scene. For example, a scene involving a couple ending their relationship in an apartment will play out very differently if that same scene is set in a restaurant. The privacy of one venue versus the public nature of the other impacts differently the behavior of the characters. People are more likely to have a huge and dramatic breakdown in private than in public. (Not coincidentally, this is one of the reasons relationship breakups and job firings often take place in restaurants.)

And don't neglect climatic conditions. On a hot, still, sticky summer night, people are more likely to lose their cool and resort to violence than they would on a breezy and comfortable day. Heat and humidity tend to sap people of their patience. A confrontation between characters on an uncomfortable night very likely will play out differently than that same confrontation on a cool and comfortable day.

Identifying the essential moments

As you get ready to get started on your play, identify the essential moments of your play by picking out the inciting incident, climax, and resolution. If you can do this, then the challenge in the writing becomes connecting the dots of your story from one milestone to another.

Inciting incident

Know the inciting incident (also called the *precipitating event*) of your play: the event or incident that sets the plot of your play in motion. It usually occurs just after your play begins. I go into the inciting incident in greater detail in the section "Firing the Starting Gun: The Inciting Incident" later in this chapter.

Climax

Have as good an idea as possible what your climactic moment will be. The climax of your story is when your two opposing forces meet in a final confrontation. Your protagonist and your antagonist come up against each other, and only one can emerge victorious, after which the plot is concluded. For example, in *Twelve Angry Men,* the climactic moment occurs with the last juror voting guilty, Juror #3 (the antagonist), who's been hanging on to his guilty vote against the other 11 jurors, led by Juror #8 (the protagonist), finally breaks down. He realizes that his opinion in the case had been skewed by personal family issues. (For a full explanation of creating the climax of your story, turn to Chapter 12.)

Resolution

See if you can envision the resolution of your play, what the landscape of your play looks like after the climactic moment. What does the new world of the characters turn out to be? How has the dust settled? For example, in the resolution of the play *Twelve Angry Men,* the jurors file out of the jury room to report their unanimous "not guilty" verdict. As a result of their deliberations and decision, a young man, very likely innocent of the murder of his father, will be set free. (You can find additional coverage of the resolution element of your play in Chapter 13.)

Putting subplots to work

A *subplot* is a relatively self-contained secondary story within the main story that impacts the main story. Subplots should have their own beginnings, middles, and ends, and they are generally resolved before the main plot comes to its conclusion. Subplots can serve the following purposes:

✔ **Subplots can enrich the main story, adding depth and complexity by showing other aspects of the characters' personalities or additional complications and consequences of the main plot.** In *Hamlet,* one of the subplots is Hamlet's relationship with Ophelia. The affection Hamlet has for Ophelia shows his softer side — until he concludes she's been sent by her father, Polonius, to spy on him. Hamlet's resulting rejection of Ophelia puts her into a funk so deep she loses her mind and accidentally drowns. The death of Ophelia, in turn, further fuels Hamlet's anger and resolve to kill his father's murderer, King Claudius, which is the main plot.

✔ **Subplots can clarify or heighten the stakes for the protagonist.** The protagonist should have a great deal to gain or lose as a result of fulfilling or failing at his mission. Subplots can emphasize the stakes. In *A Streetcar Named Desire,* the budding romantic relationship between the fragile protagonist, Blanche DuBois, and Stanley's inexperienced and naïve buddy, Mitch, seems to offer the possibility that Blanche may find peace, if not happiness, after all. But Blanche's shameful past and Stanley's enmity combine to sabotage the relationship, delivering yet another blow to Blanche's eroded psyche. It intensifies her desperation to find safety somewhere, which is Blanche's main story line.

✔ **Subplots can provide a break from the intensity and heavy drama of the main plot.** This break can be in the form of a light-hearted moment, sometimes referred to as *comic relief.* Or it can simply be a distraction that allows the audience to catch its breath. In *A Raisin in the Sun,* Walter Lee's sister, Beneatha, is being romantically pursued by Joseph Asagai, a well-to-do college student from Nigeria. Asagai gives Beneatha a colorful Nigeria shawl-type robe. Excitedly, Beneatha struggles awkwardly to drape and wear it correctly, providing a moment of levity and warmth in the otherwise dramatic play.

✔ **Subplots also can be used to illustrate and reinforce the play's themes.** For example, in *Raisin,* Walter Lee is desperate to free himself from his job as chauffer for a white man, a job he sees as servile. His attitude reinforces one of the play's themes: that many blacks feel that their lives and fortunes are governed the whims and dictates of the white majority.

One-act plays necessarily don't have subplots; a play that's only 15 or 30 minutes long really doesn't have enough time to set up and develop side stories. And as theatre's taste for shorter full-length plays grows, the extensive use of subplots may shrink accordingly.

Creating an outline

Outlining is a smart practice that produces an invaluable tool. Outlining is a good habit to get into, particularly at the beginning of your playwriting life.

What constitutes an outline of a story varies. Generally speaking, it's a plan or a roadmap created to guide you from your departure point to your destination — from the opening of your play to its conclusion. An outline can be a prose summary of the story or a list of points, in story order, that you will be incorporating into the play. Whatever form an outline takes for you, it's a tool that can keep you focused, on track, and productive. Another advantage of outlining is that it ultimately saves many more hours, even days, down the road when you're not pacing the floor, drumming your fingers, or otherwise driving yourself crazy trying to figure out what happens in the next scene.

Some writers shun outlining because they feel it locks their thinking onto a predetermined and inflexible route, but you always have the freedom to make changes as you go along. Other writers protest that, for them, part of the joy of writing is to simply write — literary free association — and see where the writing takes them. However, I caution that those writers may find that their meanderings have led them nowhere (or nowhere productive). Having an outline available is at least a good backup. You can refer to it if you need it or ignore it if you don't. In addition, writing a play is much more fun when you don't have a lot of anxiety over what's in the next scene.

Deciding Where to Start Your Play: The Point of Attack

The first important decision you make in the actual writing of your play is where to have it begin. Beginnings are critical. If you're writing a news story, the most important paragraph you write is the lead paragraph, the first paragraph. Reporters and editors know, if you don't grab readers in that first paragraph, you've lost 'em. In a novel, if the author doesn't intrigue the reader in the first chapter, chances are the reader will put the book aside forever. And moviemakers have long been aware that the first few minutes of a film are crucial in capturing the attention and interest of the moviegoer.

The most important consideration in deciding where you start your story — where it is that you admit the audience — is audience engagement. What part of the story will best draw audience members in? Where in your tale will they most effectively be hooked?

Deciding where to start your play is not as simple a question as it may seem. As you no doubt have surmised, the answer is not "at the beginning." If you look at your story as a continuum from point A to point Z, you don't always need to start telling your story at point A. In fact, it's not much of a stretch to say you should *not* start your play at point A.

Most often, the early events of your story line simply set up the situation of the play, but it's not critical that the audience *see* these occurrences. By relegating early events to backstory (which can later be revealed through exposition), you can start your play closer to the crucial action. This approach gets your play off to a running start and will engage your audience more quickly and thoroughly.

An important playwriting rule of thumb: Start your play as far into the story as possible. Starting your play in the midst of events already taking place has the major advantage of hooking the audience. Audiences are drawn into activity and a story that's underway. Curiosity is aroused: What's happening, why, and how did it start?

Imagine that you're walking down a city street and a man runs past you in the opposite direction. What do you do? Most likely you stop, turn, and watch the figure recede from sight. You also probably look in the direction from which the man came. Is he being chased? You wonder who he was and why he was running. In point of fact, you're asking yourself, "What's the story?" After all, humans are a curious species. Similarly, when an audience is brought into a story that's already in progress, they naturally wonder what's going on and who's involved. Starting in the middle of things also has the advantage of saving time. If you tell the story from the very beginning, the play will be longer but not necessarily any better.

Consider the events of your story (or look at your outline) as you envision the play. Try to identify the point in your story that will grip your audience, and see if your play can start there, as close to the middle of things as possible. What you're looking for is your point of attack.

The term for the place the playwright chooses to start his play is the *point of attack* (not to be confused, as it too often is, with the inciting incident, which is covered in the following section). The point of attack is the place in the story where the curtain rises (or the lights go up) on the stage. Following are some examples of points of attack:

- ✔ The point of attack in *A Streetcar Named Desire* shows Stanley Kowalski coming home from work, tossing to his wife, Stella, a package of meat from the butcher, and then heading off with his friend, Mitch, to the local bowling alley. These few moments introduce us to the world of the play.

- ✔ In *Twelve Angry Men,* as the lights come up, the audience hears the voice of the judge giving the jury final instructions and sees the jurors filing into the jury room. The moments between the point of attack and the inciting incident (defined in the next section) gives the audience the opportunity to get the lay of the land, to realize that this is a murder trial and the defendant is accused of killing his father.

The objective is to select a point of attack that brings the audience right into the action, a point as close to the inciting incident as possible.

Firing the Starting Gun: The Inciting Incident

One of the most interesting moments in the structuring of your story is crafting the *inciting incident.* Also referred to as the *precipitating event,* the inciting incident is the event in the play that ignites the plot of your story. It's the thing that happens that launches your protagonist on his urgent mission or quest. It creates or reveals something that must be accomplished or remedied. For example, the inciting event in *The Miracle Worker* is the arrival of Annie Sullivan, the young woman hired by the overly protective Keller family to tutor their unruly young girl, Helen, who has been deaf and blind almost from birth. Will Annie be given the freedom to do her work? Will she be able to do something with this wild child?

Because the inciting incident is what sets the plot in motion, it almost always occurs just following the point of attack, meaning just after the beginning of the play. The fact that there are exceptions to every rule is illustrated by *A Raisin in the Sun,* a play in which the inciting incident occurs offstage and before the point of attack (before the play begins). The inciting incident in Lorraine Hansberry's play is the death of the family patriarch and the resulting large life insurance check that's coming to the Younger family by mail. When the curtain rises, the family is already in conflict over what to do with this huge amount of money that's on the way.

The point of attack of a play brings the audience into the world of the play — be it a big city courtroom or the walls of Hamlet's Elsinore Castle. When the audience is admitted to the story, usually this world is at rest. The situation in the landscape of the play is relatively normal. All is going on pretty much as usual. Then something dramatic — the inciting incident — happens that disturbs this world.

Upsetting the status quo

Like an earthquake or tsunami, a sudden, life-changing event occurs in your play. Nothing can be the same. The event — the inciting incident — creates an urgent problem or challenge that upsets the status quo. It must be addressed. A new status quo must be attained.

- ✔ In Shakespeare's *Romeo and Juliet,* the inciting incident is the meeting of Romeo and Juliet. Romeo falls in love at first sight, and his world is shaken. He needs to make Juliet his own. That is his mission, and he can't rest until he has succeeded by establishing a life with Juliet which would result in a new status quo.

- ✔ Identifying the inciting incident in *The Wizard of Oz* is a snap — it's the arrival of the tornado. The tornado blows into the life of Dorothy Gale, literally upsetting her world, disturbing the status quo, and depositing Dorothy and her dog in the fantastical land of Oz. A stranger in a strange land, Dorothy's quest becomes to find her way home, and, somewhat wiser, get back to her normal life — a new status quo.

Giving your protagonist a mission

After the inciting incident occurs, the person who needs to fix the problem and restore order is your protagonist. Whether he likes it or not, the protagonist is endowed with a mission. The protagonist *must* do something. The state of affairs you create by the inciting incident must be so important, so urgent, and so relevant to your protagonist that he cannot possibly walk away from it, as in the following examples:

✔ Blanche DuBois has been driven out of every job and/or place she's been involved with. She's on the verge of physical and psychological collapse when she arrives at Stella's doorstep. She has nowhere else to go. She's on a mission to save herself, and the shelter she seeks in the crowded, rundown New Orleans apartment represents her last chance to avoid oblivion.

✔ The Pulitzer Prize– and Tony Award–winning musical *A Chorus Line* has essentially a collective protagonist. Some 17 show dancers, all in desperate need of work, have made the first cut — the inciting incident — in an audition for a Broadway show. Their mission — the objective they share but compete over — is to make the final cut and get cast in the show. The opportunity to get a gig in so highly competitive an environment is something none of the dancers can walk (or waltz) away from.

The mission the protagonist embarks on not only needs to be important to the protagonist but also needs to be important and clear for the audience. In other words, the audience needs to buy into the importance of the quest. If audience members conclude, consciously or unconsciously, that the goal of the protagonist is no big deal, their interest level and emotional involvement in the story is not likely to be very high.

If a character needs to win a chess game to satisfy his vanity, who cares? But if that character needs to win a chess game because the victory ensures he can leave the country and join his family in another country, that character is probably going to capture the hearts and sympathies of the audience. The audience will empathize and probably will be pulling for the character to win that game.

Introducing the conflict of the play

Following hard on the heels of the inciting incident is the conflict of the play. Conflict arises when the protagonist encounters obstacles to his success. The main obstacle is usually an *antagonist,* the person or thing with objectives or a purpose that opposes the quest of the protagonist. As I discuss in Chapter 7, the antagonist need not be, and generally *should* not be, viewed as "the bad guy." The antagonist is simply the character or object in the protagonist's way.

After your inciting incident has launched your protagonist on his journey, in short order you should make the conflict clear. Sometimes the conflict is obvious, particularly if it springs from the nature of the goal. For instance, Hamlet is on a mission to avenge his father's murder by, in turn, murdering the murderer, Claudius, the new king. Naturally, the object of this eye-for-an-eye justice, King Claudius, is the antagonist. What stands in the way of Hamlet's success is the king's selfish and petty desire to remain alive, particularly when his highness, the clandestine assassin, grows suspicious of Hamlet.

Identifying the antagonist and conflict in *A Raisin in the Sun* is tricky. You may jump at what seems evident — Mama Lena Younger, who stands between Walter Lee and the money he wants for the liquor store. But halfway through the play, Mama gives Walter Lee the money. So if she were the primary obstacle to Walter Lee's success, the play would essentially be over at that point. But it's far from over, so we need to look elsewhere for the antagonist.

So as not to keep you on pins and needles, as I interpret *A Raisin in the Sun,* the antagonist is not a person but a thing: racism. From the outset of the play, Walter Lee, who believes his work as a chauffeur for a white man to be demeaning, sees the potential partnership in the liquor store as a means of freeing himself that job and prevailing over the racist repression that keeps African American men from significant success in the world.

Walter Lee is in conflict with the system that keeps black people from making it. In the end, Walter Lee is tempted to make a deal with the devil — to take money from a white homeowner's association in exchange for not moving his family into a white neighborhood. This means, in an ironic turn of events, Walter Lee has the opportunity to benefit financially from white racism toward blacks. The climactic moment of the play comes when he has to make a decision whether to take the badly needed money or stand tall.

When you examine the facets of your play idea, be sure that you can readily and clearly identify the conflict of the play. To know what your conflict is is to know what your play is about. And when you understand what your play is about, chances are your audiences will too.

Incorporating the ticking clock

A very effective tool that can inject suspense and urgency into your story is the *ticking clock:* a deadline, a time limit, some form of countdown against which your protagonist must race. The ticking clock concept is used frequently and very effectively in movies and TV to help build tension and suspense. The protagonist must achieve some goal before a bomb goes off, before an asteroid strikes the earth, before the wrong man is hanged, and so on. The very popular TV series *24* was, by definition, about how the protagonist has 24 hours to achieve some objective of life-or-death, international importance. The ticking clock keeps the pressure on the protagonist and ratchets up his desperation as time winds down.

My play *Journey of the Heart* takes place in a hospital conference room in which the hospital's patient review committee is struggling to decide who gets a heart for transplant. The committee members are deeply divided between two candidates, and the atmosphere is heated. Complicating the testy deliberations is the fact that a heart extracted from a donor can remain viable for only a few hours. The longer the committee members argue, the closer they come to losing the opportunity to save either patient. The natural "life expectancy" of the harvested heart is the ticking clock.

The ticking clock tactic is not applicable to all stories, of course. But if you can work it into your play's story line, it helps keep the audience captivated.

Bringing the Audience Up to Speed: Exposition

Just about every play involves events that took place in the past, before the play begins (prior to the point of attack). These events are referred to as *backstory*. The backstory, or some portion of it, usually needs to be known so that the audience can understand more fully what's taking place. In other words, you use *exposition* to bring the audience up to speed on key events that have already happened.

Helping the audience with backstory

Providing the backstory of your play gives the audience the perspective it needs to fully appreciate the dilemma of the characters and to follow the logic of the story line.

The extensive and painful backstory for Blanche DuBois in *A Streetcar Named Desire* is essential in order to understand the peculiar and self-defeating behavior she engages in during the play. Tennessee Williams's protagonist lost the family plantation in Mississippi to debt incurred by profligate family members and by their funeral expenses. She lost her job as a teacher because of inappropriate relations with a student. She found herself living in a seedy hotel, inviting men to her room for company. Eventually Blanche is driven from the rundown hotel when management gets fed up with her behavior. Somewhere in her checkered past, she was married to a young man who turned out to be homosexual. When she expressed aversion at her discovery of this, he committed suicide. All this history is backstory, events that occurred before the point of attack, before the play begins.

When you've selected the point of attack for your play somewhere toward the middle of your story, you'll need to look at what comes before your play starts to decide how much of that backstory your audience is going to need in order to understand your characters and their story. Communicating that backstory — exposition — is a process in itself.

Getting the backstory out

Exposition is the revelation of backstory. It provides the audience with information on what has happened prior to the point of attack, before the audience is admitted to the story. Unobtrusively weaving past information into the present of the play is challenging but important for effective playwriting.

Listening to a character in a play relate past events in his life is tiresome and, in the darkness of a theatre, sleep-inducing. Therefore, your exposition has to be done in an interesting and organic way. The character must provide that information at the given juncture of the play *for a good reason*.

In bygone decades, a playwright could use domestic servants to get the backstory out. At the beginning of a play, servants would appear and begin preparing a room for a dinner or a party, all the while talking about the master losing his job or about the mistress spending an unseemly amount of time in the company of the gentlemen next door, and so forth. By the time they're finished setting up the room, you've heard enough gossip to know exactly what's gone on before and what problems are on the horizon. Today, this kind form of exposition is considered outdated and clunky (not to mention the extravagance of having to hire and pay actors just for expositional purposes).

Another unhappy form of exposition is when you have your characters recounting the backstory to each other. The problem here is the artificiality of it. People don't sit around telling each other what they already know. You don't want to write this kind of exposition:

JOAN

Arnold, dear, you remember when we got married four years ago.

ARNOLD

We got married in St. Chatterbox Chapel in Brooklyn.

JOAN

Right. We lived three years in Brooklyn before we moved here to Chappaqua.

ARNOLD

Chappaqua is where your mother lives, so it's ideal us.

JOAN

My mother is in her 90s. It's good to be nearby.

ARNOLD

Just five minutes away.

JOAN

You do realize that today is our anniversary, don't you?

ARNOLD

It totally slipped my mind that this is our fourth anniversary!

In the dialogue above, all the characters are doing is relating to each other information that's not news to either of them. Unless one of them is recovering from amnesia, such dialogue serves only one purpose (and badly at that): letting the audience in on their backstory. And if you think no one would write dialogue so overtly expositional, think again.

Below is the same scene written a tad more organically and realistically.

JOAN

I was just thinking, Arnold, about where we got married.

ARNOLD

Saint . . . what's-his-face chapel.

JOAN

St. Chatterbox. (Pause) Three of the nicest years of my life . . . in Brooklyn, I mean.

ARNOLD

Chappaqua isn't so bad.

JOAN

Yes . . . but only because mom's nearby.

ARNOLD

Amazing gal. Ninety-three years old and still going strong.
(Pause) Joan love, what brings all this up, anyway?

JOAN

Would you believe . . . our anniversary?

ARNOLD

Good lord! Not again! I've forgotten our anniversary all
four years!

Tony-winning dialogue this is not, but I expect you'll agree that the conversation sounds a little more natural while getting in the needed information. The reason for the conversation is clearer, too. Joan is reminding Arnold of their anniversary.

Another expositional technique is to break *the fourth wall:* Have a character speak directly to the audience. Neil Simon uses this device in his Eugene trilogy: *Brighton Beach Memoirs, Biloxi Blues,* and *Broadway Bound.* The main character in these plays, Eugene Jerome, occasionally speaks directly to the audience, commenting ironically and humorously on events or on the other characters. The character functions both as a participant in the play and narrator.

If you plan to break the fourth wall, do take care, however. In my estimation, a master playwright like Neil Simon choosing to break the fourth wall as a technique to achieve a heightened comedic effect is one thing. Playwrights using the device because they're having trouble coming up with a smooth way of handling the exposition is another — and lesser — thing. That's a cheat, and it usually feels that way to the audience. Clever exposition requires effort. As fun as it is, playwriting, like any other art, involves thought, effort, and creativity.

Using exposition as ammunition

Normally, as playwright, the goal is to weave into the dialogue info about the past — backstory — in small doses, as it's needed. The details of the backstory should come out when the character has a legitimate reason to bring them up. Sometimes characters, as we do in life, bring up the past to make a point, win an argument, or impress someone. This approach is known as *exposition as ammunition.* A character brings up the past to further his goals by achieving some effect on another character.

The following dialogue is an excerpt from a two-character, one-act play of mine, *A Waltz Without Turns*. It takes place in a no-frills motel in Orlando, Florida. Danny and Peggy are relatively new to each other. The scene takes place at the end of their last day of the vacation, and they've just come back to the motel room and are sitting on the edge of the bed, she in sweat shirt and sweat pants, he in T-shirt and shorts. Danny, exuberant by nature, suggests to Peggy, who tends to be somewhat moody, that they order in a bottle of champagne. Peggy's not interested. As you read what I hope comes across like natural dialogue, see how much of the backstory you can pick up.

PEGGY

(Sharply) No! You know I feel about drinking.

DANNY

That doesn't mean we can't have a sip every now and then. You're not your father, you know.

PEGGY tenses, long silence

Better a bottle in front of me than a frontal lobotomy. (The joke falls flat.) Look, I don't, you know, get crazy with booze. I'm cool. You spend as much time in clubs as I do you . . . Hey, I don't hafta explain what I do or don't do to you.

PEGGY

That's right, you don't.

DANNY

Damn. (A beat) I guess this wasn't such a good idea. Comin' here together, I mean. I needed to get away. I haven't taken a vacation in I can't remember how long. I didn't have a gig for a while, so I thought we could, like, have some fun. To be a kid again, you know. I always wanted to see this place. Disneyland. Disney World, whatever. My folks never took us anywhere. (A beat) I thought you'd like it.

PEGGY

I liked it.

DANNY

Right. Don't play poker; you'll lose your sweats.

PEGGY

Orlando wouldn't have been my choice, that's all.

DANNY

Why didn't you say somethin'?

PEGGY

You were so excited. You were looking forward to this. Anyway, you paid for the trip.

DANNY

That don't mean a thing. If *you* had money and *I* was broke, I would let *you* pay for both of us.

PEGGY looks skeptical

(Unconvincingly) Sure I would. It could happen. Hey, I'm a musician; it definitely could happen. (A beat) Hell, I guess I misread you.

PEGGY

We hardly know each other. How could you read me at all?

DANNY

That's the point! I thought this would be a great way for us to get to know each other. Quick. You know, cut to the chase. I don't have the patience anymore for dating once a week, then twice a week, and so on and so forth. (A beat) I figured this would make . . . or break us.

PEGGY suddenly turns to DANNY

PEGGY

How can you talk of love after only two weeks?

DANNY

What? When did I talk about love?

PEGGY

Before.

DANNY

I did not. When? What did I say?

PEGGY

I can't do this again!

DANNY

What exactly did I say?

PEGGY

"The Peggy we know and love."

DANNY

Oh, for pity's sake! That was a figure of speech!

PEGGY

(Building in intensity) I finally worked up the nerve to move to
New York, to get away from my father, my parents. A fat old
drunk and a dried up old biddy . . . each one of them waiting for
the other to die first. I couldn't . . . I just couldn't . . . I had to get
out of Walla Walla.

DANNY

What self-respecting adults would live in a place called Walla
Walla?

PEGGY

When I meet Edward — the poet, the guy who won a Pulitzer
Prize. I told you about him . . .

DANNY

Only once a day.

PEGGY

. . . he was . . . understanding. He encouraged me to . . . my artistic side. So I took up origami. For a while. Then he started giving me a hard time. About . . . feelings. He wanted me to show my feelings. What's so great about feelings!? He expected *everything* from me. He had no patience. I just couldn't . . . I asked him to leave. And he left. It was better that way. On my own.

DANNY

(At a loss) Okay. So . . . what are you sayin'?

PEGGY

I'm not ready to let somebody take care of me.

DANNY

Who the hell said anything about takin' care of you!?

PEGGY

What do you call all *this?* You haven't let me pay for a thing.

DANNY

Hey, that's the way I was brought up. To be *polite.* God, you can be a pain in the ass!

While Danny is trying to get Peggy to loosen up and have a good time, the bits of backstory I think you can pick up include:

- ✔ Peggy's father has (or had) a drinking problem.
- ✔ Danny has a penchant for corny jokes.
- ✔ Danny spends a lot of time in clubs because he's a musician.
- ✔ Peggy and Danny are on vacation at Disney World.
- ✔ The destination was Danny's choice.
- ✔ Danny paid for the vacation.
- ✔ Peggy and Danny have known each other for two weeks.
- ✔ Peggy is sensitive and defensive when it comes to relationships.
- ✔ Peggy's parents have (or had) a desiccated relationship.

> ✔ Peggy is from Walla Walla, Washington.
>
> ✔ Peggy was romantically involved with an accomplished poet, whom, to Danny's chagrin, she mentions constantly.

This excerpt also illustrates the use of exposition as ammunition. Each character brings up information to make or support a position or opinion. In the process, details of the backstory are communicated to the audience, giving the audience necessary background information and perspective on the characters.

Looking at Beginnings in Classic Plays

This chapter deals with a number of considerations involved in the beginning of a play, specifically the point of attack (where a play begins), the inciting incident (what gets the plot going), and exposition (how to bring the audience up to speed on the backstory). Below is a glimpse at how three classic plays handle their beginnings.

Hamlet

Perhaps William Shakespeare's best-known play, *Hamlet* provides a crystal-clear model of how to start a play. Written more than 400 years ago, the masterpiece still provides a relevant lesson in getting a play up and running.

Point of attack

Shakespeare chose as his point of attack a night the ghost of Hamlet's father, the old king, appears, which drops the audience right into the middle of the action. Events have already take place, like the death of the old king and the remarriage of his wife, Queen Gertrude, to the new king, Claudius, the brother of the recently deceased king. The play opens on the walls of Elsinore Castle, where guards see a ghost, recognize it as the old king, and decide to report what they've seen to the old king's son, Hamlet. The apparition of the frightening spirit of the old king suggests that dreadful things are about to transpire, and, more to the point, it hooks the audience.

Inciting incident

The event that shakes the world of the protagonist, Hamlet, is not so much the appearance of the ghost of his father but what that ghost tells him: that he (the old king) was poisoned by Claudius. The ghost commands Hamlet to avenge his murder, propelling Hamlet on a journey of rough justice —

revenge and murder. Hamlet has no choice. He cannot rest until he's accomplished his goal. The game, as Sherlock Holmes would say, is afoot.

Exposition

The audience finds out in the first scene of the play that the ghost of the recently dead king has been appearing to the castle guards. The chatter of the nervous guards, who are trying to make sense of what they've seen, also reveals that Denmark, led by the old king, has defeated Norway.

The next scene takes place in a reception chamber where the new king, Claudius, is receiving guests and petitioners. In other words, he's busy being king. Feeling on top of the world, he pays lip service to the tragedy of his brother's death, and he revels in his marriage to the widow. His dialogue, as it comes out in this expansive mood, fills the audience in on the what's happened since the old king died.

All this information, necessary to understanding the play and Hamlet's brooding, is revealed in dialogue that is *earned:* It's appropriate and necessary to the occasion rather than randomly thrown in simply for the benefit of the audience.

A Doll House

Henrik Ibsen's *A Doll House* is his landmark play about a dutiful wife and mother who comes to question the confining role of women in society. The play, the ending of which shocked conventional, late-19th-century audiences, was a pioneering work in modern and naturalistic theatre. The opening of the play demonstrates skillful and effective play structure.

Point of attack

Ibsen opens his play in the home of Nora and Torvald Helmer during the Christmas season. The choice of that moment introduces the audience to the normality of their middle-class existence, a placid domesticity that will be shattered at the end of the play. This opening gives the audience the opportunity to get comfortable with the comfortable circumstances of the life of the protagonist, Nora, before the past comes back to haunt her.

Opening the play during the holiday season allows the audience to witness Nora's naïveté, at least from Torvald's point of view, when it comes to spending money. The scene also underscores the fact that Nora is dependent on Torvald for money. She fawns and coos at the delighted Torvald as a means of getting from him what she wants, principally money. In addition, this particular Christmas is the eve of a significant promotion and pay raise for Torvald, who works as a manager in a bank. (Also, the frigid Scandinavian weather at Christmas time makes Nora's eventual departure into the cold, cruel world that much more an act of courage — or recklessness, depending on your point of view.)

These circumstances, in contrast to the startling and spellbinding impact of the appearance of a ghost in *Hamlet,* draw in audiences by seducing them into a sense of harmony and charming serenity — a quaint veneer that will be suddenly and shockingly destroyed.

Inciting incident

An old friend of Nora's, Mrs. Linde, comes to visit and reveals that she's looking for a job. Nora talks Torvald into giving her work at the bank.

Shortly after, Nora receives a visit from Nils Krogstad, one of Torvald's employees. He explains he's about to lose his job at the bank, which he cannot allow to happen. Nora, who had borrowed money from him years earlier to pay for Torvald's recovery from a serious illness, made the loan by forging her father's signature as cosigner. Krogstad discovers this fact, and now tells Nora he will reveal her crime if she doesn't help him keep his job. This puts Nora in the position of having try to get her husband to keep Krogstad, whom Torvald sees as rude and impertinent, or she will be disgraced and maybe even jailed for her offense, bringing ruin on Torvald and the family.

Krogstad's blackmail threat is the inciting incident. Now Nora must do something. She somehow must find a way to get Torvald to renege on the job he promised Mrs. Linde and keep Krogstad on the payroll. If she fails, her idyllic family life is doomed.

Also note that this conflict involves a ticking clock. While the time allotted to Nora to help Krogstad is not specific, she does need to act before Torvald fires Krogstad, an action that is imminent. The limited time adds urgency to Nora's mission.

Exposition

Krogstad's recounting of the Nora's naïve but desperate action — forging a legal document — is exposition, the revealing of backstory. The exchange between Nora for Krogstad is skillfully crafted. While you squirm for Nora as she falls victim to Krogstad's threat, you likely don't notice that at the same time Ibsen is filling you in on the events that put Nora at Krogstad's mercy. That's exposition as ammunition at its best!

A Raisin in the Sun

Set in Chicago, *A Raisin in the Sun* is Lorraine Hansberry's landmark play about the struggle of an African American family in the 1950s to better itself in an

America where racial segregation was still legal. The play, which captures the language and rhythm of the African American vernacular, is celebrated as one of the first plays to present a realistic portrait of black family life.

This play is a rare example in which the point of attack, inciting incident, and exposition concerning the play's backstory are almost inextricably bound up together. Though a playwright's point of attack should be as far into the story as possible, I'd say Hansberry pushed that guideline perhaps to the limit. She chose to begin her play well into this story of the powerful and divisive impact that a soon-to-arrive insurance check has on the lives and aspirations of a working-class black family crammed into a tiny Chicago ghetto apartment.

In fact, Hansberry's point of attack is so far into the story that it comes even after the inciting incident. Where most commonly the audience of a play gets to witness the event that ignites the plot, in this play the passing of the head of the family and the galvanizing news that a life-insurance check will be arriving happen before the play begins. The audience learns of the death and the money through exposition.

Only a few minutes after the curtain rises, the audience is introduced to Walter Lee Younger, who is animated, anxious, and totally preoccupied with the arrival of the large insurance check, which is expected to come the next day. The first scene of the plays reveals economically and naturally that Walter Lee wants the money to invest in a liquor store; his sister, Beneatha, anticipates that the money will help put her through medical school; and Mama has a dream of owning her own home. But when all is said and done, it's Mama who controls the money and what use it will be put to.

Placing the point of attack after the inciting incident is somewhat unconventional, but there's no right or wrong when it comes to deciding their placement. It's a matter of what works. The idea is to get your audience into the action of the play with the least preparatory material necessary. How do you know what works and what doesn't? In two ways. First, by putting yourself in the place of the audience and asking yourself what's the minimum you would need to know to get engaged in the play. And second, by observing the audience during developmental readings of your play (discussed in Chapter 15). If you're not sure, ask the audience members if they had any trouble understanding the beginning of the play.

Chapter 11

The Middle: Developing Your Story Line

Playwrights occasionally are heard to moan self-pityingly, "I've get a great idea and setup, and I know how the story ends, but I have no idea what happens in between." Or, "I've got a drawer full of first acts" (today it probably would be, "I've got a hard drive full of first acts"), referring to the beginnings of plays that stalled somewhere in the middle.

The mid-20th-century playwright and director Moss Hart, working in an era when plays were typically structured in three acts, had this to say about the woes of writing the second act — the middle of a play:

> *As a rule, the writing of a second act seems to drag on forever. It is the danger spot of every play — the soft underbelly of playwriting . . . and it is well to be aware of it. [When writing a first act] the excitement of a new play seems to supply the energy and freshness for each day's work . . . there are some first acts that literally seem to write themselves. . . . It's the second acts that separate the men from the boys.* (Moss Hart, *Act One: An Autobiography by Moss Hart*)

Writing the middles of plays can be one of the most challenging and exasperating aspects of playwriting. That being said, you can consider pointers and employ story-writing practices that will make the middle of your play less perplexing to envision and write. You find out how in this chapter. This chapter also describes how to provide challenges for the protagonist in her quest and how to instill complexity and variation into the story line to keep the audience intrigued throughout the play.

Finding Meaning in the Middle

The well-constructed play has a *beginning,* a *middle,* and an *end.* That probably seems obvious. After all, doesn't pretty much everything have a beginning, a middle, and an end — from the slithery body of the lowly earthworm to the span of a human life?

Yes, but, in structuring a story for the stage, those terms — beginning, middle, and end — have specific meanings and purposes:

- ✔ **Beginning:** The beginning is the setup of the play, including the point of attack, the introduction of your principal characters, and the inciting incident that launches the protagonist on her journey. (Check out Chapter 10 for more discussion of the beginning.)

- ✔ **Middle:** In the middle of the play, the protagonist engages in a quest toward an urgent objective. She struggles single-mindedly against the antagonist, obstacles, and reversals as she haltingly makes her way toward her objective.

- ✔ **End:** The end is the climactic moment, the final showdown between protagonist and antagonist, and the resolution, what the world of the play looks like after the dust has settled. (To find out more about the end of the play, see Chapters 12 and 13.)

There's an old storytelling chestnut that suggests that you "get a man (or woman) up a tree; throw stones at him; get him down." As hackneyed as that folksy formula is, you can draw insight from it. The steps in that overly simplified recipe are analogous to the three-part organization of a play.

- ✔ The first step — "get your protagonist up a tree" — means getting your main character into an uncomfortable, untenable position that needs action, a situation that compels him to do something. That's the "beginning" component of a story that I cover in Chapter 10.

- ✔ The third step — "get him down" — involves your protagonist solving the problem and ending the journey. (It doesn't necessarily mean the protagonist is successful in his quest. Yes, he may find his way down from the tree, but he may fall if one of the thrown stones knocks him down.) The "end" section of a play is the topic of Chapters 12 and 13.

- ✔ The middle step — "throw stones at him" — indicates the placing of obstacles and problems in the path of your protagonist. He must negotiate numerous and formidable roadblocks.

Conflicts Make the Play Go 'Round

At the core of well-written and entertaining plays is conflict — a protagonist desperately and urgently needing or wanting something versus an antagonist with contrary goals, presenting with equal desperation and urgency a series of obstacles.

To engage and maintain the hearts and minds of audiences, you need to stage and sustain conflict throughout the play. Conflict usually manifests itself in obstacles that are thrown in the path of the protagonist. The obstacles should vary in severity and pacing (ideally, escalating in difficulty and complexity) but never let up. This is expected in dramas, but it's also true of comedies.

In the uproarious comedy *Arsenic and Old Lace,* by Joseph Kesselring, the protagonist faces problem after problem. Mortimer Brewster is desperate to protect his two spinster aunts, who, out of the goodness of their hearts, have been putting lonely old men out of their misery and burying them in the basement of their Brooklyn home. His enthusiastic fiancée, his insane brothers, the intrusive local cop, and his stubborn, elderly aunts themselves present Mortimer with obstacles in his mission to look after the sweet but eccentric old gals.

This section deals with writing conflict, ensuring that the obstacles your protagonist faces are potent, plentiful, and unrelenting.

Making sure it's not easy

The obstacles that arise from the conflict you set up can vary in intensity and severity, but they should never be effortless to deal with. If an obstacle is easily overcome, the transaction will have little or no suspense or tension. If the primary obstacle standing between the Romeo and Juliet and their happiness were not the long-standing and bitter hatred between their families but only a matter of the lovers being too young to marry, they could simply wait a few years. There's hardly much drama or danger in that.

The primary obstacle that stands between Cyrano de Bergerac, the title character in Edmond Rostand's popular play, and the beautiful young woman he loves, Roxane, is his deep-seated and unshakable belief that his very large nose makes him hideous and unlovable. On the other hand, if the obstacle were, say, Cyrano's tendency dress out of fashion, the story wouldn't have much drama or suspense. A negligible obstacle like that is easily fixed by upgrading the wardrobe.

In short, the bigger and badder the obstacle, the better.

Placing obstacles every step of the way

When writing obstacles for your protagonist, to say "the more the merrier" may be an overstatement. But not by much. Your protagonist's road ought to be fraught with hills, valleys, detours, snowdrifts, fender-benders, traffic jams, and potholes. Never allow the obstacles to let up in your play. If the constant stream of conflict and obstacles ceases, your play will be like a car without gasoline: It may look good, but it's not going anywhere.

Every obstacle should present a meaningful challenge, and the overcoming of obstacles should have *consequences;* prevailing over obstacles should come at come some sacrifice to the character. There should be a price to pay.

In *Hamlet,* one of the obstacles in Hamlet's mission to avenge the murder of his father by the new king is the meddling of the king's officious adviser, Polonius. Hamlet puts an end to it by killing Polonius, albeit accidentally. The price Hamlet pays for eliminating this obstacle is the rage of Polonius's son, Laertes, who, as a result, is easily talked into helping the suspicious king plot Hamlet's death. Also, by killing Polonius, Hamlet loses his innocence. He's now done something almost as culpable as the man he seeks to punish. Hamlet's dispatch of Polonius has serious consequences.

Another way a high price can be paid for the elimination of an obstacle is in *collateral damage,* unintentional harm or injury inflicted on innocent bystand-ers or on those not directly involved in the conflict. Hamlet's indecision and rashness in dealing with obstacles in his mission to avenge his father's murder result in an impressive body count that includes such relatively innocent victims as Ophelia, Polonius, Rosencrantz and Guildenstern, Queen Gertrude, and Laertes. Their deaths were not necessary to the accomplishing of Hamlet's goal. In other words, if Hamlet had made it his business to dis-patch Claudius immediately, none of the other deaths would have occurred.

Whatever the price, when an obstacle is overcome, it shouldn't be long before another obstacle appears before the protagonist. Your protagonist should be running a gauntlet on her quest to achieve her objective.

In addition to frequency, the series of obstacles your protagonist faces should have *causality:* The surmounting of one obstacle should lead to the next obstacle. The appearance of obstacles can't be random. Looking back at the sequence of events in the middle of your play, the audience ought to be able to conclude that each obstacle arose naturally and inevitably as a complica-tion resulting from the preceding obstacle.

For example, the killing of Polonius alerts the new king to the danger Hamlet represents. The king, out of self-preservation, sends Hamlet out of the coun-try, ostensibly on a diplomatic mission to England. This enforced departure from Denmark presents Hamlet with another obstacle to his mission. If he's out of the country, he's unable get to the king to exact the revenge demanded by the ghost of his father. Thus, the removal of Polonius as an obstacle leads to the next obstacle, Hamlet's exile.

If you're able to shuffle your obstacles like playing cards in a deck and the reorder of the obstacles doesn't make any difference to your story, your story line lacks causality. Though events may occur at random in life, randomness in storytelling does not work. Strong causality in your story line keeps your audience engaged and works to gradually heighten the suspense and tension.

Knowing how far your protagonist will go

A measure of the importance of your protagonist's objective is how far she will go to achieve it. As I explain in Chapter 7, you should know and understand your protagonist as well as you know and understand your best friend. Part of this intimate awareness is knowing the extremes to which she will go and the methods she will employ to get things done.

Is your character restrained by limits and boundaries in the struggle to get what she wants, or is it total war? Does your character tend to take a wait-and-see approach, or does she "take no prisoners"? In *A Doll House,* Nora Helmer is desperate to prevent Nils Krogstad from making known her forgery of a signature on a legal document. The revelation would embarrass her husband and, conceivably, land Nora in jail. However, despite her anxiety, Nora has limits. She considers asking a close family friend, Dr. Rank, for help. But before she can bring up the subject, Dr. Rank professes his love for Nora. Nora, shaken and disappointed by Dr. Rank, refrains from asking anything of him. Clearly, Nora won't do some things. (And that self-imposed limitation presents an obstacle; she now has one fewer possible solution.)

On the other hand, in *A Raisin in the Sun,* Walter Lee Younger is unrelenting in his efforts to get his hands on a soon-to-arrive life insurance check, hoping to use the money to buy into a liquor store partnership. He sees the potential business as his one and only shot at beating the odds against African Americans by giving him the means to become his own man and provide a better life for his family. However, his mother, Lena, who controls the money, sees liquor as immoral.

Desperate to have the money, Walter Lee badgers his wife into interceding with Lena on his behalf. He bullies his sister, hoping to get her to give up her ambition to go to costly medical school. He repeatedly appeals to his mother to allow him the funds to pursue his dream. Ultimately, Walter Lee resolves to take money from a homeowners association representative who's willing to pay dearly to keep the Younger family from moving into his all-white neighborhood. It seems Walter Lee will stop at nothing to get what he wants.

In working out the story line of your play, do some brainstorming for obstacles to frustrate your protagonist. Come up with as many as you can, repeatedly asking yourself, "What obstructions can I throw down next for my protagonist?" How you organize them is discussed in the later section "Using Suspense, Setbacks, and Other Storytelling Tools."

Allowing the worst thing to happen

Occasionally you'll find yourself stuck for an adequate obstacle to come next. You've thrown impediments in the path of your protagonist, and she's dealt with all of them one way or another. And you're not sure what to try next. Here's a tool to use in those and other circumstances.

Consider your protagonist's situation: Where is she, what's around her, what's going on at the moment, where does she need to go? After you've got a good handle on the lay of the land, and ask yourself this simple question: *What's the worst thing that could happen to her at this moment?* And when you've come up with the answer, make it happen.

This worst-thing-that-could-happen tool can be used anywhere during your protagonist's journey, just so long as you're able to top it with the next obstacle. Even after the worst thing happens to your protagonist and your protagonist is at a new point in the journey, a new worst thing can always happen.

Here's how the worst-thing-that-could-happen scenario plays out in the romantic comedy *Bell, Book and Candle,* by John Van Druten. Gillian Holroyd, a modern-day witch with too much time on her hands, sets her sights on a handsome neighbor, Shep Henderson. Eventually she resorts to casting a spell, and Shep falls happily in love with Gillian. When later Shep discovers his affection for Gillian is a result of dark enchantment, he consults another witch to get the spell undone, freeing himself from Gillian. What's the worst thing that could happen?

Gillian finds, to her dismay, that she's fallen in love with Shep. And in the rules of the world in the play, a witch who falls in love and sheds a tear loses her powers. Gillian, in doing both, has become a mere mortal. Not only has she lost her man, she's lost her magical abilities as well. (Don't you hate when that happens?)

Using Suspense, Setbacks, and Other Storytelling Tools

Think of your protagonist as climbing Mount Everest. Each level of upward progress is accompanied by increasingly challenging conditions — thinner air, colder temperatures, more violent winds, greater distance from emergency assistance, and so on. If the question of your play is whether she will reach the summit, success is far from certain. The challenges steadily increase in difficulty and severity and build engaging suspense and robust tension.

Whatever the circumstances are for her, the protagonist in your play should be attempting to scale her own Mount Everest. The journey should be accompanied by escalating suspense, tension, gains, and setbacks. What you don't want involved in the story line are improbable coincidences and unnecessary elements that distract the audience.

This section describes how to build suspense and tension and how to embed into the script gains and setbacks for your protagonist. This section also cautions against some script pitfalls, including the use of coincidences and scene-stealers.

Engaging the audience with suspense and tension

Few things galvanize the interest and attention of an audience more than suspense and tension.

- ✔ **Suspense** is the anxious awaiting of the outcome of some event, particularly under circumstances in which a lot rides on how things turn out. Suspense can be generated by almost any yet-to-be-concluded situation, from politics (the result of a close and hotly contested election) to a sports event (the next pitch of a bases-loaded, two-outs-in-the-ninth-inning scenario).

- ✔ **Tension** is psychological apprehension or physical stress, a state of uneasiness that results from an event or the anticipation of an event. Tension is what an audience experiences when held in suspense. Prolonged tension (meaning tension that extends over days and weeks) is not a good thing for one's health. But tension experienced in small doses during a play is a measure of the emotional and psychological involvement of audience members.

There's an old gag about a man who insisted on wearing painfully tight shoes. When asked why he wore the tight shoes, he explained that his only joy in life was the pleasure of taking them off. Similarly (more or less), the release from tension that comes with a well-crafted climax and resolution enhances the pleasure and satisfaction of a play.

Suspense and tension are story elements you're likely to associate with drama. Here are some instances of suspense generated by the story lines of dramatic plays:

✔ Will Hamlet succeed in avenging the murder of his father, or will he be found out and eliminated?

✔ Will Tony make a life with Maria, or will racial hatred and gang warfare destroy them and their chance at happiness?

✔ Will 12 surly jurors succeed at arriving at a fair verdict, or will personal issues and prejudice send a young man to the electric chair?

But suspense and tension in theatre are not restricted to events in dramatic stories; suspense can also be achieved in comedies. In *Bell, Book and Candle,* when Gillian finds herself falling in love with her victim — a no-no for a witch — suspense builds as the audience waits to find out if she will lose her witchly powers and her man to boot.

You can infuse suspense and tension into your story by

✔ Putting your protagonist in pursuit of an ultimate objective of clear and vital importance to her

✔ Setting stakes (what happens if she achieves her goals and what happens if she doesn't) that are essential to her

✔ Continuously frustrating your protagonist's gains in achieving her objective with new and formidable obstacles and setbacks

✔ Adding the ticking clock that brings urgency to the quest (see Chapter 10 for more on this idea)

The degree of suspense and tension audiences experience during the play also is tied to the emotional investment they have in the character. If audiences don't care about the character(s), they won't feel the suspense and tension. The more audiences are engaged and invested in the protagonist's success, the more effective the rising action and setbacks will be. (See Chapter 7 for more about creating characters audiences care about.)

Following all gains with setbacks

A *reversal* is a change in fortune that adds complexity as well as suspense to a story. It's when a situation unexpectedly goes from bad to good or from good to bad. Reversals often have a tinge of irony because they usually occur when the situation appears settled one way or the other; just when things look like they'll be fine, something terrible happens. Or, at the moment things look bleak, the protagonist makes a breakthrough.

Suspense and tension can be layered into the story of your play with a series of reversals — alternating your protagonist's gains with setbacks. If you were to chart your protagonist's progress toward her objective, the line representing her progress should look like an upward-sloping zigzag line (see Figure 11-1).

The peaks of the upward-sloping zigzag line are the incremental successes, and the valleys are the setbacks.

The upward-slopping path of your protagonist's progress indicates that it's, well, an uphill battle. Each obstacle encountered is more challenging than the earlier one. Still, the overall direction of the line is upward, signifying progress despite the reversals. And the line continues upward until the climactic moment of the play is reached.

In *A Raisin in the Sun,* one of the obstacles for Walter Lee in his mission — to part-own a liquor store to provide a better life for his family — is the refusal by his mother, Lena, to give him the insurance money for that purpose. But Walter Lee's persistent and plaintive appeals to his mother, and Lena's love for her son, prompt Lena to relent. She gives the bulk of the money to Walter Lee to manage as he sees fit. Walter Lee has succeeded in overcoming a major obstacle. It is one of the peaks near the top of the upward-sloping zigzag line of his quest. In fact, it looks like his objective is all but achieved. For Walter Lee, it's a reversal of fortune. His situation has gone from bad to good.

However, after prevailing over Lena's reticence and getting the money he wants, Walter Lee naïvely entrusts money to a potential partner in the business venture who disappears with the money. The loss of the money is a major setback. This is one of the valleys near the top of the upward-sloping line. It's another reversal of fortune, but this time things go from good to bad.

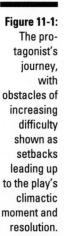

Figure 11-1: The protagonist's journey, with obstacles of increasing difficulty shown as setbacks leading up to the play's climactic moment and resolution.

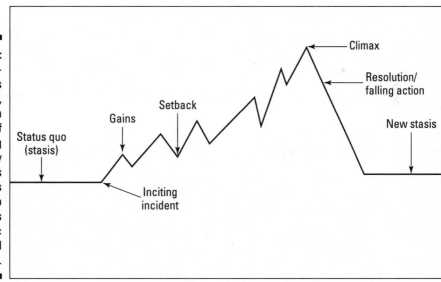

Employing coincidences and foreshadowing

As you work on the middle of your play and get your ducks — or obstacles — in a row, two concepts to keep an eye on are *coincidences* and *foreshadowing*. The first concept can be problematic; the second can be essential.

Coincidences

Coincidences are unforeseen and somehow related events that happen at the same time or place by accident. They are chance occurrences. Coincidences happen in real life all the time, and though they can be eerie, people generally take them in stride. But coincidences are not so easily accepted in storytelling. When a coincidence happens in a play — an event comes out of nowhere just when expedient to the story — the immediate audience reaction is to sneer "how convenient."

In my play *The Slope,* the protagonist, Mark, is agonizing over a telephone call he needs to make to his mother to deliver personal bad news. Throughout this play, he repeatedly moves to make the call but always backs off. At the end of the play, he finally does make the difficult phone call. But, if instead the phone had rung and it had been Mark's mother calling him, that would have constituted a colossal coincidence. Just when Mark needed but was reluctant to call his mother, she calls him? No way, José. Not only would such a turn of events be awkwardly coincidental, it would have taken the initiative out of the hands of the protagonist, a no-no.

Avoid writing coincidences into your play. Audiences are not likely to accept coincidences when they appear in "unreal life," a play. They come across as contrived. However, this advice does not preclude using a startling surprise in your play. The trick to turning an event that might seem like an artificial coincidence into an acceptable surprise is to foreshadow it.

Strategic foreshadowing or planting

When some person, place, or thing is going to be a plot point — an important part in the ending of your play — long before it's used, you should let the audience know that that person, place, or thing exists. Revealing this info is called *foreshadowing,* or *planting* a plot point. By foreshadowing or planting an object or idea, you make the later use of that object or idea feel appropriate and organic. If you don't think to foreshadow or plant an important point, you risk having the use of that object or idea feel unrealistically coincidental.

In the charming romantic comedy *Bell, Book and Candle,* the protagonist's aunt, a concerned Miss Holroyd, asks in the first scene: "Gillian, you — you haven't fallen in love with him and lost your powers, have you?" With this one seemingly innocuous but masterful line, the playwright achieves two important objectives. First, he establishes one of the rules of his world of modern-day witches: Falling in love can lose a witch her powers. Two, he plants the possibility that Gillian could lose her powers if she falls in love with her neighbor, Shep. When that dreadful fate does befall Gillian later, it seems perfectly believable and natural, because the possibility was planted early on.

The trick to successful foreshadowing and planting is to show or make reference to the relevant person, place, or thing without drawing so much attention to it that you tip your hand. You want to plant the thought without making a big deal of it. Miss Holroyd's concern is quickly dismissed by Gillian — "You don't believe that old wives' tale?" — and the subject almost immediately is eclipsed by the arrival of another character.

If you plan a surprise of some sort at the end of your play, be sure that you've at least hinted at the possibility or the means of the surprise through subtle foreshadowing or planting.

Avoiding scene stealers or hot buttons

Creating the magic of theatre — the experience of forgetting all else and becoming immersed in the world of the play — requires skillful playwriting and artful presentation (acting and staging). Unfortunately, the hypnotic effect of an entertaining and engaging play can be dissipated very easily. All it takes is the ringing of a cellphone or the decision by some audience members to discuss the scene while it's still being played out.

Additionally, you yourself — the playwright — can unintentionally take the audience out of the play. Without realizing it, you can write into your play an element that distracts the audience from the events of your play. I call these pernicious play elements *scene stealers* or *hot buttons.*

A *scene stealer* or *hot button* is the reference to some person, place, or thing that is so powerful that it moves the audience's concentration off of the play and onto that particular reference. The phenomenon being mentioned in passing, whatever it might be, evokes such strong memories and emotional connections that the events in the play gets lost or overshadowed.

The bottom line is that you need to be careful not to make a reference or raise an issue that's not essential to your story if that reference or issue is so powerful it takes the focus off of your play and sets people's thoughts on another course. Don't let scene stealers or hot buttons derail your play. However, if you want to write a play *about* major events and huge issues, please do. The world could use more of that kind of bold playwriting. Just be sure it's what you mean to be doing.

In one of my classes, a student was writing a play about untimely death and its impact on the surviving family members. Based on the playwright's own experiences, it was powerful material courageously presented. A minor point to the play's story line was that the death occurred the same day as the attack on and destruction of New York City's World Trade Center.

Unfortunately, and not to trivialize the horrendous tragedy, any reference to 9/11 in a play or in other writing can be a scene stealer. Unless the subject of your play involves 9/11 or something directly related to it, it's wise to stay away from such an evocative reference. That event is so powerfully seared into the memories of most Americans that the minds of audience members involuntarily flash back to that dark day, recalling the terrible events, the people who were lost, where they were, and other associations. Everything else immediately takes a back seat.

The solution, as proposed to my student, was to not make reference to 9/11, even if 9/11 is the day the real event on which the play is based took place. As resonant as that coincidence was to my student, it was a scene stealer that took attention away from the tragic death in the play and the family's reaction to it. You don't want to get in your own way by including so disturbing an element in a play, particularly if it has no direct relevance to the story.

Other momentous events that you probably want to avoid referencing (unless they're the subjects you're writing about) include: the assassinations of President John F. Kennedy and Martin Luther King, Jr., the AIDS epidemic, the destruction wrought by Hurricane Katrina, and the devastating earthquake and tsunami that struck Japan. These and other such cataclysmic events you yourself can identify can be so powerful on a personal and emotional level that everything else pales in comparison (and rightly so).

Varying the Mood

When theatre flourished in ancient Greece, well over 2,000 years ago, playwrights did not mix the two primary genres of tragedy and comedy. In fact, it was a hard-and-fast rule based on the ancient Greeks' sense of aesthetics. If a play was a tragedy, as is *Oedipus Rex,* by Sophocles, events were dramatic, grim, and, well, tragic. There are no yuks in that classic play of mystery, self-discovery, and violence. And if a play was a comedy, it was light-hearted and frivolous through and through. Aristotle defined comedy as ludicrous people involved in some kind of blunder that does not cause pain or disaster. Consequently, mistaken identity and the mayhem it generates were common motifs in early comedy.

Today, most dramas have humorous moments and most comedies occasionally strike a note of drama. Modern theatre places no premium on slavish purity within the genres. The mood of a play can freely swing from dramatic to comic and back (and such plays are sometimes called *dramedies*). Life has both dramatic events and comical moments, and plays today tend to reflect the yin-yang of existence. And the wide range of moods made possible by this pendulum swing from drama to comedy — covering all the stops in between — enriches plays that are written today and makes it easier to for audiences to identify with the characters.

Letting them laugh: Comic relief

Prolonged and unremitting drama can be difficult to bear both in life and in life's reflection, theatre. A continuous stream of problems and tragic events can be depressing, colloquially and clinically. In that kind of a situation, people want and need the difficulties and negativity to stop or at least let up for a while.

The theatrical change of pace — the pause that refreshes, to cite an old soft drink slogan — is most often used in plays to give audiences a breather from heavy drama. This judicious and mutually beneficial act of mercy can be accomplished through what's called *comic relief.*

Comic relief is a break from the suspense and tension that build up in dramatic moments and that can be physically and emotionally draining. Comic relief manifests in a number of forms. It can be a humorous scene or light-hearted moment astutely placed amidst dramatic scenes. Or it can be achieved through the appearance of a witty or clownish character. It also can be amusing repartee in an otherwise dramatic work.

When *West Side Story* premiered on Broadway in 1957, it shocked audiences. Musical comedy aficionados were accustomed to comparatively light content — romance, humor, a relatively benign quest for the protagonist, upbeat song and dance, and a happy ending. With its stark depiction of gangs and gang life on the west side of upper Manhattan in the mid-50s, sweetness and light fare were not what *West Side Story* gave audiences. The story line of the bold, groundbreaking musical includes racism, a knife fight, violent deaths, a near rape, and a heartbreaking ending (the death of the protagonist, Tony). For Broadway, it was nothing short of revolutionary.

But as realistic and biting as *West Side Story* is, it has its merry moments, providing comic relief in the otherwise severe story:

- In the "America" song and dance number, the girlfriends of the Sharks (the girls and the Sharks in the movie) banter the pro and cons of life in the states versus their poverty in Puerto Rico. It's an audience favorite. The amiable mood it sets serves as the calm before the storm.

- Maria's "I Feel Pretty" song, which celebrates Maria's infatuation with Tony, is joyous and playful and provides a striking contrast to the bleak events that are about to overtake Maria.

✔ The clownish "Officer Krupke" number, sung by the otherwise tough and angry Jets gang, provides, prior to the gangs' war council, an outlet for pent-up tension and emotion for the characters as well as the audience.

When envisioning or outlining your play's story, think about those spots where comic relief can be used, particularly if your play is heavily dramatic. Comic relief is an important and effective tool.

Getting serious: Dramatic relief

Though *dramatic relief* isn't a formal term, I use it here to imply that, to a lesser extent, the opposite of comic relief also is true. Prolonged and incessant laughter can be uncomfortable. At one time or another you've probably found yourself laughing so hard about something that it hurt and you had trouble breathing. Too much of a good thing. In such a situation, you need the humor to pass, or at least pause, so you can catch your breath. You need a change of pace.

In addition, a touch of drama, even in the lightest of comedies, helps ground the play in reality and gives the show an emotional center. A dramatic moment or two can help highlight and elevate the stakes for the characters.

In most full-blown comedies, the protagonist's goals are clear and uncomplicated, the action tends to be fast and furious, and nothing seriously bad happens. And inevitably, there is a happy ending. The audience can be engaged and have a good time, but, though audiences may sympathize with the protagonist and her goals, little emotional connection with the character or her dilemma is generated. This kind of comedy is a laugh fest.

But given the opportunity to meet the protagonist and get to know her goals and aspirations in a muted, sober scene — a scene during which you allow audiences to know what makes the character tick — audiences bond with the character. Such a dramatic interlude allows audiences to identify with the character and to empathize. And when the comic events resume, audiences are rested and ready and emotionally invested in the protagonist and the outcome. The play becomes a comedy with warmth and heart.

Adding the soft touch: Love

Some people posit that every play is a love story. The old idea of the one universal plot (boy meets girl, boy loses girl, boy gets girl) is evidence of that belief. If you look at love as embracing more than romantic relationships, you can argue that love is at or near the heart, pun intended, of virtually all story lines. For instance,

- In the musical *Sweeney Todd: The Demon Barber of Fleet Street,* the title character's murderous campaign of revenge is fueled by his love for the wife he believes to be dead and for his daughter.

- In *Arsenic and Old Lace,* Mortimer Brewster's vigorous and desperate efforts to protect his elderly aunts from the consequences of their homicidal eccentricities are motivated by his love for the two women who brought him up.

- *A Doll House* can certainly be characterized as a love story. The entire plot hinges on the fact that Nora so loves her husband, Torvald, that she was willing to forge a document — in other words, commit an illegal act — so that she could secure money to care for Torvald during a serious illness.

- In *A Raisin in the Sun,* Walter Lee's love of his family and son and Mama Lena's love for Walter Lee propel much, if not all, of the action of the play. Beneatha's relationship with her two romantic suitors provides the play with one of its major subplots (and some of its comic relief).

A love affair or romantic angle in a play softens and humanizes almost any story. Audiences are drawn into a story on two levels, the emotional and the intellectual. No matter how complicated, remote, or inaccessible the intellectual aspect of your story line may be, when love and romance are involved somewhere, your audiences will be able to connect. Love and romance inflame the emotions, engage the imagination, tap into our yearnings, and invite audiences to experience the love vicariously.

 Consider adding a love or romantic angle to your play if it isn't already there. A convenient way to do so is to concoct a subplot that involves characters dealing in some way with love or romance. The love threads in *Hamlet,* with the possible exception of Hamlet's love of his father, are all subplots.

Isn't it loverly?

I have trouble thinking of a play in which love doesn't play a significant part. Even the energetic insistence of the great George Bernard Shaw that his play *Pygmalion* (and, by extension, the musical version, *My Fair Lady*) was not a love story couldn't purge the romantic angle everyone else sees in it. Shaw was adamant that there was no way Eliza Doolittle, the common flower girl, and Professor Henry Higgins, a member (though a rebellious one) of the upper class, could end up as a couple. Shaw, the killjoy, even went as far as to write a postscript to his play specifying that Eliza ends up with another character in the play, the charming ne'er-do-well Freddy Eynsford-Hill.

So I suppose if you look hard enough, you can find plays in which romance or love of any sort is effectively absent. But where's the fun in that?

Making the End of Act 1 a Nail-Biter

Most contemporary full-length plays are divided into two acts — Act I and Act II. Between the acts is an intermission, a 10- or 15-minute interval during which the minds of audiences can drift back to their real-world concerns — from returning phone calls to finding the lavatories. Unfortunately, some audience members also see it as an opportunity to leave the theatre and head home.

Your best insurance against losing your audience, mentally or physically, is to structure the end of your first act so that you give audience members a clear and captivating reason to return to their seats. That they may have paid dearly for their tickets is not enough to guarantee that the audience will remain engaged, or remain at all.

In an attempt to avoid an early exodus from the theatre, I've actually heard directors suggest to playwrights that they should shorten their plays and eliminate the act break so that audiences will have no opportunity to leave. This tactic is hardly a compliment to the author or an expression of confidence in the work. And it's a silly and counterproductive solution to the intermission conundrum.

This section deals with ways in which you can meet the challenge of intriguing and hanging on to your audiences.

Heightening the protagonist's dilemma

The most productive way to keep your audiences coming back, both emotionally and physically, from an intermission is to heighten the protagonist's dilemma at the end of the first act.

End the act with a response to that handy obstacle question: What's the worst thing that can happen to the protagonist at this moment? If the worst thing does happen at the end of an act, you likely will arouse a natural curiosity in audience members. How is this dilemma going to turn out? Curiosity will help bring them back after intermission.

Amplifying the intensity with a point of no return

The *point of no return* is a landmark moment in a play when the dilemma is considerably heightened for the protagonist. It's a juncture at which there's no going back for the character. The world for the protagonist has changed, and she must continue forward no matter what the impediments are.

Here are a couple of outstanding examples of points of no return:

✔ The first act of *West Side Story,* a two-act musical, ends with one of the most breathtaking moments in American musical theatre. The lethal rumble has occurred, and the Jets and Sharks gangs scatter at the sound of a siren on an approaching police car. On the ground are the bodies of Riff and Bernardo, both stabbed to death. Wailing over them is the protagonist, Tony, who has just killed Bernardo, the brother of his lady-love, Maria. As the siren grows louder, the character Anybodys tugs at the distraught Tony, urging him to leave the scene. The desolate and somber sound of a distant chiming clock is the dirge for the dead as the curtain falls on Act I. The dilemma for Tony could hardly be more heightened. He is a killer, and nothing can change that fact. How could anyone not come back to see what happens next?

✔ *A Raisin in the Sun* is a three-act play. The second act, or middle, of *Raisin* ends with an excruciating dilemma for Walter Lee. He and his family have just been jolted to the core by the news that one of Walter Lee's business partners has run off with the insurance money entrusted to Walter Lee. This money had become the focal point of the family's dreams and aspirations, and its loss is a crushing blow to Walter Lee, his mother, who's planning to buy a house for the family, and his sister, Beneatha, who had expected to use some of that money for medical school. Walter Lee agonizes under the weight of his failure to act responsibly. He can't take it back. The disastrous loss is irreversible. What can he do? Who wouldn't want to come back to find out?

Surveying Middles in Three Plays

This chapter deals with a number of considerations involved in the development of the story line in the middle portion of your play, including obstacles, escalating action, reversals, suspense, tension, comic relief, mood, romance, foreshadowing, and points of no return. The following sections give you a glimpse at the role some of these elements play in how three classic dramas handle their middle sections.

Obstacles for Hamlet

Shakespeare's *Hamlet* provides a model for the sequencing of obstacles, impediments put in the path of the protagonist. The entire middle section of the play essentially consists of Hamlet negotiating one hurdle after another, some of his own making, in his quest to revenge the murder of his father by murdering the murderer, the new king, Claudius. The middle of the play is an unbroken chain of escalating gains and reversals.

As a tactic in his mission, Hamlet feigns madness, and, as a result, he faces an obstacle, spies. The king sends Hamlet's friends, Rosencrantz and Guildenstern, to check on Hamlet and report back. However, Hamlet sidesteps this trap when he quickly surmises what his friends are after. The price paid for skirting this obstacle is the loss of friendship. The next potential roadblock is the fair Ophelia. Polonius, the king's adviser, uses his daughter as bait to entice information from Hamlet. Again, Hamlet gets wise to the ruse, and, in anger and frustration, gives Ophelia a tongue-lashing, ultimately ordering her to a nunnery. Another hurdle cleared. The price paid for this discovery is the destruction of their relationship.

After he satisfies himself that Claudius is indeed guilty of murder, Hamlet comes across the new king alone in a chapel in prayer. Hamlet could easily slay the slayer and be done with his mission. But instead he bypasses the opportunity because he's afraid he'd send the king to heaven if the king dies while praying. Here the obstacle really is Hamlet's lack of resolve, and the price he pays for not putting aside this arbitrary obstacle is the prolonging of the quest (with fatal consequences to others).

Hamlet visits his mother's chambers and badgers his mother about her remarriage to Claudius. Thinking a figure hiding behind a curtain is King Claudius, Hamlet stabs through the curtain and kills the meddlesome Polonius. The price Hamlet pays for removing this obstacle is the melancholy and subsequent death of Ophelia; the hatred of Polonius's son, Laertes; and an enforced trip to England, where the king has ordered Hamlet's death. And so on. The events of Shakespeare's immensely popular play continue in tight causality, one obstacle leading to another until the climax, the final confrontation between Hamlet and Laertes (the king's surrogate) and between Hamlet and King Claudius himself.

Suspense and tension in A Doll House

In Henrik Ibsen's *A Doll House,* suspense and tension build as Nils Krogstad, who is blackmailing the protagonist, Nora Helmer, using documents she forged years earlier, sends a letter to Nora's prim and proper husband, Torvald, revealing all. Krogstad threatens Torvald with ruin (by making Nora's crime public) if Torvald does not continue to employ him at the bank Torvald manages.

Nora knows that Torvald soon will get and read Krogstad's explosive letter. Meanwhile, Nora's friend, Mrs. Linde, has gone to make an appeal to Krogstad to take back the letter. Tension and suspense build as Nora tries tactic after tactic to delay Torvald from retrieving his mail, including frantically performing for him a dance she will do at a costume party later.

If Torvald reads the letter, it will destroy his trust in Nora and devastate their marriage. The Helmers' "doll house" existence is hanging in the balance, building the suspense and tension. Will the letter be intercepted or will Helmer's disillusionment come and his idyllic house of cards collapse?

Comic relief in A Raisin in the Sun

The second act of *A Raisin in the Sun* (the middle of this three-act play) immediately follows the taut ending of the first act, a scene in which Walter Lee refuses to interfere with the plans of his wife, Ruth, to get an illegal abortion. Ruth is emotionally strung out, Mama Lena is scandalized and in a rage, and Walter Lee is shaken yet unmoved in his resolve to put his liquor store dream above all else. After this emotional, gut-wrenching ending to Act I, Act II opens with a moment of comic relief.

Walter Lee's sister, Beneatha, enters the stage from a bedroom dressed in authentic African garb, a gift from an admirer — a college student from Nigeria. After proudly promenading around the room for Ruth's benefit, Beneatha plays a record of African drumming and chanting and dances a folk dance. Walter Lee enters the apartment, drunk, and gets into the drumming. He leaps up onto the kitchen table and extemporizes an African scene. Another of Beneatha's admirers, a preppy, very much assimilated college student, walks into this chaotic scene. He's stunned and none too happy about what he sees Beneath doing, putting a comic button on the scene. The scene is a masterful blend of respect for African traditions and Beneatha's overly ardent and thus humorous attempt to look the part of a well-dressed Nigerian woman.

This moment of levity allows the audience to catch its breath after the drama of the previous scene, and, refreshed, the audience is readied for the powerful and emotionally jarring events to come.

Chapter 12

The Climax: Bringing the Conflict to a Head

In This Chapter

▶ Creating the climactic moment

▶ Knowing how your play ends

▶ Avoiding inferior endings

▶ Making sure your audiences are satisfied

*I*f the middle of a play is the place in a script where many writers get bogged down, then the finale of a play is the second-most dicey terrain to cover. As a playwright, you're continually challenged to come up with an ending for your play that's

✔ Appropriate to the story you're telling

✔ Satisfying to the audience you're writing for

✔ Somewhat surprising or unexpected

Even Anton Pavlovich Chekhov, one of the world's great playwrights, was bedeviled by the seeming impossibility of coming up with fresh endings to plays. In an 1892 letter to a friend, he complained: "The hero either gets married or shoots himself."

Undoubtedly, in moments of less stress, Chekhov would have acknowledged at least a handful of ways to end a play that don't involve matrimony or suicide. But his frustration illustrates the difficulty you may face in meeting the challenge of coming up with an ending for a play.

This chapter assists you in bringing your play to a satisfying and justified conclusion. It details how to bring the opposing energies of the play to a head and provides advice in avoiding common pitfalls in play endings.

Acknowledging Where Your Story Stands

In the opening of your play, you introduce your characters, and, through an inciting incident, you launch your protagonist on his vital and urgent quest. In the middle of your play, your protagonist contends with a series of obstacles, increasing in difficulty, on his way to the goal of his quest. Okay, now what?

Some playwrights (and writers of all sorts, for that matter) begin their work not knowing where it will end. For this kind of playwright, the task of writing is also a journey of exploration. The writer works with the confidence that he and his protagonist will discover their way to a fitting conclusion for the trek.

Other playwrights embark on their projects with their stories comprehensively outlined; they travel with a detailed road map. For such a playwright, the skeleton of the play is in place; he needs only to put the flesh and blood on the bare bones to bring his creation to life.

In practical fact, most playwrights work somewhere in between these two extremes. They begin with at least a tangible sense of direction and a maybe slightly hazy vision of the play's destination, written or not. And at the same time, they're willing to make discoveries along the way.

By the time you've written the beginning and middle of your play, either by a process of discovery or through planning, you've arrived at the third and final leg of the journey — the ending. For the purposes of this exploration, the *ending* of a play is both the climax (addressed in this chapter) and the resolution (discussed in Chapter 13).

One of the responsibilities of the playwright is to deliver to his audiences a satisfactory and fulfilling ending. But a good ending doesn't necessarily mean a happy ending or even the ending audiences want. It means an ending, surprising or not, that brings the story to an artistically satisfying conclusion. You must write a finale that, in retrospect, will seem to the audience truthful, plausible (given the circumstances), and maybe even inevitable.

The ending is the play's moment of truth. And the end begins with the climax.

Crafting the Play's Climax

As with the other main segments of stage storytelling — the beginning and the middle — writing the ending of your play takes thought, preparation, and craft. The good news is that you're at least two-thirds of the way through your play, and you know the moment that's coming — the climax.

Your climactic scene is the moment the entire play has been building toward, whether you were conscious of that or just taking it step by step. It's the moment when your protagonist succeeds or fails in his mission, after which a new stasis or stability (the resolution) will be achieved in the landscape of your play.

This section deals with the writing an effective climax, the ultimate confrontation of the play. (I cover the resolution, which comes after the climax, in Chapter 13.)

Building to the climax

The *climax* or *climactic moment* is a point near the end of your play when the protagonist and antagonist confront each other for the final time. Only one emerges victorious. (For a recap of protagonist and antagonist, turn to Chapter 6.)

The climactic event can involve almost any kind of confrontation, from a grand physical showdown — as in the final duel in Neverland between Peter Pan and Captain Hook — to the touchy and touching ending of John Van Druten's *Bell, Book and Candle* in which, after much turmoil and confusion, the protagonist finds that the man she loves accepts her and returns her love.

Don't confuse the climax of the play with moments of high passion or frantic activity. Though those moments may be peaks in the upward-sloping zigzag line of story, the climax is the ultimate peak, the culminating event that ends your protagonist's journey. At the climax, the spine of the play, the plot of your story, comes to an end. The audience now knows what it's been waiting to find out — how things turn out for the protagonist in the end.

In a play where the protagonist is destined to fail to achieve his goal — a story in which the protagonist heroically goes down in flames — the climactic moment often is preceded by an achievement or noticeable gain toward the goal. This short-lived positive note sets the audience up to experience, along with the protagonist, the distress and disappointment of the final defeat.

In *A Doll House,* as the play barrels toward its climactic scene, the audience believes for a moment that the blackmail letter to Torvald (the note that will destroy Nora's marriage and her idyllic existence) may be intercepted before it reaches Torvald. But this glint of hope is dashed by, of all people, Nora's friend and ally, Christine Linde. Mrs. Linde decides that Torvald should know about Nora's long-hidden crime, and she discourages Krogstad from retrieving the letter because she believes airing the truth will be much better for all than perpetuating the secret. (With friends like that . . .)

In plays where the protagonist is going to succeed his mission, the climactic moment — his victory — is often preceded by a low point, a negative reversal from which it looks like the protagonist cannot recover. Then in a final reversal of fortunes, the protagonist triumphs.

For example, in *A Raisin in the Sun,* Walter Lee Younger, who has been desperate to get his hands on family insurance money so that he can invest in a liquor store, is at his lowest point just before the climactic scene. He discovers that one of his potential business partners has absconded with the money. Walter Lee has been scammed, costing his mother and sister the financial resources that might have helped them fulfill their dreams. However, in the play's climactic moment, Walter Lee, emotionally and spiritually devastated, rises up from the ashes of his thwarted aspirations and finds the moral strength to refuse money intended to buy the Younger family out of moving into an all-white neighborhood.

Pitting the protagonist against the antagonist: Mano a mano

The climactic scene the play has been heading for brings together the protagonist — your main character — with the antagonist — the person or thing that has opposed the protagonist's mission. It's a *mano a mano* battle that can be an emotional, psychological, and/or physical showdown.

Emotional climax

The climactic moment can be an emotional scene, as in *The Miracle Worker,* by William Gibson. Annie Sullivan has been hired by the Keller family to try to communicate with and instruct the wild young Helen, who has been deaf and blind from early childhood. The process has been emotionally and physically difficult for Annie and Helen, and has tried the patience of the Keller family, particularly the patriarch of the family, Captain Keller.

In Act III, Annie Sullivan (the miracle worker of the title) is at a low point. It appears Annie's slow and painful progress with Helen is about to be undone by Helen's well-meaning but overindulgent father. Nevertheless, against the will of the autocratic Captain Keller, Annie drags Helen out of the house to a water pump. In what the characters and the audience suspect will be Annie's last hand-to-hand struggle (literally) with young Helen before she's fired, Annie forces Helen to refill a water pitcher she dumped on Annie.

As Helen pumps the water, the physical contact with the flowing water awakens in Helen vestigial memory from her infancy (prior to the illness that took her sight and hearing). In one of the most emotionally powerful scenes in theatre, Helen makes the connection between a remembered baby word, "wah-wah" (water), and the liquid gushing from the pump. At that moment, Helen realizes that everything has a name, and the world is opened to her. Annie, the protagonist, emerges victorious from her climactic confrontation with the forces, Helen's stubbornness included, that had kept the child isolated and in the dark.

Psychological climax

In *Twelve Angry Men,* the climactic moment is more psychological than emotional, but it still packs an emotional wallop. Juror #8 (the characters in the play are not given names, only jury numbers), who starts out as the lone not-guilty vote among the jurors, has been waging a campaign to get his fellow jurors to look more closely at the evidence from the trial, in which a young man stands accused of killing his father. As the jury members struggle to be meticulous and objective, one by one they see huge flaws in the evidence and begin arriving at not-guilty verdicts.

If any juror alone is the antagonist, it's Juror #3, who throughout the play cajoles, badgers, and bullies the other jurors to stay the course and vote guilty, a verdict that would send the young man to the electric chair. The climax approaches as Juror #3 remains the lone guilty vote and vows to hold his ground in spite of the opinions of the other 11 jurors.

The stalemate continues as the jurors, led by Juror #8, demand to know Juror #3's thinking. In the climactic moment of the play, in a rage and unable to present a coherent argument for his point of view, Juror #3 breaks down into tears, finally realizing that his stubbornness stems from his anger at his own son, from whom he is estranged. Juror #3 votes not guilty, and the jury is unanimous. The plot is concluded. The audience now knows how things turn out for the protagonist, Juror #8. He attentively and persistently did his civic duty as a juror, and he saved the life of an innocent young man.

Physical climax

Few climactic moments in plays turn on a physical confrontation more vividly than *A Streetcar Named Desire.* In the play's explosive confrontation, one that is brewing from the beginning, the delicate but exasperating protagonist, Blanche DuBois, is assaulted and raped by her brother-in-law, Stanley Kowalski, whom she antagonizes almost from the start of the play. Blanche's irritating and self-destructive ways don't justify the brutality visited upon her, an attack that drives her over the brink into insanity. But you know what they say about playing with fire. In this physical climactic confrontation, the protagonist loses, her flaws contributing to her downfall.

The last character standing

To use a combat metaphor, in the final showdown between the protagonist and antagonist — be the antagonist a person or thing — only the victor should remain standing. One side is triumphant and the other is defeated. Consider these three examples:

✔ *The Miracle Worker:* Annie Sullivan stubbornly struggled against the forces, sometimes well-meaning, that kept Helen Keller in an almost impenetrable shell. Annie's unrelenting efforts to reach and teach Helen lead finally to the breakthrough in spite of the obstacles presented by Helen's family and by Helen's disabilities. In the end, Annie wins.

✔ *Twelve Angry Men:* Juror #8 doggedly fights to overcome lethargy, obstinacy, and prejudice, principally represented by Jurors #10, #4, and #3, and successfully gets the jury to do its job. The result is a not-guilty verdict for the defendant and a victory for Juror #8, overcoming his fellow jurors' opposition.

✔ *A Streetcar Named Desire:* Protagonist Blanche DuBois, in desperate need of help, support, and love, undermines herself with her instinctive attitudes of superiority and with her meddling in her sister's marriage. Like a wolf protecting its territory against interlopers, Stanley Kowalski fiercely defends his turf and vanquishes the invader. Here the antagonist, Stanley, remains standing, and what's left of Blanche, physically and psychologically, is removed to an asylum.

Firing Chekhov's gun

The great 19th-century Russian playwright Anton Chekhov famously said that if in Act I you have a pistol hanging on a wall, then it must be fired in the last act. The quote has several variations, but the point is that the noticeable presence of a gun creates the expectation that it will be used. The prominent existence onstage of so strong a symbol of violence and death cannot be ignored or easily forgotten by the audience. It creates, if not an obligatory scene (see Chapter 3), an obligatory moment in which the weapon will be used in some way. Otherwise why is it there?

The phrase *Chekhov's gun* is sometimes used to mean foreshadowing, describing a person, place, thing, or idea that comes up early in a play but doesn't play a significant role until later on. However, most Chekhov aficionados agree that he wasn't suggesting foreshadowing.

Chekhov's statement is more commonly understood to mean that you should never write into your script the presence of any powerful or attention-getting item, like a gun, if it's not going to be used later in the play. The audience naturally develops the expectation that this riveting item will come into play at some point.

For example, if a medieval suit of armor is standing upright some place onstage, it's going to attract notice. Inevitably, audience members will wonder why it's there and come to the conclusion that it will play some role in the coming events. And if that suit of armor isn't worn by a character, used as a hiding place for something, or put to use some other way, the audience will leave puzzled or disappointed.

Although audiences willingly accept the set on a stage as representing reality, still they are aware on some level that what's seen on the stage was put there by conscious choice, be it a gun, suit of armor, or a portrait of a giant rabbit hung over a fireplace. The audience will rightfully infer that the conspicuous object was put there for a reason and will have a function in the play.

Finding the Ending to Your Story

Playwrights are sometimes undecided about whether their story should end happily or not. Deciding whether the protagonist achieves his goal or not can be difficult.

Working on a full-length play takes time, often much more time than you may suppose — many months and even years. Therefore, you may lose sight of your destination even when you're so close to the end of the play. At such a point, referring back to your outline is helpful. Your answer may be right there on paper (or on your screen). If you haven't outlined your play, a close review of your play to this point may refresh you on your initial impulses concerning the plot and its conclusion. This careful rereading of your play may reveal to you the direction in which your play is heading, even if you've not been conscious of it. In other words, see where your initial instincts take you.

Also consider your play's theme. Endings have ramifications. What kind of ending best drives home the underlying message of your play? If your play truly can go either way, with your protagonist succeeding or not, you have a problem. All the events of your play, particularly those in the middle of the play, should have been building, even if it's not obvious, to a particular ending. If you find your ending can go either way, then your causality is flawed, and you should revisit and revise the chain of events leading to the climax (see Chapter 11).

This section helps you consider the best type of conclusion for your play by examining the appropriateness and justification of various types of endings.

Identifying whether your play ends happily

Does your play end happily, unhappily, or neither? Yes, "neither" is an option. Though most people, including me, find ambiguous endings frustrating, sometimes stories do end inconclusively, leaving the audience to fill in the blanks and come up with answers for themselves.

According to the great playwright George Bernard Shaw, Henrik Ibsen's *A Doll House* is an example of how a play can end indeterminately. The play closes with the protagonist, Nora, literally walking out on her husband, Torvald, and leaving her children behind. She's leaving her doll house existence to find herself and to discover her rightful role in life. Does her journey end happily? Only Ibsen knew, and he isn't talking.

Shaw, however, felt the indeterminate ending to *A Doll House* served a positive purpose. He believed that leaving audiences up in the air, rather than simply supplying them with a neatly resolved conclusion, led them to reflect more on character and theme than specific events. Ibsen's indeterminate ending, as Shaw saw it, essentially says that no one knows what the role for women is in this new modern world. It's something that's yet to be discovered.

Twelve Angry Men ends happily, meaning successfully for the protagonist, Juror #8. The evidence presented in the trial is closely scrutinized, and the jury arrives at a fair verdict. A young man, the accused, is set free. The positive ending of Reginald Rose's courtroom drama helps illustrate the theme that one man (person) *can* make a difference. And it makes the point that, if we don't pay close attention and make an effort to do the right thing, injustice can hold sway. A negative ending would not have made these points.

On the other hand, *A Streetcar Named Desire* ends unhappily for the protagonist, Blanche DuBois. She's failed in her quest to find a safe haven for herself. Her thin grasp on reality has been destroyed, and she's carted off to a mental institution. The Tennessee Williams masterpiece depicts an American South that's changing from an idealized agrarian and genteel culture to a modern industrial and coarser society, a world that can be pitiless and brutal to the vulnerable. Blanche clings to a South that no longer exists. Much of the malevolence that she experiences results from shameful behavior that takes its toll. Blanche's fantasy world proves to be as flimsy as the colorful Chinese paper lanterns she hung on light bulbs.

Clearly, Williams saw the new South as inhospitable, and a positive ending for Blanche would have undermined that sentiment. The play's grim ending mirrors the playwright's grim take on the transformation of the South.

Mixing emotions: Bittersweet finales

Plays can have endings that are both happy and unhappy. This type of ending can be referred to as *bittersweet,* a conclusion that's happy with overtones of sadness or regret, or an ending that's sad but tinged with a sense of joy or optimism for the future.

The ending of *Cyrano de Bergerac* clearly qualifies as bittersweet. Cyrano, a soldier, poet, and one of the most feared swordsmen in Paris, is in love with his cousin, Roxane. But he dares not reveal to her his love because he believes that his extremely large nose makes him hideous and impossible to love. Roxane instead falls in love with a young, handsome soldier, Christian. Because Christian is totally inarticulate when it comes to women, Cyrano hides himself and feeds Christian the poetic words of love that Christian, in turn, professes aloud to Roxane. Cyrano can only speak his love to Roxane through the poems and letters he composes for Christian's use. When Christian is killed in battle, Roxane, in her grief, so idolizes Christian's poetic nature that Cyrano cannot bring himself to shatter the myth and tell Roxane the truth. Roxane retires to a convent.

Fifteen years later, Cyrano, who visits Roxane weekly, is ambushed by his enemies and is struck a fatal blow to the head. Cyrano manages one last visit to Roxane during which, in the climactic moment of the play, she realizes that the man whose poetic soul she's loved all along was Cyrano. She declares her love for Cyrano, who dies happy, comforted that he is loved and will be remembered. So sad, and yet Cyrano finally gets to bask in the warmth of Roxane's love, even if only briefly.

What the bittersweet ending of *Cyrano* accomplishes is twofold. It emphasizes the sacrifice Cyrano was willing to make, even after Christian's death, to preserve, for her sake, the illusion with which Roxane was in love. And at the same time, it allows Cyrano to be rewarded for his unselfishness without diminishing the magnitude of his sacrifice.

Bittersweet endings can be touching and poignant, and if you're going for emotional impact on a personal level, this kind of ending can achieve that. The downside is that very likely some audience members will negatively label the ending as "sentimental." But if you see the ending of your play as double-edged — with a combination of happy and sad elements — go for it. If it's truthful (unforced), most audiences will respond to it.

Making sense of surprise endings

A surprise ending is a conclusion to your story that the audience didn't see coming. Or if the final events were indeed anticipated, it can be an ending that was reached in an unexpected way, as in *The Miracle Worker*. In that play, the audience has to assume, from the title if from nothing else, that Annie Sullivan will work a miracle. The audience takes for granted she will find a way to lift the opaque curtain of deafness and blindness that has kept young Helen Keller from understanding and interacting with the world. But *how* Annie does it is what surprises the audience.

Throughout the play, which is based on a true story, Annie Sullivan works tirelessly to spell words into Helen's hand using a specialized hand-in-hand alphabet. Annie's enormous quest is to get the uncooperative and often unmanageable child to understand and communicate. But though Helen can repeat back the hand spellings, she's just mimicking Annie. Helen has no idea that she's spelling words and that the words have meaning.

Despite Annie Sullivan's determination and best efforts, she's unable to make a breakthrough with Helen. The patience of the Keller family has run out, and the feisty Annie may very well be dismissed. Just as all seems lost, Helen and Annie engage in what appears to be just another one of their many battles of will — but this one, involving a foreshadowed faint memory of water, leads to the surprising "miracle" breakthrough.

The key to making the moment believable is the foreshadowing. *Foreshadowing,* or *planting,* is the unobtrusive embedding into the script of a seemingly unimportant idea or event that later pays off big time. It makes the later moment plausible, and it's an especially important tool if you're planning to use a surprise ending.

At little past halfway through *The Miracle Worker,* Helen's mother, Kate, pleads with Annie to continue her work. She points out that Helen, despite outward appearances, is an intelligent little girl. She was a smart baby, beginning to speak when she was only six months old.

> *"She could say the word 'water.' Not really — 'wah-wah.' 'Wah-wah,' but she knew what it meant."*

In those few lines, playwright William Gibson inconspicuously plants the idea that as an infant Helen knew what water is and understood it has a name. This ostensibly minor tidbit, which is now lodged in the back of the minds of audience members, enables the surprise ending — Helen's memory of her baby word for water — to work. The surprise ending, given Kate's explanation above, makes sense and is believable.

Without the foreshadowing — the recollection of the word "wah-wah" by Helen — the concluding event would have seemed to come out of nowhere. It would have come across as a convenient event just added on to the story to wrap things up. Such an ending is known as *deus ex machina,* and I explain it in the next section.

Avoiding the Problematic Deus ex Machina Ending

When engaged by storytelling of almost any kind, contemporary audiences expect that the protagonist will solve (or not solve) his problem or reach (or not reach) his goal by his own efforts. Modern audiences do not find it satisfying to follow the progress of the main character through thick and thin only to have him rescued, or have his problem solved, at the end by some person or thing that had little or no relationship to the story.

A person or thing that is introduced suddenly and unexpectedly, providing a contrived and convenient solution to an apparently insoluble difficulty, is called a *deus ex machina* event. The Latin phrase translates as "god out of a machine." It refers to a plot device, used by some ancient Greek playwrights, by which a god materializes at the end of the play to solve the problems of the characters. The god character would appear onstage lowered by a crane, as if descending from the heavens, and the deity would bring order to the chaos, deciding the play's outcome. That technique may have worked for audiences a couple millennia ago, but a contemporary story with a deus ex machina ending is considered flawed.

The deus ex machina ending can be seen in the old clichéd western films in which cowboys and Indians do battle, only to have the outcome decided by the last-minute arrival of the cavalry. The Indians are routed and the cowboys are saved. (Of course, most westerns never dealt with the likelihood that the cowboys got themselves into that tight spot by encroaching on Native American lands.) This last-minute, something-out-of-nowhere-saves-the-day ending cheats the audience out of the opportunity to see how the opponents would have solved the problem themselves.

At the end of the classic 1939 film *The Wizard of Oz* and the stage play based on it, just after Dorothy misses the Wizard's balloon that was to carry her home to Kansas, the good witch, Glinda, very conveniently appears again. She tells Dorothy she had the power to return home all along simply by using the power of the magic slippers she's wearing. Dorothy's mission is accomplished through the unexpected intervention of a relatively minor character, Glinda.

In the original story by L. Frank Baum, this deus ex machina ending is even more blatant. Glinda appears only once, and it's at the end of the story, just when Dorothy is in need of a miracle. Talk about good timing.

In Joseph Kesselring's timeless farce comedy, *Arsenic and Old Lace,* Mortimer Brewster is about to get married to the local minister's daughter, Elaine. However, Mortimer's dreams of wedded bliss are derailed when he accidentally finds out that his charming and considerate aunties, who brought him up, have been poisoning sad and lonely old men and burying the gents in the basement of their Brooklyn home. This discovery, added to the fact that Mortimer's two brothers are loony, convinces Mortimer he can't marry the lovely and innocent Elaine because "Insanity runs in the family. It practically gallops!" His engagement and happiness on the rocks, Mortimer strives to protect his aunts by getting the precious but dangerous old ladies and one of his brothers committed to the cozy local mental asylum.

Deus ex machina rears its ugly head in this comic masterpiece to lift the roadblock to Mortimer's marriage to Elaine. As they are about to be committed, Aunt Abby and Aunt Martha reveal a long-held and sad secret: As an infant, Mortimer was taken in by them. Mortimer is not a blood member of the Brewster family. While revelations of this kind — the mistaken identity — are a staple of farce comedy, it's a solution to Mortimer's dilemma that's provided by someone other than himself and it comes out of nowhere. Textbook deus ex machina. (But don't let that stop you from enjoying this madcap play.)

Satisfying the Audience

One of the trickiest and sometimes most awkward questions to ask and answer about the climax and ending of your play is: Will this satisfy audiences? Will they go home feeling they've witnessed a complete and satisfying story with an appropriate conclusion? Or will they go home frustrated and unhappy with the experience?

A number of considerations are involved in dealing with making the ending of your play satisfying and fulfilling to the audience. Audiences can be disappointed with the ending for the following three reasons:

- **The conclusion doesn't seem earned:** Audiences are discontent if the ending seems tacked on rather than logically arrived at.

- **The ending isn't what they wanted:** Even if your ending is earned, if it's not what the audiences crave, they're likely to be unhappy.

- **The ending isn't standard for the genre of your play:** Audiences are likely to be thrown if the ending isn't what's expected from the genre you're working in.

Knowing the potential problems can help you deal with any uneasiness (or potential uneasiness) about writing an ending and any issues your climax may have. The following sections discuss these main problems so you can craft an ending that satisfies audiences and does you proud.

Building up to an earned conclusion

Plays have a cause-and-effect structure. Unlike life, in which good and bad things can happen at random, events in created stories should occur in a cause-and-effect pattern. One event, choice, decision, or action should lead directly to another event, choice, decision, or action, and so on. If any of these elements is changed, the direction of the play must be changed accordingly.

This causality that links the events of your play leads you to an *earned conclusion.* The earned conclusion is an ending to your play that's justified by the events that came before. It's a relevant and plausible ending that is appropriate to the story you're telling.

An earned conclusion sometimes, in retrospect, can be seen as inevitable. In other words, given the events of the plot, this particular ending seems unavoidable. It's the ending to which the play was heading all along, whether it was anticipated by the audience or not.

But inevitable does not equate with predictable. The sense that this ending is right for the story, that it's an earned conclusion, should come to the audience at the end. The ending should not be predictable from the start.

Think of the inevitability as analogous to the criminal trial process. At the beginning of the trial, you, as a juror, don't know if the defendant is guilty or innocent. The verdict is not predictable. But after hearing the evidence presented by the prosecution and defense, you and your juror colleagues come to a decision. The specific verdict is the equivalent of a story's earned conclusion. Looking back over the testimony given in the trial, it seems unavoidable that this verdict would be reached. But that clarity comes only after going through the process, after all the evidence was examined.

- In *Hamlet,* given Hamlet's foot dragging about avenging the murder of dear old dad, more and more people get involved and the body count climbs, making it almost inevitable that Hamlet himself, in the end, will go down in a blaze of glory. After being the cause, directly or indirectly, of the death of others, it seems unavoidable that Hamlet will pay for his bungling and procrastination with his own life. In retrospect, it's clear the events Hamlet brings about earn, fairly or not, what comes to him.

- In *A Streetcar Named Desire,* the flawed protagonist, Blanche DuBois, who desperately needs a place to crash and get away from the ghosts of her tarnished past, digs her own grave. Rather than being grateful for the hospitality, she insults and actively expresses disapproval of her host, her coarse brother-in-law, Stanley Kowalski. Blanche has entered a wolf's den, and, rather than making nice, she continuously pokes the wolf with a stick. She inevitably will be devoured. So looking back at the events of the play, Blanche's psychological destruction and physical humiliation is an earned conclusion — an inevitability — even though Stanley's actions are brutal and unpardonable.

These endings aren't predictable at the start, but, given the actions of the characters and the courses of events, the conclusions are justifiable or earned.

Revising to avoid an unearned conclusion

If the failure or potential failure to satisfy an audience with the end of your play is due to a conclusion that's unearned, the ball's in your court. If your ending is of the deus ex machina variety — a wrap-up that comes out of nowhere — then the solution is within your power. (Refer to the earlier section "Avoiding the Problematic Deus ex Machina Ending" for more explanation.) Fix the end of the play. Be sure that where your play ends is where the play had been heading. Let your protagonist overcome (or fail to overcome) his obstacles by his own efforts and not through convenient coincidence (as in *Arsenic and Old Lace*) or through the actions of a new or minor character (like Glinda in *The Wizard of Oz*).

If you're dead set on a particular ending that feels deus ex machina-ish, open the hood, go back into the engine of your play, and add some new parts. Foreshadow the end. Plant a person, place, thing, idea, or statement earlier in the play that hints at the possibilities related to your ending. But be subtle. You don't want to give away your ending. Just mention in passing, for example, the legend that a treasure was lost in the area centuries ago, so when your protagonist later uncovers a treasure and it's the key to his success, that plot point won't come out of nowhere.

Breakin' the audience's heart

Another cause of audience dissatisfaction is an ending that's not that what audiences were hoping for. For the most part, audiences naturally lean toward happy endings. Usually, they want the protagonist to succeed and live happily ever after. But the story lines of some plays, like many of life's situations, do not end happily.

For example, my play, *Journey of the Heart,* which dramatizes the tense deliberations of a hospital committee deciding which of two patients gets an available heart for transplant, does not end happily. Audiences yearn for a different result. But my ending is truthful and dramatizes the no-win and sometimes tragic decisions that are made every day in the field of organ transplantation.

Standing firm with an unhappy ending comes at a cost. Most ticketholders enjoy seeing upbeat or feel-good plays and are more likely to recommend to others plays with happy endings. Therefore, if your play ends sadly, it may not sell as many tickets as a comparable play with an upbeat ending. To change or not to change the ending is the question, and it was a question that *A Chorus Line* faced.

The creative team of *A Chorus Line,* one of the most successful musicals of all time, was in a quandary when the show premiered. The musical explores the difficult lives of show dancers as they audition for a new musical. Though it's an ensemble piece, one of the dancers, Cassie, gets a bit more attention than the others. The audience gets to know Cassie and pulls for her to land a job, but, in the end, she did not get a part in the show.

Marvin Hamlisch, the composer of the wonderful music for *A Chorus Line,* said that audiences left early performances of the show dissatisfied and disappointed that Cassie wasn't cast. Audiences identify with Cassie's desperation and hopes, and, when she failed to get the job, audiences felt let down. The creative team made a quick and simple fix: Cassie gets the job. Genius! And the rest, as they say, is history. Decades after its debut, the *A Chorus Line* is still the longest-running American-made Broadway musical.

When *A Doll House* was to open in Germany, the actress playing Nora considered the ending (Nora leaving her children) immoral. The playwright, Henrik Ibsen, fearing his play might be tampered with, himself changed the ending of the play so that Nora ultimately remains. The play was produced in a number of cities in Germany, but, without Ibsen's controversial ending, ticket sales dropped off. Ibsen restored his original ending, and the play became a classic of world theatre.

The change in ending in *A Chorus Line* worked, oddly enough, because of a lack of causality. The play doesn't build to an inevitable ending; it could have gone either way. So in that respect, the structure of the play was flawed, and the creators, no doubt, cried all the way to the bank. In short, the many other strengths of the marvelous show eclipsed that structural weakness. Ibsen's experience, on the other hand, demonstrates that when the conclusion is not truthful to the story you're staging, audiences will sense it and realize you backed off.

Should you change the ending of a play to accommodate the opinions and yearnings of others? There is no one answer to that question. Ask yourself how much violence the proposed alternate ending does to your play and to what you want to say with the play. I turned down a Minneapolis production of one of my plays because the director wanted to make changes in the play that I thought unnecessarily changed the tone. What *you* do in such a situation is, frankly, up to you and how badly you want or need a production. (See Chapter 3 for more on when to compromise and when to stand your ground.)

Exploring new ground with revolutionary material

Another type of ending can leave audiences startled, if not dissatisfied. Using in your ending any subject matter that's very different or unusual for the genre can, if well written and appropriately presented, catch the audience members' attention and make them think in a new way.

West Side Story is an example of play that contains material and events that made it revolutionary in its time. Broadway musicals generally are festive events with bouncy music, clever lyrics, sparkling dancing, and lighthearted and uplifting stories. But *West Side Story* not only ends sadly but also stages events that were unheard of in musicals at the time of its debut. *West Side Story* features racism, a gang rumble with a deadly knife fight, the violent deaths of three key characters, an attempted rape, and the shooting death of the protagonist. This is a Broadway musical comedy?

Legend has it that at the end of the premiere performance of the musical, the closing curtain was greeted by a disquieting stunned silence. The audience was shocked and unprepared for this kind of in-your-face reality in a musical. The actors backstage, waiting to trot out for their curtain call, were sure the audience hated the show. But, presently, the audience broke into wild and prolonged applause that signaled an enthusiastic, if slightly belated, acceptance of this new kind of Broadway play.

Surveying Climaxes in Three Plays

The moment of truth arrives in every play. The moment is the climax, the final confrontation between the protagonist and the antagonist, the latter being the person or thing that's been giving the protagonist a hard time. This chapter covers such considerations in wrapping up your play as the earned conclusion; sad, happy, bittersweet, surprise, and problematic endings; and audience satisfaction. In this section, I discuss how three classic plays handle some of these elements.

Hamlet's earned fate

Shakespeare's title character, Hamlet, essentially broods and bungles his way through his quest to avenge the murder of this father. Hamlet's decision not to kill King Claudius (the murderer) while he is praying leads directly to the killing of Polonius, the executions of Rosencrantz and Guildenstern, Ophelia's drowning, Hamlet's lethal duel with Laertes, and the poisoning of Queen Gertrude. Finally, Hamlet stabs and poisons King Claudius, as he himself is dying from a wound from a poisoned sword. The collateral damage is extensive.

That Hamlet, the protagonist, dies completing his quest, is an earned conclusion. The trail of bodies Hamlet leaves in his wake establishes the deadly gravity and consequences of his quest, and it seems appropriate that Hamlet should share the fate that his bungling caused others.

The procrastination of Hamlet, who had contemplated suicide earlier in the play, virtually ensured that Hamlet, ironically, would not survive the killing of King Claudius.

A Doll House rocks the boat

A Doll House, a play that seems tame by today's standards, shook society to its core with its revolutionary material. The ending of Henrik Ibsen's play changed theatre, and maybe even societal perceptions, forever.

When Torvald receives Krogstad's blackmail letter citing Nora's forgery of her father's signature, Torvald, to use an anachronistic phrase, goes ballistic. He rages at Nora for her naïveté, for what he considers her "irresponsible" actions (which probably saved his life), and for allegedly being a corrupting influence on their children. But contrary to what you may suppose, this highly emotional moment of alarm and outrage is not the play's climax. The story is not yet over.

The climactic moment is muted but powerful. It almost gets lost in the relative quiet that follows Torvald's venomous outburst at his wife. Torvald receives a second letter from Krogstad that takes back the threats in the first letter. Krogstad, who's found happiness again with a long lost love, calls the whole thing off. The blackmail thing? Eh, nevermind. As a result, Torvald is off the hook, and he magnanimously forgives Nora. But unbeknownst to him, the damage is done.

Torvald cannot take back the terrible things he said to Nora, and those words bring about the climactic moment. He violated the unwritten domestic compact of the time: The wife takes care of the children, the home, and the husband's needs, while the man of the house provides for and protects his family. Torvald, rather than standing up for his wife against Krogstad, turned on Nora. He had unintentionally exposed the shallowness and inequality of the traditional family arrangement. And for Nora there was no going back.

She tells Torvald that the blackmail crisis and his vicious response to it have made her see that she doesn't understand the social order and what her role is. She doesn't really know herself. All her life, she's lived like a toy doll in a doll house — first her father's and then Torvald's. Then the bombshell explodes. Nora tells Torvald that she's leaving him and the children. With this climax, the spine of the play is at its end. Nora's quest to prevent her past actions from destroying their conventional domesticity is over, and, ironically, in the end it is she who ends up tearing apart the sham existence.

This ending shocked audiences. Ending a play with a woman leaving her family was unheard of. Many critics excoriated the play, and for a time it was banned in England and elsewhere. So immense was the pressure of this overwhelmingly unhappy public reaction that Ibsen composed an alternative ending in which Nora is forgiven and resumes her customary role in the household, but Ibsen regretted and got rid of that rewritten ending.

A happy ending to A Raisin in the Sun

Unlike *Hamlet,* which ends in tragedy (which is to say unhappily), and *A Doll House,* which ends controversially (at least in its time), *A Raisin in the Sun* ends optimistically (happily).

Walter Lee Younger, who agitated the family in his quest to get his hands on an insurance check to finance his scheme to partner in a liquor store, gets his wish. Mama (Lena) Younger puts Walter Lee in charge of the family's precious resources. Walter Lee promptly loses it all by entrusting it to one of his business partners who runs off with the money.

Walter Lee, devastated and desperate to redeem himself with his family, contacts a representative of a homeowner's association who had offered to buy back, at a handsome profit to the Youngers, a house they recently purchased in his all-white neighborhood. Walter Lee is determined to take the money being offered even though it means capitalizing on racist fears.

The climactic moment comes when Mr. Lindner, the association rep, shows up ready to make the deal. Walter Lee, still reeling from the betrayal, at the last minute manages to summon the courage and self-respect to tell Mr. Lindner that he is refusing the deal and that the Youngers plan to be good neighbors. In the final analysis, Walter Lee has acted admirably and has taken his place as the head of the family. Even though the lost money isn't recovered, audiences leave this play feeling good because Walter Lee and his family are sticking together.

Chapter 13

The Resolution: Wrapping It All Up

In This Chapter

▶ Writing a final moment for your play

▶ Taking a look at how other plays settle into a new status quo

*Y*our play has had its climactic moment (see Chapter 12). The final confrontation has taken place, and the story line is at its end. Audiences now know what they've been waiting to find out — how things turn out for the protagonist. Your audiences have found out whether she's succeeded or fallen short in her quest. So what's left? What remains to be written? The resolution.

After the climax, consequences generally follow as the aftermath to the concluding event. In a play, a last brief moment or scene usually comes after the play is, for all intents and purposes, over, during which the audience gets to see how things have come to rest. This final glimpse, the *resolution,* is in essence an epilogue that gives the audience a peek at the new landscape of the world of the play.

The resolution is what remains after the climax. If you want to impress your friends, you can refer to the resolution as the *dénouement* (day-noo-*mah*), which translates as "untying." (Why call the resolution, during which you tie up loose ends, an "untying"? In Europe, the plot is seen as a complicated knot that needs untying. In the U.S., playwrights tend to think of the resolution as picking up the pieces, or "tying up the loose ends."

This chapter describes how to dramatize the consequences of the play's climax, the aftermath of the final protagonist/antagonist confrontation.

Picking Up the Pieces

Just before the curtain falls on your play, you can build in a moment of resolution. The resolution can follow seamlessly at the end of the climactic scene, or it can take place in an independent scene, usually short, after the climactic scene.

Whether as a coda to the climactic scene or in a scene of its own, the play's resolution gives the audience the chance to see how the world of the play has been altered and what becomes of the characters' efforts and/or situation. This section deals with writing your play's resolution, tying up all loose ends, and returning the world of your story to a new equilibrium.

Revealing how the dust settles

Imagine your play's climactic moment as a tornado. A number of weather factors come together to create the conditions that spawn the funnel cloud. The violent storm visits havoc upon anything in its path, and then it disappears. When the dust settles, inevitably things are changed. Some have been hit hard by the twister, and others are spared. Either way, the community is not the same, and never again will be, after the cataclysm.

A play's resolution is the landscape in the world of the play after the climactic storm, big or small. The resolution of a story can be immense and in your face or it can be diminutive and simple.

A dramatic resolution

In the final scene of *A Streetcar Named Desire,* the resolution is large, dramatic, and heartrending. It comes in an independent scene set several weeks after the climactic scene. Two representatives of a mental asylum come to fetch Blanche DuBois, who's been mentally and physically devastated by Stanley in the climactic scene. Now, lost in her fantasy world, Blanche at first panics and struggles fiercely against her new custodians. Finally, however, she submits to the kindness of one of the strangers and is taken away. Her sister, Stella, who chooses not to believe Blanche's story that Stanley raped her, resumes her passionate relationship with her husband. Blanche is gone and, as far as we can tell, Stanley and Stella and their new baby live happily ever after.

Forcing a "moral" resolution

When the 1951 film of *A Streetcar Named Desire* was made, Hollywood censors forced a different resolution on the story. According to the Hays, or Production, Code (which existed from the 1930s through most of the 1960s), a film could not allow a wrongdoer to get away with his crime; the miscreant had to get what was coming to him. Consequently, in the movie, which was also written by Tennessee Williams, Stella apparently chooses to believe Blanche's allegations of rape and moves out, leaving Stanley to suffer the consequences of his transgression.

A subtle resolution

Instead of destruction wrought by a tornado, the resolution of a play can be as soft as the sunshine after a rainstorm: restrained, uncomplicated, and positive, as it is in John Van Druten's *Bell, Book and Candle*. Gillian, the ex-witch, and Shep, the upstairs neighbor formerly bewitched by her, come to a startling (to them) realization. With the old dark magic gone, the real magic of love is beginning. In the play's resolution, Gillian and Shep melt into each other's arms as the curtain falls. The dust settles very comfortably for the lovers in this play.

Tying up loose ends

The resolution allows the playwright the chance to tie up loose ends if some of the threads in the play remain dangling. If your play has subplots — and most full-length plays do — the resolution is your last opportunity to bring closure to the stories within your main story.

In *The Miracle Worker,* the climactic moment has passed; young Helen Keller has realized that things have names and that Annie Sullivan has been trying to teach her the names. The story line is concluded. The audience has seen Annie work the miracle.

But a loose end remains. What about the relationship between Helen and Annie? For almost the entire play, Helen and Annie struggle both psychologically and physically as Annie persists in teaching Helen words and table manners while Helen aggressively resisted. Now that the breakthrough has occurred and Helen understands what Annie was doing, is Annie's involvement with Helen over? Is this where their story ends?

In the resolution, which comes as a coda to the climactic scene, Helen, after her initial burst of discovery and excitement, breaks away from the embrace of her joyful and weeping parents and gropes her way back to Annie. Annie spells *teacher* into Helen's hand, and Annie spells it back. With that simple action, the bond between them is sealed.

In the musical *West Side Story,* the audience waits to find out if Tony (formerly of the white gang, the Jets) will succeed in his quest to love Maria (sister of the Sharks' leader, Bernardo) and make a life with her. Given the escalating gang rivalry and the racial tension (and the tragic ending in the source material — Shakespeare's *Romeo and Juliet*), the odds are steeply against Tony and Maria. In the climactic moment in the final scene, Tony, racing toward Maria, is shot and killed just as he's about to embrace Maria. The story is over. The question of whether Tony will be able to have a life with Maria has been answered, negatively and irrevocably.

But what about the gang warfare that's been the backdrop of show? It's been the subplot that's provided the biggest obstacle to Tony and Maria. How does that play out? The creative team, fortunately, did not come up with some unrealistic happy ending in which, as a result of the tragedy, the gangs put aside their differences and prejudices in favor of a game of basketball. Instead, the Sharks help the Jets carry away Tony's body. So for that brief instant the gangs come together, striking a muted note of optimism, resolving the gang warfare subplot as positively as possible without moving the resolution into the realm of the implausible.

Returning your world to equilibrium

You open your play with the world of your play in balance. You give the audience a glimpse of the play's landscape at rest — a status quo. In short order, your inciting incident occurs: An event disturbs the landscape of your play; the world you've given the audience is thrown out of balance. Now your protagonist is out to return her world to balance. By righting the wrong, meeting the challenge, or solving the urgent problem, your protagonist is restoring the world of the play to equilibrium. The resolution can be a return to the state of affairs at the beginning of the play, or it can be a new landscape, a new stasis in a different place.

For example, the status quo at the beginning of William Gibson's *The Miracle Worker* is that a six-year-old girl, blind and deaf, gropes her way around her home, grasping and clawing at people and things, disrupting the activities of the members of her family. Helen lives in a world of her own, unable to communicate or interact with anyone in any meaningful way.

A teacher is sent for, and Annie Sullivan arrives from Boston to try to teach Helen how to behave and, more importantly, to communicate. The status quo has been upset. Annie is on a mission to get through to Helen, and she lets nothing and no one stand in her way. And in the climactic moment of the play, Annie makes a breakthrough with Helen, who comes to understand the concept of names and words.

The crisis has passed. Helen is now changed forever. The landscape has changed; there is no going back. In the resolution of the play, Helen and Annie Sullivan settle into a new balance, an enduring teacher/pupil relationship. The world of the play has been returned to equilibrium, a new equilibrium.

A Streetcar Named Desire has a different kind of resolution: one that returns the world of the play to its original equilibrium, more or less. The status quo at the beginning of the play is that Stanley, a rugged and down-to-earth man, arrives at his apartment from a day on the job just long enough to pitch to his wife, Stella, a parcel of meat from the butcher shop. Then he leaves with a friend for an evening of bowling, and Stella tags along after.

Blanche DuBois, Stella's sister, shows up, fleeing bad memories and unhappy experiences. She hopes to find shelter with her sister. The arrival of Blanche upsets the status quo. The lives and existence of Stanley and Stella are thrown out of balance. As needy as she is, Blanche can't help criticizing and belittling her host, Stanley, putting the two of them on a collision course. In the climax of the play, Stanley assaults his sister-in-law, leaving her psychologically defeated and physically devastated.

The final scene provides the resolution of the play. Blanche is taken away to a mental institution. The lives of Stanley and Stella, which now include an infant, settle back into a routine, a new stasis for the Kowalskis as passionate lovers and parents. Their world, now free of Blanche's disruptive influence, has returned to an equilibrium that is very much like their original state.

Emphasizing your theme

If part of the impulse to write your play involves a theme or message you want to get across (see Chapter 5), then you want to be sure that the resolution of your play is consistent with your theme. Your resolution should support your point of view and provide a dramatic example of the validity of the theme that motivated you. If it doesn't, look again at the plot of your play to determine if the events of your story took an inharmonious detour from your intended track. Or consider the possibility that your play proves a point other than the one intended. It's not uncommon for a playwright to fully understand what her play is about only after it's completed.

The consequences of your play's climax should be a direct result of the climactic events. If your resolution is unrelated, or only marginally related, to the culminating moment of your play, look again at the possible results of your climax to be sure you've focused on the end result that relates to your theme.

Inherit the Wind, by Jerome Lawrence and Robert E. Lee, debuted on Broadway in 1955. The play, about a high school teacher, Bertram Cates, who was arrested and put on trial for teaching the theory of evolution, is based on the notorious Scopes "Monkey Trial" in Tennessee 30 years earlier. The theme of the play celebrates the right to think for oneself and to hold opinions strongly, even if they are generally disliked and controversial. The play underscores the importance of standing up for what one believes, even in the face of popular condemnation.

Inherit the Wind ends with the accused found guilty of breaking state law by teaching evolution. But the convicted man, heading toward an appeal, is able to take solace in the fact that the trial raised awareness of the issue throughout the country. And more to the point, he stood his ground for what he believed and will continue to do so.

A powerful resolution to a topical theme

The great American playwright Arthur Miller was appalled at the machinations of Senator Joe McCarthy of Wisconsin, who spearheaded a hysterical campaign in the 1950s to root Communists out of American government. He made unsubstantiated claims that large numbers of Communists and Soviet spies and sympathizers were inside the United States federal government and elsewhere. His principal tools in his unrelenting and very public campaign were subpoena power, intimidation, and character assassination.

Many writers and entertainers were labeled communist sympathizers and were unable to continue working. Among those well-known artists accused of communist sympathies or called to testify were Dashiell Hammett, Lillian Hellman, Lena Horne, Paul Robeson, Elia Kazan, Aaron Copland, Leonard Bernstein, Charlie Chaplin, and Arthur Miller. In all, 320 artists were blacklisted (ostracized by employers), and for many of them this meant the end of their careers.

Arthur Miller was so profoundly shocked and angered by this violation of constitutional rights that in 1953 he wrote a play, *The Crucible,* as his response to "McCarthyism." *The Crucible,* an allegory, is set in 1692 Salem, Massachusetts, and is a fact-based portrayal of the frenzied and deadly hunt for witches, ignited by jealousy, lies, and fear.

Miller's themes include the dangers of lies, intolerance, and hysteria, the abuse of power, the ruination of reputation, and the trampling of rights and justice. In the play, the protagonist, John Proctor, would rather die than bow to pressure to confess to false accusations and allow his good name to be destroyed.

Proctor, in the end, stands up to the wickedness. In the resolution of the play, he and others go to the gallows. The courage and sacrifice of the protagonist dramatizes the terrible consequences of unbridled lies, hysteria, and character assassination, and justice run amok. Had Proctor been spared in the play's resolution, the evil of the injustices would not have been conveyed with the same impact.

Though Cates lost the trial, the resolution — his planned appeal of the negative verdict — emphasizes his self-sacrifice and continuing heroism, supporting and validating the play's theme, the right to speak and act on one's beliefs, even if controversial. The resolution says, this battle may have been lost, but the war is far from over.

Resolving Three Classic Plays

The resolution of a play is what's left after the smoke clears. Who's left standing? What is the effect of the climax on the people, places, and things of the play? What does the play's altered world look like?

The resolution of *Hamlet* is tragic; the resolution of *A Doll House* is, in part, inconclusive and subject to interpretation; and the resolution of *A Raisin in the Sun* is one of optimism.

Hamlet

The climactic scene of *Hamlet* leaves bodies strewn throughout the great hall of Elsinore Castle. Laertes, Queen Gertrude, King Claudius, and Hamlet are dead of stab wounds and poison. Earlier in the play others lost their lives — Polonius, Ophelia, Rosencrantz, and Guildenstern — the victims, innocent or not, of royal intrigue, treachery, and revenge.

With the demise of Hamlet, the spine (arc or through line) of the play has come to an end. Hamlet's world was thrown out of balance by the revelation of the murder of the old king by Claudius, and by the old king's ghost's demand to be avenged. After the climactic and deadly duel, Hamlet's world has come to a new balance.

The resolution of the play involves the arrival of Prince Fortinbras of Norway, a country with which Denmark has been at war. He brings an entourage. The message of Fortinbras is essentially: "Let's get this mess cleaned up, and, oh, by the way, I'm taking over." With the leadership vacuum in Denmark, Norway is now free to exert dominion over its old enemy. The resolution of the tragedy of Hamlet is a remarkable body count and a new political order, the subjugation of Denmark.

A Doll House

In Ibsen's *A Doll House,* equilibrium is upset as Nora Helmer struggles desperately to keep her husband, Torvald, from discovering that she forged a signature to borrow money. The money was used to pay for Torvald's convalescence from a serious illness, but Nora knows that won't cut it with Torvald. He's stern and inflexible when it comes to what he sees as wrong.

In the end, Nora is unable to prevent Torvald from reading a blackmail letter from his employee, Nils Krogstad. The letter divulges Nora's crime and threatens public exposure if he, Krogstad, is not kept employed at Torvald's bank. Torvald explodes in a torrent of rage and recrimination directed at Nora. When Krogstad calls off the extortion, Torvald breathes a sigh of relief, but Nora has been traumatized. She's past the point of no return. She's realized she cannot trust Torvald to protect her or to be on her side. Both her husband and the system (under which husbands provide their wives with shelter and protection) have failed her.

The resolution for Nora is to try to understand who she is and what her role in life should be. And she needs to work this out for herself. Alone. Consequently, she announces to Torvald, shocking and devastating him, that she's leaving him, her children, and her home. After explaining to him — at some length — what she's doing and why, she immediately leaves. And that action is the resolution of the play. Nora removes herself from the circumstances she can no longer tolerate and goes out into the world, with no preparation or resources, to find her future.

The audience, whether it understands and supports her decision or not, is left to wonder what becomes of Nora. It's an ending that George Bernard Shaw called indeterminate and, as a result, thought-provoking. Nora's departure provides a new equilibrium — a household without a wife and mother, and a woman who's on a journey of self-discovery that's only just begun.

A Raisin in the Sun

In *A Raisin in the Sun,* an African American family in a Chicago tenement apartment struggles to come to terms with its future. It's a new future made possible by the arrival of a large insurance check. This is one of the few plays in which the inciting incident — the news that a large check is coming — occurs before the start of the play. Consequently, when the curtain rises (the point of attack), the status quo in the Younger household already has been upset.

The play's protagonist, Walter Lee Younger, wants to use the money as his share of an investment in a liquor store, which he sees as his one shot at bettering himself and his family. But his mother and sister have plans to use the money to help the family in other ways.

After Walter Lee unwisely entrusts the money to one of his business partners who absconds with the cash, the family's dreams are shattered and Walter Lee is in a funk of guilt and despair. Yet he manages to rally and turn down the opportunity to cash in on the racist fears of a suburban homeowner's group.

After the play's climax, the world of the play, thrown into turmoil by the insurance money and Walter Lee's obsession with it, has now returned to a new equilibrium. Walter Lee and his family have grown stronger from the debacle. In the resolution of this resurrection story, the family goes ahead with its plan to move into a new home in the white neighborhood despite the potential problems.

The resolution further illustrates that Walter Lee has discovered that being a man is not about what job he has or his earning potential. He learns that being a man is about having self-respect and doing the right thing, particularly in difficult times. And having stood tall, he has taken his place as the head of the Younger family.

Chapter 14

Giving the Musical Special Consideration

*T*he Broadway musical, also referred to as *musical comedy,* is today one of the most popular of the performing arts. Musicals have something for everybody: catchy music, clever lyrics, lively dance, and, if you're lucky, an engaging story. A musical provides a well-rounded evening of entertainment.

When out-of-towners come to New York City on business or vacation, one of the top items on their lists of things to do is see a Broadway show. And by a "Broadway show," they usually mean a musical. (If you lump straight plays in with musicals, almost two-thirds of Broadway show audiences are tourists.) Countless thousands of tickets are sold every day for musical shows on or near Manhattan's Great White Way. As this book goes to press, throngs of theatergoers are lining up to see such popular and enduring shows as *Wicked, The Lion King, Phantom of the Opera, Billy Elliot, Mary Poppins, Jersey Boys, Mamma Mia!, Chicago,* and, Off-Broadway, *Avenue Q.*

Musicals are not only popular with theatregoers; they're also a staple of school and community productions throughout the country. Musicals generally involve large casts, making them ideal for high school, college, and amateur theatre productions where an important criterion in selecting a show is a large number of parts to accommodate as many performers as possible.

This chapter explores this popular stage storytelling form, clarifying the similarities and differences between musicals and straight plays (nonmusicals), explaining who's involved in their creation, and providing a crash course on writing the book (the story and dialogue) for a musical.

Taking a Look at the Medium of Musicals

What is a musical? Well, a musical is *not* a play with music added. A musical, technically called a *book musical,* is a stage story in which the music (melodies and lyrics) is an integral part of the storytelling. The songs, like the dialogue and action, advance the plot.

In a well-structured musical, if you take a song out, you lose part of the story. Something will be missing. If you can take a song out of a musical, or if the order of the songs can be changed without making a difference to the story, then the song or songs are not integrated with the story and probably aren't needed.

The obvious defining feature of musicals is that the characters sing and dance as well as speak and behave. Dance is, to one extent or another, also a component of most musicals. Some musicals are song-and-dance heavy, whereas others are light in that respect. But all musicals have songs and most have dance that are *indispensable* to the story. Both the singing and dancing are expressions of powerful emotions in the characters.

Some audience members find engaging themselves in musicals difficult if not impossible. They're not able to process the fact that characters apparently can break out in song and dance at any minute. "It's just not realistic," some would say. "You don't see people singing and dancing around in real life!"

Oh, no? What do people do when they're happy and in a good mood? They very often hum to themselves or even sing a song out loud. Music and song are natural means of expressing our emotions. We sing at religious holidays and ceremonies and at weddings and funerals. We sing songs that express our patriotism. And of course we commonly sing, even if only in the shower, songs that express our feelings of love.

When characters sing in musicals, it's nothing more than an artistic extension of what most people do in life. Musicals take artistic license. They push our natural inclination to express emotion through song to the level of art.

And what about dance? Granted, most people don't have many opportunities to go into a fully choreographed dance supported by the music of an orchestra. But like singing, dancing is a natural expression of positive emotion. What does a wide receiver do when he catches a quarterback's pass in the end zone? He breaks out into spontaneous dance. He expresses his joy and triumph with a little improvised footwork, even at the risk of a yellow flag and a 15-yard penalty.

The Broadway show

The Broadway show, which includes straight plays as well as musicals, is a theatrical presentation that takes place in one of about 40 professional theatres with 500 seats or more located in the Theatre District and in Lincoln Center for the Performing Arts in New York City. Shows presented "on Broadway" and in London's West End are generally considered the top plays and musicals in the Western world.

In addition to its role as a Mecca for theatregoers, Broadway also attracts the best and brightest actors, singers, dancers, directors, composers, lyricists, librettists and playwrights, and stagecraft people from around the world. The Broadway theatre scene is to theatre aficionados what Hollywood is to film buffs.

Here are some impressive facts and figures about Broadway compiled by The Broadway League:

- The annual attendance at Broadway shows averages about 12 million, grossing something like $1 *billion* dollars a year.

- Broadway is one of the greatest tourist destinations in New York City; visitors purchase around 6 million tickets per year.

- Broadway attendance tops that of the ten local professional sports teams (Mets, Yankees, Rangers, Islanders, Knicks, Liberty, Giants, Jets, Devils, and Nets) *combined!*

- Broadway theatre supports almost 85,000 local jobs and contributes close to $10 *billion* to New York City's economy.

And dance is also part of many important ceremonies — religious and secular — from weddings to birthday parties and bar mitzvahs to the dancing in New Orleans jazz funerals. Singing and dancing are natural and realistic, almost reflexive, behaviors that are elevated to a higher degree of artistry in musicals.

Another explanation for the acceptance of characters singing and dancing is the suspension of disbelief. As I discuss in Chapter 3, *willing suspension of disbelief* allows you to put aside the knowledge that what you're watching is not real, that you're only watching actors and dancers performing. Without thinking about it, you forget literal reality and you go with the flow. It's not so hard if you allow it to happen.

Writing the Libretto

From outward appearances, you may not think that writing the script for a play and writing the script — called the *book* or *libretto* (Italian for "little book") — for a musical are very different. (In this section, I use the term *libretto,* as opposed to *book,* to avoid confusion.) In both a play script and in a libretto, you arrange dialogue and stage directions similarly on the pages. However, in a libretto you also include the lyrics for the show's songs. The lyrics in a libretto are broken into their sung phraseology, looking to the eye like a poem. Following is a page of the script for my show *The Devil's Music: The Life and Blues of Bessie Smith*. This page begins with stage directions and some dialogue; then has the lyrics to a song; and then goes back to dialogue.

> PICKLE plays a few intro bars to "Dirty No-Gooders Blues."

BESSIE

Yeah, that's a good one — 'cause I wrote that too! I don't play the pi-ana or nothin'. I just sings it and they sets it down for me. Writin' don't mean usin' your hands; it means using your heart.

> BESSIE sings "Dirty No-Gooders Blues."

Did you ever fall in love with a man that was no good?
Did you ever fall in love with a man that was no good?
No matter what you did for him, he never understood

The meanest thing he could say would thrill you through and through
The meanest thing he could say would thrill you through and through

And there wasn't nothing too dirty for that man to do

He'll treat you nice and kind til he wins your heart in hand
He'll treat you nice and kind til he wins your heart in hand
Then he'll treat you so cruel, that man you just can't stand
Then he'll treat you so cruel, that man you just can't stand

There's nineteen men livin' in my neighborhood
There's nineteen men livin' in my neighborhood
Eighteen of them are fools and the one ain't no doggone good

Oh Lawd, Lawd, Lawd, Lawd, Lawd, Lawd, Lawd, Lawd
Lawd, Lawd, Lawd, Lawd, Lawd
That dirty no-good man treats me just like I'm a dog

(Directly to the crowd/audience) Now that ain't no kind of welcome a'tall! You want me to sing for y'all, don't ya? Well, put your hands together for me or I'll walk my ass right outta here. I already done it once tonight. So let me hear it now!

The mystique of musicals

Musicals are about dreams and flights of fancy. Maybe more than other forms of stage entertainment, musicals are escapist by nature. They should not only help you forget your mundane cares but also take you to intriguing places and times that capture your imagination. At the very least, a musical should take you somewhere away from your everyday world.

For example, in the last decade, the Tony-winning best musicals of year all took audiences to many other places, from fantasy to the simply unfamiliar:

- *The Producers* (2001): A fanciful and comic look at a Broadway show produced in 1959.

- *Thoroughly Modern Millie* (2002): A Midwest girl comes to New York City in the Roaring Twenties determined to become a success.

- *Hairspray* (2003): The rock 'n roll and television world of 1960s Baltimore with an undercurrent of disharmony between the races.

- *Avenue Q* (2004): An adult *Sesame Street*–like coming-of-age story involving human and puppet characters in New York City.

- *Monty Python's Spamalot* (2005): A highly irreverent parody of the King Arthur legend intertwined with Broadway-show satire.

- *Jersey Boys* (2006): Based on the lives of the 1960s hit singing group The Four Seasons, from their lowly New Jersey origins to the big time.

- *Spring Awakening* (2007): Depicts teenagers coming of age and discovering sexuality in late-19th-century Germany.

- *In the Heights* (2008): Three days in the lives of the residents in the Dominican-American and Nuyorican neighborhood of Washington Heights in New York City.

- *Billy Elliot the Musical* (2009): A young working-class boy in Northern England finds and persists in his love of dancing in spite of his father's disapproval.

- *Memphis* (2010): Based on the experiences of Dewey Phillips, one of the first white disc jockeys to play black music in the 1950s.

Incorporating the elements of a solid libretto

Many of the elements that make for a well-structured play also are found in the librettos of musicals, but perhaps with greater emphasis. The story elements of a libretto need to be heightened and made more distinct because there is less script time to develop subtleties. The script, which provides the skeleton of the show, is only one part of the musical equation, which involves libretto, music, lyrics, and, usually, choreography.

Following are some of the hallmarks of a successful musical libretto:

✔ **A simple story:** Because much of the story in a musical is told through song and dance, the libretto is much shorter than the script for a play of equal length. Though the number of songs and dances in musicals vary, it's fair to say that a good half, if not more, of the show is comprised of singing and dancing. Therefore, the scriptwriter — the librettist — has half as much script space to develop story lines or characters as he would have in an average full-length play. As a consequence, the stories in musicals are much less complex.

✔ **Uncomplicated subplots:** The subplots in musicals, like the main story, tend to be uncomplicated and most often involve romance or comic situations that impact the main plot. In *The Music Man,* Harold Hill, the something-of-a-scoundrel protagonist, sells musical instruments to the children of a small town by making shallow promises to teach the kids their instruments. His mission to sell and run is complicated by a couple of subplots. He finds himself attracted to the town's librarian, Marian, and he gets involved in helping her young brother, Winthrop, who lisps, find his self-confidence. These subplots add dimension to the story line without being intricate or extensive.

✔ **A fascinating milieu:** A musical usually, but not always, takes the audience to some place and/or some time different from everyday existence — be it the Dickensian England of *Oliver* or Siam of the 1860s in *The King and I.* This relocation to some "exotic" locale heightens audience interest level and enables audiences to more easily accept some of the artificialities of the genre, like singing and dancing.

✔ **A strong central character with a passionate mission:** Although the protagonist of any play should be passionate, this trait is even more important in musicals because passion and strong emotions are what prompt characters to sing and dance. Emile de Becque of *South Pacific,* Tony in *West Side Story,* Jean Valjean of *Les Misérables,* the title character Sweeney Todd, and Cassie of *A Chorus Line* are all strong, passionate characters who wear their hearts on their sleeves.

✔ **An unambiguous antagonist who's a worthy opponent:** The stronger the antagonist, the more consequential the struggle for the protagonist. And the greater and more important the challenge, the more the audience will care. Jean Valjean, an escaped prisoner trying to make a new life for himself and a young girl entrusted to his care, is being doggedly pursued by the police officer, Javert. Javert has vowed to recapture the escapee, making him a man dedicated to his job and a worthy and dangerous antagonist.

✔ **A point of no return:** This is a moment in the protagonist's journey where a decision is made or an event occurs from which there is no retreat. It's the crossing of the Rubicon, the burning of bridges behind the character. At the end of the first act of *West Side Story,* Tony has killed Bernardo, the leader of the Sharks gang, but, more significantly, he's stabbed to death the brother of Maria, the woman he loves. Tony has passed the point of no return. He's forced move forward and deal with his actions. This kind of defining moment helps bring audiences back after intermission, wondering, for example, what lies ahead for the unfortunate Tony.

✔ **Love:** Love, if not romance, is an vital in musicals. Unlike plays, which can be driven by the urge to communicate esoteric themes, musicals need to *entertain,* and few elements entertain and engage audiences more than romance. If love isn't the primary story line of a musical, it's one of the main subplots. *South Pacific, West Side Story, The Music Man, Phantom of the Opera, A Chorus Line, Oklahoma*, and *In the Heights*, among many, many others, all are essentially love stories. *My Fair Lady* and *The King and I* are stories of love that can never be consummated. Even the grim and darkly humorous *Sweeney Todd: The Demon Barber of Fleet Street* has love. Todd is fortunate enough to find a lady companion, Mrs. Lovett, who appreciates his murderous efforts, and she uses the fruit of his labors in her pies. Todd also is driven by the love of the wife he believes to be dead. If romantic love is absent in a show, you're sure to find some other form of love, be it love of family or friends.

✔ **Humor:** Like love, humor is an indispensable element of musicals because of its entertainment value. Just about every Broadway musical has a humorous scene or character or a comic or novelty number, like Ado Annie singing "I'm Just a Girl Who Can't Say No" in *Oklahoma* or "Adelaide's Lament" in *Guys and Dolls.* Or musicals can be primarily humorous, like *A Funny Thing Happened on the Way to the Forum, The Producers,* or *Spamalot.*

✔ **High stakes:** If love and passionate pursuits are characteristic of the librettos of musicals, then the stakes must be high enough to arouse that kind of fervor. What's being pursued by the protagonist and why need to be urgent and important. What's to be gained if the protagonist succeeds, and what stands to be lost if he fails? These questions point you to the stakes.

Exploring different sources of material for musicals

A rule of thumb when it comes to the creation of musicals asserts, "It all begins with the book (libretto)." The process of creating a musical should begin by scripting the story, dialogue, and action.

A musical should begin with a good story that captures the imagination of the collaborative team. The librettist then isolates the essential events of the story and puts them into script form, appearing very much like the script for a straight play. But although starting with the libretto is the norm, there are exceptions, like jukebox musicals.

Jukebox musicals

In recent years a trend has emerged of acquiring the rights to the body of work of some composer, band, or singing group and creating a musical around it. Referred to as *jukebox musicals,* these projects, rather than beginning with the libretto, instead start with the music. Unfortunately, the songs being used, as popular as they may be, were not written to be part of the storytelling in musicals, and that makes writing a serviceable libretto problematic.

When beginning with the songs of a given composer or group, a libretto has to be constructed that strings the songs together in some logical order. The songs need to feel like they arise from the story and the character's needs, not just from the desire of the creators to make use of the songs.

The Broadway musical *Mamma Mia!* stitches together more than 20 popular ABBA songs in a story about a young bride-to-be seeking to know which of three men is her father. Though not a perfect fit in all cases, the songs work well as a whole in the immensely successful Broadway show and movie version.

A way around the challenge of creating story moments to justify the already-written songs is to write a libretto about the group or singers themselves and use their music in the show during the relevant periods of their history. This approach is what the mega-hit show *Jersey Boys* does with 1960s rock 'n roll group Frankie Valli and the Four Seasons. The show recaps the group's career, and the songs are sung at the times in their career when they were recorded.

Though these two shows are successful, jukebox musicals often fare poorly because the stories written to hang the songs together tend to be weak or silly. But there's no sign that the trend toward jukebox musicals is letting up. Recently two more opened on Broadway: *Million Dollar Quartet* and *Rain: A Tribute to the Beatles on Broadway.* The first stages a historic 1956 impromptu jam session involving Elvis Presley, Jerry Lee Lewis, Carl Perkins, and Johnny Cash. The latter, *Rain,* makes no attempt at all to tell a story; it's a concert presentation featuring performers giving musical impersonations of The Beatles.

Adaptations

Most Broadway musicals are adaptations of preexisting stories, referred to as the *source material.* Musicals are expensive and complex to create and stage. Any weak element in a show can sink it.

But a way to help reduce the risk is to start the project with proven material. When working with a story that has succeeded in another medium, you can have a degree of confidence that, if a problem emerges, it probably won't be with the underlying story or characters, assuming the librettist did a good job with his adaptation.

Also, the use of proven material from another medium brings to the project public name recognition, a marketing advantage. When potential audiences know of the successful source material, they're more easily sold on the idea of seeing a musical version of the popular work.

The stories upon which musicals are based come from a variety of sources:

- ✔ **Novels:** *Oliver (Oliver Twist), Wicked, Phantom of the Opera, Les Misérables, Jekyll & Hyde (The Strange Case of Dr. Jekyll and Mr. Hyde),* and *The Man Who Would Be King*

- ✔ **Movies:** *Billy Elliot, Catch Me If You Can, Chitty Chitty Bang Bang, Fame: The Musical (Fame), The Full Monty, Hairspray, Legally Blonde, The Lion King,* and *The Producers*

- ✔ **Plays:** *West Side Story (Romeo and Juliet), Raisin (A Raisin in the Sun), Kiss Me, Kate (The Taming of the Shrew), High Society (The Philadelphia Story),* and *My Fair Lady (Pygmalion)*

- ✔ **Television shows:** *The Addams Family* and *Happy Days*

- ✔ **Cartoons and comic books:** *Spider-Man: Turn Off the Dark, Li'l Abner, Annie (Orphan Annie),* and *You're a Good Man, Charlie Brown (Peanuts)*

- ✔ **Poetry:** *Cats (Old Possum's Book of Practical Cats)* and *The Wild Party*

- ✔ **Historical events and biographies:** *Titanic, 1776, Fiorello, Barnum,* and *Evita*

All that being said, musicals can be, and have been, created from ideas not related to preexisting material. If you have an original idea and you think it's solid, feel free to start from scratch. Some successful musicals built around original ideas include *A Chorus Line, The Drowsy Chaperone, Grease, In the Heights, Memphis, The Music Man,* and *Sunday in the Park with George.*

Outlining the structure of a musical

As varied as Broadway musicals are, they are, for the most part, tightly structured works that follow a time-tested formula. Musicals, with the diverse artistic disciplines that are involved, are complicated machines that must be tightly synchronized and made fully functional.

If the tires of your car are flat, if you run out of fuel, if the engine tends to stall, and so on, your automobile is going nowhere. It fails to serve its purpose. Similarly, if any one of the artistic elements of a musical fails — the libretto, music, lyrics, dance, or staging — the show is very likely to tank. Like the proverbial chain, a musical is only as strong as its weakest link.

And though some very successful exceptions do break these rules, following are some of the major infrastructure elements that comprise and support the modern musical.

Opening number

Musicals usually begin with a song. The opening musical number has a very specific function: It introduces and sets up the world of the show. The opening song and/or dance literally sets the stage for the audience, informing the audience of the type of show that's being presented. The opening number has the following functions:

✔ Sets the tone, letting the audience know if the show is primarily dramatic or essentially comedic

✔ Establishes the milieu, telling where the story of the show takes place

✔ Indicates the time period — past or present

✔ Establishes the style of the show as natural or fantastical

✔ Introduces the characters of the show, though not necessarily all of them

"I want" song

Following closely after the opening number is the "I want" song. The function of this song is very straightforward. It defines the main character and reveals what he wants. And what the character wants is directly related to the character's journey — what the protagonist is out to achieve.

In *My Fair Lady,* Eliza Doolittle sings, "All I want is a room somewhere, far away from the cold night air" in "Wouldn't it Be Loverly." Her "I want" song expresses her dream of a life better than that of a street vendor.

Sometimes "I want" songs aren't so specific. In *West Side Story,* Tony sings in "Something's Coming" that he wants something more out of life than gang warfare and expresses the premonition that something good and important is going to happen to him. (The something turns out to be love in the form of the character of Maria.)

Production number

The production number is a common, though not essential, component of most musicals. It's an elaborately staged song, usually involving dancing and a lot of people.

A good example of a production number is the closing number of *A Chorus Line,* in which the entire cast, dressed in gold-colored formalwear complete with top hats, sings and dances a reprise of the song "One." Another example is the "Tonight Quintet and Chorus" near the end of the first act of *West Side Story* in which the Jets, Sharks, Tony, Maria, and Anita, in different venues but all on stage at one time, sing a stirring reprise of "Tonight."

The eleven o'clock number

The "eleven o'clock number" is a song sung late in the second act (of a two-act show) that expresses the main character's strong emotions as the show nears its climactic moment. It can express a low point for the character just before his final success in the climax, reminding the audience of what's at stake for the character. And it can raise the emotional level in anticipation of the play's conclusion.

In *South Pacific,* the eleven o'clock number is "This Nearly was Mine." It expresses Emile de Becque's heartbreak and longing for his lost love, Nellie Forbush, just before he departs on a dangerous military mission.

Another eleven o'clock number is "I've Grown Accustomed to Her Face," from *My Fair Lady.* It expresses Henry Higgins's sorrow and discontent that his star pupil, Eliza Doolittle, has struck out on her own. It sets up the emotional moment when, to his surprise and smug satisfaction, Eliza returns at the conclusion of the show.

Finale

The finale is what it sounds like: the final number of the show. It usually provides an emotional punch at the end. It can be a reprise of an earlier song, like breathtaking "The Impossible Dream" at the end of *Man of La Mancha* as Miguel de Cervantes dramatically exits to face trial before the Spanish Inquisition. Or it can be a powerful new song, like "You Can't Stop the Beat" in *Hairspray,* that leaves audiences smiling and tapping their feet to the driving and infectious rhythm of the upbeat number.

Specialized numbers

In addition to the structural numbers mentioned above, musicals have specialty songs. According to the late Lehman Engel, who used to teach in the BMI Musical Theatre Workshop now named after him, the three kinds of songs in musical theatre are as follows:

- **Ballads:** Ballads are reflective numbers, usually about love or some other strong emotion, that allow characters to express and explore their innermost feelings. "Can You Feel the Love Tonight" from *The Lion King,* "What I Did for Love" from *A Chorus Line,* "Some Enchanted Evening" from *South Pacific,* and "I Don't Know How to Love Him" from *Jesus Christ Superstar* are examples of ballads.

- **Charm songs:** These songs let a character charm an audience. They often introduce and help define a character, and allow the character to share his motivations and priorities. Examples are "Wouldn't It Be Loverly" from *My Fair Lady* and "I Feel Pretty" from *West Side Story.*

- **Comedy numbers:** These songs are calculated to put a smile on the faces of audience members, like "Master of the House" in *Les Misérables,* "Honey Bun" from *South Pacific,* and "Officer Krupke" from *West Side Story.* They put the comedy in musical comedy.

Knowing when a character should sing

People who have little patience with musicals may feel that characters burst out in song and dance at the oddest moments, making the convention of singing and dancing hard to swallow. For instance, as Tony lies dying in the arms of Maria at the end of *West Side Story,* the distraught Maria sings a brief reprise of "Somewhere" (you know, the one that begins "There's a place for us . . ."). As crazy as that may seem, there's method to the madness. A rule helps define the moment when characters sing.

Characters sing and dance in musicals when words alone aren't enough to express the emotion. When characters feel great joy, happiness, anticipation, excitement, sadness, regret, and even anger and hate that are too big for just words, they are moved to convey their emotions through song and dance.

Finding the right balance of dialogue and songs

No set-in-stone rule can tell you how to balance dialogue and songs. Some shows are song-and-dance heavy, meaning that the bulk of the show involves music as opposed to dialogue, and others feature few songs and dances. The rock operas *Jesus Christ Superstar* and *Rent* have 25 to 30 or more songs, but *Peter Pan* and *1776* have about 15 musical numbers each. These numbers illustrate that there is no prescribed number of songs in a musical.

Some musicals are sung throughout, including the dialogue, much like opera. Referred to as, surprisingly, sung-through shows, they include Broadway hits like *Cats, Evita, Joseph and the Amazing Technicolor Dreamcoat, Les Misérables,*

Miss Saigon, and *Chess.* In sung-through musicals, the song moments are bridged by dialogue that is set to music, referred to as *recitative.*

The sung-through musical is a style choice. I know of no particular advantage in choosing to write a sung-through musical, but they have some disadvantages. As powerful as some sung-through shows are, the singing of dialogue strains the tolerance of audience members who already have trouble processing characters breaking out into song. In addition, the work of the librettist, who already works in the long shadow of the song writer and lyricist in standard musicals, is further eclipsed in sung-through musicals in which almost all the words are lyrics.

Partnering in the Creative Team

Musicals don't have authors; they have creative teams. A musical is an even more collaborative medium than a play. Unlike plays, which are usually the work of a sole creator — the playwright — at least at the start, musicals are projects created by a team of artists, each of whom brings a specific and necessary skill to the table.

Following are the theatre artists you'll find involved with musicals:

- **Librettist:** Writes the script — the story, dialogue, and action.
- **Composer:** Writes the melodies of the music.
- **Lyricist:** Writes the lyrics, the words to the songs.
- **Choreographer:** Creates the dances for the show. (Most often, unless the show is conceived of as dance-heavy, a choreographer enters late in the process, after the show largely done.)

Working together as a team

The creative team for a musical usually ranges from two to four members.

- **One-person team:** Rarely, you'll have a musical in which the music, lyrics, and libretto were all created by the same person. One example is Meredith Willson, who wrote the music, lyrics, and libretto for *The Music Man,* which won the Tony Award for best musical in 1957.
- **Two-person team:** A team of only two people can consist of a person who is both composer and lyricist in collaboration with a librettist. Or it can encompass a composer and a librettist/lyricist.
- **Three-person team:** The most common arrangement of creators consists of three individuals — a librettist, a composer, and a lyricist.

✔ **Four-person team:** Occasionally, a choreographer can be part of the creative team, particularly if the show is to feature a lot of dance. In some instances, the choreographer comes up with the concept of the show, as did Jerome Robbins with *West Side Story*. And stellar choreographer Bob Fosse was a prime mover in the creation of the hit musical, *Chicago*.

As a rule, the first step in the creation of a musical — after the creative team has selected and agreed to the subject matter — is the writing of the libretto (the story, dialogue, and action). Theoretically, as the librettist works, he shouldn't concern himself with where songs might be sung. That's the job of the composer and the lyricist. The librettist essentially writes a play.

After the libretto is drafted, the composer and lyricist go to work. They find the moments in the script that sing. They isolate and musicalize the scenes in which the emotions of the characters are so strong that they need to be expressed in song. The librettist may be involved in the song-placement discussion, but he typically defers to the expertise of the composer and lyricist.

Generally, the next step is for the composer to write the music. The music is turned over to the lyricist, who commandeers much of the dialogue from the libretto and transforms it into lyrics for the songs. Some of the best moments and dialogue the librettist writes may be subsumed by the songs. And that's a good thing. A smart librettist isn't territorial when it comes to his contribution to the project.

After the songs are in place in the script, the script is ready for the choreographer. The choreographer finds the moments in the show where the characters express their feelings through dance, and then he creates dances.

Covering all bases with a collaboration agreement

Whatever arrangement of creators you have in a musical, choose your collaborators carefully. A collaboration on a musical is like a marriage: easy to get into and heaven when it's working, but painful and awkward to dissolve when things go bad. After you're committed to a collaboration, you're bound and obligated to do your part. If personality conflicts turn up or you discover you all have different visions of the work being created, the experience can become a nightmare.

The creative team of a musical, if it's smart, works under what's referred to as a *collaboration agreement*. This contract specifies the responsibilities of each of the collaborators, what happens if the collaboration falls apart, how the royalties from the show are divided, and so on.

It's unwise to invest a lot of time and creative effort in a collaboration without a formal agreement. When a project begins to achieve some success, you may be amazed how oral agreements and promises tend to become confused. You can save yourself a major headache by using a very handy collaboration agreement template available to members of the Dramatists Guild (www.dramatistsguild.com).

I've had potential collaborators say to me, "Who needs a contract? We're all friends here." My answer to that is, "If we're all such good friends, then what's the problem in executing a collaboration agreement?" Collaboration agreements are a way of ensuring that the collaborators stay friends.

If you have trouble compromising and difficulty giving others their creative space in projects you're involved in, then collaboration in musicals may not be right for you. Control freaks do not do well in collaborations.

Hey, where's my name? Keeping your pride in check

To be a successful librettist, you need a good degree of humility. When you look at the marquee of the theatre hosting your new musical, what you're likely to see are the names of the composer and lyricist above the title of the show. In other words, among the members of the creative team in musicals, the librettist is usually the least visible. Musicals are commonly billed as the work of the composer and lyricist. Consider these examples:

- **Rodgers and Hart's** *Pal Joey:* Music, Richard Rodgers; lyrics, Lorenz Hart. But who wrote the libretto? John O'Hara, based on his novel of the same name.

- **Rodgers and Hammerstein's** *The Sound of Music:* Music, Richard Rodgers; lyrics, Oscar Hammerstein II. The libretto? Howard Lindsay and Russel Crouse, based on Maria Trapp's book, *The Story of the Trapp Family Singers.*

- **Kander and Ebb's** *Cabaret:* Music, John Kander; lyrics, Fred Ebb. And the libretto by John Masteroff, based on John Van Druten's novel *I Am a Camera.*

- **Stephen Sondheim's** *Sweeney Todd: The Demon Barber of Fleet Street:* Music and lyrics by Stephen Sondheim. And who wrote the libretto? Hugh Wheeler, based on a play by the same name.

The librettist tends to have a higher profile when he's also the lyricist, as is the case with the team of Lerner and Loewe — Alan Jay Lerner, lyricist and librettist, and Fredrick Loewe, composer — who created the often-revived hits *My Fair Lady, Camelot,* and *Brigadoon.*

The intoxicating but often very frustrating world of musical theatre is not for scriptwriters who must be in sole, total control of projects. It's also not a comfortable environment for playwrights who crave seeing their names in big letters on marquees, posters, and flyers. Humility, a trait that doesn't come naturally to show-business people, is much needed by playwrights who venture into musical theatre.

Part IV

The Show Must Go On

"Normally at a first table reading of a play, we just assume the corpse in the room."

In this part . . .

When you've finished a draft of your play, pat yourself on the back for a job well done — and then get back to work. The process of playwriting isn't finished with the completion of a draft. In this part you find out about the several important steps involved in getting the play out of your computer and onto a stage. You need to have your play read and critiqued by knowledgeable individuals, do public readings to get feedback, revise the play, and then interest a producer or producing theatre company in doing your play. And, when your play goes into production, you need to know the do's and don'ts for playwrights involved in that process (particularly in rehearsals). The chapters in this part guide you through these important final phases of playwriting.

Chapter 15

Getting Your Play Read and Making Revisions

In This Chapter

▶ Finding out why revising your first draft is so important

▶ Listening to critiques from theatre people and audiences

▶ Applying feedback and revising your script

▶ Doing the whole process again

As you've worked on your play, the experience has likely been a joy . . . at times. At other times, you probably were ready to tear out your hair. Join the club. The process of creation can be very rewarding, but it's seldom easy or without its frustrations.

But despite the highs and lows, if you stick with it, the point will come when you key in the words, "End of Play." You've completed a draft of your script — a major milestone. The long hours of hard work in solitary confinement have paid off. You can sit back and, for a moment at least, bask in the warm glow of achievement. Congratulations! You did it!

In short order, the reality will sink in that your work is far from over. The completion of a draft of a play is an accomplishment, but the work of creating a play is not over until the play is performed for an audience. Theatre is a collaborative medium (which I discuss in Chapter 3), and you'll get your first taste of that in revising and developing your play. The process necessitates the involvement of many other people.

Getting your script from your computer into the hands of people who are equipped and willing to critique your play is the next step in the journey to performance. It's a multifaceted challenge with rewards and frustrations of its own.

This chapter underscores the unavoidable need for knowledgeable input and constructive feedback in the refinement of your play. You'll find out what revisions your play might need and explore how and where to find practical development advice and support.

Readying Your Play for the World

A play is a mechanism that must function efficiently if it's to succeed in engaging an audience and telling your story. A playwright, maybe more than writers of other literary forms, needs to be pragmatic and objective when writing and refining a script. The playwright has to consider the endpoint — the performance of the play — and the many practical factors that affect its success.

When you read a poem, short story, or novel, you can pause at any time to ponder a point or reread a section. After viewing a movie in a theatre, you can see it again on television or DVD if you missed something the first time. These days you can even rewind a television show or watch it again on the Internet if a moment went by too fast or wasn't clear.

None of these options is available to audience members watching a play in a theatre. Therefore, a play must be experienced fully and according to the playwright's vision the first time. Like parachuting from a plane, things better work as planned, or, in the end, the experience will be disappointing.

For this reason, playwrights, more than other writers, test their work, actively seek input and feedback, and then embark on revisions to ensure that their work is, well, working. And playwrights have a variety of ways, direct and indirect, to get help, ranging from one-on-one criticism to readings of the script by actors before selected audiences.

The opportunities to have your play critiqued by people who know what they're looking at or to have your play read by actors can be few and far between. Most people who can offer valuable feedback or conduct a reading for you are likely to be busy. You may have to wait your turn to get attention. While you're waiting, you don't want to be spinning your wheels or letting your newly acquired playwriting skills get rusty. So do what playwrights do to keep momentum going: Start on your next play. Continuing to work shows others that you're serious about playwriting and don't intend to be one of those often-tiresome one-play wonders.

Even if you get quality feedback and revise your play accordingly, keep your expectations modest. To be perfectly blunt, in most cases a playwright's first play is the one she cuts her teeth on. You can expect to make the mistakes you'll learn from while working on your first play. My first two plays were good stabs at the craft, but they're still "in the drawer" (in my computer, to be more precise).

The first play I wrote was a drama, and the recurring criticism I received was that it was much too similar to Edward Albee's *Who's Afraid of Virginia Woolf?*

Hardly surprising, because that's one of my favorite plays. My second play was a comedy, and the repeated criticism was that the play was very funny but not really about anything. Every now and then I pull those two early plays out the drawer, imaging that with the experience I have now I could fix their problems. But just the opposite occurs. My expertise inevitably indicates that the troubles with those plays are so fundamental that my time would be better spent working on new plays.

However, my early failures shouldn't discourage you from fully committing to your first play. The first play of a former student of mine, now a colleague, appears headed for a Broadway production. Not bad for a first play.

Getting Feedback on the Early Draft

In the autobiography aptly entitled *Rewrites: A Memoir,* Neil Simon, arguably the greatest living playwright, points out:

> . . . *a playwright has one advantage over screenwriters. An audience will tell you immediately what's wrong, and you can go home and fix it.*

A playwright is able to test his work and then act upon the results. He can solicit reactions both from people in the know and from general audiences to see for himself how well the script is working long before the play leaves the nest forever. Testing and getting early feedback is a prudent and common-sense measure. After all, if you can improve your play, why wouldn't you want to?

This section covers how to get expert opinions, participate in playwrights' workshops, benefit from readings (closed and open), and get back to the keyboard to do your rewrites.

Preparing your draft

When preparing to harvest other people's expertise and viewpoints on your play, consider the following tips:

- ✔ **Check your script for misspellings and typos and have someone other than yourself proofread your work.** My initial proofreader is my wife, Sandy. She's good at catching grammatical errors, typos, omitted words, and redundant redundancies. And having lived with a playwright for many years now, her input on the play itself is, I sometimes grudgingly acknowledge, very good. (Sandy's graciousness in reading my scrib-blings serves other purposes. It keeps her in the loop and reassures her that what hubby is working at behind the closed door is not Texas Hold 'Em online. Not all the time, anyway.)

If you can sweet-talk, bribe, or guilt anyone into proofing your script, read the material aloud. For some reason, when you read a script or manuscript of your own out loud, as opposed to reading silently to yourself, your eyes and mind look more closely at the actual words on the page rather than assuming what's there is what you meant to put there. Though reading aloud is slower and consumes more energy, you tend to spot errors more easily.

✔ **Make your play as good as you can before you start showing it around.** Work and rework your story and dialogue until you're satisfied that they're as good as you know how to make them. Be honest with yourself about the state of your script. You need to put your best foot forward for two important reasons.

- First, you don't want to get feedback suggesting fixes that you already know you need to make. That redundant feedback wastes everyone's time and energy. If you know about problems, take care of them before you trot out the play. If your play is as tight as you can make it, then the feedback you'll get, rather than being basic and obvious, probably will be more sophisticated and valuable.

- Second, a lot of playwrights out there are trying to get handy feedback on their plays. In other words, you have a lot of competition for the time and energy of people who are in a position to help. Unless you happen to strike a very responsive chord, you're unlikely to be able to go back to those sources of feedback a second time with the same play. You'll probably get one shot, so you want your play to be as ready for critiquing as possible.

✔ **Be open to criticism.** Hearing someone raise concerns about the play you've worked so hard on is never easy. The experience is like having one of your children analyzed and criticized by strangers. Some playwrights handle it better than others. I've seen playwrights get into defensive postures and testy debates over the feedback they get. Rather than listening and trying to extract useful meaning from what they're being told, they reflexively argue and explain. All that kind of response does is waste time and, what's worse, discourage people from working with you.

Don't behave like a playwright I witnessed who, in response to criticism, literally pointed to a line in his script and argued, "but it says that right here." You never want to say, in essence, "I don't like your comments or ideas" to anyone who's given you time and effort. Feedback and input are gifts. Take them, thank the giver for his generosity, and move on. Taking criticism graciously can be hard to do sometimes, I know. But you don't want to develop a reputation for being stubborn, inflexible, or overly protective. When you get back to your keyboard, you can use the comments that make sense to you and discard the rest. You're under no obligation to implement any suggestion you get.

✔ **Format your script correctly.** Your script must look like a professional script. You wouldn't go to a job interview in flip-flops, cut-off jeans, and a holey T-shirt (unless you're applying for a job as a beachcomber); you'd dress to look like you'd fit in with the people you want to work with. The same is true in preparing a script. Turning in a sloppy or confusingly formatted script may try the patience of script evaluators before they've even read the first lines of dialogue. Present your material in a format that says "this person knows what she's doing" by using proper play script format. (See the appendix for an example of a formatted script.)

Getting expert opinions

One of the most obvious ways of getting useful feedback on your play is to show it to people who know and understand plays; namely directors, actors, or other playwrights. Writing, directing, or acting in a play does not automatically make someone a play script expert, but chances are you'll get a more informed opinion from a theatre person than from a layman.

So how do you go about finding these people? You can use a number of strategies:

✔ **Check out the theatre or performing arts department at your local college.** Find out who teaches theatre or playwriting there. (You may find the playwriting teacher, if there is one, in the English Department. I earned my MFA [master of fine arts] in playwriting under the late veteran playwright Jack Gelber in the English Department of Brooklyn College.) If you have the time and financial resources, taking a course with the appropriate person will provide you with additional playwriting training and give you access to the instructor. If you can't take a course, contact the professor and ask whether she would mind reading and offering feedback on your new play. You may want to sweeten the request by offering a small honorarium.

Also see whether you can find any relevant courses or theatre professionals in local adult- or continuing-education centers.

✔ **Investigate your local professional or community theatre or performing arts center.** Sometimes these organizations have associated theatre education programs. Take a course or try to establish a relationship with an experienced theatre person there. Or see whether you can find someone there, like the artistic director or literary manager, who might be willing to work with you.

✔ **Ask around to see whether your area has an unaffiliated playwrights workshop.** You may be able to find a group of likeminded playwrights who meet regularly to read and critique each other's work. In addition to checking with the usual suspects — theatre organizations — ask at your local library.

Typically, I belong to two workshops at one time so that I can work on two different plays in tandem. Rather than increasing pressure on me, as you may suppose, this arrangement actually reduces pressure. When I go cold on one play (which is not an unusual occurrence), I can focus on the other project until the first play recaptures my imagination.

✔ **See lots of plays, be they professional, amateur, or scholastic.** Not only is attending theatre good for your playwriting education, but it also gives you the opportunity, after the performance, to introduce yourself to the directors and actors at the theatre and ask about playwriting resources in your area.

✔ **Offer to volunteer at a theatre in some capacity.** Community theatres and even professional companies are always looking for volunteer help. You can offer to run the lights, work the sound system, help build sets, usher, staff the box office, and so on. Volunteering gives you the opportunity to be around theatre people and make contacts.

✔ **Join The Dramatists Guild.** The Dramatists Guild is the national association for writers of plays and musicals. The Guild describes itself as "a community of playwrights, composers, and lyricists dedicated to protecting, informing, and promoting the interests of dramatists everywhere." Among other benefits, the Guild publishes a sensational magazine, *The Dramatist,* for members and issues an invaluable annual resource directory of theatres and other valuable information. Basic membership is $75 a year. Go to www.dramatistsguild.com for more information.

Should you pay per view?

Freelance dramaturges read and critique scripts for a fee. I myself have rendered this service on rare occasions. Is hiring a freelancer for feedback worthwhile? It depends on the quality and thoroughness of the feedback, the fee being asked, and the individual's background. For instance, if the playwright, director, or playwriting teacher is primarily experienced in heavy drama, she may not be the best person to critique a farce comedy. If you're considering hiring a freelancer, ask for references. Find out whether you can speak to one of the dramaturge's satisfied customers. All this being said, paying a freelancer for a critique is my least favorite method for getting feedback. Why should you pay for it when you can get it for free?

Whichever path or paths you take in terms of getting feedback, don't put all your money on one horse. Don't take any one person's comments — positive or negative — as gospel. Try to get as many opinions as possible. What may be seen as a problem by one person may be no problem at all for others.

Arranging play readings for feedback

Readings are a very useful way to get a feel for how well your play is working. A play reading is what it sounds like: People, preferably actors, read aloud your play.

Understanding the reading process

Generally, a reading is organized this way: You, a director, or someone else with contacts rounds up the required number of actors to read the characters in your play. An additional person is asked to read the stage directions. The participants are given copies of the script in advance so that they can familiarize themselves with the story and their character.

At the appointed place and day, chairs are set out for the readers. The actors sit with the scripts in their hands and read for you and whatever audience you've arranged — select or public.

Readings can take place in any of the following venues:

- **Private residences:** A reading can be something informal arranged by you in your home. A friend and very successful colleague, Tom Dudzick, has the first reading of any play he writes in his living room. He asks actor friends to read the parts and invites knowledgeable friends to offer feedback afterwards. (He usually puts out a spread of bagels, which is a nice touch.)

- **Libraries:** Many public libraries have reading series. They schedule poets and novelists to read from their works. Some also host — or can be sold on the idea of hosting — a play reading with actors. Because libraries are public institutions, these readings usually must be open to the public.

- **Theatres:** Some theatres offer readings of new plays as part of their season to provide additional programming for their audiences. A theatre reading allows the artistic staff of the theatre to hear — and see audience reaction to — a play that the theatre may be considering for full production. Theatre readings can have a small admission fee, or they can be free to the public. Theatre readings are often, but not always, followed by a *talk-back,* a discussion of the work between the audience and the playwright.

- **Guild readings:** The Dramatists Guild and other playwright organizations and play development groups host readings for the benefit of their playwright members. Check out your local playwright organization, usually located in or near a metropolitan area, for information on programs they offer.

Here are some things you should know before organizing or asking for a reading of your new play:

- ✔ **Actors should be given the scripts as far in advance as possible so that they can acquaint themselves with their characters and with the story.** If you want to really learn from the reading, you don't want to hand out scripts to actors as they walk in the door for the reading. When actors are reading the script for the first time as they're doing the reading, it's called a *cold reading*. Cold readings are inferior because the actors have no clue as to what the characters are about or where the story line is taking them. Consequently, the actors can read lines incorrectly (with the wrong intentions or emotions) because they haven't had the opportunity to discover what the play is about.

- ✔ **Don't expect full acting in a reading.** Yes, the actors, having reviewed the script beforehand, should be able to make informed choices on how to play their characters and their scenes. But they haven't had the benefit of weeks of rehearsals with a director, which they need in order to do fully developed performances.

- ✔ **Readings get minimal rehearsal.** You or your director should try to get the cast in a room at least once before the official reading to minimally rehearse the script. (Twice is better, if possible. Often a rehearsal is scheduled a week before the reading, and another rehearsal is held the day the reading itself at the reading site.) This quick-and-dirty rehearsal plan is primarily aimed at making sure everyone understands the play and their roles. You're not going to get a finished, polished performance for a reading, so don't expect it.

- ✔ **Actors do not and should not memorize their parts for a reading.** Some actors feel that they'll impress the playwright and director if they can recite some of the lines from memory. I strongly discourage actors from attempting to learn their lines in so short a period because it distracts them from concentrating on how best to deliver the lines. The reading should be a test of how well the play works, not a test of whether the actors can remember their lines without looking at the script.

- ✔ **Actors generally don't get paid for doing readings.** Actors do not expect payment, per se, for the reading. Actors can be reimbursed for travel expenses and a meal if they're working during or around mealtime, and sometimes the reading cast gets a small stipend for their time if the budget allows it. Reimbursement and stipends are more likely to be involved if the reading is being conducted by a theatre organization that has some resources at its disposal. If you're organizing the reading yourself, donuts and coffee and a hearty "thank you" afterward are all that you need to provide. Emerging actors and emerging playwrights usually have one thing in common — no money.

Never promise or even hint to an actor in a reading that she may get the role in your play if it gets produced. Even if you'd give your right hand to have a certain actor play a certain role, making or implying any promises is unwise. If you're fortunate enough to get a production of your play, you're going to want to hold auditions for all roles. You may even be *required* by the theatre company or Actors' Equity (the theatre actors' union) to hold auditions. And the producer, the person who's putting up the money to do your show, may very well have in mind an actor she may want for a role. If you feel you can't stop yourself from making some kind of commitment to an actor, promise only that you will invite her to audition for the role if the play gets done sometime down the road. The best policy, however, is to make no promises at all.

Avoiding the "staged" reading

People often confuse a reading of the play with a "staged" reading. A *reading*, as discussed in the preceding section, is a sit-down affair in which the actors are simply reading, not moving.

A *staged reading* involves the attempt to act out the play as much as is logistically feasible. The actors, with scripts in hand, move around the stage as directed in rehearsal. The actors may be asked to make entrances and exits. They may pick up and use props, which can get a little awkward when holding a script. The idea is to show as much of the physicality of the play as is possible, assuming that audiences appreciate the play more if it includes action.

I find staged readings clumsy. In a staged reading the actors have to remember what they need to be *doing* as well as how to read the lines. Even if the actors make notations in their scripts concerning the blocking (where they should be onstage at any given moment), a staged reading means that they will be doing two things at one time — reading the script and glancing at their notations.

You'll be lucky to get two rehearsals for a reading, so you probably want the actors to focus on how to deliver the lines, not on where they should be when delivering the lines. After all, the crucial task in any reading is to assess the success of the fundamental components of your play — the characters and the conflict. And the way I see it, having the stage directions reader tell the audience the essential physical activities is more than adequate. Audiences are able to process the words "Carol throws her glass at Tom" without seeing Carol throw her glass at Tom.

In all fairness, some theatre people swear by staged readings. They feel they get good results. Who's right? In time, you'll come to your own conclusion.

Knowing what to look for in a reading

For you, the playwright, the most important part of any reading is what you learn about your play through the process. Always keep in mind that the reading is not being conducted for your enjoyment or for the entertainment of the audience. If the reading turns out to be entertaining, all the better, but remember that this is a working event for you.

Arm yourself with a pen and notepad and find an inconspicuous seat somewhere. Your job is to listen, watch, and make notes, based on your reactions and those of the audience, on how well your play works and what you can improve.

Because you are there to observe the play in action, you should *not* be onstage reading a part or reading the stage directions. Even if you've written a role for yourself in the play, which is not uncommon, during a reading you're the playwright, not an actor. Sometimes you'll hear an actor-playwright say "But I *have* to read the role; *I* know how it's supposed to be read." That's rationalizing. The dialogue should be written well enough that any actor can read the role correctly. Trust me: You'll be a much happier actor down the road if you focus on being the playwright during your readings. Your script will end up in better shape, and, as a result, your performance as an actor will be enhanced.

To get the most out of a reading, you need to hear your play without the distraction. You need to listen to your lines and watch the audience reaction, and you can't do those things well if you're onstage with your eyes on the script. Following are the tasks you should be doing during a reading:

1. **Listen to the lines of dialogue as they come out of the actors' mouths.** Do they sound like natural language with a conversational rhythm? Or do the lines sound artificial and forced, written because the characters need to say this or that to keep the play moving? Often dialogue that sounds great in your head or looks terrific on the page sounds stiff, dull, overly complicated, too linguistically correct, or overwritten when people are actually saying the lines. Try to put yourself in the audience's place. What would you think of this dialogue if you hadn't yourself written it?

2. **Watch the audience.** As unobtrusively as possible, look at faces. Do people seem interested and engaged in the story? Or are they looking around, glancing at their watches or programs? Are they yawning, or, heaven forbid, dozing off? Are audiences laughing at your funny lines? Do they look emotionally involved at the dramatic points? Make specific notes about points of the play at which the audience is reacting as hoped and where the audience appears unengaged.

Don't get so involved in enjoying your work — a big temptation — that you forget to evaluate to your dialogue and study the audience. Years ago I knew a playwright who would roar with laughter and squirm in his seat with unrestrained delight during readings of his plays. He was his own biggest fan and had a whale of a time at his readings. Consequently, he also had a lot of trouble revising and improving his scripts. If you genuinely want to make your script better (and if you don't, why are you having a reading?), be sure to stay focused, be your own constructive critic, and stay alert to the audience's input throughout the reading.

3. **Conduct a feedback session with the audience after the reading.** If possible, have a theatre-savvy individual moderate the discussion. The moderator should throw out constructive questions to the audience, like

   • Were you able to follow the story line?

   • Were any moments unclear or confusing?

   • Did your attention drift at any point?

   • Were the characters' motivations clear?

   • Did any of the characters do or say anything that seemed out of character?

   • Did the conclusion of the play seem appropriate to the story?

   • What worked best for you?

   After probing the audience for reactions, the moderator can throw the floor open for questions (if you're willing). But don't let the feedback period (which should be no more than 30 minutes) degrade into an unstructured, free-for-all discussion that doesn't address the important questions you need to have answered. (The next section delves deeper into creating an effective feedback session after your play reading.)

4. **Ask the audience questions about anything that concerns you.** If you suspect that some aspect of the work is a problem, don't kid yourself that everything's fine just because no one brought up the problem. You know your play better than anyone, and if you're concerned about whether something is working or not, now is your chance to poll an audience. "I was wondering," you may say, "whether anyone had a problem with Carol throwing a glass at Tom. Did you feel she was provoked enough to do that? Did that seem out of character for Carol? Did Carol lose your sympathy at that moment?" And so on.

A reading of your play in progress, with a specially invited audience or in a public venue, is a great gift and privilege. Make the most of it.

Getting the most from post-reading feedback sessions

Before the reading, discuss with your moderator the kinds of questions you'd like asked of the audience. To keep the comments on the right track, the moderator can give the audience some guidelines before things get rolling.

If you want feedback on only a specific aspect of the play, like the story line or on the clarity of the characters' motivations, because that's where you feel you need to most input, you can tell the moderator to only allow that type of feedback. However, I don't advise that approach, because you may avoid hearing feedback that you should be hearing. Denial is not helpful in assessing the state of your work.

In feedback sessions, some comments and observations are helpful, and other remarks and opinions are not only unhelpful but maybe even damaging for a playwright to hear. The moderator must be unafraid to step in to guide the discussion or get clarification if an out-of-bounds remark is made, such as "I think the character of Amanda is stupid." She may ask the person who made the well-intentioned but useless comment questions like

- ✔ Do you mean the character seems uneducated?
- ✔ Do you mean the dialogue written for the character doesn't seem appropriate for the character?
- ✔ Do you mean that the character makes poor choices?

The moderator needs to find the constructive idea behind the poorly worded criticism. This intervention protects you and helps you understand what the person was really trying to say.

Don't let the feedback segment of your reading become a free-ranging question-and-answer session. The playwright isn't at the feedback session to clarify script points for the audience. The play should speak for itself. If audience members are not clear about certain aspects of the play, explaining them to the audience does not help you with the script.

For example, if an audience member asks you why your protagonist shoots the antagonist at the ballet, the appropriate response by you is not to answer the question but to say something like "So it's not clear why she does that. Thank you; that's a great point. I'll work to make that clearer." While the questioner may be somewhat disappointed not to get an answer, she probably will be gratified that she provided you with a "great point."

Tackling the Grisly Task of Rewriting

"Writing is rewriting," successful novelist Richard North Patterson has said. "To fall in love with a first draft to the point where one cannot change it is to greatly enhance the prospects of never publishing." The same is true for playwrights and productions.

Some playwrights have no problem reworking and rewriting their scripts. They enjoy it. For them, revisiting their dialogue and story development is part of the fun of writing. Unfortunately, I am not one of those playwrights. For me, rewriting is hard work. But it comes with the territory, so all playwrights need to make their peace with the process.

When you get down to rewriting, save your new work as a new draft. By preserving the earlier drafts, you can refer back to them in the event you later want to see what you had early on.

After you've had a successful reading of your play and you're back at your computer with a pad full of notes and observations, you're ready to knuckle down to the task of rewriting your play. How do you make sense of everything you heard and took down?

Taking the gut-feeling test

If you have a gut reaction that what you heard from someone, or from a lot of someones, is on the nose, then address it. Consider what was said, and, if you agree with the comments, no matter how uncomfortable, work on the problem.

Give yourself permission to make wholesale changes. Don't be tied to anything you wrote earlier if it doesn't seem right anymore. Dare to make the big changes that your instincts tell you are needed. You can always go back to your earlier version if later you decide that the rewriting took you in a wrong direction.

After a reading of *Canvases,* a full-length, two-character play *(two-hander)* that I wrote, people suggested I ought to add the people who were referred to in the play. One of the two characters in *Canvases,* Carol, mentions her mother and a girlfriend, and audience members thought I should actually write them into the script as characters. So I did. I did a total rewrite of the play, adding the new characters. After a reading of the new, larger-cast version, I took an objective look at what I had. I concluded that my gut had been right the first time. The revised play was indeed different, but it was no better. Expanding the cast did not enhance the play, and (from a potential producer's point of view) it made the play less attractive commercially (it required more actors to pay). So I set aside the new draft and concentrated on refining the two-character version. Had the experiment been a waste of time? No, not at all. When I decided to go back to the play as a two-hander, I went back to it more confident that I had the right structure for the story I wanted to tell. When you come back to something after moving away from it for a while, sometimes you come back with a stronger sense that you were on the right track the first time.

Remembering that the majority doesn't always rule

If a good number of people at your reading expressed the same concerns or reservations about the play, clearly you need to look at those issues. But don't assume that all those people were right.

Playwriting is not a popularity contest or a numbers game. Simply because a majority of the people who spoke up articulated the same or similar concern doesn't mean you *must* make changes. But I very strongly suggest you take a dispassionate look at what you're being told. Never ignore what you're hearing out of laziness or, what's more likely, stubbornness. There's a big difference between a carefully considered conviction that you're right and the understandable but insidious reluctance to change anything.

Remember that a play must *function:* The buggy needs to cart the ticket-holding folks from point A to point Z in an engaging and entertaining fashion. If a number of people in the audience express reservations about the ride in any way, looking closely at the problem is to your advantage. You may find that the real problem is something different than the audience identified, but you'll never be able to fix things unless you thoroughly investigate the issue.

Allowing yourself a fresh perspective

Finding booboos and problems in your own work is problematic. When you read your own work, your mind plays tricks on you. Your eye, in cahoots with your brain, assumes what's on the page is what you meant to put there, so you very likely won't see errors and problems that others would immediately spot. But the good news is that you have ways to deal with this.

You can self-critique your writing more efficiently and accurately if you put the pages (or scene, or entire play) aside for a while.

If you try to get a handle on how things are going, in whole or in part, immediately after finishing the work, you're apt to miss what issues may be there. When work is fresh in your mind, you're less likely to home in on problems, from omissions to clumsy transitions to clunky dialogue.

The best way around this "blindsight" is hindsight. Put the work away for a day or two. Work on an new scene, another part of the play, or even another play entirely for a while. And then go back for a look at the writing you put aside. When you come back to your writing after some time away, you'll see the scene or the play in a fresh light. The distance of only a day or two helps you bring a more objective perspective to the work.

The playwright Neil Simon incubates his work for longer periods. "Over the years I have found that putting a play, or even one act, into a drawer and not looking at it for at least a few weeks makes wondrous things happen. Its faults suddenly become very clear," he wrote in *Rewrites: A Memoir.* "When I take it out and reread it . . . what's good remains good, but what's bad jumps off the page and smacks me right across my ego. My thin black indelible pen puts a line through every inferior word and sentence, blocking it out forever. . . ."

If you don't have the luxury of leaving your work for a couple of days or weeks, then at least allow a few hours to pass before you go over the work with a critical eye. A little bit of distance goes a long way.

Going Another Round with Your Advanced Draft

After you've labored, happily or not, over your script and produced a strong revised draft, guess what? You're still not done. To be prudent, you want to undergo another round of opinions, critiques, and readings.

You probably don't want to impose on those theatre colleagues and readings hosts who have already assisted you with this play. Therefore, if possible, approach other individuals and organizations. Not only does finding new helpers avoid wearing out your welcome with any one person or institution, but using other resources gives you fresh, new feedback on your play.

Essentially repeat the process of showing your play around and arranging a public reading of your play. And you should again honestly and rigorously weigh the pros and cons of the comments you get and make the appropriate revisions.

When you get to the point of rewriting later drafts of your play, avoid a pitfall that can sink an otherwise assiduous effort at rewriting: the natural tendency to want to change as little as possible. Some playwrights are practically incapable of doing rewrites because they become enamored with their early work.

The prescription is to stop trying to fix the problems by changing a word here and a phrase there. Put the whole scene or act aside and start again as if you hadn't written it before. Totally rewrite it. Don't waste time and energy trying to save this or that section. You don't necessarily have to permanently discard the malfunctioning scene or act, but work as though you will and start fresh. Though this approach is, yes, a lot more work than tinkering, the result of getting a new start will probably be fresher and stronger and clearer than it would be if you take the patching approach.

At this point, you may be wondering whether the revising process ever ends. When a script is finished is a subjective judgment, but you can probably feel comfortable with your script when it reaches the point at which

✔ Audiences are fully engaged in the story.

✔ The characters' motivations are clear.

✔ Audiences know what they're waiting to find out (the outcome).

✔ The ending feels appropriate for your story.

You're then ready to move on to the process of going public with your play.

Chapter 16

Rehearsals and Premieres: Nail Biting 101

In This Chapter

▶ Knowing and understanding your theatre collaborators

▶ Making the most of the rehearsal process

▶ Maximizing what you learn from previews

▶ Anticipating and enjoying your play's opening night

*L*ike the proverbial hardworking mother, a playwright's work is never done. Or so it seems. You've put your play — and yourself — through the painstaking and time-consuming process of play development, involving a series of critiques, readings, and rewrites (see Chapter 15). The result is a tight draft (yes, you still call it a *draft*) of your play that's ready to take its first tottering steps on its own on the path to production.

In this chapter, I assume that a producer or producers have stepped forward to finance a production of your play. (If you're wondering how to make that very important step happen, flip ahead to Chapter 17 to read about finding a producer.) Now begins the mostly fun — sometimes frustrating — part: getting the show on its feet.

This chapter explores the satisfying and trying process of rehearsals. You find out how you can attend, participate in, and survive rehearsals, maximizing the opportunity presented by rehearsals, all leading to the crowning moment — your official opening night.

Getting Acquainted: Who's Who in Your Production

Before delving into the magical and mundane process of rehearsing a play, you need to identify who's who. Knowing who the significant players in the game are and what they're supposed to do (and *not* do) will keep you from making unnecessary mistakes and looking unprofessional.

Producer

The producer's principle business is to raise the money to put on the play. *Commercial producers* hope to make a profit for themselves and/or the investors they round up. Producers in nonprofit theatre (often the artistic directors or executive directors of their organizations) simply hope to cover their expenses and have some money left over to seed the theatre's next production.

The producer, who has picked a play he wants to produce, hires the director. After the director is on board, the producer may or may not get involved in assembling the balance of the creative team — the actors and the stagecraft (sets, lighting, sound, costumes, and so on) people. However, the producer does get involved in spending a good deal of money on the following necessities:

✔ Renting rehearsal space

✔ Renting the theatre to be used (if he doesn't have one at his disposal)

✔ Paying salaries of the cast (including the director), crew, and theatre staff

✔ Paying for sets, costumes, props, sound effects, and so on

✔ Advertising and promoting the play

✔ Paying an advance and royalties to the playwright (or creative team)

A lot of money is laid out long before the first ticket is sold. (You can find more on producers in Chapter 17.)

Your producer, in a perfect world, should have little or nothing to say about changing anything in your play. But the producer has the power of the purse, so he may suggest changes. Don't be so quick to get your hackles up. The producer has a lot riding on the success of the play, so he's not going to introduce into the project an element that could sabotage things. If he's an experienced producer, his feedback is likely to be practical and possibly invaluable, so carefully consider what he has to say.

Producers also have been known to insist on casting an actor they want for the roles. The actor most likely will be right for the role. Remember, the producer, too, wants the play to succeed, so he's not going to insist on an inappropriate actor. But what do you do when you're offered an actor or "suggestion" from the producer that, after honest and objective consideration, you feel is wrong for your play? You weigh the potential "damage" of the producer's proposal against the possibility of blowing the production by rebuffing the producer.

If you're stymied, check in with your director. If he agrees with you, he may be willing to speak to the producer on your behalf. Then again, the director may see much less of a problem than you do. If the director isn't able to support your objection, unless you want to risk imploding your production, you probably will just need to let go of your discomfort, particularly as a new playwright. After you've gotten a production or two under your belt, you'll be seen as having more authority behind your judgment.

Theatre is a collaborative medium, and, unfortunately, the collaborative input isn't always what it should be. But you can take solace — cold comfort though it may be — in the knowledge that nothing can be changed in your script without your permission. However, do be careful about digging in your heels on small points. Productions have been lost owing to pride and stubbornness. Producers always have other fish they can fry in your stead.

Director

The director, like a ship's captain, charts the course and destination of theatrical production. And like the skipper, the director chooses his crew and determines what supplies are needed for the journey.

The director begins by studying and envisioning the play: what it says, how it should look, and what kind of cast it should have. If he's smart and secure in his work, the director will consult with you about his vision. To help the production run smoothly, being open to new ideas this early in the process is very important.

After the director has formed his vision for the play, he holds auditions to cast the play. You, as playwright, can choose to be involved in the audition process, listening quietly and privately providing the director with input. Ultimately, you should trust the judgment of your director. You do have the power to veto a casting choice, but like detonating a nuclear weapon, it's not the way you want to resolve a disagreement. Vetoing a casting choice is a last resort, and I recommend that you never do it.

After the play is cast, the director works out a rehearsal schedule (in accordance with union rules, if they apply). You have the right to attend rehearsals, but you must be mindful of things you should do and, more importantly, things you should *not* do in rehearsals, which I discuss later in this chapter. Also, the director usually is responsible for hiring, in consultation with the producer, the stagecraft professionals: the lighting, sound, set, and costume designers and the stage manager.

As captain of the entire crew, the director praises and cajoles, pushes and prods, critiques and coaches everyone involved until the play is ready to open. When the play has begun its run, the director usually departs for his next project, leaving the stage manager in charge.

Stage manager

If the director is captain, then the stage manager is first mate. The stage manager coordinates the rehearsal schedule, ensuring everyone is in place and ready for rehearsals. He works with the stagecraft people on behalf of the director. Most of all, he makes detailed notes of the play's staging and every decision, choice, and adjustment the director makes. The real work of the stage manager begins when the show has opened and the director has departed. At that juncture, the stage manager is in full control of the production, and he must ensure that all personnel — cast and production crew (light and sound operators, costumer, stagehands, and so on) — show up on time and do their jobs properly. If an actor grows weak on his lines, the stage manager works with the actor to get back up to speed. If an actor is replaced, the stage manager rehearses the replacement into the show.

The stage manager also *calls the show,* meaning that he, armed with a copy of the script and a headset connecting him to the entire operation, gives the cues for light changes, sound use, set changes, actor entrances and exits, and so on. The better coordinated the production is, the more hands-off the stage manager can be.

Actors

Actors are faced with the challenge of inhabiting your characters and breathing life into your dialogue. Acting requires training and dedication and, most importantly, artistry to make your characters live and love and laugh and weep. All actors hit rough patches during rehearsal. And an actor must be sharp and confident to hear and put to use a director's feedback aimed at helping him through the rough patches.

As easy as some of them make it seem, theatre actors do a difficult job — becoming and convincingly behaving like someone else for hours. And they do it before an audience, without the safety net of a shouted "cut" if something goes wrong.

Respect your actors. Praise your actors. They are eager to please. And they are vulnerable and sometimes easily discouraged. Make them feel as important as they are. Because when all is said and done, when the playwright and director are nowhere to be seen, the actors are out there onstage in front of maybe hundreds of people, night after night during the run of a play.

Conducting Auditions

The producer and/or director spread the word about auditions for your play through casting agents, industry publications and websites, word of mouth, or a combination of all three methods.

The director gets inundated with photo-résumés from actors and from the agents for actors who'd like to be seen for the roles. The photo-résumé provides an idea of each candidate's experience, training, skills, qualifications, and appearance. (But don't be surprised if your candidates look little like their photos. Actors too often use glamorous or, what's worse, outdated photos of themselves, which, by misleading the director, is a self-defeating practice.) The director (with your participation, if you like) sifts through the mountain of photo-résumés to decide whom to call in for auditions. Figure 16-1 is an example of a photo-résumé; the photo appears on one side, and the résumé content on the other side.

If you choose to attend auditions, you'll join the producer, director, and stage manager at a table in an audition room or studio. Situated a comfortable distance in front of the table is a chair for use by the auditioning actor. Outside the room is a waiting area.

As with most aspects of theatre, the audition process varies. Actors may be asked to prepare in advance and perform a monologue or two (anywhere from one to two minutes in length each) — dramatic, comic, or Shakespearean — from other plays. Or, actors may be provided with pages from your script, *sides,* which they will be asked to read with some intention (acting) in the audition room. Or, actors may do a combination of monologues and readings. For example, the first round of auditions may involve candidates doing prepared monologues, and the second round of auditions may have the actors work with sides. The approach used is usually determined by the director.

After the first round of auditions, the producer, director, and playwright discuss their notes and the actors' photo-résumés and narrow down the pool to a small number of candidates for callbacks. *Callbacks* are invitations to the next round of auditions, and actors are ecstatic when they get a callback. The team conducting the auditioning chooses the cast from the pool of callbacks. (Auditions rarely go more than two rounds. However, the 2006 revival of *A Chorus Line* went three rounds because the producers began the process with an *open call,* disparagingly referred to as a *cattle call,* meaning that auditions were open to anyone who showed up. The show's audition team saw 3,000 dancer/actors in the first round!)

Figure 16-1: An example of an actor's photo-résumé.

Attending Rehearsals

Rehearsals, particularly your first time through the process, can be the acid test not only for the play you wrote but for you as the playwright. Your play will be envisioned, conceptualized, studied, planned, rehearsed, learned, memorized, and staged, all in a matter of weeks. The undertaking involves hard work, trial-and-error experimentation, long hours, artistic license, and creative space.

The process of putting together the production of a play can vary somewhat from play to play. Professional, community (amateur), and school productions differ in many of the rehearsal rules governing the responsibilities and rights of producers, directors, actors, stagecraft people, playwrights, and anyone else involved. (For the purposes of this discussion, the producer of a play can be an individual or individuals or it can be a theatre company.) In any situation, a good rehearsal process operates like a well-trimmed sailing vessel. What the rehearsal process requires of you, the playwright, is patience, participation when appropriate, and professionalism. You do not want to get in the way, which, unfortunately, is easy to do.

For simplicity's sake, in this section, I assume that you've chosen to be part of the process. Participation of the playwright usually isn't required in the production of a play. New playwrights tend to glom onto their productions like white on rice. Veteran playwrights often let the productions take care of themselves, with the possible exception of new plays. If a producer insists that you be involved in the production of the play, an uncommon but not impossible scenario if the play is brand new, you're entitled to reimbursement of your expenses. Your contract, which I cover in Chapter 17, usually includes such a provision.

Working through rehearsal steps

Theatrical rehearsal involves a number of steps, each distinct and each with its own objectives. The rehearsals take place in a rehearsal studio or other such large room that's quiet and private. About a week before the play opens, the director and the cast get to rehearse in the set onstage. Though rehearsal plans differ according to the process of the director, they all tend to include these steps:

- ✔ **A table reading:** The process begins with a sit-down reading of the play by the cast around a table. The actors familiarize themselves with the play and with their fellow actors and then usually have an open discussion of the play.

- ✔ **Script-in-hand rehearsals:** These rehearsals go over small chunks of the play, or *beats,* with scripts in the hands of the actors. The actors can explore the emotional content and the physicality of the play without the burden of memorizing lines.

- ✔ **Off-book rehearsals:** In these later rehearsals, the actors know their lines, which is referred to as being *off book.*

- **Technical rehearsal:** This stop-and-go rehearsal allows the director and the stagecraft people to adjust sound levels and to ensure that the lights are aimed and adjusted properly. This rehearsal goes *cue to cue,* meaning it goes from a point where the lights or sound change to another point in the play where the lights and sound change, skipping the dialogue and action in between.

- **Run-throughs:** In these rehearsals, the entire play is done from start to finish with as little stopping as possible, allowing the director and cast to see what shape the play is in. Run-throughs can be halted and resumed by the director to address any problems or issues he sees.

- **Dress rehearsal:** This run-through of the entire play with the actors in their costumes is usually one of the final rehearsals. Sometimes a dress rehearsal is conducted with an invited audience, giving the actors the opportunity to experience audience reaction to their work.

- **Speed-throughs:** In these sit-down rehearsals, the actors speed through their lines without acting or movement. The objective is to have the actors brush up on their lines if the show has had a few days off.

Good directors often give their actors a high degree of freedom at the beginning of the rehearsal process. The director comes into rehearsal with a clear vision of the play and a solid plan for the day's work, but if he's confident, he can allow actors to experiment by doing the scene as *they* see it. Wise directors don't force their vision on the actors, because that would stifle spontaneity and creativity. Instead, through rehearsals' process of trial, error, and directorial feedback, the actors experiment their way to a performance that artistically satisfies them and their director, and, eventually, an audience. Almost as if by magic, the finished product often exceeds the expectations of everyone involved.

During the whole rehearsal process, among other backstage activities, the actors are learning their lines at home; costumers are making and fitting the costumes; publicity photos are being taken; sometimes press interviews are given by the playwright, director, and or cast; and the set and props are being designed and built or acquired.

Supporting the director

From the director's point of view, staging a brand-new play is very different from directing plays that have been produced before, classic or contemporary. In the case of previously produced plays, the playwright usually isn't present — he's either gone to that big theatre in the sky or he simply chooses not to participate in the production of a play that's already proven itself. The director can do his work without feeling anyone's looking over his shoulder. Additionally, he has the advantage of being able to reference prior productions to see how other directors have done them.

A director working on a new play has no previous productions of the play to research. He's on his own. For some directors, being the first director is a thrilling prospect — he has the opportunity to put his stamp on how the play will be done in future productions. For other directors, this thrill of doing a new play can be accompanied by a sense of insecurity if they're unsure of themselves.

Having the playwright in attendance also makes the experience different for directors. Most of the time, directors are delighted to have the playwright in attendance because the playwright is another resource to be mined. But the blending of an uncertain director and a new playwright can be dicey. It can result in unnecessary anxiety and conflict. The director can feel threatened by a playwright hovering in the background, and the director's shakiness may manifest in a request that the playwright not attend rehearsals.

Dealing with a request to absent yourself is thorny. I've handled it in two ways:

✓ **The deferential approach:** Adopt a placating and supportive posture. Acknowledge that the director is the boss and that everything goes through him — questions from the actors and any ideas you may have. Assure him that you know the time to offer input is during breaks or before or after the rehearsal, in private, and only to him. In essence, promise to sit somewhere out of sight to be both not seen and not heard.

This assuaging approach generally reassures the director enough to withdraw his request for the playwright to stay away from rehearsals. If it doesn't, negotiate a point at which you can begin sitting in. The very fact of giving the director his way goes a long way toward establishing trust. It says, in effect, if I can trust you to hold a few closed rehearsals, then you can trust that I can sit in on future rehearsals with interfering. This approach can be hard for new playwrights.

✓ **The cooperative approach:** If a director you know and respect asks you to skip the first few rehearsals because he sincerely believes the process would benefit from a couple of private and intimate sessions, smile and cheerfully accede. You may not be happy about such a request, but if you know that the director knows what he's doing, you can agree and rest assured that the world won't end because you aren't present for every rehearsal.

Holding your tongue with the actors

Working in such a concentrated way, the director, cast, production staff, and playwright usually develop a tight-knit bond. Every member of this temporary family strives to respect and help each other toward the common goal: a hit play. This spirit of camaraderie and cooperation is something to be valued and nurtured.

However, unlike the domestic family in which, theoretically at least, both parents share power and responsibility, the play production family has only one parent, the director. Every decision is either made or cleared by the director. All questions and problems should be presented to the director for solutions. And that includes any questions, problems, or ideas you have.

 Never get between the cast and the director. If an actor asks you a question about the play, always defer to the director, allowing him to field the questions. If an actor comes to you privately, politely and supportively respond, "You probably should be asking [director's name] about that. If he wants me to work with you on it, I'd be happy to." When you take that tack, your director will love you for it, and potential irritation and divisiveness are averted.

If your director has done his homework adequately, you may be surprised at how well he knows the play and how perceptive his answers are. He may even come up with inspiring responses and ideas that never occurred to you, which can be thrilling. You just need to give the director his elbow room and be open to his ideas.

Getting the play on its feet

When rehearsals begin in earnest, the director selects a number of pages of the script, a section of the play called a *beat,* to be the focus of each rehearsal session. In other words, the play is rehearsed, at least initially, in bite-size chunks. The rehearsals proceed in this fashion, section by section, until an entire scene has been worked. Then that scene may be worked from start to finish. Then the director moves on to a beat in the next scene, and so on.

Early in the process, the actors rehearse with scripts in their hands. As the rehearsal period progresses, the actors do their homework — learning their lines.

In addition to working out the characters' actions and emotional cores, the rehearsals also deal with blocking. *Blocking* is where on the stage the characters (actors) are at any given moment in the play. Early on, the actors usually are free to move about the stage, working out where the lines are best and most logically said. The director watches and offers *adjustments,* suggestions to improve a moment or a line. These small adjustments, this fine-tuning by the director, is often what makes the difference between a flat or lively moment.

Being associated with Penguin Rep Theatre in Stony Point, New York, I dropped by one afternoon to unobtrusively watch the rehearsal of an upcoming production, directed by the theatre's artistic director, Joe Brancato. The beat they were working on involved two characters uttering some potentially powerful lines six or eight feet from each other. But even to my untrained eye, the beat felt lifeless. It wasn't working well.

Joe, seated in the orchestra section of the theatre, pondered a moment and then gave an adjustment. He changed the blocking, suggesting that the actors say their lines face to face, within arm's length of each other. I thought they would crowd each other and restrict the energy between them, but just the opposite happened. Standing within striking distance of each other, the lines sizzled. An urgency and power sprung from the proximity of the actors. The minor repositioning of the actors made a huge difference. That effective adjustment is what astute and experienced directors can do.

Finding ways to enhance the way the story's told is what rehearsals are about. The director and actors try different alternatives to find the best means of realizing the moments of your script. This trial-and-error process can be frightening at first . . . but relax. Patience is key here.

Preparing yourself for the play to be different than you imagined it

The process of producing a play is a step-by-step affair. It takes time, patience, and intelligence to get through the rehearsal process with a minimum of anxiety and stress.

A way of reducing the tension level for everyone involved is for you, the playwright, to sit back and let the stew simmer. In other words, don't rush to judge what you're seeing early in rehearsal. The finished production will be the result of a great deal of work by everyone involved. Don't expect too much too soon. Early in the process, the play won't look like what you had in mind. It doesn't even look like what the director has in mind. You can't judge the butterfly by the appearance of the caterpillar.

Lepidopterological (look it up) analogies aside, the point is that you need to restrain yourself from badgering the director with your concerns that a moment or a scene isn't what you had in mind. With time and patience, the play will come around. You need to trust the process and the people involved.

That being said, the chances of the play ever looking exactly how you envisioned it are slim. Each of the dozens of people working to bring your work to life has a vision of the play that can't possibly be identical with yours. You need to be confident that your work will benefit from the contributions of others. Develop the restraint to allow other professionals to impact your play, even in ways you couldn't imagine, so long as their choices do not *significantly* distort your vision.

The most common reaction I have had when I see how my plays shape up is astonished excitement and enthusiasm. In fact, in my 25 years of playwriting, I can count on one hand the number of times I felt compelled to speak to a director about the direction in which the play was going. And in those cases, either I was given an explanation that I accepted or the director made the appropriate adjustments. But my concerns were expressed only after the director had ample time to see his plan mature and I had the chance to see how the play worked as he saw it.

Should you direct your own play?

No matter how much some playwrights are cautioned against trying to have it all their own way, some will persist in it. Which, if you're one of those playwrights, raises the question: Should you direct your own play? The answer is no, never . . . well, maybe.

The answer is definitely *no* if your sole motivation in considering directing your own play is to be sure it will be 100 percent how you conceived of it. A better alternative to directing is to learn the art of compromise and come to terms with the reality that theatre is a collaborative medium. Directing is an exceptionally challenging profession full of responsibility and pressure. A director

- ✔ Needs to intimately know and understand theatre — both its history and in the present — and have seen or read lots and lots of plays.

- ✔ Needs to know acting, acting approaches, acting problems, and how to coach actors (the last a very specific skill).

- ✔ Needs to have excellent people skills. He should to be able to deal effectively and diplomatically with producers, actors, playwrights, stagecraft people, and many others.

- ✔ Needs to be a "detail person," able to analyze a script minutely so that he can make informed judgments and answer questions.

- ✔ Needs to be a jack-of-all-trades. He has to make judgments on variety of different arts and crafts, like set design, lighting, sound, and costumes. He doesn't need to be an expert in these and other areas, but he does need to know enough to make good choices.

- ✔ Needs to be able to research thoroughly the circumstances and time period of the play to bring authenticity to the production.

In addition to these challenges, directing your own play robs you of a talented and creative production partner. By not working with a skilled director, you eliminate the opportunity to benefit from the experience and expertise of another theatre professional. You cut out one corner of the theatre collaboration diamond: the playwright; the director; the actors; and the stagecraft people.

So unless you have twin passions — playwriting and directing— avoid the temptation to "take over" the production just to be able to control things. You may be shooting yourself in the foot, not to mention squandering time during which you could be playwriting.

Doing more rewrites (Gulp!)

Rehearsals can be invaluable for polishing your play. A big benefit of experiencing the rehearsal process is the opportunity to see how your play, as the director and actors bring it to life, is working. You can sit in the back of the rehearsal room with your script and take notes. Then, with the blessing of the director, you can go home and fix what seems not to be working.

Always consult with the director before you do rewrites. The problems you want to fix may not be problems at all, just issues that the director hasn't yet addressed. Or, the director may want to hold off on changes until the actors are more solid on their characters and performance. In other words, coordinate your efforts with the director's plan. You don't want to be a loose cannon, disrupting the process of realizing of the script.

At some point toward the end of the rehearsal period, the director will *freeze the script.* This means that no more changes can be made in the script for this particular production. Exactly when this point comes is up to the director, who's balancing your opportunity to improve the script with the need of the actors to have adequate time to learn the "final" version.

Seeing Your Play Performed — Finally

Seeing your play fully performed in front of an audience is a thrilling — and scary — experience. Most of the time when I watch the performance of one of my plays, I can't sit. I find myself anxiously pacing in the back like an expectant father outside a delivery room. And when you get down to it, that comparison is very apt.

The play is your baby. You conceived it and gave birth to it (even if you're a guy). The baby has gone to school (the rehearsal process), and now your offspring is walking and talking and out in the world on its own. When your play finally opens, you can't do anything but watch it like everyone else. Or *can* you do something? Yes — if your play has a preview period, more rewrites are possible.

Testing the waters out of town

In the early to middle portions of the last century, major productions of plays and musicals commonly opened out of town. *Opening out of town* means fully presenting the play for paying audiences in communities and theatres outside of New York City.

The theory is that an out-of-town opening allows you to try out the play or musical under real-world conditions but in a less-important market than New York City, which is the Mecca, the Holy Grail, the big kahuna of theatre in the U.S. The producers, director, playwright, or creative team then has the opportunity to — yes, yet again — rewrite and rework the play before the New York reviewers get their critical hands on it.

Productions often opened out of town in cities like Philadelphia, Boston, Hartford, or New Haven, among many others. The theatre community understood, and still does, that the play or musical was not yet *set* (finalized) and could be modified — in major or minor ways — as a result of the out-of-town tryout.

The practice, while less common today, has not disappeared. Some recent shows that had out-of-town tryouts include *The 39 Steps* (Boston), *American Idiot* (Berkeley, California), *Catch Me if You Can* (Seattle), and *Wonderland* (Houston). But the people behind *Spider-Man: Turn Off the Dark* brought the show directly to Broadway. The staging of the show is so expensive, elaborate, and technically complicated, it was decided to mount the show once, where it counts.

Performing previews

Besides out-of-town openings, another more convenient and common way of testing a play before letting the critical hounds loose is to open in previews. *Previews* are fully presented performances of the show for paying audiences (though tickets sometimes are discounted). By theatre tradition, critics usually refrain from publishing reviews of the play until after previews, when the play officially opens.

Audiences understand that during previews the show can be interrupted to address issues or problems (artistic or technical) that crop up. They also know that the show isn't yet set. Changes, significant or not, can be made before the show has its official opening performance.

Preview periods have no prescribed length; it's decided for each production by the producers in conjunction with the director. The preview period may be a handful of shows or several weeks of performances. *Spider-Man: Turn Off the Dark* has shattered all preview records with months and months of trial-and-error presentations.

More rewrites? Will it never end?

Is rewriting ever over? Well, that's up to you . . . and maybe the director and producer, too. With so much riding on the success of the play, it's hard to turn down the opportunity to do some repair work and polishing whenever the opportunity presents itself. The great American playwright Tennessee Williams was known to rewrite his plays even after major productions.

What you don't want to do is become a tinkerer. As the old saying goes, if it ain't broke, don't fix it. You can drive yourself crazy tinkering and tweaking and making changes that, in essence, make the play different but not any better. You can better utilize that energy in composing a new play.

Surviving Opening Night

Eventually opening night arrives. After your best development efforts and out-of-town tryouts or previews or both, the play is ready for the first official performance.

What do you do during the opening performance? Usually you're seated in the audience with proud family members and friends. You fasten your seatbelt, grip the armrests, and try to enjoy the performance. Even the most experienced and confident of playwrights is nervous during the premiere performance. You've done your best, and all you can do is hope that the audience responds in the way you and your collaborators want.

After the official opening performance, many productions have a party for the cast, director, playwright, producer(s), and invited guests. Though most of the praise will be heaped upon the actors — the most visible corner of theatre's creative diamond — don't feel neglected. There will be credit enough to go around.

What a playwright does at subsequent performances is essentially up to him. He can, as I do, stand in the back of the theatre and pace. Even after decades writing plays, knowing that the play's ultimate success depends heavily on the performance of others — directors, actors, and stagecraft people — is still both nerve-racking and thrilling. As with sports teams, the success or not of the effort usually doesn't rely on the performance of any one participant.

Reacting to missteps or problems

What the playwright should not be doing during the first performance is gesticulating, rolling his eyes, shaking his head, or otherwise indicating rough spots during a performance. Display confidence and appreciation of the play for people around you. Save your reactions for a private discussion with the director. Opening night is an occasion for appreciation, not criticism.

Another no-no is placing blame. If the play, for whatever reason, isn't as well-received as you had hoped, never — and I mean *never* —attempt to put blame on others (the actors, the director, or whomever). Pointing fingers only makes a bad situation worse. I once witnessed a disgruntled playwright grumbling that his actors let him down and his director didn't know what he was doing, and so on. That kind of reaction is ugly and ungracious, and it reflects badly on the playwright himself. Behavior like that brings everyone down. What's worse, word will get around the theatre community that the playwright is a stinker and his work is to be avoided.

When things go badly, keep in mind that everyone has done his best. Appreciate the weeks upon weeks of work everyone put in. If you have the chance to quickly rework the play to fix what didn't work, go ahead and take it. But keep in mind that if you've gone about pinning responsibility for the problems on the director or cast, they may not be very enthusiastic about helping.

Dealing with reviews

Not all plays get reviewed. If your play is opening on Broadway, the newspaper, television, radio, and Internet critics will be there. That's their job. But if your play opens Off Broadway, or Off-Off Broadway, or in any one of the thousands of large and small theatres around the country, you'll likely have to do a selling job — using news releases, e-mail blasts, promotional kits, websites, and personal invitations — to get the critics to attend your opening. And it doesn't always work.

Why do you want reviewers? Reviews are an invaluable form of publicity and promotion. If reviewers praise your play, you'll sell more tickets. It's that simple. Many theatregoers choose the plays they see based on what the critics say about the plays. It may not be fair that a small number of individuals — the critics — have so much power over what succeeds or not, but that's the way it is.

In addition, getting your play reviewed puts it on the map. Unlike the now cliché phrase from the film *Field of Dreams,* "If you build it, they will come," the fact that your play is being done does not mean audiences will come. One of the biggest components of a producer's production budget is advertising, because audiences need to know your play exists in order to even consider it. A lot of shows are being performed on any given evening, so you're going to need all the promotion and visibility you can get, including reviews.

If your play gets generally positive reviews, it stands a good chance of having a successful run. Praise by critics, even universal acclaim, doesn't necessarily guarantee success, but it sure helps. Unfortunately, one of theatre's ironies is that unanimous critical praise does not ensure success, but universally negative reviews almost always mean disaster.

If your play gets generally negative reviews, your play stands a very good chance of folding. Some critically excoriated plays have closed within a few days of the bad reviews. Even lukewarm reviews can be fatal. Poor or lackluster reviews can cause ticket sales to drop off precipitously and tempt the producers to take the financially prudent step of cutting their losses by closing the show.

In 1988, $8 million (an enormous amount at the time) was invested to bring to Broadway the musical *Carrie,* based on the Stephen King horror novel of the same name. Beleaguered by technical problems and, more to the point, ripped to shreds by the critics, the show closed after only 16 previews and 5 official performances. Even the immense talent of Broadway luminary Betty Buckley as Carrie's peculiar mother couldn't save the show. *Carrie* became theatre legend as one of the quickest and costliest failures in Broadway history.

What do you do if you find yourself and your play on the south side of critics' reviews? Probably not much. The producers have to decide if they want to stick it out or put the show out of its misery, and you don't get a say in that matter. Rarely, producers of an ineffective play have the playwright and director significantly rewrite and rework it and attempt another production. But when a show has been branded unsuccessful by the critics, getting those critics back for a second look is almost impossible. Reconceiving a play and bringing it back is an uphill battle, and such attempts should not be undertaken out of anger, frustration, or pure stubbornness. (That being said, according to recent reports, productions of *Carrie* have been taking place around the country. So never say never.)

Generally, the most productive route to take after a shellacking is to put the piece aside, lick your wounds, and move on to your next play. Often you learn as much, if not more, from a failure than you do from a success. And approached with more experience and confidence, your next play will very likely do better.

Chapter 17

Promoting Your Play and Getting a Production

*I*n theatre, writing the play is only the first step. The second step is staging or producing the play, and that part involves a multitude of other people, including actors, directors, and stagecraft designers and technicians. But this second step never gets to happen unless someone foots the bill. Your play will never get to see the light of a stage without this indispensible collaborator.

A sobering fact about theatre — a reality applicable to all of the performing arts, actually — is that little happens without money. Someone or some organization needs to round up the many, many dollars it takes to bring your work to life — from rehearsal to opening night and beyond.

Another stark truth about playwriting and theatre is that you're facing a good deal of competition from other playwrights, ranging from newcomers to Tony winners and everyone in between. In theatre, there are no minor leagues in which to cut your teeth. The moment you take on the role of playwright, you're competing against the best the field has to offer. The prize for which you contend is financial support. And the competition is stiff and unending.

This situation is daunting, yes, but not hopeless. If your author, a Bronx boy of Hispanic heritage from a low-income family, who grew up in city housing projects, can learn to write plays well enough to attract the support of producers and theatres around the country, then getting your play produced is far from impossible. If you're organized, methodical, and persistent about it, getting produced is very doable. In fact, I can truly say that every playwright I know personally who has really worked at promoting his or her play has had success. You can, too.

This chapter goes through the steps involved in getting your play produced, exploring where and how to submit your play for production consideration.

Considering the Producer's Perspective

The first place to start your visit with the realities of the theatre world is with a look at the business side of theatre, specifically producing. No play, no matter how good, can be enjoyed by audiences without a producer to make it happen. But it's important to understand that the producer isn't just some anonymous source of cash. The producer is a theatre-savvy person with a love of plays and specific tastes, who enjoys being directly involved in theatre and has the monetary resources and contacts to finance a play, maybe yours. So always keep in mind that the producer is an integral and essential member of the theatre family.

Understanding roles of producers and artistic directors

Attracting the interest of a producer is a challenge common to all playwrights. Many eager playwrights with plays in their hands are vying for the attention of a relatively small number of producers. And by *producers* I mean an individual, a collection of investors, a theatre company, or an organization that can provide the necessary resources to make your play happen.

Producers

The principal task of a theatrical producer is to raise (or in rare cases, provide out of pocket) the money to finance a production of a play or musical. The money covers all the expenses involved from day one.

When choosing a play, what does a producer look for? A producer's decision to produce a particular play is based on a combination of the producer's personal taste in plays and the project's artistic merit and potential earnings. In other words, is the play good and will it sell tickets?

The big problem is that investing in a theatrical production is a money-losing proposition (see the later section "Tallying up the financial side"), but people still do invest in theatre, thank the theatre goddesses (Thalia and Melpomene)!

General rules always have exceptions, but here's how, for the most part, the producing process works:

1. **A producer comes across a script she likes and is willing to finance.** The play may have been submitted to her directly through a playwright's agent. Or a director or other theatre person may have recommended the play. Or the producer may have seen a reading of a certain play.

2. **The producer negotiates an option or some similar contractual agreement with the playwright (or whoever holds the rights to the play).** See the later section "Making friends with contracts" for more on this step.

3. **The producer works up a production budget, arriving at a figure that will finance the entire production from the rehearsal period well into the production run.** The budget usually includes a reserve, an amount of money held aside for unanticipated urgent situations, like slow ticket sales early in the run.

4. **The producer goes about rounding up a sufficient number of investors to achieve the level of financing needed to produce the show.** Shows are very expensive to produce, so the risk is shared with others. It's uncommon for a producer take on the entire financing of a project. (Sometimes none of the producer's own money is put into the production, but she takes a percentage of the show's profit as compensation for her work.)

5. **The producer hires a director.** The director, in turn, casts the actors, hires the stagecraft people (set, lighting, sound, and costume designers, among others), and determines the rehearsal schedule.

6. **The producer rents the theatre and hires the house staff and the backstage personnel (stage hands, electricians, carpenters, and so on).**

7. **The producer brings on the publicity and marketing team to tout and advertize the show.** This area is one of the producer's biggest expenses.

8. **The producer keeps track of and handles all the financial aspects of the show.** These aspects range from the production funding to expenditures to ticket sales income to weekly expenses to the playwright's royalties, and so on.

All in all, the producer's job is to provide the financial foundation through which your play will be rehearsed, staged, and performed. Be appreciative of what your producer is doing for you and the play, because chances are she's going to lose money. (Check out the sidebar "Should you produce your own play?" later in this chapter if you're contemplating taking the risk of producing your own play.)

Artistic directors

Like commercial producers, artistic directors (ADs) of not-for-profit theatres are the individuals who make the decisions concerning which plays will be supported for production. ADs, however, make their decisions in the context of the theatrical season they're planning.

To be selected for production by a not-for-profit theatre company, a play has to be judged worthwhile, but it also needs to fit in with the AD's vision of the upcoming season. The AD may be trying to provide a balance between plays with serious tones and themes with comedies. The AD may also need, for budgetary reasons, a small-cast play because his other candidates for the season have large casts. The AD may also be looking to provide a balance between brand-new plays and previously produced works. In other words, the artistic director's considerations can be more complicated that a judgment about merit and marketability.

For example, David Saint, the artistic director of a prestigious regional theatre, the George Street Playhouse in New Brunswick, New Jersey, considers between 50 and 100 plays annually for his season's offerings. (He doesn't accept unsolicited scripts.) As many as three or four of the selections for his five-play season can be new plays, but always at least one is new. The George Street Playhouse also hosts readings of new plays in progress.

Tallying up the financial side

Investing in theatrical productions is not for the faint of heart. Unfortunately, most plays and musicals lose money. It's no secret. If you decide to put some money into the production of a play or musical, the likelihood is strong that you'll never see that money again.

The Holy Grail for producers is *recoupment,* the point at which a play or musical has earned enough money to reimburse the backers all the money they invested. At recoupment a producer can exhale after holding her breath for months and months, maybe even years.

By the time a show opens, the producer's upfront investment is pretty much exhausted (except maybe for a reserve of cash for emergencies, like slow ticket sales early on). The show needs to begin supporting itself ASAP through ticket sales. Reaching recoupment and moving into the black is the producer's goal. Most shows don't reach recoupment, ergo they lose money.

Recoupment is challenging because the money taken in on ticket sales is not pure profit. Out of the box-office revenues the playwright gets her royalties; the actors get paid; the stage crew and staff get paid; the stage manager gets paid; in a musical, the conductor and orchestra get paid; the theatre rental is paid; the advertising and publicity is paid for, and so on. What little is left, if anything, after all expenses are paid, goes to the producer and investors.

With profit dribbling in small doses, investors wait a long while to get back what they put in. Even an artistically successful, critically acclaimed play can lose money if it doesn't run long enough.

Statistics vary, but theatre folks have estimated that out of every ten Broadway plays, eight lose money, one breaks even, and one makes money. More specifically, as many as 75 percent of musicals lose money and 80 percent of plays lose their capitalization. The percentage of shows that fail to break even is even higher for Off Broadway productions.

So why would anyone in her right mind want to put money into a theatrical production? Well, there are as many explanations as there are producers, but the reasons probably fall into these three categories.

- ✔ **What I did for love:** Some producers invest in theatre because they have a passion for the art form. They're well-to-do enough that they can afford to put some money into supporting the medium they love. If they make money, fine, but their principal interest is providing resources for projects they believe in.

- ✔ **Rubbing elbows:** Some producers invest in plays because they want to be part of the world of theatre. They get satisfaction out of seeing their names in Playbills, attending cast parties, and rubbing elbows with actors and directors. Investing is their ticket to the backstage of theatre.

- ✔ **Jackpot:** Some producers hope to hit the jackpot. Though they know the odds are against them, they hope to back the show that becomes the next megahit. Producers who invested in *Cats, A Chorus Line, Phantom of the Opera,* or *Wicked* made millions. Successes like that are few and far between, but as the lottery slogan goes, "You've got to be in it to win it."

Theatre is definitely *not* the place to invest junior's college money or the retirement nest egg. Theatre producing is for those who have a love of theatre and some "play money," pun intended, at their disposal.

The bottom line is this: The show that gets the money gets produced; the show that fails to attract a producer does not get done. The best and most meritorious projects aren't always the ones that get produced. How well tickets will sell is a crucial factor in most theatrical investing decisions. Producers are free to put their resources behind any project they like, worthwhile or not.

Being a playwright, I can't see how anyone would bypass a play of potentially enduring merit — like mine — in favor of a play with strong ticket-selling prospects. Whining aside, the grown-up in me has to admit that I understand why producers feel the need to lean in that direction. It costs an arm and a leg and a pound of flesh from the midsection to produce a play. Production costs can range from $75,000 to $100,000 for a small professional production to many millions for shows in large regional theatres. And unfortunately, these sums will only rise.

Maybe your first instinct is to react, "The cost of a production is the producer's headache. What's it to me?" There huge sums impact playwrights in significant ways, including the negative impact of increased ticket prices, which leads to potentially smaller audiences.

The high price of tickets — even for the nosebleed seats — puts the magic of live theatre out of the reach people of modest means, young people and students, those on fixed incomes, and many others with limited discretionary spending. And when it comes to young people and students, high ticket prices inhibit the development of future theatre audiences.

Because playwright royalties are based on ticket income, you may be tempted to turn a blind eye to the problem of rising ticket prices. Unfortunately, however, the more expensive the tickets are, the smaller the market for theatre tickets is. So in the long run, you may not do better at all.

Another effect of the high cost of producing theatrical works is that fewer plays and musicals get produced. The more one show eats up available investment money, the less there is to go around for other projects.

Taking the First Steps toward a Production

Perhaps the most challenging and frustrating aspect of playwriting is getting your work into the hands of people who can produce your play or help get it produced. You can't just drop your script into an envelope or e-mail it to a producer or producing theatre company unsolicited. It won't get read. And it won't be sent back. It'll just disappear into the black hole of unwanted scripts known as the circular file.

Producers and producing organizations are inundated with scripts. Hundreds and even thousands of scripts turn up in the mail or in their e-mail inboxes every year. Producers, even those with staffs, couldn't possibly read everything they get. As a consequence, most have adopted the policy of not reading unsolicited scripts.

Producers do read scripts that are submitted by agents. Agents know, or should know, the type of plays particular producers or producing theatres prefer, and that's what agents send them to read. (More on agents in the later section "Getting yourself represented by an agent.")

What follows is a discussion of strategies and tactics you can employ to get your play noticed, considered, and, ultimately, produced.

Copyrighting your play

Before you begin showing your play around, copyright it. Copyrighting your play gives you the peace of mind that comes from documenting ownership of your work.

Also, it's cool to receive in the mail an official document (the copyright certificate) that proclaims for all to see that you own and control the play entitled _____ (fill in the blank), written by you.

By law, anything you write, a play for example, is automatically legally and exclusively yours to control. So why copyright the play? Because the copyright provides you with the documentation that you or your heirs can use to prove ownership if a question about that arises. The copyright process is simple and relatively inexpensive, so don't pass it up. Turn to Chapter 4 for more on how to copyright your play.

Submitting to contests and competitions

Theatres, arts organizations, and agencies throughout the country provide recognition for plays — and sometimes prizes, readings, or productions — by sponsoring play contests and competitions or by offering grants and fellowships. Submitting your new play to contests and competitions is a simple way to get your feet wet and get some attention for your work. Winning a prize or award adds credibility to the work when you submit it for production consideration. Not to mention that prizes and awards help you build a résumé.

My very first success as a playwright came in 1989 when I submitted a long one-act play (about 45 minutes long), *Casino,* to the New York Foundation for the Arts biennial Artists' Fellowship competition, an opportunity designed for artists living in New York State. I was one of 13 awardees in the scriptwriting category that year. The fellowship came with a $6,000 award! But the more important part of the distinction to me was the fact that a panel of strangers decided that my work was worthwhile.

Contests and competitions vary widely. Some contests are for 10-minute plays; others are for one-act plays, full-length plays, or musicals. You can find competitions for children's plays; for plays by and about women, gays, people of color, and the disabled and for new writers and experienced writers, and so on. Competitions and contests are also organized by subject matter: for example, plays on the Civil War or plays about love. You and your work undoubtedly fall into some available category.

When submitting a play to a contest or competition, carefully read the guidelines and parameters. If your play doesn't fit the category *exactly,* don't waste postage, your time, and the time of the contest organizers by submitting. The competition evaluators are not going to make an exception for you because your play is good.

Some contests and competitions charge an entry fee, which is controversial among playwrights. The Dramatists Guild of America strong opposes the charging of fees to enter competitions (usually somewhere between $10 and $25, but some as high as $35 and $50). The Guild doesn't ban its members from submitting to contests and competitions sponsored by organizations that require a fee, but it does call for fee-charging contests and competitions to make full disclosure concerning the use of the fees (preferably put toward prize money) and any rights demanded of, or obligations placed on, the winning scripts. (For more information on its policy on entry fees, visit www.dramatistsguild.com.) So, when submitting your play to contests and competitions, it makes sense to submit first to those sponsoring organizations that don't charge a fee.

You can find out about contest and competition opportunities in a number of ways. Here are some sources of playwriting competitions and contests:

- ✔ **The Dramatists Guild Resource Directory:** The official annual reference for playwrights compiled by the Dramatists Guild of America and available free to its members (and purchasable at bookstores) is an authoritative reference for any serious or casual playwright. It contains lots of useful resources for playwrights: a calendar with submission opportunities, submission opportunities for special interests, 10-minute play opportunities, a sample writer's resume, and sample letters for inquiries and submissions, among other valuable resources. You can find out how to join the Guild at www.dramatistsguild.com.

- ✔ **The Dramatists Sourcebook:** This biennial reference contains more than 800 opportunities for playwrights, translators, composers, lyricists, and librettists, including script submission procedures for over 300 professional theatres, more than 100 contests, and information on scores of publishers, fellowships, residencies, agents, and reference publications.

- ✔ **Screenwriter's and Playwright's Market:** This publication is a wealth of info concerning script agents, script managers, production companies, screenwriting contests, play markets, play competitions, playwright resources, and more. The listings offer more than 250 markets for plays (including all the fringe festivals), over 100 playwriting contests, 50 plus regional playwriting groups, agents, TV markets, screenwriting conferences, and production companies.

- ✔ **Playwrights' Center's Writer's Opportunities:** For an annual membership fee of $50, the Center give you access to what the organization claims is the best collection of information for working dramatists in the United States. The database of over 200 entries contains information on contests, theatres, publication opportunities, and more. The listings can be searched by date, special interest, or state. You can become a member at `www.pwcenter.org`.

- ✔ **Playbill Online:** `www.playbill.com` is crammed with news and information on theatre in New York City, in regional theatres throughout the country, in London, in Canada, and elsewhere. Playwrights can find a limited number of submission opportunities by clicking "Job Listings" under "Casting & Jobs." Under "Browse by Category," click on "Editorial/Writing."

- ✔ **NYC Playwrights:** This organization bills itself as a group of writers, actors, and others who develop new work for the stage and other media. It provides a long list of a variety of submission opportunities at `www.nycplaywrights.org`.

- ✔ **The Loop:** This social network (`www.thelooponline.net`) is a community of playwrights, lyricists, librettists, composers, and other theatre artists. The Loop Online provides several types of resources for playwrights, including a long, searchable list of submission opportunities.

- ✔ **Doollee.com:** This free, online guide to modern playwrights and plays claims to provide information on 37,658 playwrights and 125,547 of their plays. You can enter information about yourself and your work at this site. You can also find lists of agents, play publishers, and the names and address of theatres.

- ✔ **Insight for Playwrights:** For an annual membership fee of $35, `www.insightforplaywrights.com` provides access to its database of play submission opportunities, along with other info and services.

There are too many more submission sites, some of them focusing on special interests, to attempt to list them all here. You can find more leads by doing an online search of a phrase like "listings of play submission opportunities."

Websites come and go, and, as with any web searching, be alert to opportunities that look too good to be true, particularly when money is involved. Some legitimate contest and competition opportunities do come with submission fees. But in general, avoid or carefully check any site that asks for money to read or evaluate your script.

Submitting to play festivals

Play festivals are special events, generally annual, during which a group of plays are performed for the public. Getting your play done in a festival is a good way to get exposure for the work, and, in some of the bigger festivals, you may even attract a potential agent or producer.

Festivals vary from those presenting full-length plays to a few specializing in one-minute plays (which are incomprehensible to me). The shows in a festival may be grouped by theme (for example, romance at the library) or by type of play (according to length or genre), but some festivals have no such guidelines for entries. Festivals range in length from one day to several weeks.

Festivals also differ widely in how they're designed. Some select their entries from submissions; others are open to whomever wants to participate. Some charge a fee to participate; others are free. Some produce the plays involved; others expect the show to come in fully rehearsed and ready to go.

Some theatre festivals are organized and publicized well; others are not. If you're interested in participating in a festival, do these two very important things:

- ✓ **Learn everything you can about how the festival operates and what's expected of you.** You don't want show up to enjoy a production of your play only to find out that you were responsible for staging it. Obviously that's an extreme example, but crazy things can happen if you're unprepared.

- ✓ **Speak with people who have participated in the past in that particular festival, not just any festival.** Ask questions about their experiences, good and bad. Especially try to get candid opinions on whether they feel the experience was worth the effort. Unfortunately, with some festivals, when all is said and done, there's really not much to gain.

Submitting your play to a theatre

Every theatre that accepts submission of plays for consideration has its own procedure to be followed — and followed to the letter. Play submission listings, like those mentioned in the earlier section "Submitting to contests and competitions," usually give the method to use to submit to each of its listings, or they refer you to the website of the theatre or organization for the specifics. Although the details vary, the submission procedures you encounter fall into the categories below:

- ✓ **Unsolicited scripts accepted:** Unfortunately, very few theatres accept unsolicited scripts (scripts submitted without invitation) anymore. There was a time when a greater number of theatres were willing to accept open submissions of plays for consideration. But today most artistic directors, dramaturgs, and other people making production decisions have concluded they cannot handle the resulting volume of plays they would get. If you find a theatre that takes unsolicited scripts — and its preferences match your play — go for it. Otherwise, you need to go through one of the more complicated routes that follow.

✔ **Queries:** Today, the most common approach required by theatres involves a query or cover letter with a synopsis of the play (the requested length varies), your résumé, and, often, ten pages of the script. Some theatres ask for a self-addressed, stamped envelope for use in replying to you and/or returning the script.

This process is more elaborate than just sending out your script unsolicited with a cover letter. And though it's understandable that theatres need to receive queries in ways they find manageable, personally I balk at the synopsis requirement. If I could tell the story I want to tell in a couple of paragraphs, I wouldn't have spent many months writing the darned play! However, after my snit passes, I compose the synopsis as instructed.

✔ **Agent submissions only:** This alternative is exactly what it sounds like. In order to submit to theatres with this policy, you need to provide the script through a recognized theatrical agent. Of course, if you don't have an agent, as is the case with most playwrights, particularly newcomers, you're out of luck. (See more about agents in "Getting yourself represented by an agent.")

Sending via e-mail versus snail mail

A growing trend on the part of organizations that receive play submissions is to request that the script be provided as an attachment to an e-mail as opposed to a hardcopy of the play delivered by mail. This practice saves trees and helps keep the offices of these theatre entities clear of stacks and stacks of scripts.

E-mailing a script also saves playwrights money. Making a copy of a script, putting it into a report cover of some sort, and sending it via priority mail can easily amount to over $10 per submission, even more if you include a stamped, self-addressed return envelope for the script.

(Many submission opportunities that accept hardcopy scripts give you the choice of providing a stamped envelope for return of the script or allowing them to discard and/or shred the script if they decide to pass on it. To save the cost of the return postage for a script that may be dog-eared and coffee-stained and consequently useless to me, I choose the latter option.)

Getting the bad news about submitting

There's some bad news about submitting your work for prize or production consideration, and it involves the processing of submissions.

Unfortunately, too many organizations that receive scripts for consideration relegate the first round of reviews to interns or other relatively inexperienced staffers. The expertise and wealth of experience you hope would be brought to bear in evaluating the precious fruit of your labors may not be involved in this first round of cuts. Furthermore, if your play is experimental or avant-garde, the merits of your efforts are much less likely to be recognized by the theatre student from the local college.

My Edinburgh experience

In 1993, I put two of my one-act plays together as a 90-minute show and took the program to the Edinburgh International Festival. The opportunity to see my plays performed in a small theatre six times a week and be appreciated by international audiences was exciting, as was the opportunity to spend three weeks in the historic city of Edinburgh, Scotland. However, the six months that preceded that experience were pure heck, to put it mildly.

The Edinburgh festival, which chooses participants from submissions, expects its shows to come in fully rehearsed and ready to rumble. And because the theatre spaces used in the festival operate almost around the clock, you need to install your minimal set just before the performance and *strike* (remove) it immediately afterward.

In the half year or so before the trip, I functioned as producer of the program. I worked out a budget of $31,000 to cover theatre rental, advertising, transportation, housing, and meals for seven performers, the director, and myself. The money was raised through a combination of sources. One was successful grant solicitations; the largest grant came from Sandoz (now Novartis) Pharmaceuticals for which, at the time, I was working as a freelance writer. Additional money came from fundraising performances of the plays that were staged in New York City and Rockland County (a NYC suburb). I threw in a few thousand of my own to hit the target amount.

But the problem was, for the six months preceding our departure, I was deeply involved in the overwhelming tasks of:

- Submitting application materials to the festival
- Writing grant applications
- Participating in casting the play
- Making travel preparations (flights and trains)
- Ensuring that everyone in the cast had a passport
- Renting housing in another country
- Working out meal money and a small stipends for each of the actors
- Buying insurance to cover everyone involved for the festival period
- Attending rehearsals of the play
- Organizing fundraising performances
- Composing the description of the plays for the festival program
- Writing publicity material

All this, and more, on top of my life as a teacher, freelance writer, and playwright. Thank goodness I could share the responsibilities with the director, Pat Weber Sones, who was my collaborator in the venture. Without her above-and-beyond-the-call-of-duty efforts, I would have ended the grueling adventure in a padded cell.

Be sure that your submission follows the organization's guidelines to the letter, because any oversight on your part can be fatal to your chances of even being looked at, never mind carefully read. The root of this problem lies in another discouraging reality in submitting scripts, the volume of scripts received by the evaluating organization. Obviously, you're facing a great deal of competition. What's worse, the sheer volume of scripts received leads to regrettable time-saving devices.

Should you produce your own play?

Should a playwright produce her own play? The answer, in my estimation, is similar to that of "should I direct my own play" question in Chapter 16: Do it only if producing is something you want to do. My experience shared in the sidebar "My Edinburgh jaunt" should give you a taste of what's involved in producing a play. Producing is a complicated and demanding business, whether you're doing a play abroad or close to home.

If you have the stamina, are knowledgeable about theatre, are interested in producing, and have access to funding sources, self-producing

is not out of the question. In fact, it's not all that rare for small productions. If you're thinking about giving it a shot, I suggest you talk with others who have self-produced on the same level you're contemplating. Producing, particularly because it usually involves other people's money, is not something you want to take on lightly, naïvely, or on a whim.

As far as I'm concerned, the months before my Edinburgh experience taught me that, unlike Leo Bloom in the Mel Brooks hit film and musical *The Producers,* "I *don't* wanna be a producer."

With piles and piles of scripts to go through, script "readers" look for any reason, superficial reasons included, *not* to consider scripts. They weed out scripts using any criteria your script violates. Is the script longer or shorter than the prescribed length? Is the script bound in a way other than the required method? Is the play not in the proper script format? Did you forget to include your résumé or the 10-page excerpt? Yes to any of those questions, and out it goes. It may not be fair, but that's the reality you're facing.

Championing Your Play (And Getting Others to Join You)

One of the most important bits of advice I share with new playwrights is to "join the club." By that, I mean start showing up where playwrights and other theatre people show up. Look for workshops, seminars, and classes on playwriting and theatre in your area and participate in them. Introduce yourself as a new playwright to the people involved. Make your interests and aspirations known to people already in the business.

Go to plays, and afterward introduce yourself to the actors, director, and, if she's in attendance, the playwright. Again, don't be shy about introducing yourself and talking shop.

Take an acting class and a directing class. In the process of studying acting for four years and directing for two years, I learned a great deal about how actors and directors approach plays. The classes also gave me the opportunity to become acquainted with actors John Leguizamo, Gary Perez, William Charles Mitchell, and Edward Norton and veteran theatre director Terry Schreiber, among a legion of up-and-coming and experienced theatre folks. These connections put me in a position to be recommended should any one of them come across an opportunity he believes is right for me. And it has happened.

To put yourself in a position to benefit from ideas and leads for opportunities that theatre people may be able to share with you, start showing up where theatre people show up. Become a familiar face. Let people know who you are and what you'd like to do. You never know who may one day open a door for you.

Approaching producers

Producers are people who have financial resources or who can gain access the resources to finance the production of a play or musical. As you may imagine, producers are besieged by playwrights and agents with plays they want produced. When it comes to the question of getting your play done or not, producers — be they individuals or theatre companies — are royalty. How do you approach these princes of production, monarchs of money, kings of cash? The answer: very carefully.

In the interests of full disclosure, I must warn you that if you're a beginning playwright, getting the attention of these busy and much sought-after people is nearly impossible. But not impossible.

You can employ strategies to respectfully and effectively approach potential backers of your play. None of these strategies involves sending producers your play unsolicited, phone calling or e-mailing them, or visiting their offices uninvited.

First, take the time to research the producers you want to contact. Go online and check out their projects. Make sure they produce plays similar to yours. If you go after a producer whose résumé includes only dramas and your play is a farce comedy, you're probably wasting your time. Though you never know what will catch the eye of any individual, the most efficient course of action is to pitch to a producer the kind of project she tends to involve herself in. Hopefully, the subject matter of your play will connect with the interests of the producer.

Following are some constructive ways to approach producers:

✔ **Query letters:** Write a brief letter describing your play and asking if she would be willing to read it. It can't hurt to demonstrate some knowledge of her productions by mentioning some of her previous successes, particularly if you've seen any of them. Include your résumé if you have some theatre experience. Do keep the letter short and sweet and focused. Keep in mind that the producer receives hundreds of such letters. You'll score no points with her by meandering and being longwinded.

✔ **Showcase productions:** A more complicated and relatively expensive strategy is to mount a *showcase production* of your play, a short run of the show in a small theatre in a convenient-to-the-industry location. Lots of small theatre companies, mostly in metropolitan areas, do new work on a small scale. Consult the theatre submission resources above and try contacting a few. Keep in mind that the process of getting selected even for a short run of your play is, of course, competitive.

In showcase productions, usually no one gets paid. Everyone — the director, actors, designers, and you — is involved in the production to showcase his or her talents. The key to making this effort pay off, from your point of view, is to send out invitations to producers to see the show as your guests. Because producers get a ton of such invitations, your invitation needs to be persuasive. After the showcase, you can speak with the producers in attendance to thank them for coming. If they're interested in your project, they will ask about it. Don't push; you may want them to visit with you again on another project.

✔ **Backers auditions:** A more specialized and targeted approach is to mount a *backers audition,* a rehearsed presentation of the play, or a good part of it, to stimulate interest of producers in the project. A backers audition is usually a one-shot affair done in a studio for an invited audience. Potential producers, naturally, are among the people you invite. Ask your invitees to RSVP. You don't want to put in this kind of effort if no producers are planning to be there.

Playwrights often invite some theatre-savvy friends to the backers audition to help build up the audience. Having an appreciatively applauding audience helps sell your play.

After the reading, mingle with your special guests. Engage the producers in no-pressure conversation about the play. Ask where they felt the piece was strong and where some work might be needed. If someone wants to pursue the possibility of production, she'll let you know. Again, don't push.

✔ **Readings:** Probably the easiest way to exhibit your play for potential backers is to arrange for a reading of the play. You can hold a reading at any of a number of venues, ranging from libraries to rented studios to theatres that select plays for their reading series. The reading should be rehearsed at least once, preferably twice, before it's done for the invited audience. Again, a non-aggressive chat with the producers after the event should signal if someone is interested in your play.

✔ **Recommendations by mutual friends:** If you have friends, particularly theatre acquaintances, who are enthusiastic about your play, these friends can serve as contacts and intermediaries on behalf of you and your play. Don't be shy about asking someone you know if she would be willing to speak to so and so about considering your play. It works. Advertisers have long known that third-party endorsements carry a lot more persuasion power than do self-promotion efforts. Networking in theatre is as important and effective as it is in any other enterprise.

Getting an agent to represent you

From playwrights who don't have an agent, you frequently hear complaints along the lines of, "If I had an agent pushing my play, it would be in production right now." From playwrights who do have an agent, you frequently hear, "My agent does nothing for me. Every production I've had I found myself." So are agents worth it or not?

Having an agent is better than not having one. An agent can open doors for your work that you can't open yourself. Most major theatres and producers won't read a script unless it comes from an agent. And agents are able to zero in on theatres that are more likely than others to be interested in your kind of play.

Agents know that if they submit plays that aren't appropriate to the theatre/producer or that aren't ready for production consideration, theatres and producers will cease accepting scripts from them. Therefore, good agents works with their playwrights to be sure their scripts are ready for submission, and theatres and producers benefit by receiving for consideration only plays that have been somewhat vetted.

On the other hand, an agent is not the key to your success. The quality of your play is always the most important thing. And having an agent doesn't mean you can sit back and wait for the contracts to start crowding your mailbox. To be shrewd, you must continue to market yourself and scout out possibilities for your plays, even when you have an agent. And if you hit on something, you turn the lead over to your agent.

Decades ago, theatrical agents represented the body of work of a playwright. When you wrote a play, your agent would work with you on getting it into the hands of producers. Today, agents cherry-pick projects. They don't, in essence, sign you up. Instead, they sign up your play if they feel it's marketable. If not, they pass on the play. This policy is both bad and good. If your agent chooses not to take on your newest project, it's a bit of a slap down. However, you really don't want an agent representing your play if she doesn't fully believe in it. Her heart and priority won't be devoted to the project, and that does no one any good. Instead, if your agent passes on your new play, you're free to find another agent who sees potential that your first agent didn't.

But here's the Catch-22: Getting an agent is hard unless you've had a production of your work. A production shows a potential agent that you're a working playwright and your work is far enough along to be produced. But getting a production, particularly a major production, is difficult if you don't have an agent. As mentioned before, nowadays most producers and producing theatres consider only agent-submitted work.

All this being said, how do you get an agent? By using the same tools you employed in approaching producers (see "Approaching producers" to review in more detail):

- ✔ **Query letters:** You can send a brief letter describing your play and your background, accompanied by your theatre résumé if you have one.

- ✔ **Showcase productions:** Stage a short run of your show and invite potential agents and other theatre professionals.

- ✔ **Backers auditions:** Set up a rehearsed presentation of the play (or excerpts) explicitly for agents (with friends to supplement the audience) to stimulate interest in the project.

- ✔ **Readings:** Do a reading of the play for an invited audience, including agents.

- ✔ **Recommendations by colleagues and mutual friends:** Theatre-savvy acquaintances and friends can serve as contacts. Don't be shy about asking. I got my agent through an introduction by a playwright friend.

Networking with directors and actors

When you get to know directors through theatre activities, keep these contacts fresh. See their work. Send them a congratulatory note or e-mail. Similarly, let them know what you're doing, particularly when you have developmental readings of your play. (But make your contacts sparingly. Overdoing it can lead to the impression that you're badgering them.) Directors can give you invaluable feedback on your play. The sharp eye of a savvy director can pick up a detail or identify a weak spot in your script, something you may not have noticed that may make a big difference to the success of the play.

If you're lucky, a director may be so intrigued by your play that she wants to set up a reading of the play with actors. As I discuss in the following section, a reading itself can be a step toward a production of your play.

If you're acquainted with any actors and can show them your script, they may also be able to help. It's not uncommon for an actor to get excited about a script because it has a part that she wants to do. When this happens, the actor may just run the script over to a director or producer she knows. (While you should be appreciative of an actor's excitement over your play, keep in mind you shouldn't make promises to actors you probably can't keep. You can tell an actor that you'll try your best to get her an audition if the show happens, but anything more than that is ultimately out of your control.)

In this business, you never know what contact may become an advocate for your play. A third-party endorsement is always stronger than good things you yourself say about your play, and the genuine enthusiasm of a director or actor may very well lead to a production of your play.

Increasing your visibility

Theatre is not for the bashful. You've got to make every effort feasible to promote your play and yourself as a playwright. Others can do missionary work for you, but when push comes to shove — and it often does in this competitive business — you need to be your own best advocate.

You can get visibility for yourself and your play in a number of practical ways, including the following suggestions. And they don't necessarily involve a lot of money.

- **Aggressively develop your play:** As you work and rework your play, take every opportunity to show it to savvy theatre people and have readings of your play in progress. Don't be secretive about your play when it's in good shape and copyrighted. The more exposure your play gets, the more likely it is to be seen by someone who may be interested in producing a play like yours. You never know where that crucial contact may be made.

- **Network:** Without being boorish about it, let every actor and director and theatre person you come across know that you have a new play, especially any actor or director you think might be right for the project. An actor who wants to do the play or a director who'd like to stage it can be a very powerful advocate for you. Very frequently, productions of plays come about due to the self-interest of an actor or director. (But remember, don't make promises only a producer can keep.)

- **Attend industry events:** Show up where people you want to be like show up. Get yourself out to theatre industry seminars, workshops, retreats, and conventions. Not only will these events be opportunities to learn, particularly about marketing, but you can meet and get to know your new playwriting and theatre colleagues. In my experience, people in the industry are usually very willing to share with colleagues information on theatres that may be right for a given play.

✔ **Join the Dramatists Guild:** You'll find no better resource for playwrights, new or experienced, than the Dramatists Guild (`www.dramatistsguild.com`). The membership fee is more than reasonable, and you get a ton of useful and important information and advice for your buck. The Guild offers a variety of outreach events to members across the country. Guild programs include the Dramatists Guild Fellows Program, DG Academy seminars, Director/Dramatist and Songwriter/Bookwriter Exchanges (networking meetings), Friday Night Footlights play readings, and town hall member meetings across the country.

✔ **Send your play out:** As discussed in the earlier section "Taking the First Steps toward a Production," submit — appropriately — your play to contests, competitions, festivals, theatres, and producers. Even when you don't get selected for production, you may get noticed. Often, rejected plays come back to the playwright with a notation saying, "Unfortunately, this play is not right for our needs, but please do send us your next play" or something of that nature. This kind of encouragement means you made an impression. When you're ready with your next play, send it to that person or organization with a note of your own, saying something like, "I really appreciated your encouraging note on my last submission, suggesting I send to you my next work. Please find attached my play. . . ."

✔ **Send out postcards or e-blasts:** Send out to appropriate theatres, producers, and agents an announcement that your new play is available for consideration. The message should contain a carefully crafted paragraph describing the play and, in case anyone wants to reach you to discuss the play, your contact information.

Safeguarding your reputation

To be attractive to a potential producer, you need to safeguard your reputation. Many, many people are involved in theatre, but it's really a small community. How you behave, well or badly, will get around and will not likely be forgotten. If you earn a reputation of stubbornly refusing to consider changes in your script, refusing to do rewrites, making a nuisance of yourself during rehearsals, blaming everyone else if things go badly, and so on, you will probably not get as many productions of your plays as someone who has a good reputation will. In other words, you want to be seen as a smart writer who knows a good suggestion when she hears one. You want to be known as a team player and a person who knows when and how to provide input during rehearsals. And most importantly, you want to cultivate the reputation for being extremely appreciative of the talents and skills of all the people who contributed to your production, whether the play hit the heights you wanted or not. Remember, word gets around.

Years ago, during a production of one of my plays in New York City, I was elated to be working with an actor I admired. Rehearsals were thrilling, and he and his costar were magic together. But come the first performance, the actor (I'll call him Max) stumbled through his lines and looked very unsure of himself. Max's shaky acting didn't ruin the play, but it wasn't what I knew it could be. Night after night, Max turned in the same unsteady and uninspiring performance, despite the director's efforts to get something more out of him. Sometime long after the show had ended its run, I found out that Max had been "fortifying" himself by drinking before every performance.

After that experience, I would never, ever work with Max again. Too much is at stake in a production, too many people's hopes, aspirations, and efforts are involved, to take a needless chance on someone who can't be relied upon. Max earned a negative reputation, and I could never in good conscience recommend him to anyone.

Furthermore, in this age of social media and Twitter, word gets around lightning fast. Like potential employers, many theatres also do Internet searches to get a handle on the kind of person you are. Take care of your rep and it'll take care of you.

Dealing with rejection

Rejection is the norm in theatre. The vast majority of submissions of your play to theatres will be declined. Just about every playwright, with the possible exception of the big names in theatre, has to face this fact. To preserve your sanity, you cannot get emotionally invested in every submission you make, and you cannot take rejection personally.

Look at play submissions as auditions. Committed, working actors and dancers audition constantly for roles in plays and musicals. Most of the time, they come away empty. (In 2006, the producers of the revival of *A Chorus Line* saw about 3,000 dancers audition for the show's 25 parts!) The situation is similar for the submission of plays to contests, competitions, festivals, theatres, and producers. All these entities get hundreds and even thousands of plays to consider. As a playwright, you can't go bonkers or give it all up if you don't encounter immediate success. The odds against any one play getting produced are not favorable.

Just about every playwright I know — myself included — has a file of rejection letters. They vary from the rare personal note to the ubiquitous "Dear Playwright" form letter. When I get a rejection letter, I put it away, and fantasize that one day I will send a note to every one of those short-sighted and unimaginative artistic directors, trumpeting my success and thumbing my nose at them. Of course I will never do that. Neither should you. But save those rejection letters. One day you'll find them amusing.

Making friends with contracts

Contracts are an important part of a playwright's life. When you're offered a contract by a theatre or producer for a production of your play, you'll be on cloud nine. It's finally happened! You're getting your play produced!

Contracts specify what you can expect from the producer and what the producer expects of you. The first time you see a production contract, very likely you will find it bewildering. What you should not do is sign a contract without some representation or knowledgeable advice. A producer or theatre company is not out to cheat you, but that doesn't mean that the contract you're offered isn't stacked in the other party's favor. The following resources can help you check out the contract:

✔ **An attorney:** Some lawyers specialize in theatrical contracts and will review your contract and advise you (for a fee, of course). If you use an attorney, shop around. Find out what experience the attorney or law firm has with theatre. Ask what the fees are. In other words, don't be intimidated. Be as smart a shopper as you would be with a flat-screen TV. Don't ask Cousin Louie, the defense attorney, to review your contract. You want someone who knows what's customary in theatre to look at the paperwork.

✔ **The Dramatists Guild:** One of the services offered — and a very valuable one at that — by the Dramatist Guild to its members is a review of a contract you're negotiating. The Guild's law department won't represent you, but it will advise you about what is standard and acceptable in a contract and what isn't. You can join the Guild and take advantage of this service at www.dramatistsguild.com.

The Dramatists Guild also provides its members with DG-approved contracts for your use with all levels of theatrical production. You can use the sample contracts as your template in negotiating with a producer, and then you can go back and run it past the DG lawyers.

✔ **An agent:** Your agent, if you're fortunate enough to have one, will negotiate the contract for you and get you the best terms possible. An agent will charge 10 percent of your royalties on this play . . . *forever.* For the privilege of having an agent represent your play, the standard agency contract requires that the right to represent this play — and collect 10 percent of your royalties on it — belongs to that agency, for a long as the agency exists. And the agency is entitled to its 10 percent even if it's not involved in the contract negotiations. In other words, you can't do an end run around the agency. (The earlier section "Getting yourself represented by an agent" provides more info on working with agents.)

On the positive side, the agency will negotiate for you the highest possible royalty percentage (the agency's income depends on that, too).

Keeping Pace with the Theatre World

Theatre is always evolving. What some producers want to produce and what some audiences want to see changes, slowly but surely. As a playwright, you should never decide to write a play to fit a trend. Before all else, you should have a story you're passionate about telling.

However, being up-to-date on the changing face of theatre can be helpful. You need to be particularly aware of contemporary expectations concerning cast size, set restrictions, and length expectations. You don't want to impede your chances by not knowing what's going on. If you find yourself working against the trends, it should be by choice and not because you didn't know the transformations that have been taking place.

Following trends

In this section, I discuss some of the more dominant trends readily observable in theatre.

- ✔ **Smaller cast sizes:** In an attempt to keep production expenses down, producers and some producing theatres more and more are opting for plays requiring four or fewer actors. Sadly, this trend inhibits playwrights from writing the kinds of wonderful medium and large-cast shows that are characteristic of great playwrights from Shakespeare to Chekhov to Tennessee Williams to Neil Simon. Reducing the canvas with which contemporary playwrights can work reduces the theatrical experience. Small casts often result in small plays.

  Musicals are somewhat of an exception. Theatre people understand that musicals, which include actors, singers, dancers, and musicians, need larger casts than do plays. Even so, the pressure is on for creative teams (composers, lyricists, and librettists) to keep the casts of new musicals as compact as possible.

- ✔ **One set:** Another money-saving trend is the preference of producers for a play that uses only one set, sometimes referred to as the *unit set.* Not having to change sets between scenes and/or acts saves the expense of having to build and dress additional sets. However, this trend limits the scope of the story a playwright can tell. "Show, don't tell" is a maxim in theatre, but when playwrights are restricted to one set, what they can show is restricted.

- ✔ **90-minute wonders:** The length of plays is shrinking. Instead of producing the lengthy plays of past centuries, a growing number of producers feel that a play of 90 minutes is adequate and maybe even preferable. Perhaps this trend is caused by a desire to accommodate what they may believe is the shorter attention spans of audiences more used to television and Internet entertainment. With a 90-minute play, the audience is entertained in a short period of time, and everyone's home in front of the TV for the 10 o'clock news. Less is more? In this case I'm not so sure. While writing shorter plays drives playwrights to make every scene really count — a good thing — it also may limit the scope and complexity of the stories playwrights want to tell.

✓ **One-person shows:** Another movement in theatre is toward the one-person show, a play in which one actor performs what's essentially a monologue for the audience. The actor may play different characters in the play. Inarguably, a one-person show is more economical — you have to pay only one performer. And some one-person shows work like gangbusters (or maybe it should be *gangbuster*), like Carrie Fisher's *Wishful Drinking* and John Leguizamo's *Mambo Mouth*. But the impression of conflict, the essence of playwriting, is challenging to maintain with one actor, as are romance and a sense of urgency and danger, so one-person shows can feel undramatic if not extremely well done.

✓ **Multimedia:** Modern plays are not shying away from using nontraditional (for theatre) media in their storytelling, employing tools like music, projected slides, film, and video. Recent Broadway shows that can be considered "multimedia" include:

  • *Sondheim on Sondheim,* which was a combination of live performance of the songs written by Stephen Sondheim and projected images and video of the master composer/lyricist himself.

  • *Wishful Drinking,* a one-person show written and performed by Carrie Fisher (of *Star Wars* fame), chronicling her career and various family and relationship entanglements through live performance and projected images and video.

  • *Brief Encounter,* by Emma Rice, an inventive stage adaptation of Noël Coward's romantic story of forbidden love, recreated though live stage performance and projected images and film.

✓ **Catering to youth:** A spate of shows, mostly musicals, have been aimed at people in their late teens to early 20s. These shows include *The Lion King, In the Heights, Avenue Q, Hairspray, Spring Awakening,* and *The 25th Annual Putnam County Spelling Bee.* Theatre must attract young people to build the audiences of the future. But playwrights need to take care not to pander to the TV- and Internet-bred youth by writing down to them in the shallow sitcom style and dialogue they may be accustomed to. Theatre should challenge, educate, elevate, and motivate, not compromise the things theatre does best — intimate and provocative storytelling with live actors before a live audience

✓ **Jukebox musicals:** Producers have not yet lost their appetite for jukebox musicals, shows that take music of a popular band or singing group and attempt to wrap a show around them. Because the traditional Broadway musical, in theory at least, begins with the story and not with the music, jukebox musicals tend to feel light on story and heavy on music. Some of the more successful jukebox shows include *Jersey Boys* (Frankie Valli and the Four Seasons), *Mamma Mia!* (ABBA), *Movin' Out*

(Billy Joel), and *Million Dollar Quartet* (Elvis Presley, Jerry Lee Lewis, Carl Perkins, and Johnny Cash). Although this type of show goes back as far as the '70s, the first decade of the 2000s witnessed more than three times the number of jukebox musicals as were produced in the three preceding decades combined.

Making sense of Broadway, Off Broadway, and Off-Off Broadway

In New York City, the scale of a theatrical production is usually described by the terms *Broadway* show, *Off Broadway* show, and *Off-Off Broadway* show. Those labels relate to the theatres in which the shows are presented. Counterintuitively, however, these labels have less to do with the location of the theatres as with their size.

- A Broadway house is a theatre with 500 or more seats. Most major musicals and some large-cast straight plays are booked into these huge barns. Most of these theatres are located in or near the Times Square area of New York City.

- An Off Broadway theatre accommodates 100–499 ticketholders. This medium-size theatre is ideal for intimate straight plays, where proximity to the audience is advantageous. These theatres can be pretty much anywhere in Manhattan.

- Off-Off Broadway theatres cater to as many as 99 patrons. These small theatres are ideal for experimental and off-beat shows that draw small audiences, and they provides relatively inexpensive venues for trying out new shows that have ambitions to move up. Theses spaces can be storefronts, or upstairs lofts, or black boxes. (A *black box* is what it sounds like, a rectangular space, usually painted black, that has no fixed seating or stage area. The seating and playing areas can be arranged to suit the vision of the director.) Economy, intimacy, and flexibility are the advantages of this kind of theatre.

Historically, the Off Broadway theatre category materialized after World War II as a reaction to the expense, commerciality, and high-priced tickets of Broadway shows. Off Broadway provided a more intimate and less costly venue for new, less commercial, and innovative theatre. The Off Broadway movement peaked in the 1980s.

Eventually, Off Broadway productions became more mainstream and commercial, resulting in the rise of production costs and ticket prices. As Off Broadway became more conventional, history repeated itself. The small Off-Off Broadway theatre became the refuge for novel and inexpensive theatre productions. Scores, maybe even hundreds, of Off Broadway productions are going on at any given time. For people with a taste for new works and for pieces that push the envelope, Off-Off Broadway is the place to go.

Exploring regional theatre

The destination at the end of the playwright's yellow brick road is not the Emerald City but "The City That Never Sleeps," so many people in the theatre community speak of theatre and plays in terms of the New York City scene. But theatre is very much alive and well outside of the Big Apple. And outside of NYC is where many playwrights first get their work produced. Chicago, Minneapolis, Los Angeles, San Francisco, Philadelphia, Boston, and Toronto all have thriving theatre communities, and countless other cities have flourishing theatre scenes.

The big category of theatre away from Broadway and its kin is what's called *regional* or *resident theatre*. These terms usually refer to professional, non-profit theatre companies that offer multishow seasons.

Theatre companies throughout the United States produce a variety of works, including new plays, classic dramas, popular comedies, and musicals, and they sometimes host the touring companies of Broadway shows.

Much of the success of these independent theatre companies depends on attracting and maintaining a strong base of season subscribers. Regional theatres that have loyal subscribers (meaning many, if not most, of the season's tickets are sold in advance) have more freedom than others venues to stage new work from unknown playwrights and to experiment with noncommercial works (plays that aren't likely to be Broadway moneymakers).

As a playwright, you may want to research the regional theatre(s) near you, if there are any, to find out if the organization's mission includes a play development program, readings, and/or second-stage productions of new works that you may be able to participate in. Many regionals have, in addition to their main stage, a smaller auditorium or studio space called the *second stage* for new or small or experimental works.

Most of the largest regional theatres are members of LORT, the League of Resident Theatres, and a visit to the organization's website (www.lort.org) explains its mission and provides web links to its 80 or so resident theatre members, located in about 30 states.

London's West End

The West End theatre quarter is London's equivalent of New York's Broadway district. As London's main theatre district, the West End (of central London) contains approximately 40 venues. Along with Broadway theatres, theatres in the West End, now also referred to as *Theatreland,* present most of the best commercial shows in the world.

Some people think West End Theatre is limited to commercial productions. But a good deal of noncommercial (government subsidized) theatres also operate in London, including the National Theatre, the Royal Shakespeare Company, the Globe Theatre, the Old Vic, the Young Vic, the Royal Court Theatre, the Almeida Theatre, and the Open Air Theatre. These prestigious and, in some cases, historic theatres stage Shakespearean works, other classic plays, and the premieres of new plays by leading playwrights. Hit plays from these noncommercial theatres sometimes transfer to Theatreland for commercial runs, and even to New York.

Any trip to London by a playwright serious about her craft should include a visit with several West End productions. By watching the best, you can only get better.

Part V
The Part of Tens

The 5th Wave   By Rich Tennant

"If you must know, the reason you're
not in any of my plays is that you're
not a believable character."

In this part . . .

They say wisdom is born of pain. Well, I say you can save yourself a lot of bumps and bruises by learning from the playwrights who came before you. This final part saves you having to reinvent the wheel. You pick up time-tested pointers and helpful hints, including playwriting realities every playwright should be aware of, the features and characteristics that make a play great, and some playwrights whose work you should be familiar with.

Chapter 18

Ten Things Every Playwright Should Know

*P*laywrights have a lot on their plates: concocting a story line, considering a theme, creating characters, selecting a setting, establishing high stakes, building to a climax, devising a satisfying climax and resolution, developing the play in readings, working on rewrites, marketing the play and finding a producer, participating in rehearsals, working on more rewrites, and attending the play's opening (whew!). So a playwright, after all this, can be forgiven if he loses sight of some the constructive notions, the common-sense advice, and the principles and techniques involved in plays and playwriting.

What follows are ten things every playwright should know — wisdom born of pain, if you will. Keeping these tidbits in the front of your mind will help you stay on track, preserve your mental health, and get you through the sometimes harrowing production process.

Why People Do the Things They Do

As a playwright, you need a decent working understanding of human behavior. You ought to have a good feel for why people do the things they do. You don't need to be a PhD in psychology to write good plays, but taking a psychology course at your local community college or investing in a copy of *Psychology For Dummies* by Adam Cash (Wiley) couldn't hurt. For those of you who may feel a bit intimidated by the idea of delving into psychology, I'm here to tell you that finding out what makes people tick is very interesting and even fun.

For example, one notion in psychology is that people behave out of self interest. In other words, they do the things that are good for themselves. You may think that this idea is cynical and labels all people as selfish, but take a closer look before you balk. If, for instance, you were to decide to make dinner for yourself and your significant other, and you chose to make your favorite dish, say meatloaf, clearly you'd be acting out of self interest. You like meatloaf. On the other hand, if you were to decide to bake a quiche because your significant other loves it (even though you're not crazy about it), that's lovely, but it's still acting out of self interest: Making your significant other happy is rewarding to yourself.

A playwright creates characters and writes about their behavior, emotions, motivations, and objectives. A general knowledge of psychological processes can help you identify a broader range of behaviors available to your characters, and help you feel more secure and grounded in the choices you and your characters make in the circumstances set forth in your plays.

Plays Should Show, Not Tell

Behavior is the currency of plays. What audiences *see* characters do to each other — their motivated behavior — is the stuff of drama. Characters *telling* audiences their feelings is nowhere as effective as audiences being shown those feelings through the characters' actions.

Few things are more stultifying in a play than long stretches of dialogue that amount to characters telling each other facts or relating the past. A certain amount of this type of dialogue is necessary as exposition, but it should be *motivated* exposition — the character should have a strong need to bring up the subject(s). (This is called *exposition as ammunition;* see Chapter 10 for more on the topic.) But beyond what's needed as exposition to reveal the backstory of the play, long meandering conversations, long telephone calls, the reading of a letter by a character, and so on are all inherently undramatic. Theatre audiences expect to see events unfold and they expect to see the characters battling — overtly or subtly — over something important in the here and now. In short, theatregoers should be shown the story, not told.

Writing Is Rewriting

The real work of writing, especially playwriting, is rewriting. A playwright has many opportunities to rework and rewrite his play during the process of development. First, you write and rewrite the early draft of the play before anyone gets to see the script. Then you rewrite after the play has had the benefit of a reading and the educated feedback of theatre-savvy people. After that, you may have additional readings of the play, resulting in more rewriting. An astute playwright takes advantage of these opportunities.

When the play is in rehearsal for its first production, you can learn a lot about the script by watching the director and actors work to bring the play to life. If the cast struggles at some point in the play with a script problem, the play needs rewriting. If you're not able to be near the production to see those problem spots, sometimes phone conferences with the director can result in some rewriting of the play. And the rewriting doesn't necessarily end with rehearsals. When a play goes into previews for paying audiences, the playwright can improve the script based on the audience reactions he observes. Nothing can simulate the experience of watching an audience respond, or not, to what you've put in the script. And if there are weak spots, the preview period provides one last time to address them.

A play is a vehicle that's designed to take an audience on a nonstop, two-hour journey, and the play needs to function to make the journey successfully. As a dedicated playwright, you must be attentive. You need to watch for any squeaking, rattling, or hesitation, anything that can interfere with the efficiency of the ride. As challenging as it may be, a willingness to rewrite and rework the play until all the kinks are out is a characteristic of a committed playwright.

Plays Aren't for Preaching

The primary purpose of a play is to entertain by engaging the attention of the audience. Entertained audiences lose themselves in the story. The magic of theatrical storytelling is absorbing entertainment, but that's not to suggest that the play shouldn't have an agenda. Playwriting is a medium of expression, and, in addition to spinning a good yarn, a play is able to say something about the human condition. But in order to get your message heard, you need to entertain.

Plays are not a soapbox. People don't go to theatre to be taught, preached at, or lectured to, even if audiences happen to agree with your message. If, in the process of entertaining audiences, your play communicates a point of view about something, great. But your message won't be received if audiences aren't engaged. Entertainment is the key that opens the door to the mind. Audiences will sit for just about anything you have to say, any point you're trying to make, so long as they're entertained.

On the other hand, audiences tune out any message, controversial or not, if they're not entertained. If people aren't engaged, they check their watches, think about a spot for a post-show drink, plan to call the babysitter, and so on. When this happens, you've lost the opportunity to speak to them, because you can't reach an audience that's not paying attention.

Characters Shouldn't Be Interchangeable

Every character in your play should be an individual, with a distinct and specific point of view and objective. Characters should not be in a play simply to populate the set, and they shouldn't be interchangeable. In life, people aren't interchangeable, and, in your play, they shouldn't be interchangeable either.

Many new playwrights are tempted to create nonspecific characters, as in "This character can be a man or a woman; it doesn't really matter." But it does matter. How a man reacts to given situations can be very different from how a woman responds. Men tend to have different interests than women. Men tend to react to threats in ways that women don't. This difference may be cultural or generic — nature or nurture — but it's undeniable.

How a young person deals with a problem can be very different from how a senior citizen processes the issue. A young person may be facing a situation for the first time, with little experience handling that kind of problem, whereas an older person may have handled such situations in the past and would be better able to deal with it. Their responses likely will be very different and specific to who they are.

In short, it *does* matter who your characters are. Every character should have needs and manifest behaviors that are unique and specific to who he is. And if the character doesn't serve a significant and relevant purpose, the character should get the axe.

Problems Won't Be Solved in Production

It up to you, the playwright, to address and remedy any problems you identify in your script. Don't expect others to do your job for you, not even the talented people you work with in production.

I occasionally hear a playwright assert, "Oh, the actors will figure out how to handle that in rehearsal," or, "The director will come up with a way of making the scene work." These sentiments aren't constructive. Yes, a shrewd director can sometimes come up with an idea or adjustment to make a problem scene work. And yes, talented actors often can play a scene better than it's written. But you don't want to count on actors and directors having the expertise to patch the holes in your boat.

Directors have their jobs; actors have theirs; and you have yours: to write a tight and functioning play. Your responsibility is to come up with as finished as script as you can. Leave no stones for others to turn. If you do find yourself stumped, the time to consult with others — directors, actors, or anyone — for suggestions is long before rehearsals begin. Rehearsal schedules tend to be tight, and you have no guarantee of time to deal with script problems. So roll up your sleeves, get under the hood, and fix any problems you know of before you get into production.

Money Talks

Producers wield the power of the purse. One of the sad realities of theatre — of most arts, for that matter — is that money plays a key role in which projects come to fruition. Someone has to come up with the financing to get the production process rolling. That person is the producer, and he who pays the bills gets to call the shots.

The quality of the script isn't necessarily what ultimately decides whether you snag a producer. The potential marketability of your play can be a big factor in whether you get financing for a production. Does the producer believe he can successfully market the show and sell tickets? Many thousands of dollars, perhaps millions, can be involved, so you can't blame a producer for leaning toward projects that have better chances of succeeding financially.

I don't include this fact to suggest that you shy away from what moves you and instead write plays that may be more marketable. You need to write what you need to write. Anything less than your most truthful work ultimately will be unsatisfying. You just need to know that some plays are more marketable than others, and you might have to look and work harder to find that producer who will enthusiastically open his wallet for your play.

You Have Strengths and Weaknesses

Knowing yourself isn't easy. Understanding the urges and issues that move you can take objectivity and a lot of thought (and maybe years of psychotherapy). Many people aren't motivated (or courageous enough) to devote a lot of time to self-scrutiny. But knowing yourself — your strengths and weaknesses as a person and as a writer — can be advantageous. It can help you focus on the issues about which you feel most strongly. And if you're going to spend months and years on a play, it better be a play involving something that dovetails with who you are and what you can do best.

Years ago, a reporter asked me what I thought was the common theme in my work. I told her I didn't think there *was* any common thread to my work. To me, my plays were as individual as children; yes, they sprang from the same source, but they have distinct personalities and different things to say. The reporter surprised me (and flattered me with her knowledge of my work) by isolating a motif common to my plays. She suggested that my plays deal with injustice, characters struggling to overcome unfairness and prejudice. After a moment's thought, I realized she was right. I have a low tolerance for injustice, personally and in society, and that characteristic was coming through in my work without my realizing it. Her astute observation elevated my self-awareness.

Self-awareness can enable you to apply your best creativity and skills to your work. For example, in addition to having a clearer perspective of my work, I've come to accept the fact that I can't write an out-and-out comedy. On those occasions when I've tried, I haven't produced anything worthwhile. Since I'm better at writing dramas that include humor, that's what I focus on.

What you, as a playwright, have to give to the world through your work is who you are and what you believe. Anyone, to one degree or another, can figure out plotting and character development. What will set you apart and make your plays memorable is how much of yourself you're willing to share — I don't mean your biography; I mean your thoughts, emotions, beliefs, and passions. How naked and vulnerable are you willing to make yourself? How unafraid are you to deal with delicate or controversial issue without trying to shield yourself? When you dare to write truthfully, to write from who you are and how you observe the world, audiences will respond.

Patience Is a Virtue

Making your way around the vagaries of the theatre business takes a good deal of patience. Things tend to happen slowly in theatre. To keep costs down, staffs are lean and, consequently, overworked. Schedules of activities are worked out many months, even a year or more in advance. And you can rely on unanticipated snafus to cause delays.

Many moons ago, a wine company marketed its products under the slogan, "We will sell no wine before its time." Plays, like wine, need time to develop and mature to reach their full potential. Many months, and sometimes years, are required to draft and rework a play, guiding it through all its developmental paces. Like rushing a wine, rushing a play results in a rough and less satisfying product. If you trot your play out before you have made it as good as you can, the bad taste it may leave could close doors to you in the future.

Patience is also required when marketing of your play. You send out queries, or the play itself, to various contests, competitions, festivals, theatres, producers, and so on (as detailed in Chapter 17), and then you wait. And wait. Organizations typically respond in three to nine months, if they reply at all. Some explicitly announce that their response time is a year. These waiting times are long, but have patience and don't sit at the window just waiting for the letter carrier to bring a response. While your work is being evaluated, move on to your next play. Make productive use of the time.

When you finally attract interest in your play, the lead times between a decision to produce the play and the actual production can be many months if you're working with a commercial producer, and a year or more if you're being slotted into a theatre company's season. When your play finally moves into production, again patience is going to be required, because the director and the actors require time and effort to get the play looking something like the show you had in mind. You won't see your play in the first days or first week or two. Rehearsals are a process — a creative, trial-and-error process — that takes time. So sit back and let the artists do their thing, or go home and work on your next play.

Natural to you or learned, patience is a handy attribute.

When to Take a Vacation

As challenging and sometimes maddening as playwriting can be, I can't recall a time when I wanted to get away from it entirely. I enjoy playwriting, and my life would have a big hole if I were to stop. However, a vacation every now and then is a good thing. When you have just finished writing a play and are about to embark on another, a short period of downtime between plays can help you recharge your batteries, so to speak. Yes, you run the risk of breaking some momentum you may have going for you, but a respite to clear your head can be as valuable as continuous enthusiasm and drive.

A writer's resource is his life. And if you're going to have meaningful experiences to draw from, you must live life. Be social and get out of the house for events and recreation and, more importantly, leave your comfort zone now and then to experience new and different people, places, and things. Travel.

Vacations, therefore, serve the purpose of temporarily lifting the pressure to produce while giving the little gray cells a rest. In addition, vacations can be opportunities to expand your horizons, to restock your mental shelves with new ideas, and get ready for the next project awaiting you.

Chapter 19

Ten Hallmarks of a Great Play

In This Chapter

▶ Giving audiences intriguing characters and stories

▶ Providing audiences with an escape from their day-to-day lives

▶ Writing plays with simplicity and honesty

*T*he presentation of a play can vary from the minimal — a bare stage and a spotlight — to the complex, like the cross-section of an almost fully furnished home. The work of actors can range from unremarkable to Tony-winning-caliber performances. The directing of the show can be hands-off and subtle or stylized and highly conceptual. But when you get right down to it, a great evening of theatre is less dependent on staging, acting, and direction than it is on the power of the story — the play itself. Unforgettable plays and the ones audiences want to see again and again have specific characteristics that make them great.

This chapter highlights some of the qualities and attributes typical of highly successful and enduring plays. No play, even the outstanding ones, necessarily exhibits all the following traits, but you'd be hard pressed to find a great play that doesn't conform to at least a few of these elements.

Characters the Audience Can Care About

One of the thrills and attractions of strong storytelling is the opportunity for the audience to go on a psychological and emotional journey with the protagonist. In most plays, the audience is meant to be pulling for the main character to succeed in her mission, investing hopes and aspirations in that character's success. In a powerful play, the audience members unconsciously choose sides and become cheerleaders for the protagonist.

This process of *identifying* with the protagonist — putting yourself in the character's place — makes the experience of the play more personal. If you set up well the protagonist and her goals, and if what's at stake is important to the protagonist, the psychic connection between her and the audience is made automatically and unconsciously.

Here's the recipe: An individual presented sympathetically plus meaningful goals that an audience can endorse equal a character the audience can care about.

A Story Line that Keeps 'Em Guessing

Few faults weaken a story line more than predictability. Strong stories usually have a degree of mystery or suspense. The inciting incident of the play sets the protagonist on a challenging journey, and, with much at stake for her, the audience watches and wonders whether the protagonist will achieve her goals. That ongoing question of the play is what helps keep the audience paying attention and guessing.

As I explain in Chapter 6, an audience eagerly anticipating the destination of the journey is focused on the "what." What is the protagonist's problem, and what will be the outcome? But suppose the audience knows the end of the story. Where's the suspense or mystery? How do you keep audiences guessing if they know the story's end? In most such cases, you focus on *how* the protagonist manages to get to that (known) ending.

For example, a smart and fun show with an outcome already known by every American is *1776*. The 1969 Tony Award–winning musical deals with a divided Congress and the events leading to the signing of the Declaration of Independence. We all know that the Congressional representatives of the 13 colonies did vote for independence and did sign the famous document; so what's issue of the play? It's the *how*. How did John Adams manage to convince a split and acrimonious group of proud and successful men — many of them loyal to England — to agree to vote for independence? The engaging and clever libretto (script) by Peter Stone and the music and lyrics of Sherman Edwards put a fresh and enjoyable spin on those events.

Great plays keep a step ahead of the audience, providing unanticipated events in the plot, story twists and turns, reversals and setbacks, and formidable challenges to meet. Whether you let the audience speculate as to the protagonist's future success or failure or whether you have the audience focus on how the main characters achieve the outcome, as much as possible, you want to keep audiences guessing.

A Timely and Relevant Subject

Great plays are remembered for many reasons, but among the important qualities of an outstanding play are the timeliness and relevance of the subject matter. The plays that get produced decade after decade are the ones that speak to audiences in a meaningful way. They say something vital about human nature, our place in the world then and now, and how we live and love and get along with each other, among other important themes that are as valid and evocative today as they were when the plays were written.

When playwrights get down to the business of writing plays and when producers and artistic directors pick the plays they wish to produce, two of the major considerations in the process of selection are timeliness and relevance.

- ✔ **Timeliness:** Is this the right moment in time for this particular subject matter? Can audiences benefit from exposure to this kind of material now? Or is the topic passé and moot? Has the world moved beyond the issues raised by the play?

- ✔ **Relevance:** Is the topic of the play related to events, movements, and trends taking place now? Will audiences make the connection between the play's message and the world at large today? Does the play present parallels to the events shaping society, comparisons that say or teach us something useful? Does the play matter to contemporary audiences?

In the late 1980s, I saw Henrik Ibsen's audacious play *Ghosts* produced by the Roundabout Theatre Company. Ibsen had written the play more than a century earlier, in 1881, and it deals with the bitter legacies left to a family after the death of the profligate head of the household. In the play, Helen Alving discovers that her son is dying of a sexually transmitted disease that he inherited from her late, philandering husband. In the heartrending climactic moment, her son, who is terrified about the inevitable decline of his body and mind, asks her to kill him rather than allowing him to deteriorate into incapacity and madness.

Why stage a century-old play that ends with the impending tragic and slow death of a young man to whom was unknowingly transmitted a fatal disease (syphilis), a disease that today is curable? Because its situation was relevant in the 1980s. Many Americans, mostly men, were dying of a mysterious and incurable sexually communicated disease unknowingly transmitted to them (AIDS). And families and friends could do little more than to stand by and watch them die. The ending of *Ghosts,* a play that was condemned and, in some places, banned in the 1880s, still spoke eloquently 100 years later, and because of its timeliness and relevance it was a heartrending to play to experience.

A Time and Place that Transport Audiences

One of the charms of going to the theatre is that for the duration of the play you're taken out of your daily life and transported to another time or place. You're shown a person, location, or era that is unfamiliar to you, or you may see a familiar person, place, or time period presented in an unfamiliar way.

In this sense, plays can be considered *escapist literature*. Escapist literature is usually defined as imaginative entertainment that distracts or diverts people from the stress and trying circumstances of their lives. The term has a belittling connotation, implying that literature that provokes serious thought or deals with social issues is superior.

I would argue, in area of theatre at least, that plays can do both. They can offer the respite from the mundane and the pleasure that escapist literature is intended to provide. But plays also can, in the process of transporting audiences, expose audiences to ideas and issues of consequence. The great plays do this.

For example, *Inherit the Wind,* the 1955 play by Jerome Lawrence and Robert Edwin Lee, takes the audience to the fictional, quiet Southern town of Hillsborough of the 1920s, where a young schoolteacher is arrested for teaching Darwin's theory of evolution, illegal under state law. Not only is the audience taken back to an earlier, simpler time in the American past, but it's also confronted with the issue of the right of individuals to think for themselves. Even today, the question of unfettered academic and scientific inquiry versus religious perspectives is still not fully resolved.

Musicals, almost by definition, take audiences to different times and places. Although there are always exceptions to any rule, consider the example of *South Pacific,* the beloved 1949 Rodgers and Hammerstein musical, which conveys the audience to a U.S. military base on a tropical island in the South Pacific during World War II. What might have been a lighthearted romantic excursion to that exotic locale is deepened and enriched by important themes, like war versus pacifism, prejudice and its sources, and the exploitation, intentional or not, of indigenous peoples. The show won the Tony for Best Musical and the Pulitzer Prize for Drama.

Dialogue Expressing Inspiring Sentiments

Art provides a forum in which artists can express inspiring and evocative sentiments. As a playwright, you're able to use your skills and the medium to (hopefully) reach thousands of people with your particular slant on the world. Find the right words, and you'll be able to provoke, challenge, edify, and inspire audiences. Consider these excerpts of moving dialogue:

> **Hamlet:** What a piece of work is a man, how noble in reason, how infinite in faculties, in form and moving how express and admirable, in action how like an angel, in apprehension how like a god! the beauty of the world, the paragon of animals — and yet, to me, what is this quintessence of dust? (*Hamlet,* William Shakespeare)

Helmer: Before all else, you're a wife and a mother.
Nora: I don't believe in that anymore. I believe that, before all else, I'm a human being, no less than you — or anyway, I ought to try to become one. I know the majority thinks you're right, Torvald, and plenty of books agree with you, too. But I can't go on believing what the majority says, or what's written in books. I have to think over these things for myself and try to understand them. (*A Doll House,* Henrik Ibsen)

Mama: Crazy 'bout his children! God knows there was plenty wrong with Walter Younger — hard-headed, mean, kind of wild with women — plenty wrong with him. But he sure loved his children. Always wanted them to have something — be something. That's where Brother gets all these notions, I reckon. Big Walter used to say, he'd get right wet in the eyes sometimes, lean his head back with the water standing in his eyes and say, "Seem like God didn't see fit to give the black man nothing but dreams — but He did give us children to make them dreams seem worthwhile." (*A Raisin in the Sun,* Lorraine Hansberry)

Blanche: But some things are not forgivable. Deliberate cruelty is not forgivable! It is the one unforgivable thing, in my opinion, and the one thing of which I have never, never been guilty. (*A Streetcar Named Desire,* Tennessee Williams)

Honesty and Openness

Theatre is no place to hide. To win over audiences, actors must make themselves emotionally naked and vulnerable. An earnest director must share and implement her vision of the play she's staging, no matter how controversial that vision may be. And the playwright must be open and truthful in her writing. Who you are and what you believe are your unique gifts to the world. Your writing, be it prose or poetry, must have the ring of truth and sincerity, or it will be recognized by audiences as either contrived or empty of genuine emotional content.

The American masterpiece *Long Day's Journey into Night,* by Eugene O'Neill, premiered in 1956 and was awarded the 1957 Pulitzer Prize in Drama. What's significant about those dates is that O'Neill died a few years earlier, in 1953. The play is to a large extent autobiographical. The painful story of the play's tormented Tyrone family mirrors the flawed people and difficult events of the playwright's own life. So honest and open was O'Neill in this play that when it was completed in 1942, he had the play locked away with instructions that it not see the light of day until well after his death. If he couldn't hide as an artist, he could at least attempt to hide his art.

Specificity that Can Be Universal

A new playwright writing a play based on, for example, events in her family history may be tempted to omit specifics that would pinpoint the characters in the play as being of a particular race or religion or geographic location. Many playwrights do this in the belief that the more general and nonspecific they makes the characters and events, the more likely audiences members of different backgrounds are to identify with the characters of the play. However, the exact opposite is true.

It's a paradox in playwriting that the more specific your play is, the more universal it is. If the playwright writes a play truthfully dramatizing incidents in a Hispanic family story (as I did), surprisingly, people of other ethnic and racial backgrounds will identify with the characters. Though the specifics of language, dress, customs, cuisine, and other manifestations of culture can differ between the characters and audiences, the challenges of the family in the play can be those of any family, regardless of the superficial differences.

Lorraine Hansberry's *A Raisin in the Sun* is the story of a specific African American family in Chicago in the 1950s struggling to realize the dreams of higher education, a move from a tenement apartment to the suburbs, and employment with dignity. Though the particulars of the Younger family may differ with the specifics of audiences and their families, the struggle to provide a better life for one's loved ones is universal. Audiences identify and empathize with the Youngers and their aspirations.

Simplicity and Clarity in Storytelling

The great plays, whether their story lines are straightforward or relatively complex, feature an essential simplicity and clarity. The core of a great play — who the protagonist is, what the protagonist wants, and how the protagonist goes about getting it — is simple and unambiguous. The stakes and the urgency of the protagonist's dilemma are readily apparent. For example:

✔ Hamlet is on a mission to avenge the murder of his father, the late king of Denmark. He goes about it haltingly and clumsily, but, goaded on by the ghost of the murdered king, Hamlet seeks a rough justice that will remove a fratricidal usurper and put to rest his father's spirit. The numerous subplots — Hamlet's attachment to Ophelia, his relationship with his mother, Polonius's bond with his son Laertes, and so on — provide Shakespeare's *Hamlet* with dimension, but they don't distract or detract from the play's central clarity and simplicity.

✔ On the lighter side, in the Joseph Kesselring comedy *Arsenic and Old Lace,* Mortimer Brewster is desperate to protect his dear, sweet aunts from the consequences of their peculiar homicidal habit so that he can proceed with his marriage and move on with his new life. Although the madcap subplots (involving his uncle, "Teddy Roosevelt;" his relationship with his murderous and maniacal brother Jonathan; and the intrusion of the local beat cop) all up the ante, they don't muddy or eclipse Mortimer's clear and simple goal.

A Surprising, Yet Inevitable, Ending

In plays, as in most storytelling, you want to keep the audience wondering about, and watching for, how things will turn out for the protagonist. And you want to provide an answer to these questions, an ending to your play that surprises and yet feels justified, earned, and even inevitable. You want your audiences to look back at the events of the play and, though surprised, be able to conclude: "Of course it had to come to this."

The tumultuous ending of *A Streetcar Named Desire* surprised and shocked audiences. Blanche DuBois's continual meddling and supercilious attitude toward Stanley Kowalski put her on a collision course with her uncouth brother-in-law. In retaliation, Stanley sexually assaults Blanche, and, as a result, in the final scene Blanche is removed to a mental institution. As unforgivable and brutal as the climactic events are, they have a certain inevitability. It was obvious on Blanche's arrival that she had only a flimsy grasp on reality. It was equally obvious that Stanley would take only so much interference from his unwelcome houseguest. Blanche was the china shop and Stanley was the proverbial bull, who, when provoked, remorselessly shattered everything inside that shop. In retrospect, given the behavior of the characters, Blanche's destruction was destined to take place.

Themes Illustrating the Human Condition

Whether or not a playwright consciously considers theme or message as part of the playwriting process, audiences usually will find a thesis or point to the play. The great plays make a statement. They say something meaningful about the human condition; they add to society's understanding of people and life. The great plays leave audiences with something to think about.

In *Cyrano de Bergerac,* the swashbuckling character Cyrano, arrogant and confident in his swordsmanship, is, at the same time, insecure about his looks, which keeps him from wooing the beautiful Roxane. Instead, Cyrano assists the handsome but unimaginative Christian in courting Roxane, thereby demonstrating admirable generosity and selfless love. Cyrano puts the happiness of the woman he loves ahead of his own romantic fulfillment, illustrating the noble human traits of concern for others and self-sacrifice. Whether or not Edmond Rostand intended these qualities to convey a theme of the play, audiences come away from the play with the author's perspective on love and personal fulfillment as illustrated by Cyrano.

Chapter 20

Ten Playwrights You Should Know and Emulate

• •

In This Chapter

▶ Checking out playwrights who have had a big impact on theatre

▶ Considering their greatest plays, recurring themes, and influences

• •

Selecting ten playwrights to hold up for examination and emulation is as subjective as attempting to name the greatest baseball players of all time or the most important figures in world history. Anyone's list of names can be argued.

Ultimately, the list of playwrights I compiled reflects who I am and my play-writing biases almost as much as the prominence of the individual writers. And if compiling such a list wasn't daring enough, I further stuck my neck out by selecting a must-read play for some of my choices.

If you're inclined to dispute my pick of playwrights and plays, know that I freely admit my list to be imperfect. If, in your view, I haven't selected the perfect ten, I hope you'll nevertheless agree that you can learn much from the exceptional playwrights and plays discussed in this chapter.

Sophocles

Sophocles (circa 496–406 BC) is probably the best known of the ancient Greek playwrights. Records indicate that he wrote as many as 123 plays, but only 7 have survived the millennia intact: *Ajax, Antigone, Trachinian Women, Oedipus the King, Electra, Philoctetes,* and *Oedipus at Colonus.*

In his day, Sophocles was the Babe Ruth or Wayne Gretzky of Greek theatre. He participated in maybe 30 of the annual dramatic competitions that were held in Athens during religious festivals, and he is thought to have won 18 to 24 of them. *Oedipus the King* (or *Oedipus Rex*), a delightful family drama (if you're into Stephen King or Wes Craven), is the playwright's most recognized work and perhaps the most famous of the surviving Greek plays.

Oedipus the King tells the story of the King of Thebes, who needs to find a way to end a deadly pestilence afflicting his people. In the process of investigating the cause of the plague, Oedipus learns of a prophesy that he would kill his father and marry his mother. (This is where Sigmund Freud sits up and takes notice.) Oedipus recalls having killed a man in a fight years earlier. The local blind seer is consulted but warns Oedipus to drop the matter. When Oedipus persists and learns that he was adopted — and the people he thought were his parents aren't — the pieces fall into their awful places. The man he killed was the old king Laius, his biological father. To make things worse, Oedipus unknowingly married the victim's widow, Jocasta, his mother and now his queen. Bummed over these inconvenient truths, Jocasta hangs herself, and Oedipus stabs his eyes with pins, blinding himself. He further imposes upon himself the penalty of exile.

Oedipus the King falls into the first of ancient Greece's two primary forms of theatre, tragedy and comedy. (For more on these forms, turn to Chapter 6.) Almost a century after its first performance, *Oedipus the King* was cited by the Greek philosopher Aristotle in his *Poetics* as the epitome of theatrical tragedy. For newcomers to playwriting, becoming familiar with the drama, ingenuity, and irony in this granddaddy of tragedies is a smart move.

William Shakespeare

If great plays are those that stand the test of time, then Will Shakespeare (1564–1616) is truly the greatest playwright. He's the author of 38 plays that are considered some of the greatest plays in the English language. *Hamlet, Macbeth, Romeo and Juliet, Othello, The Merchant of Venice,* and *The Taming of the Shrew,* among others, are household names.

Shakespeare's plays, the delight of generations of scholars and English teachers and the bane of centuries of high school students, are so popular and so frequently performed for many reasons. His dialogue has poetry and lyrical language. His story lines, many borrowed from history, myths, legends, and preexisting stories, are ingenious and well crafted. His understanding of human nature is insightful and exhaustive.

What's equally impressive is that Shakespeare dealt with real issues, universal issues that trouble us today and still provide grist for the playwriting mill:

✔ **Revenge** (example: *Hamlet*)

✔ **Overreaching ambition** (example: *Macbeth*)

✔ **Hatred and unbridled enmity** (example: *Romeo and Juliet*)

✔ **Jealousy** (example: *Othello*)

✔ **Racism and prejudice** (example: *The Merchant of Venice*)

If William Shakespeare didn't write about some characteristic of human nature, the trait probably isn't significant.

Anton Chekhov

Russian playwright Anton Pavlovich Chekhov (1860–1904), famous as one of the world's great short-story writers, also carved out a place for himself in the history of world theatre. By the time of his death at age 44 of tuberculosis, in Russia he was second in literary celebrity only to Leo Tolstoy.

Chekhov's body of work includes more than 200 short stories, two novels, and plays that are among theatre's great works, including: *The Sea-Gull, The Three Sisters, Uncle Vanya,* and *The Cherry Orchard.* Some scholars consider him the father of the modern short story and the modern play.

Along with contemporaries Henrik Ibsen, August Strindberg, and George Bernard Shaw, Chekhov was a trailblazer in modern drama, writing tragicomic plays that portray life as it is and hold up social issues for inspection. His themes include feelings of disillusionment and disappointment, monotony of daily life, the class system, and changing times. Chekhov revealed he was very much aware that he was breaking new ground by writing "plotless" plays that depict the real world:

> After all, in real life people don't spend every minute shooting at each other, hanging themselves and making confessions of love. They don't spend all the time saying clever things. They're more occupied with eating, drinking, flirting and talking stupidities — and these are the things which ought to be shown on the stage. A play should be written in which people arrive, go away, have dinner, talk about the weather and play cards. Life must be exactly as it is.

Lillian Hellman

Lillian Hellman (1905–1984) was a controversial playwright who espoused liberal and left-wing causes. Her most famous plays include *The Children's Hour, The Little Foxes,* and *Toys in the Attic.*

The Children's Hour is perhaps the play for which Lillian Hellman is most remembered. It tells the story of two women, Karen and Martha, who run a private boarding school for girls. When Karen is forced to discipline a chronic mischief-maker, Mary, the girl, in a ruse to get herself removed from the school, distorts overheard comments and recounts them to her well-to-do, influential, and doting grandmother. Mary's tale suggests that Karen, engaged to be married to local doctor, and Martha have a lesbian relationship. The grandmother spreads the story, and in short order, the school and Karen's engagement are destroyed by the lie. In a final irony, Martha confesses that, throughout the years of their intimate but innocent friendship, she has secretly been in love with Karen. Martha, who can no longer bear it, takes her own life.

The first production of *The Children's Hour* on Broadway, though it ran for two years, broke the law. It was illegal in New York State to refer to the subject of homosexuality on stage. Probably due the immense success of the play, the regulation was not enforced. But the controversy had only just begun. The Pulitzer Prize committee refused to consider the play, and the play was initially banned in Boston, Chicago, and London. Lillian Hellman was subjected to further scandal when she was blacklisted by Hollywood after being called to appear before the House Un-American Activities Committee in 1950.

Hellman's work is one good example of how theatre throughout its history has been a forum in which it's been possible to push the envelope by staging plays involving controversial issues like homosexuality, racism, and government abuses.

Tennessee Williams

When playwrights argue about whom the greatest American playwright was, Tennessee Williams (1911–1983) usually heads the list of suspects. Williams, a native of — no, not Tennessee — Mississippi, is the author of one of the most impressive and successful canons of plays by any American writer. His now classic plays include *The Glass Menagerie, A Streetcar Named Desire, Summer and Smoke, The Rose Tattoo, Camino Real, Cat on a Hot Tin Roof, Suddenly Last Summer, Sweet Bird of Youth,* and *The Night of the Iguana.*

The magic of the plays of Tennessee Williams is that they're a mixture of lyrical language, haunting characters, and provocative subject matter (like love, sex, lust, rape, human frailty, homosexuality, alcoholism, disability, death, and, even cannibalism).

Tennessee Williams let it all hang out. Many of the characters that populate his plays are thinly veiled replicas of the central people in his life. His mentally ill sister, Rose, is said to be the model for the handicapped and insecure Laura of *The Glass Menagerie.* The now discredited medical procedure, prefrontal lobotomy, which was performed on Rose, is an element in the play *Suddenly, Last Summer.* Amanda Wingfield, the domineering and self-deluding mother of Laura in *The Glass Menagerie,* may be based on Williams's own mother, Edwina. The issue of homosexuality that appears in some of Williams's plays, including *A Streetcar Named Desire* and *Cat on a Hot Tin Roof,* no doubt emerges from the playwright's own experience. And the guilt-ridden Tom, who flees the madness of the Wingfield household, is said to be a reflection of the author, Tennessee (*Thomas* Lanier) Williams.

Arthur Miller

Arthur Miller (1915–2005) was, for more than half a century, one of the great working playwrights of American and world theatre. His work is familiar not only to theatre buffs but also to millions of high school and college students who've studied his plays. His celebrated and timeless pieces include *All My Sons, Death of a Salesman, The Crucible,* and *A View from the Bridge.*

Unlike many playwrights who tend to look inward for inspiration, Miller's gaze was outward, and his work grew out of some of the momentous events and issues of the second half of the 20th century. His award-winning *All My Sons* deals with the questions of guilt and responsibility involving Joe Keller, a producer of substandard World War II military materials. The defective parts were responsible for the deaths of a number of pilots, including, in a terrible irony, his own son.

Miller's Pulitzer Prize– and Tony Award–winning drama *Death of a Salesman* exposes the underbelly of the American Dream and is one of two classic plays for which Miller is most remembered. It centers on Willy Loman, who bought into the shallow values of appearance and popularity over substance and hard work. As a result, he's a failure in business, as a father, and as provider for his wife. Now, at the end of his career, the callousness of the dog-eat-dog world of sales, his delusions of grandeur, and the unsuccessful lives of his sons catch up with him. He reacts by providing for his wife in the only way he can; he commits suicide so that his wife will benefit from his life insurance.

Miller's second monumental and probably most-performed play is *The Crucible.* The play is a dramatization of the hysteria of the Salem witch trials that led to the deaths of innocent citizens. However, the play was clearly intended by Miller to mirror the destruction of the careers and lives then taking place as a result of the hysterical and unprincipled search for Communists conducted by Senator Joe McCarthy and others in the 1950s.

For Miller, playwriting provided a platform from which he could expose the hypocrisies of society and comment on governmental abuse of power.

Samuel Beckett

The poet, writer, and playwright Samuel Beckett (1908–1989) was born in Dublin, Ireland. He was a student and friend of the modernist, avant-garde novelist and poet, James Joyce. In 1969, Beckett was awarded the 1969 Nobel Prize in literature.

Beckett's landmark work, one which changed assumptions about playwriting and the nature of theatre, if not life itself, is *Waiting for Godot: A Tragicomedy in Two Acts.* First performed in France in 1953, the two-act play has been described as a play in which nothing happens, twice.

In *Waiting for Godot,* the play's two main characters, Vladimir and Estragon, wait on a country road for someone named Godot to arrive. Godot repeatedly sends word he is about to appear, but he never does. The pair complain, argue, sleep, and consider suicide, but they do very little. They are joined for a time, in both acts, by Pozzo and his slave, Lucky, enigmatic characters that temporarily break the monotony for Vladimir and Estragon. The play ends with a message from Godot that he will not come today but surely tomorrow.

Waiting for Godot, along with some of Beckett's other works, like *Endgame, Krapp's Last Tape,* and *Happy Days,* are considered part of the Theatre of the Absurd movement, popular from the late-1940s to the 1960s. In this genre of literature, in an atheistic universe, life is purposeless and meaningless, and anything can and does happen at random.

Edward Albee

Edward Albee (1928–) is widely known for *The Zoo Story, The Sandbox, Who's Afraid of Virginia Woolf?,* and *Three Tall Women,* and is another writer in the Theatre of the Absurd genre (see the preceding section for more on that movement).

As a young man, Albee rebelled against his comfortable and conventional existence in Connecticut and at various schools. He ran away to Greenwich Village in New York City, a haven for the rebellious and offbeat, where he wrote his first successful play, *The Zoo Story.* Over his career, Albee received multiple Pulitzer Prizes for Drama and other awards and honors, and today he's considered a grandmaster of American theatre.

Albee's theatrical calling card is the early 1960s play *Who's Afraid of Virginia Woolf?* At times shocking and frightening and at other moments funny and poignant, the play tells the story of a mature college professor, George, and his boisterous wife, Martha, who, after a late party on campus, are visited immediately afterward by a young and newly arrived instructor, Nick, and his timid and tipsy wife, Honey. Martha and George continue to drink. Old wounds surface as the hosts engage in psychological and verbal no-holds-barred combat that repels and fascinates the younger couple. Soon Nick and Honey are drawn into the festivities, as foibles and secrets are revealed and used as daggers in the four-way duel. By dawn, the couples are exhausted, remorseful, and, most important, stripped of their illusions and façades.

Despite the play's bleak depiction of marriage, the sexual references, and harsh language, *Who's Afraid of Virginia Wolf?* won the 1963 Tony for Best Play and the New York Drama Critics' Circle Award for Best Play. However, though it was also chosen for the 1963 Pulitzer Prize for Drama, the prize trustee objected to the profanity and sexual themes and awarded no Pulitzer Prize for Drama that year.

August Wilson

August Wilson (1945–2005) grew up in Pittsburgh's Hill District, an African American neighborhood that later provided the backdrop for many of his plays. Wilson's best-known plays are *Fences,* which won a Pulitzer Prize and a Tony Award, and *The Piano Lesson,* which won a Pulitzer Prize and the New York Drama Critics' Circle Award.

Wilson set himself the goal of writing ten plays dramatizing the African American experience over the ten decades of the 20th century. This project is referred to as the "Pittsburgh Cycle" or his "Century Cycle." Nine of the plays are set in the Hill District. The plays in Wilson's decade-by-decade are

- 1900s: *Gem of the Ocean* (2003)
- 1910s: *Joe Turner's Come and Gone* (1988)
- 1920s: *Ma Rainey's Black Bottom* (1984)
- 1930s: *The Piano Lesson* (1990)
- 1940s: *Seven Guitars* (1995)
- 1950s: *Fences* (1987)
- 1960s: *Two Trains Running* (1991)
- 1970s: *Jitney* (1982)
- 1980s: *King Hedley II* (1999)
- 1990s: *Radio Golf* (2005)

Fences tells the story of a frustrated and bitter Troy Maxson, who had been a fine baseball player in his younger days but, to his unending resentment, was barred from the major league because he is black. Troy struggles with racism, family issues, infidelity, and a fear of death.

Neil Simon

Neil Simon (1927–) is probably the most successful playwright on the planet. His long string of hit plays, dating back to the early 1960s, is unrivaled in modern theatre. He is the author of more than 30 successful plays and over 30 screenplays. Some say that a Neil Simon play is being performed at any given time somewhere in the world. For any playwright who's inclined toward comedies, Neil Simon is the playwright to study.

Simon's remarkable body of work has earned just about every scriptwriting award imaginable. Having begun his career as a TV comedy writer, he's won Emmy Awards, as well as Tony Awards, Writers Guild of America Awards, a Golden Globe Award, a New York Drama Critics Circle Award, an Outer Critics Circle Award, a Drama Desk Award, the 2006 Mark Twain Prize for American Humor, and a Pulitzer Prize for Drama.

In 1966, Simon had four shows on Broadway at the same time: *Sweet Charity* (for which he wrote the libretto), *The Star-Spangled Girl*, *The Odd Couple,* and *Barefoot in the Park.* His works include such hits as *The Sunshine Boys, The Good Doctor, God's Favorite, Chapter Two, They're Playing Our Song* (a musical), *I Ought to Be in Pictures, Brighton Beach Memoirs, Biloxi Blues, Broadway Bound, Jake's Women, The Goodbye Girl,* and *Laughter on the 23rd Floor.*

Simon's play *The Odd Couple,* which was so popular that it spun off a long-running hit TV series by the same name, follows two men, one divorced and one separated, who share an apartment. Though friends, their differences in habits and outlooks on life quickly have them at each other's throat. The names of the two main characters have come to be synonymous with either obsessive cleanliness and neatness — Felix Unger — or with mindless messiness and scruffiness — Oscar Madison.

Appendix

Formatting a Script

*P*laywrights, like many artists, tend to be nonconformists. If you didn't march to the beat of your own drummer, you probably wouldn't be writing plays. However, in some areas it doesn't pay to stray from the prescribed path, and one of them is in formatting your play.

Format is important. Expressing your individuality in formatting is not appreciated and can actually impede your chances of getting serious consideration. People who read and evaluate plays for possible production expect your play to be submitted in professional play script form (which is different from screenplay and teleplay formatting). With hundreds, even thousands, of scripts competing for production support, you want your script to look professional, not give a script evaluator the impression that you don't know what you're doing. Straying from the accepted format can get your script tossed into the discard pile even before a single line is read.

The good news is that formatting a play is simple. Here's an explanation of the elements of a script, in the order you should arrange them:

The cover page:

- ✔ Put the title of your play and your name.

- ✔ Include your contact information (if and when you have an agent, include the agent's contact information rather than your own).

The cast of characters page:

- ✔ Put the title of your play and your name.

- ✔ List *all* the characters in your play (no matter how minor) and give a minimal description of the characters. Don't hamper your director with specifics like blonde or tall or blue-eyed if those specifics don't matter to the play. You don't want to unnecessarily restrict the pool of actors if the character's appearance doesn't make a difference.

- ✔ Add a minimal description of the physical setting for the play (leaving out any unimportant details).

✔ Add a reference to the time in which the play takes place (year, month, day, day of the week, time of day, and so on). Again, don't get too specific if it doesn't matter to the play.

The following pages:

✔ Put the title and your name on the first page of the script (in case the cover page gets separated).

✔ On every page, use a header that shows two pieces of information:

• The title of the play (if you're submitting to a contest or competition that wants the entries to be unidentifiable, simply eliminate the header for that submission).

• A code that tells you which draft you're looking at. Over time, you'll likely have a number of drafts of your play, and annotating your drafts can help you keep them straight. The code I use, which you can see on the sample script pages in this appendix, indicates that this is the fourth draft, done in August of 2008.

✔ Number the pages, starting with the first page of the actual play (not the title page). A simple command does this in every word processing program I know of. (If someone reading your play should happen to drop some loose pages, the numbering will come in handy.)

✔ Set the left margin to 1½ inches to allow for three-hole punching for a binder, and set the right margin to 1 inch.

✔ Open the play with stage directions. Add stage directions as needed between lines of dialogue. Except for a word or two that suggests how a line may be read (for example, "Merrily"), you don't want to have stage directions embedded in the dialogue.

Indent stage directions 2½ or 3 inches in from the left margin, and single space the lines. (Single space all text in the document.)

✔ After the opening stage directions, skip a line and center the name of the character who speaks. The name of characters should be in all CAPS.

✔ Directly below the name of the character is the character's dialogue. The dialogue is justified left.

✔ After the character's dialogue, a line is skipped and the next character to speak appears in the same format as above.

The following figure shows the cover page, cast listing, and the first two pages from one of my one-act plays as an example of the standard playwriting format. (If it seems like a lot of trouble to set your play up as modeled below, there are a number of script writing programs — some free — you can get your hands on that can make it simpler to adhere to the right format.)

Midnight Kiss
by Angelo Parra

Characters

HAROLD: About 30 years of age; dressed in slacks and a sports jacket.

ROBERTA: Late-20s, dressed attractively for a holiday office party.

Setting

A comfortable and quiet parlor with a loveseat, adjacent to a room where a party's in progress.

Time

Present, around Christmas.

Midnight Kiss

A new play by

Angelo Parra

111 Main Street
Our Town, MA 10000
(212) 555-XXXX
greatplaywright@yourparticulardomain.com

Midnight Kiss
by Angelo Parra

HAROLD sits alone on a loveseat. He restlessly clutches an almost empty glass of eggnog. There are party sounds coming from an adjacent room. He looks at his watch. After a moment, ROBERTA casually enters, carrying an almost empty glass of wine.

ROBERTA

Being aloof, are we?

HAROLD

Me? No. I'm just not big on . . .

ROBERTA

Parties?

HAROLD

. . . making cocktail party chitchat.

ROBERTA

(Merrily) 'Tis the season to be jolly.

HAROLD

Yeah, well, fa-la-la-la.

ROBERTA settles on to the arm of a loveseat opposite HAROLD. There's a burst of laughter from the other room.

ROBERTA

I suppose they can be kind of a drag. Stiff office types desperately trying to look casual.

HAROLD

Don't let me be a downer, Roberta, I'm just not a party guy.

ROBERTA

Oh, damn.

HAROLD

What?

1

ROBERTA

You remembered my name. I feel like such a dumb-dumb.

HAROLD

Harold.

ROBERTA

I'm sorry. That's embarrassing.

HAROLD

You walk in a door; strangers are shoved in your face. How's anybody supposed to remember anybody?

ROBERTA

Yes, but you remembered me. Bobbie.

HAROLD

(Correcting her) Harold.

ROBERTA

(Laughs) No. Me. Bobbie. I prefer Bobbie. Roberta sounds like a man's name with a grunt. Robert–uh. I mean it's okay (indicating the other room) with those guys, but not with . . . friends . . . Harold.

HAROLD

Okay. Bobbie.

ROBERTA

Funny, I don't remember seeing you around the office.

HAROLD

No. I was invited by Ed. Ed Carson. My neighbor.

ROBERTA

Yes, Ed of Accounts Receivable. Nice man.

HAROLD

The best.

ROBERTA

(Pause) So . . . here we are. Alone on Christmas Eve.

2

Index

• C •

• D •

Internet

Blogging For Dummies,
3rd Edition
978-0-470-61996-4

eBay For Dummies,
6th Edition
978-0-470-49741-8

Facebook For Dummies,
3rd Edition
978-0-470-87804-0

Web Marketing
For Dummies,
2nd Edition
978-0-470-37181-7

WordPress
For Dummies,
3rd Edition
978-0-470-59274-8

Language & Foreign Language

French For Dummies
978-0-7645-5193-2

Italian Phrases
For Dummies
978-0-7645-7203-6

Spanish For Dummies,
2nd Edition
978-0-470-87855-2

Spanish
For Dummies,
Audio Set
978-0-470-09585-0

Math & Science

Algebra I
For Dummies,
2nd Edition
978-0-470-55964-2

Biology For Dummies,
2nd Edition
978-0-470-59875-7

Calculus For Dummies
978-0-7645-2498-1

Chemistry For Dummies
978-0-7645-5430-8

Microsoft Office

Excel 2010 For Dummies
978-0-470-48953-6

Office 2010 All-in-One
For Dummies
978-0-470-49748-7

Office 2010 For Dummies,
Book + DVD Bundle
978-0-470-62698-6

Word 2010 For Dummies
978-0-470-48772-3

Music

Guitar For Dummies,
2nd Edition
978-0-7645-9904-0

iPod & iTunes For
Dummies, 8th Edition
978-0-470-87871-2

Piano Exercises
For Dummies
978-0-470-38765-8

Parenting & Education

Parenting For Dummies,
2nd Edition
978-0-7645-5418-6

Type 1 Diabetes
For Dummies
978-0-470-17811-9

Pets

Cats For Dummies,
2nd Edition
978-0-7645-5275-5

Dog Training For Dummies,
3rd Edition
978-0-470-60029-0

Puppies For Dummies,
2nd Edition
978-0-470-03717-1

Religion & Inspiration

The Bible For Dummies
978-0-7645-5296-0

Catholicism For Dummies
978-0-7645-5391-2

Women in the Bible
For Dummies
978-0-7645-8475-6

Self-Help & Relationship

Anger Management
For Dummies
978-0-470-03715-7

Overcoming Anxiety
For Dummies,
2nd Edition
978-0-470-57441-6

Sports

Baseball
For Dummies,
3rd Edition
978-0-7645-7537-2

Basketball
For Dummies,
2nd Edition
978-0-7645-5248-9

Golf For Dummies,
3rd Edition
978-0-471-76871-5

Web Development

Web Design
All-in-One
For Dummies
978-0-470-41796-6

Web Sites
Do-It-Yourself
For Dummies,
2nd Edition
978-0-470-56520-9

Windows 7

Windows 7
For Dummies
978-0-470-49743-2

Windows 7
For Dummies,
Book + DVD Bundle
978-0-470-52398-8

Windows 7 All-in-One
For Dummies
978-0-470-48763-1

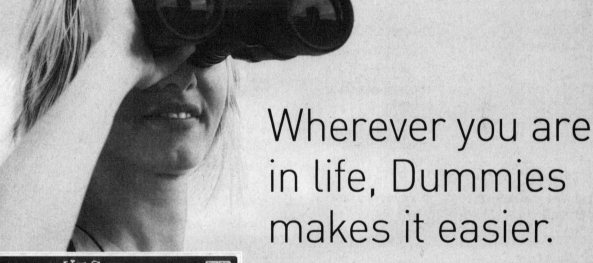

Wherever you are
in life, Dummies
makes it easier.

From fashion to Facebook®,
wine to Windows®, and everything in between,
Dummies makes it easier.

Visit us at Dummies.com

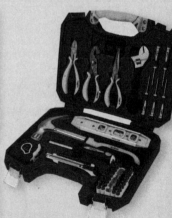